Conflict Inflation

This book brings together distinguished scholars who analyze the recent resurgence of inflation from the point of view of conflict among social classes over the appropriate distribution of income.

For the better part of the past four decades, inflation remained low and stable in most industrialized economies—certainly close to the various inflation targets. As a result, inflation did not pose much of a policy threat, and economists' attention was drawn elsewhere. Since 2020, however, the picture is very different. A pandemic followed by a war has led to a surge in inflation throughout the globe, the result of war, climate change emergencies, supply chain deficiencies, and other cost-related post-COVID problems (so-called greedflation). This surge in inflation has left many economists bewildered. Post-Keynesians, however, have proposed a sound explanation. For them, inflation is 'always and everywhere' a conflict phenomenon, and they have applied this view to the post-pandemic era.

This book is a must-read to understand inflation not only in normal times but also in times of crises. It is an essential read for students, policymakers, and scholars in the fields of economics, social sciences, and public policy.

The chapters in this book were originally published as a special issue of *Review of Political Economy.*

Maria Cristina Barbieri Góes is Assistant Professor at LINK Campus University, Rome, Italy, and the co-editor of the *Review of Political Economy.* Her research activity is focused on post-Keynesian economics, growth theory, fiscal and monetary policies, income distribution, macroeconomics, and regional economics. Her scientific contributions were published in various journals.

Sylvio Antonio Kappes is Professor of Macroeconomics at the Federal University of Alagoas, Brazil. His main areas of research are Stock-Flow Consistent models, Monetary Economics, and Post-Keynesian Economics. He is the co-editor of the *Review of Political Economy.*

Louis-Philippe Rochon is Full Professor of Economics at Laurentian University, Sudbury, Canada, where he has been teaching since 2004. He is the editor-in-chief of the *Review of Political Economy.* He is the founding editor (now Emeritus) of the *Review of Keynesian Economics.* He has widely published in post-Keynesian economics, and monetary theory and policy. He has been Visiting Professor in over a dozen universities around the world.

Conflict Inflation

Edited by
Maria Cristina Barbieri Góes, Sylvio Antonio Kappes, Louis-Philippe Rochon

Routledge
Taylor & Francis Group
LONDON AND NEW YORK

First published 2025
by Routledge
4 Park Square, Milton Park, Abingdon, Oxon, OX14 4RN

and by Routledge
605 Third Avenue, New York, NY 10158

Routledge is an imprint of the Taylor & Francis Group, an informa business

British Library Cataloguing-in-Publication Data
A catalogue record for this book is available from the British Library

ISBN13: 978-1-032-98800-9 (hbk)
ISBN13: 978-1-032-98808-5 (pbk)
ISBN13: 978-1-003-60073-2 (ebk)

DOI: 10.4324/9781003600732

Typeset in Minion Pro
by codeMantra

Publisher's Note
The publisher accepts responsibility for any inconsistencies that may have arisen during the conversion of this book from journal articles to book chapters, namely the inclusion of journal terminology.

Contents

Citation Information

The following chapters in this book were originally published in *Review of Political Economy*, volume 36, issue 4 (2024). When citing this material, please use the original page numbering for each article, as follows:

Introduction
Conflict Inflation
Maria Cristina Barbieri Góes, Sylvio Antonio Kappes and Louis-Philippe Rochon
Review of Political Economy, volume 36, issue 4 (2024), pp. 1299–1301

Chapter 1
The Conflict Theory of Inflation Revisited
Robert Rowthorn
Review of Political Economy, volume 36, issue 4 (2024), pp. 1302–1313

Chapter 2
Conflictual Distributional Struggles and Inflation
Malcolm Sawyer
Review of Political Economy, volume 36, issue 4 (2024), pp. 1314–1330

Chapter 3
Sellers' Inflation and Distributive Conflict: Lessons from the Post-COVID Recovery
Ettore Gallo and Louis-Philippe Rochon
Review of Political Economy, volume 36, issue 4 (2024), pp. 1331–1350

Chapter 4
Cost-Push and Conflict Inflation: A Discussion of the Italian Case
Davide Romaniello and Antonella Stirati
Review of Political Economy, volume 36, issue 4 (2024), pp. 1351–1380

Chapter 5
Inflation, Unemployment, and Inequality: Beyond the Traditional Phillips Curve
Lilian Rolim
Review of Political Economy, volume 36, issue 4 (2024), pp. 1381–1396

Chapter 6

Conflictual Inflation and the Phillips Curve
Marc Lavoie
Review of Political Economy, volume 36, issue 4 (2024), pp. 1397–1419

Chapter 7

Which Policies Against Inflation After Covid-19 and the War in Ukraine: The Italian Case
Luigi Salvati and Pasquale Tridico
Review of Political Economy, volume 36, issue 4 (2024), pp. 1420–1435

Chapter 8

Kaleckian Models of Conflict Inflation, Distribution and Employment: A Comparative Analysis
Eckhard Hein and Christoph Häusler
Review of Political Economy, volume 36, issue 4 (2024), pp. 1436–1464

Chapter 9

'Sellers' Inflation' and Monetary Policy Interventions: A Critical Analysis
Giuseppe Mastromatteo and Sergio Rossi
Review of Political Economy, volume 36, issue 4 (2024), pp. 1465–1485

Chapter 10

Conflict Inflation and the Role of Monetary Policy
Pedro Clavijo-Cortes
Review of Political Economy, volume 36, issue 4 (2024), pp. 1486–1509

Chapter 11

Conflict, Inertia, and Phillips Curve from a Sraffian Standpoint
Franklin Serrano, Ricardo Summa and Guilherme Spinato Morlin
Review of Political Economy, volume 36, issue 4 (2024), pp. 1510–1535

List of Contributors

Maria Cristina Barbieri Góes, LINK Campus University, Rome, Italy.

Pedro Clavijo-Cortes, New Mexico Taxation and Revenue Department, Santa Fe, USA; Universidad Católica de Colombia, Bogotá, Colombia.

Ettore Gallo, University of Parma, Italy.

Christoph Häusler, Berlin School of Economics and Law, Germany; University of Technology of Compiègne, France; Sorbonne University, Paris, France; Université Paris Cité, France.

Eckhard Hein, Berlin School of Economics and Law, Institute for International Political Economy (IPE), Germany.

Sylvio Antonio Kappes, Federal University of Alagoas, Brazil.

Marc Lavoie, University of Ottawa, Canada; University Sorbonne Paris Nord, Villetaneuse, France.

Giuseppe Mastromatteo, Università Cattolica del Sacro Cuore, Milan, Italy.

Louis-Philippe Rochon, Laurentian University, Sudbury, Canada.

Lilian Rolim, Instituto de Economia, Universidade Estadual de Campinas (UNICAMP), Brazil.

Davide Romaniello, Vanvitelli University, Naples, Italy.

Sergio Rossi, University of Fribourg, Switzerland.

Robert Rowthorn, University of Cambridge, UK.

Luigi Salvati, Università Telematica, Pegaso, Italy.

Malcolm Sawyer, University of Leeds, UK; FMM, Dusseldorf, Germany.

Franklin Serrano, Universidade Federal do Rio de Janeiro, Brazil.

Antonella Stirati, Roma Tre University, Italy.

Ricardo Summa, Universidade Federal do Rio de Janeiro, Brazil.

Guilherme Spinato Morlin, Universita' di Pisa, Italy.

Pasquale Tridico, Roma Tre University, Italy.

Introduction: Conflict Inflation

Maria Cristina Barbieri Góes, Sylvio Antonio Kappes and Louis-Philippe Rochon

For the better part of the past four decades, inflation remained low and stable in most industrialized economies — certainly close to the various inflation targets. As a result, inflation did not pose much of a policy threat, and economists' attention was drawn elsewhere. This said, the study of the so-called 'great inflation moderation' would have been advantageous in knowing why there were no inflationary forces. After all, the last 4 decades have seen it all: bursts of growth and recessions, a financial crisis, and intermittent injections of liquidity through unconventional policy interventions by central banks, which in mainstream theory, should have been accompanied by some inflation — some say even in the double-digits.

But if this lack of inflation poses a number of interesting challenges for mainstream theorists, post-Keynesians and heterodox economists have not been taken aback. First and foremost, if inflation is cost-pushed, the lack of inflation must be caused by weakened cost forces. This is precisely what Perry and Cline (2016) found — that low inflation during this period was attributed to across-the-board wage declines over the same period, as well as to low import prices.

Since 2020, however, the picture is very different. A pandemic followed by a war has led to a surge in inflation throughout the globe. The lockdowns implemented at asynchronous times disrupted global supply chains, leading to a shortage of many inputs, chips being the most dramatic example (Igan, Rungcharoenkitkul, and Takahashi 2022; Rees and Rungcharoenkitkul 2021). The Russia-Ukraine war affected several important commodities such as oil, gas, wheat, and corn, leading to a surge in the prices of food, energy, and fertilizers (Avalos and Huang 2022). Moreover, the climate emergency brings three additional inflationary pressures: 'climateflation' from climate change costs, 'fossilflation' from reliance on fossil fuels, and 'greenflation' from the high demand for metals and minerals needed for green technologies (Schnabel 2022).

Once again, mainstream and heterodox interpretations are in opposite poles. The first sees inflation as a demand phenomenon. This diagnosis is the basis of all major central banks' responses to inflation: by raising interest rates, they hope to cool down the economy and, then, reduce inflation. The second group, by its turn, argues that inflation is cost-push, or conflict-driven. Accordingly, alternative policy measures like targeted price controls as part of a comprehensive strategy to address the severe macroeconomic disruptions have been advocated instead of interest rate hikes triggering heated debate (Weber

2021). According to this second group, the sources of the recent surge in inflation are to be attributed to the above-mentioned events (lockdowns, war, climate emergency etc.) and to the so-called 'sellers inflation' (Weber and Wasner 2023), meaning an increase in prices led by rising mark-ups. This is the basis of the conflict view of inflation, by which all price increases happen due to the desire of a group to increase its income share.

The mainstream makes a small concession to the idea of conflict when they discuss wage-price spirals. In this view, the wage demands come first, and leave firms with no other choice but to raise prices. Therefore, workers are seen as the instigators of the conflict. But, in reality, workers are more often than not simply reacting to inflation, and demand higher wages in order to catch up. In this sense, we should refer to price-wage spiral, if anything.

Post-Keynesians see the conflictive nature of inflation in a very different angle. The concept of conflictual inflation within heterodox economics has roots extending back to the 1950s. Joan Robinson (1956), the 'founding mother of post-Keynesians' (Rochon 2023), is one of the first to address this issue. In the 1970s, following the oil shock and subsequent inflation surge, Cripps and Godley (1976) and Rowthorn (1977) pioneered conflict inflation models. Subsequently, various post-Keynesian economists have further developed these models (Blecker and Setterfield 2019; Dutt 1987, 1990; Lavoie 2022; Taylor 1985), including those incorporating the 'conflict-augmented Phillips curve' (Summa and Braga 2020).

As Hein (2023, p. 1) puts it, 'inflation is always and everywhere a conflict phenomenon, with different potential triggers'. One such triggers can be wages increases, as some in the mainstream put it (see Storm 2024), but that would be fighting against the data. On one hand, there is little historical evidence on the existence of wage-prince spirals (Alvarez et al. 2022); on the other, the recent episode of inflation shows that one of the main triggers were not rising wages, but rising mark-ups (Weber and Wasner 2023).

This symposium is dedicated to the post-Keynesian conflictual view of inflation. The contributions offer interpretations of the post-Covid surge in prices, as well as make theoretical advances. On this last point, we are glad to present a wide variety of different post-Keynesian strands, from Kaleckian to Sraffian. We wish to acknowledge all authors and reviewers who contributed to this important and necessary symposium.

Disclosure Statement

No potential conflict of interest was reported by the author(s).

ORCID

Maria Cristina Barbieri Góes http://orcid.org/0000-0001-8953-5412
Sylvio Antonio Kappes http://orcid.org/0000-0001-8886-9365

References

Alvarez, J., J. Bluedorn, N. J. Hansen, Y. Huang, E. Pugacheva, and A. Sollaci. 2022. 'Wage-Price Spirals: What is the Historical Evidence?' IMF Working Paper no. 2022/221.

Avalos, F., and W. Huang. 2022. 'Commodity Markets: Shocks and Spillovers.' *BIS Quarterly Review* 19: 15–29.

Blecker, R. A., and M. Setterfield. 2019. *Heterodox Macroeconomics: Models of Demand, Distribution and Growth.* Edward Elgar Publishing.

Cripps, F., and W. Godley. 1976. 'A Formal Analysis of the Cambridge Economic Policy Group Model.' *Economica* 43 (172): 335–348.

Dutt, A. K. 1987. 'Alternative Closures Again: A Comment on 'Growth, Distribution and Inflation'.' *Cambridge Journal of Economics* 11 (1): 75–82.

Dutt, A. K. 1990. *Growth, Distribution, and Uneven Development.* Cambridge: Cambridge University Press.

Hein, E. 2023. 'Inflation is Always and Everywhere ... a Conflict Phenomenon: Post-Keynesian Inflation Theory and Energy Price Driven Conflict Inflation.' IPE Working Papers (224/2023).

Igan, D., P. Rungcharoenkitkul, and K. Takahashi. 2022. 'Global Supply Chain Disruptions: Evolution, Impact, Outlook.' *Bank for International Settlements Bulletin* no. 61.

Lavoie, M. 2022. *Post-Keynesian Economics: New Foundations.* Edward Elgar Publishing.

Perry, N., and N. Cline. 2016. 'What Caused the Great Inflation Moderation in the US? A Post-Keynesian View.' *Review of Keynesian Economics* 4 (4): 475–502.

Rees, D., and P. Rungcharoenkitkul. 2021. 'Bottlenecks: Causes and Macroeconomic Implications.' *Bank for International Settlements Bulletin* no 48.

Robinson, J. 1956. *The Accumulation of Capital.* London: Macmillan.

Rochon, L. P. 2023. 'On the Theoretical and Institutional Roots of Post-Keynesian Economics.' *Review of Political Economy* 35 (1): 6–27.

Rowthorn, R. E. 1977. 'Conflict, Inflation and Money.' *Cambridge Journal of Economics* 1 (3): 215–239.

Schnabel, I. 2022. 'A New Age of Energy Inflation: Climateflation, Fossilflation and Greenflation.' Speech by Isabel Schnabel, Member of the Executive Board of the ECB, at a panel on "Monetary Policy and Climate Change" at The ECB and its Watchers XXII Conference, Frankfurt am Main, European Central Bank, March 17, 2022. https://www.ecb.europa.eu/press/key/date/2022/html/ecb.sp220317_2~dbb3582f0a.en.html.

Storm, S. 2024. 'Tilting at Windmills: Bernanke and Blanchard's Obsession with the Wage-Price Spiral.' *International Journal of Political Economy* 53 (2): 126–148.

Summa, R., and J. Braga. 2020. 'Two Routes Back to the Old Phillips Curve: The Amended Mainstream Model and the Conflict-augmented Alternative.' *Bulletin of Political Economy* 14 (1): 81–115.

Taylor, L. 1985. 'A Stagnationist Model of Economic Growth.' *Cambridge Journal of Economics* 9 (4): 383–403.

Weber, I. M. 2021. 'Could Strategic Price Controls Help Fight Inflation?' *The Guardian*, December 29. https://www.theguardian.com/business/commentisfree/2021/dec/29/inflation-price-controls-time-we-use-it.

Weber, I. M., and E. Wasner. 2023. 'Sellers' Inflation, Profits and Conflict: Why Can Large Firms Hike Prices in an Emergency?' *Review of Keynesian Economics* 11 (2): 183–213.

ȃ OPEN ACCESS

The Conflict Theory of Inflation Revisited

Robert Rowthorn

ABSTRACT

This article develops ideas contained in a previous paper on conflict inflation (Rowthorn [1977]. 'Conflict, Inflation and Money.' *Cambridge Journal of Economics* 1 (3): 215–239). It begins with a summary of that paper, stressing the importance of staggered markets, conflicting aspirations and unanticipated inflation. It then examines three recent articles that share a similar perspective. In the light of this discussion, it makes some general observations about the nature of conflict inflation. Finally It concludes with an application of conflict theory to the recent cost of living crisis in the UK. It argues that private companies have used their market power to defend their profit margins and ensure that the entire burden of higher world prices is borne by consumers, in particular wage and salary earners.

1. Introduction

For economists of my generation the present conjuncture is a matter of déjà vu: massive increases in the prices of imported fuels and other commodities; rapid growth in domestic prices as firms defend their profit margins and in wages as workers seek to preserve their standard of living; higher interest rates as central banks restrain demand so as to break the wage-price spiral.

All of the above were visible following the oil shocks of the 1970s and are visible today. However, there are some important differences. Globalisation and the decline of industrial employment, especially in manufacturing, have greatly weakened the power of organised labour. In many western countries, trade unions are now largely confined to the public sector. There has also been a decline in the reach and authority of the centralised trade union and business federations that played a major role in implementing government-sponsored income policies during the 1970s.

In the wake of the first oil shock, following debates with Joan Robinson and other Keynesians, I constructed a simple model of what has become known as the conflict theory of inflation (Rowthorn 1977). The following is a condensed version of the model. The notation differs somewhat from the original.

1.1. Rowthorn

There is one type of final output in the economy. Total output is constant and equal to 1. There are four types of competing claims on final output: workers (wages), firms (profits), foreigners (net import costs) and government (taxes). The shares of import costs and taxes in final output are exogenous and equal to F and T respectively.

Real wage determination is a two-stage process. In the first stage, in the labour market, workers negotiate a money wage which takes some account of future inflation. If prices rise as anticipated, workers will receive a share W^{lab} of final output. In the next stage, firms set prices in the product market that in aggregate give them a share Π^{prod} of final output. This implies that the share that workers actually receive, after firms have set their prices, is given by

$$W^{prod} = 1 - \Pi^{prod} - F - T$$

The difference between these two quantities is the 'aspiration gap' which is defined as follows:

$$\begin{aligned} gap &= W^{lab} - W^{prod} \\ &= W^{lab} + \Pi^{prod} + F + T - 1 \end{aligned}$$

The aspiration gap is positive if prices increase by more than was anticipated in the wage bargain. In fact, with the pricing behaviour assumed in my model, unanticipated inflation is proportional to the aspiration gap:

$$p^{un} = \lambda \times gap$$

If agents respond to unanticipated inflation by revising their price expectations upwards, the result may be a potentially explosive wage-price spiral.

Note that the model does not determine the actual rate of inflation, merely its unanticipated component. The above equation would continue to hold if all wages and prices rose by an additional x per cent per annum.

To analyse the impact of a shock to import prices or taxes we proceed as follows. Let the unemployment rate U be a proxy for economic slack and suppose that both W^{lab} and Π^{prod} depend negatively on U. When there is slack in the economy, workers are less able to get higher wages and firms are less able to raise prices.

Bringing these elements together, the aspiration gap is

$$gap(U, F, T) = W^{lab}(U) + \Pi^{prod}(U) + F + T - 1$$

Hence

$$p^{un}(U, F, T) = \lambda \times gap(U, F, T)$$

Holding F and T constant, we get a downward sloping Phillips curve relating unanticipated inflation to unemployment.

The above equations have obvious implications for public policy. Consider an economy with initially a zero aspiration gap, so that unanticipated inflation is zero. Suppose there is a large increase in the cost of imports (F). This will reduce the amount of output to be shared amongst workers and firms. Suppose that neither workers nor firms are prepared to absorb these higher import costs by accepting a lower real income. The total claims on national output will therefore increase and the aspiration gap will become positive. As a result, there will be unanticipated inflation, culminating possibly in an explosive wage-price spiral. One response, popular in the 1970s, is for the government to implement wage and price controls, thereby reducing the various claims on national output and closing the aspiration gap. An alternative, that is popular today, is for the central bank to use monetary policy to reduce the rate of inflation by increasing the amount of slack in the economy. The aim is to engineer a recession or near recession so as to induce workers and (maybe) firms to modify their aims and settle for lower wage and price increases. Such a policy uses the compulsion of economic slack to close the aspiration gap and eliminate undesired inflation. This is what the Oxford economist Thomas Balogh called the 'incomes policy of Karl Marx'.

The above was the essence of my argument. For illustrative purposes, I supplemented the argument by assuming that the central bank could control the level of demand by manipulating the stock of money. This was not crucial to my argument, and in retrospect was a diplomatic mistake. Milton Friedman, a famous advocate of this view, was anathema in Cambridge at the time. I could just as well have assumed, more realistically, that the central bank operated through its control of the interest rate. I should also have stressed my debt to Michael Kalecki, whose influence on my paper is evident. Nevertheless, I believe that my model was rather original at the time, in particular its notion of an aspiration gap and the linkage of this gap to unanticipated inflation. But its main ideas were well-known even then, as can be seen from the following passage from the 1973 Report of the Deutsche Bundesbank.[1]

> The oil-producing countries striving for a larger share in the national product and national income of the industrial countries need not necessarily result in further acceleration in the pace of price rises. Whether this occurs depends in every country very greatly on whether it is made easier or more difficult to pass on the higher prices of these (and other) major imports — in other words, on whether the intensification of the international distribution struggle triggered off by the oil countries' price agreement is followed by an intensification of the domestic struggle for the distribution of the national income, which in real terms is hardly growing. The aim of the Bundesbank's policy, in full agreement with the Federal Government, is to restrict the scope for passing on the higher prices as far as possible from the monetary angle. This is not in marked conflict with other goals of domestic economic policy. Such a conflict is the easier to avoid, the more the participants in the economic process — in conformity with the overall course of economic policy — for their part give priority to the fight against inflation and act accordingly. (DBB 1973, p. 1)

Today's IMF reports say much the same thing.

2. Later Contributions

Since I wrote my 1977 paper, there have been numerous papers on the same theme, many published in so-called heterodox journals. For example, Dutt (1992) uses a

---

[1] I am grateful to Wendy Carlin for bringing this passage to my attention.

conflict theory to analyse accumulation and crises. Carlin and Soskice have done so much to develop the conflict theory of inflation, and conflict between firms and workers lies at the heart of the three-equation model of inflation use to such effect in their textbook (Carlin and Soskice 2014). In the New Keynesian tradition, Erceg, Henderson, and Levin (2000) have used a conflict theory to explore monetary policy. I cannot review the whole of this literature, so I shall confine myself to three recent papers which connect directly with my 1977 article. For a general survey of conflict inflation see chapter 8 of Lavoie (2022).

2.1. Martin

Martin (2023) considers a discrete model in which expectations play no overt role. He uses what he calls a 'rudimentary' model to highlight the essentials of conflict theory, which are often hidden by the detail.

Martin starts by considering two basic regimes which I shall call 'wage-led' and 'price-led'. In both regimes, workers and firms have targets equal to X^* and Z^* respectively. The aspiration gap is X^*Z^*. There is conflict and inflation if $X^*Z^* > 1$.

In the wage-led regime, all workers receive a money wage that allows them to achieve their target X^* at the new average price P_t. Thus, $W_t = X^*P_t$. However, for contractual reasons, only a fraction v of firms is able to set a new price $P_t^* = Z^*W_t$ so as to achieve their target Z^*. The remaining firms are contracted to sell at the old price P_{t-1}. The (geometric) average price is therefore:

$$P_t = (P_t^*)^v e(P_{t-1})^{1-v}$$

Since $P_t^* = Z^*X^*P_t$, it follows that:

$$P_t = P_{t-1}(X^*Z^*)^{v/(1-v)}$$

Note that $P_t > P_{t-1}$ if $X^*Z^* > 1$. Using lower case to denote logs, the above equation can be written

$$p_t - p_{t-1} = \frac{v}{1-\text{v}}(x^* + z^*)$$

The left-hand side is the rate of inflation. There is conflict and inflation if $x^* + z^* > 0$.

In the profit-led regime, the roles of wages and prices are reversed, but otherwise the argument is the same.

Martin is dissatisfied with the above models for the following reasons.

> Inflation occurs in these rudimentary models when at least one of the parties to the real income conflict remains permanently dissatisfied and aggregate real income aspirations are excessive. Behind this prediction lies the assumption that price and wage setting behaviour remains unmoved by the continuing frustrations of the aggrieved. That assumption is questionable. Consider, for example, the first rudimentary model in which firms never achieve their target margin in the presence of inflation. Why would firms willingly accept such a shortfall not only in the current period but in all past periods? ... The same question in principle may be asked of all conflict models in which the real income aspirations of one or both of the competing groups, construed as workers and firms, are persistently thwarted. (Martin 2023, p. 11)

As an illustration, Martin suggests the following pricing rule for firms that reset their prices in period t:

$$P_t^* = Z^* W_t \left[\frac{Z^*}{\frac{P_t}{W_t}} \right]^{\phi t}$$

Since $P_t = (P_t^*)^v (P_{t-1})^{1-v}$ and $W_t = X^* P_t$ the above equation implies that:

$$P`_t = P_{t-1} (X^* Z^*)^{(1+\phi t) \frac{v}{1-v}}$$

If $X^* Z^* > 1$ and $\phi > 0$ there is accelerating inflation as firms try ever harder to make up for past failings.

Using lower case to denote logs, the above equation can be written

$$p_t - p_{t-1} = \frac{v}{1 - \mathrm{v}} (1 + \phi t)(x^* + z^*)$$

There is conflict and inflation if $x^* + z^* > 0$.

> Martin's illustrative adjustment (error correction) mechanism incorporates both 'proportional' and 'integral' control, the latter to make good the cumulative effect of all past margin shortfalls. In the conflict inflation literature, an allowance for 'proportional' control, to address a recent shortfall, is commonplace, but the scarcity (absence?) of 'integral' control is puzzling. Why would firms confine their attention to the most recent profits shortfall and ignore all previous shortfalls? (Martin 2023, p. 11)

The idea that pricing (and wage setting) may have an error correction dimension is important, and Martin is justified in his criticism of the conflict inflation literature for neglecting this issue.

2.2. Michl

The next paper is by Michl (2023). A dynamic version of the aspiration gap based on growth rates is appropriate in this case.

Money wages are determined first and then prices. The growth rate of money wages is

$$\hat{W} = R^w + \alpha_w (e - e^*)$$

where e is the employment rate and e^* is a constant. The variable R^w is the rate of inflation that bargainers assume during wage negotiations. It is conventionally known as expected inflation.

The growth rate of prices is

$$\hat{P} = R^p + \alpha_p (u - 1)$$

where R^p is the rate of inflation that individual firms expect when they set their own prices, and u is capacity utilisation.

The third equation is

$$R^p = \delta R^w + (1 - \delta) \hat{W}$$

This equation indicates how firms' expectations about inflation are influenced by the scale of wage settlements.

If prices grow at the rate anticipated in labour market negotiations, real wages grow at the following rate:

$$\hat{w}^{\text{lab}} = \hat{W} - R^{w} = \alpha_w(e - e^*)$$

The actual growth of real wages depends on the prices that firms set in the product market:

$$\hat{w}^{\text{prod}} = \hat{W} - \hat{P} = \delta\alpha_w(e - e^*) - \alpha_p(u - 1)$$

The aspiration gap (my terminology) is defined as follows:

$$gap = \hat{w}^{\text{lab}} - \hat{w}^{\text{prod}}$$

The gap is the difference between anticipated and actual real wage growth. Unanticipated inflation is

$$\hat{P}^{u} = \hat{P} - R^{w} = gap$$

Michl assumes that $u = e/\kappa$. In this case, $\hat{P}^{u} = 0$ when $e = e_n$ where

$$e_n = e^* + \frac{\alpha_p(1 - e^*/\kappa)}{(1 - \delta)\alpha_w + \alpha_p/\kappa}$$

When e is at this 'neutral' level, the aspiration gap is zero. If the authorities seek to keep e above this level, there will be excess claims on national output (positive aspiration gap) and persistent unanticipated inflation. If expectations are adaptive, the eventual result of such a policy could be explosive inflation.

2.3. Lorenzoni and Werning

Lorenzoni and Werning (2023) — henceforth known as 'L&W' — use a continuous time model to analyse conflict inflation in a network economy. The following is a concise summary of their elegant analysis.

L&W consider an N-sector network in which sectors are linked to each other by an input-output matrix $M = [m_{ij}]$. Some of the sectors may provide labour services, in which case the selling price is a wage. The matrix is irreducible and its rows sum to unity. There is a unique strictly positive vector γ such that for all j:

$$\gamma_j = \Sigma_i \gamma_i m_{ij} \text{ and } \Sigma_i \gamma_i = 1$$

This vector is used to weight the various sectors.

To capture the notion of staggered decision-making, L&W assume Calvo pricing whereby individual agents in sector i can reset their selling price with probability λ_i per unit of time. This probability may vary across sectors but is constant through time. Prices are measured in logarithms.

An agent in sector i who is setting the new price at time t will choose the following reset price:

$$p_{it}^* = a_{it} + \sum_j m_{ij} p_{jt}$$

where a_{it} is the current 'aspiration' of agents in this sector. The nature of this aspiration is unspecified. The aspiration gap (my terminology) for the economy as a whole is defined as follows:

$$gap_t = \Sigma_i \gamma_i a_{it}$$

There is a conflict in aspirations if $gap_t > 0$.

The inflation rate in sector i is given by the following equation:

$$\pi_{it} = \lambda_i (p_{it}^* - p_{it})$$

It can be shown that average inflation is

$$\bar{\pi}_t = \lambda \times gap_t$$

where

$$\lambda = \left(\Sigma_i \frac{\gamma_i}{\lambda_i} \right)^{-1}$$

Thus, average inflation is proportional to the aspiration gap. For this reason, L&W refer to average inflation as conflict inflation.

L&W distinguish between intrinsic aspirations and defensive aspirations. Intrinsic aspirations refer to a situation in which expected prices are constant. A defensive aspiration is the additional amount that a price-setting agent will charge to compensate for expected growth in the cost of inputs. L&W give the following formula for the total aspiration of an agent in sector I at time t.

$$a_{it} = E_{it} \int_t^{\infty} e^{-(\rho+\lambda_i)(s-t)} ((\rho + \lambda_i) a_{is}^* + \Sigma_j m_{ij} \pi_{js}) ds$$

where a_{is}^* is an intrinsic aspiration and ρ is the discount rate.

To illustrate the implications of the above formula, assume that all intrinsic aspirations are constant ($a_{is}^* = a_i^*$ for all s), that all expected prices grow at the same constant rate $\bar{\pi}^e$, and that $\lambda_i = \lambda$ for all i. Then

$$a_{it} = a_i^* + \frac{\bar{\pi}^e}{\rho + \lambda}$$

and average inflation is

$$\bar{\pi}_t = \lambda \left(\Sigma_i \gamma_i a_i^* + \frac{\bar{\pi}^e}{\rho + \lambda} \right)$$

If $\Sigma_i \gamma a_i^* = 0$ there is no intrinsic conflict, but fear of future inflation may cause agents to seek higher prices and hence cause inflation and conflict.

L&W do not discuss unanticipated inflation, but it can be derived from the above equation by subtracting $\bar{\pi}^e$ from each side:

$$\bar{\pi}_t - \bar{\pi}^e = \lambda(\Sigma_i \gamma_i a_i^*) - \frac{\rho\bar{\pi}^e}{\rho + \lambda}$$

Note that $\lambda(\Sigma_i \gamma_i a_i^*)$ is equal to unanticipated inflation when $\rho = 0$ and to actual inflation when $\rho = \infty$.

2.4. Comparison

(1) Unanticipated inflation in my paper is proportional to the intrinsic aspiration gap. The same is true in Michl and, under certain restrictive conditions, in L&W. Martin does not consider expectations explicitly. He is more concerned with the catch-up process, whereby firms (and workers) seek to recoup past losses. Actual inflation in his model is proportional to the aspiration gap.
(2) Defensive pricing plays a similar role in Rowthorn, Michl and L&W. Fearing future inflation, agents increase their prices, thereby provoking what they fear. As Franklin Roosevelt said in another context, 'We have nothing to fear except fear itself'.
(3) In Rowthorn, Michl and L&W, expectations influence inflation and lend a degree of indeterminacy to their predictions.

3. What is the Conflict Theory of Inflation?

The term 'conflict theory' is often used to denote any theory which explains inflation as the outcome of conflict between organised or semi-organised groupings, typically capital and labour. From this perspective, it is a variant of institutional economics. However, many conflict theories, including those reviewed in this article, have another feature. In pursuing their conflicting aims, the parties involved interact within a specific kind of market framework. This framework consists of staggered and uncoordinated markets in which various types of agents have differential powers over price (and wage) setting. The existence of staggered and uncoordinated markets promotes the establishment of wage-wage, wage-price or price-price spirals, in which gains by some types of agent in one market are later partially or fully negated by reverses in some other market. This possibility allows conflicting aims to manifest themselves as inflation.

Incomes policies were popular in the 1970s. They served two purposes. One was to establish some target distribution of income. The other was to coordinate wage and price decisions, so that this outcome could be achieved without inflation.

The conflict theory has been associated with class conflict, as in the case of a wage-price spiral, but it might well apply in other contexts. An example would be a tug of war between oil producers and consuming countries. If the consuming countries raise their own prices in response to a higher oil price, the producing countries may retaliate by raising the oil price a second time, and so on.

Martin, Michl and Rowthorn identify the agents involved as workers and firms. In contrast, L&W ignore the identity of agents and focus exclusively on the market framework within which agents interact. Their contribution should not therefore be classified as a conflict theory, but as a general foundation for such theories. This, indeed, is their stated aim.

3.1. An Example

To illustrate the conflict theory in action, I shall examine the recent inflation and cost of living crisis. I shall concentrate on the UK, which is the economy I know best, although the experience of many other advanced economies is similar.

It will be useful to consider the claims on national output under four headings: foreign trade (net cost of imports), taxation, profits, wages.

The inflation was set off by Covid and the war in the Ukraine. The resulting disruption of supply chains caused a sharp spike in world commodity prices. The IMF index of energy prices rose from 126 in January 2020 to a peak of 370 in August 2022 and, for other commodities, the index peaked at 178 in April 2022. Commodity prices have fallen somewhat since then, but remain high by historical standards.

Reflecting these developments, UK import prices increased by 12.2 per cent during the course of 2022 when the cost of living became a hot political issue. Export prices rose by 11.7 per cent over the same period. I estimate that the net cost to the UK of higher world prices in 2022 was equivalent to 3.4 per cent of the national wage and salary bill.[2] Higher world prices were reflected in higher consumer prices. During the course of 2022, real wages fell by 3.4 per cent because money wages were not able to keep up with prices (Figures 1 and 2).[3] Thus, the loss to the UK due to higher world prices accounts numerically for the entire reduction in real wages that occurred during 2022.

What of the other claims on national output? During the crisis years of 2021 and 2022, the official series indicate that the share of private sector profits in GDP remained virtually constant throughout this period, but rose sharply towards the end. The closing surge may be a statistical anomaly due to the alignment adjustment of private non-financial company profits. When the gross operating surplus is calculated without adjustment, it remains flat as a percentage of GDP right through 2023 (Figure 3). The typical firm, it seems, was able to pass on higher costs with a normal profit margin to the wage earning consumer. A result that would not have surprised Kalecki!

Figure 4 plots the ratio of taxes to the national wage and salary bill. There is a wave-like motion, reflecting the surge in income tax payments towards the end of the tax year. Total taxes rose somewhat faster than the wage bill during this period. This is partly explained by increased receipts from the corporation tax levied on private companies. The government also introduced a 25 per cent Energy Profits Levy in May 2022. Conversely, there was a temporary Energy Support Scheme which gave every household a £400 discount on their energy bills for winters 2022 and 2023. This shielded households from the full impact of higher energy prices at the expense of the energy companies. However, these measures were both too little and too late to prevent a significant reduction in the material standard of living of the average worker.

---

[2]The net cost was estimated as follows. Exports and imports for the period 2020–2023 were revalued at 1st quarter 2020 prices and the results subtracted from the actual 2020–2023 figures.

[3]The series for earnings is from ONS (2023a). It refers to total weekly pay, seasonally adjusted excluding arrears. The series for consumer prices is from ONS (2023b). All series plotted in Figures 2–4 are from ONS (2023c).

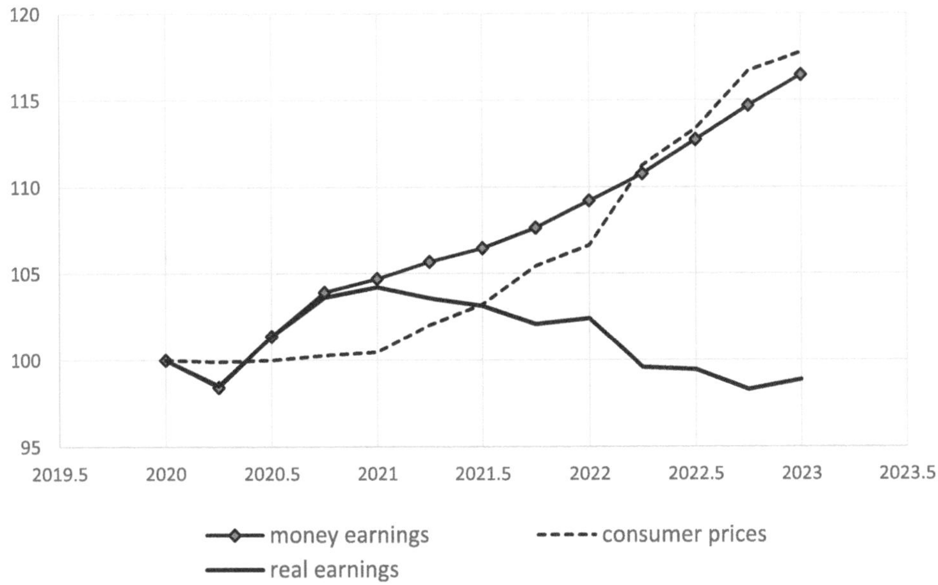

Figure 1. Earnings and prices.

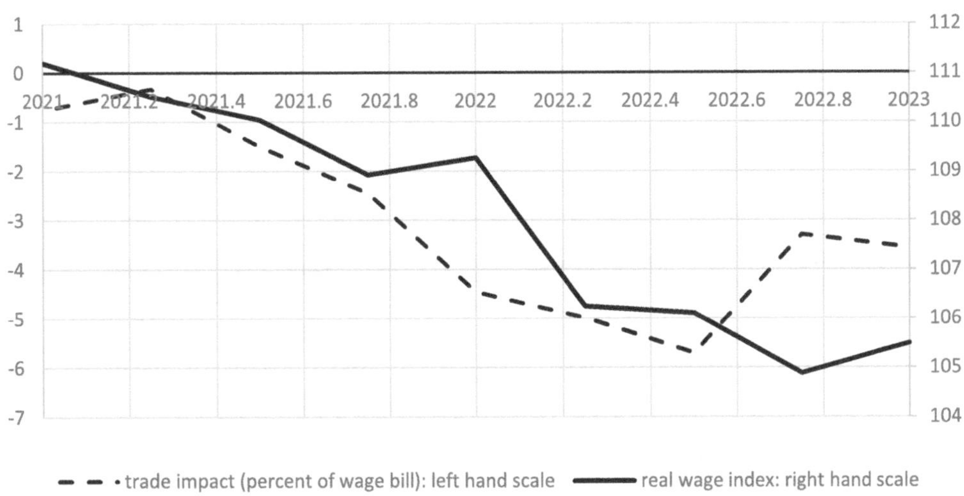

Figure 2. Trade loss and real wages compared.

To sum up. The evidence suggests that the burden of higher world prices was borne largely by wage and salary earners. Private firms were able to maintain their profit margins by passing on their higher costs to consumers.

These developments took place against a background of economic stagnation. Once the economy had bounced back from Covid, annual GDP growth slowed down to an average 0.5 per cent. Given stagnant productivity, the rising claims of import costs and taxes, plus the resilience of profits, it was inevitable that real wages would fall. Money wages increased but not enough to offset the higher cost of living.

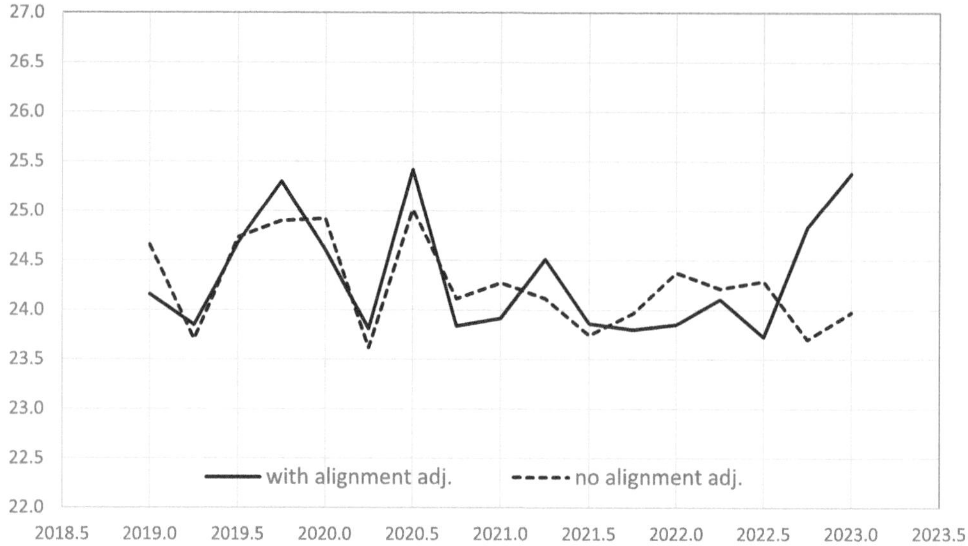

Figure 3. Gross operating surplus of private companies as per cent of GDP.

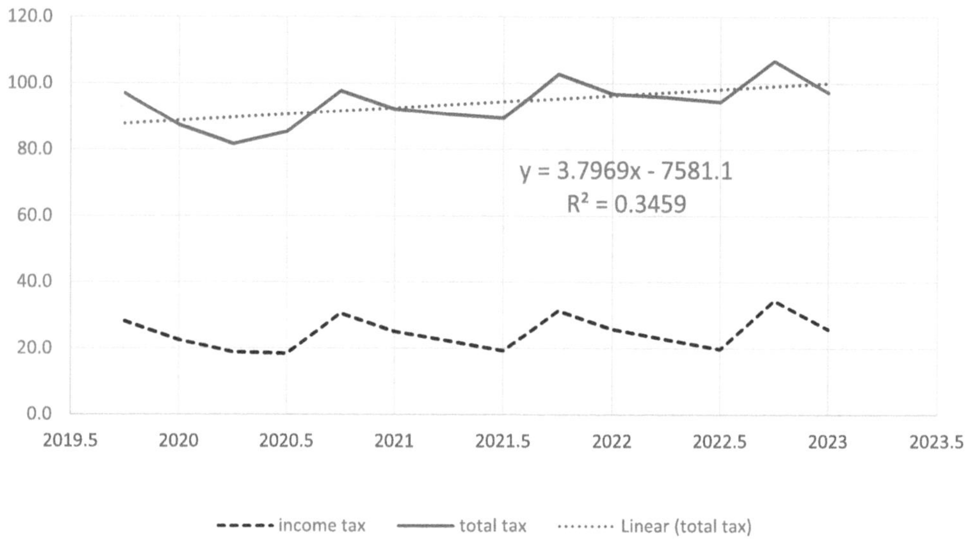

Figure 4. UK taxes as percentage of national wage bill.

At the time of writing, the cost of living crisis is ongoing. Workers in the private sector, being mostly without trade unions, must accept what the market offers. But workers in the highly unionised public sector, or the quasi-public sector such as the railways, can resist. There has been a spate of strikes by teachers, university lecturers, ambulance drivers, doctors, nurses, train drivers and others. Many of these public sector workers have settled for below-inflation pay rises, but they will be back for more. To stem the inflation, the Bank of England has taken an increasingly hawkish stance, raising the interest rate dramatically. The resulting fall in demand will reduce inflationary pressures in the private sector, although at uncertain cost in terms of lost output.

4. Conclusion

Conflict theories explain inflation as the outcome of conflicting claims in staggered markets. The extent to which claims conflict can in principle be measured by some variant of the aspiration gap. The recent cost of living crisis in the United Kingdom (and many other advanced economies) can be usefully analysed from a conflict theory perspective.

Acknowledgements

I should like to thank Wendy Carlin, Bill Martin and Ivan Werning for many valuable discussions on the topic of conflict inflation.

Disclosure Statement

No potential conflict of interest was reported by the author(s).

References

Carlin, W., and D. Soskice. 2014. *Macroeconomics: Institutions, Instability, and the Financial System*. Oxford: Oxford University Press.

DBB. 1973. 'Report of the Deutsche Bundesbank 1973.'

Dutt, A. K. 1992. 'Conflict, Inflation, Distribution, Cyclical Accumulation and Crises.' *European Journal of Political Economy* 8 (4): 579–597.

Erceg, C., D. Henderson, and A. Levin. 2000. 'Optimal Monetary Policy with Staggered Wage and Price Contracts.' *Journal of Monetary Economics* 46 (2): 281–313.

Lavoie, M. 2022. *Post-Keynesian Economics. New Foundations*. 2nd ed. Cheltenham: Edward Elgar. 744 Pages.

Lorenzoni, G., and I. Werning. 2023. 'Inflation is Conflict.' https://conference.nber.org/conf_papers/f188954.pdf.

Martin, B. 2023. 'Rudimentary Inflation Conflict Models: A Note.' Centre for Business Research, University of Cambridge, Working Paper No. 535. 24 Pages.

Michl, T. 2023. 'Inflation Stabilization and Normal Utilization.' *Journal of Post-Keynesian Economics.*

ONS. 2023a. 'AWE: Whole Economy Level (£): Seasonally Adjusted Total Pay Excluding Arrears.' Office for National Statistics, August 15.

ONS. 2023b. 'Inflation and Price Indices.' Office for National Statistics, August 16.

ONS. 2023c. 'GDP: Quarterly National Accounts UK: January to March 2023.' Office for National Statistics, June 30.

Rowthorn, R. E. 1977. 'Conflict, Inflation and Money.' *Cambridge Journal of Economics* 1 (3): 215–239.

Conflictual Distributional Struggles and Inflation

Malcolm Sawyer

ABSTRACT
The article is focused on what it terms a conflictual distributional approach to inflation and economic activity. It presents a brief discussion of the relationships between conflictual approaches and the mainstream approaches. It then makes some remarks on the macro-economic and micro-economic aspects of the analysis of inflation and the role of money. Analyses of price setting and wage determination are brought together to provide employment and real wage levels whereby claims on income are mutually consistent. The framework is utilised to discuss sources of inflationary pressure and the roles of capacity and demand.

1. Introduction

This article considers the contributions of perspectives on inflation in which distributional struggles play a major role. There is often what is termed a conflict theory of inflation; however, it can be expanded to include a conflictual distributional approach to inflation. It is also recognised that the conflictual approach builds on a general perspective of a conflictual society, and that there are many formulations of such an approach that share some common features but also differ in terms of specific representation.

The article begins with reflections on discussions of inflation (Section Two) and the ways in which conflictual claims over income distribution have been downplayed in most approaches to analysis of inflation. When price setting and wage determination are considered, there appear to be divergent claims regarding income shares that have to be reconciled in some way. However, mainstream analyses have ignored or downplayed the consequences of these divergent claims. Section Three provides some general considerations to bear in mind when analysing inflation. Section Four presents a discussion of the analysis of price and wage determination and the factors that influence the outcomes. Section Five brings together price and wage determination to consider what is termed an inflation barrier (a constant inflation level of employment) and discuss inflation dynamics. Section Six provides some concluding commentary.

2. Historical Reflections

Although conflict approaches to inflation became explicit during the 1970s and some contrast with dominant approaches at the time involving some form of Phillips curve and monetarism (with the stock of money being the major causal factor for inflation), they played a rather limited role in general macro-economic discussions on inflation. For example, Laidler and Parkin (1975), in their major review of inflation, placed monetarism, expectations on inflation and excess demand centre stage, and largely ignored any approach that could be linked with a conflict approach, with the exception that studies of wage inflation and trade union strength were included. According to them, 'Inflation is a process of continuously rising prices, or equivalently, of a continuously falling value of money. .... Inflation is, then, fundamentally a monetary phenomenon' (p. 741). A statement such as this casts the study of inflation within the macro-economic realm; that is, it is a study between two aggregates (money and price level) for which there is no micro-economic counterpart. It places the relationship between money and prices as central rather than, say, prices and wages — a monetary phenomenon rather than an income distribution issue. Laidler and Parkin made little suggestion of a conflictual approach, although the role played by trade unions in wage inflation was brought in. They quoted Harrod — '[the] new wage–price explosion is altogether unprecedented ... the causes [of which] are sociological [and] first cousins to the causes of such things as student unrest' (I972, p. 44) — and then ignored the point.

Approaches to inflation have often been formulated in terms of a Phillips curve, though what is meant by that curve (price or wage inflation, role of expectations, measure of economic activity) and the perceived mechanism underlying it has various explanations. The Phillips curve being a single-equation approach is not suggestive of a conflict concerning income shares. And, in its Friedman (1968) formulation, it becomes associated with a 'natural rate of unemployment', which bears a strong similarity to labour market clearing and full employment, and lack of a medium to long-run trade-off between inflation and unemployment. The new Keynesian Phillips curve focuses mainly on price inflation and its relationship with expected inflation and the output gap, and makes the assumption of marginal costs increasing with output. An extension to wage inflation is provided in Galí (2015, Chapter 6), based on the assumption that workers 'face Calvo-type constraints on the frequency with which they can adjust nominal wages'. Price and wage inflation equations can be placed together to yield equilibrium involving output gap and profit share. However, in comparison to the conflict approach discussed below, this is analysed in the context of a closed economy. Approaches such as those represented in Blanchard, Amighini, and Giavazzi (2021) utilise a wage and price level equation. Here, the equality of the wage–price ratio is asserted, from which a 'natural rate of unemployment' is then derived, though one which bears little resemblance to Friedman's concept. In the simple formulation, the wage–price ratio is effectively set by the pricing decision and the wage decision has to be brought into line through the rate of unemployment. While there is potential conflict regarding the wage–price ratio, little attention is paid to that. Formulations such as that of Layard, Nickell, and Jackman ([1991] 2005) were based on price- and wage-setting behaviour and claims regarding income shares (real product wage) were conflictual but seen to be mutually compatible at the so-called (and mis-named) non-accelerating inflation rate of unemployment (NAIRU). When price- and wage-setting behaviour are portrayed in terms of a relationship between prices and wages, then there is inevitably a degree of conflict. The conflict has tended to be downplayed, and little attention has been given to inflationary processes. Instead, the focus shifted to the operations of the labour market, role of employment protection, etc. and implications for the rate of unemployment.

The emergence of a conflict approach to inflation largely arose on the political left (at least within the UK). Rowthorn (1977b), in the chapter entitled 'Inflation and crisis', cites debates in *Marxism Today* and provides a general perspective. In his paper entitled 'Conflict, inflation and money', Rowthorn (1977a) started from the view that 'conflict is endemic in the capitalist system and concerns all aspects of economic life' (p. 215). In his approach, inflation rises as a result of the competing claims of workers and capitalists, summarised by the term 'aspiration gap'. 'The aspiration gap is determined by the market power of workers and capitalists, and their willingness to use this power. Thus, anything which affects the extent or use of power will affect the aspiration gap and, through it, the rate of inflation' (215). The scale of the aspiration gap depends on the level of demand providing a route through which level of demand impacts inflation. Taxes and the terms of trade impact the share of income available for post-tax wages and profits, and workers and capitalists seek higher wages or prices to compensate for reduction in real disposable income arising from higher taxes and higher import costs.

My own thinking about inflation and a conflict approach was strongly influenced by the results of empirical work on wage and price inflation in the UK in which I was involved in the second half of the 1970s and into the 1980s. In Henry, Sawyer, and Smith (1976) a range of inflation theories, including both price and wage inflation estimations, were empirically tested for the UK during the period from the late 1940s to the mid-1970s. Simple versions of the Phillips curve (rate of wage change as a function of the unemployment rate and expected inflation) and a monetarist formulation with the stock of money influencing the rate of price inflation were examined and found empirically wanting in our study. We estimated a 'target real wage' approach (as, for example, equation 5 below). This approach had not been extensively used at the time, and we drew on Sargan (1964), which had been more of an econometric exploration. It incorporated an error correction mechanism, and indeed was one of the first applications of that technique. As such, it portrays money wages adjusting towards a 'target' real wage in light of price inflation expectations, with the process of adjustment influenced by the rate of unemployment. Unemployment plays a constraining role in relation to wage inflation but unemployment reflects (inversely) workers' bargaining power. In the Phillips curve, unemployment is generally seen as reflecting demand (or, as in Lipsey 1960, excess demand for labour). One of the properties of the simple Phillips curve is that, for low rates of unemployment, wages rise faster than (expected) prices, and the real wage (wage to price ratio) rises. Low unemployment would lead to real wages rising year after year. In the excess demand view, a higher real wage would lead to a fall in demand for labour and thereby a rise in unemployment. This adjustment process is clearly absent in the target real wage approach, the implications of which are described below.

In Sawyer with Aaronovitch and Samson (1983) (and also Sawyer et al., 1982), price change equations were estimated for 40 UK manufacturing industries over the period

1966 to 1975 on a quarterly basis. In Chapter 2 they argued that price determination can be viewed as a mark-up over unit costs from a wide range of theoretical perspectives. Lee (1998), in his survey of pricing behaviour, confirms that. With 'target' price (that is, the price the firm believes to be in its own interests) set as a mark-up over costs, then change in price is related to change in costs and adjustment of price towards the 'target' relationship with costs. For example, using a profit maximisation approach, the target price would be a mark-up (depending on price elasticity of demand) over (marginal) costs. One feature of looking at price change at the industry level is that differences between industries in terms of response of price to cost and demand changes. It also reveals that, at the firm/industry level, changes in unit labour costs are relatively unimportant to price changes (to the extent that, on average, a 1 per cent change in unit labour costs leads to a circa 0.2 per cent change in price; this relates to manufacturing) and input prices are rather more important. This is perhaps not surprising in light of the ratio of labour costs to sales revenue.

These empirical studies indicated that price and wage formation had to be approached separately (and hence any single-equation representation, however arrived at, would be inadequate), and conflicting claims would exist regarding income shares. It becomes self-evident that the 'target' relationship between price and costs has an implication for the wage–price ratio and the 'target real wage' has implications for the wage–price ratio. There is an inevitable conflict between the income claims of these two groups.[1] On the price determination side, while there was a basic mark-up pricing approach, the patterns differed across industries, including whether higher economic activity would be associated with higher prices.

The conflict concerning income shares between workers and capital is placed centre stage in the domestic economy. The pricing decisions, however, depend on wages, domestic input prices and prices of imported goods and services, including commodities, semi-finished and finished goods. The sometimes dramatic rise in some global prices (and often subsequent reversals) has substantial effects on domestic inflation through pricing decisions. Government, via taxation decisions, can affect conflictual claims, as will be briefly mentioned below.

3. Some General Considerations on Inflation Analysis

3.1. Inflation and Macro-economics

The study of inflation is regarded as belonging in macro-economics rather than micro-economics textbooks. As Weber and Wasner (2023) note, 'the dominant view of inflation holds that it is macroeconomic in origin and must always be tackled with macroeconomic tightening' (p. 103). The macro-economic origins are located in the level of aggregate demand and/or the stock of money. The policy responses to inflation currently focus on the use of monetary policy and interest rates, but at other times have included deflationary fiscal policies and control of the growth of the money supply.

Pasinetti (1974) described his approach to analysis as

[1] See Sawyer (1982) for my first attempt to place price and wage determination together.

> not 'macro-economic' in the sense of representing a first simplified rough step towards a more detailed and disaggregated analysis. It is macro-economic because it could not be otherwise. Only problems have been discussed which are of a macro-economic nature; an accurate investigation of them has nothing to do with disaggregation. They would remain the same — i.e. they would still arise at a macro-economic level — even if we were to break down the model into a disaggregated analysis and therefore introduce the necessary additional information (or assumption) about consumers' choice of goods and producers' choice of techniques. (p. 118)

Prices and wages are settled at the micro-economic and meso-economic levels, and respond to level and composition of demand (relative to capacity) and costs. The price level is merely a weighted average of an appropriate range of prices of goods and services. The rate of price inflation is derived from price changes at the micro-economic level, which is viewed as a micro-economic rather than a macro-economic (in the sense of Pasinetti) phenomenon. Within an overall rate of inflation, changes in relative prices may occur via the structure of demand, differences in cost changes, etc. A sharp change in some prices has often had implications for general change in prices. Rapid rises in commodity prices have been major contributory factors to inflationary episodes in industrialised countries, such as in 1950/51, 1972/74 and 2021/23. In the other direction, though often less spectacularly, decline in commodity prices in the 1980s (e.g., Beckerman and Jenkinson 1986) could aid in lowering inflation. Downward pressure on the prices of many manufactured products exported by China were argued to aid the low inflation climate of the 2000s.

The monetarist approach to inflation is macro-economic in nature: a relationship such as $MV = PT$ is macro-economic, and the implied direction of causation runs from M to P. As monetarists argue, an upward change to some prices will not cause inflation for a given money supply because some other prices will need to fall to ensure consistency with $MV = PT$. Post-Keynesians and many others would, of course, deny the perceived exogenous nature of money and would view the direction of causation running from changes in some prices to changes in money stock (as evidenced in, for example, Hasan 1999; Hoover 1991).

A change in the general level of demand ('aggregate demand') would have widespread effects on prices, production and employment. The effects of such a general change occur via decisions made by firms and others on price. Changes in relative prices can exist as firms may be in different positions in terms of output relative to capacity, and variations across different sectors of the economy may occur in response to how far level of demand has changed.

Viewed in this way, counter-inflation policies could focus on control of individual prices. Attempts at price and incomes policies, particularly from the 1950s to the 1970s, did indeed seek to limit price rises (over a year say) in line with the government's inflation target.

The macro-economic relations in a conflict approach (as indeed in the NAIRU approach) relate to the derivation of what is termed the constant inflation rate of employment (CIRE), which relates to the level of economic activity (measured by employment rate) and income distribution at which inflation would be constant. This is macro-economic in the sense that there is no corresponding micro-economic relationship.

3.2. Money

A conflict approach to inflation, like most theories of inflation, has to be located within an endogenous money framework. Higher prices and wages have to be financed and paid for, and that applies to all theories of inflation other than a monetarist theory from some form of 'helicopter money'. Specifically, money in the form of commercial bank deposits (in a current account) is created through the loans process, and destroyed though the repayment of loans. Producers require initial finance (to use circuitist terminology) to cover costs of production, and rising costs of production (whether as a result of costs rising or through purchase of inputs to enable higher output) and banks can provide loans to enable that initial financing. With a reflux mechanism, the loans would be repaid and the stock of money would not rise. Any desire by the public to hold ('demand') more money (in the form of bank deposits), say for transaction demand purposes, would mean the reflux mechanism would be incomplete and there would be some increase in the stock of money.

3.3. Conflictual, Income Distribution and Inflation

Conflictual claims over income shares are ever present, with degrees of reconciliation between the competing claims, as suggested in the model below (and many others). When competing claims are mutually consistent, which can be interpreted as a form of 'stand-off', each party views the cost of pushing up their share of income as too much. In the CIRE below, there is a possible reconciliation between employment level and the wage–price ratio, and inflation (price and wage inflation) is portrayed as constant when the economy operates at that employment level and wage–price ratio. The reconciliation of income shares can be disturbed in many ways: shifts in the target real wage and pressures to achieve it, shifts in target profit margins, and moves in the prices of imported goods and services are amongst the factors mentioned below. A move in the level of demand from that consistent with the CIRE would involve rising (higher demand) or falling (lower demand) inflation. It is rising inflation rather than level of inflation that arises from conflict when one party pushes for an increased income share. The level of inflation that eventually results is path dependent when inflation rises and, subsequently, when measures such as demand deflation are taken to reduce it.

4. Price and Wage Behaviour

This section considers price-setting behaviour and then wage determination. In each case, I start with a general formulation. It must be stressed that price setting is undertaken in numerous ways, depending on firms' motivation, interdependences between firms, industrial structure, etc. In a similar vein, wage determination comes in many forms ranging from close to a spot market through to collective bargaining. Seeking to provide an aggregate representation of price and wage setting necessarily involves severe aggregation issues thus, at best, the economy-level representation below can only be indicative. It also the case that there are differences in price and wage determination over time and space, and social, political and institutional factors will have a bearing on those determinations. As argued above, the aggregate representation of price setting is not a macro-economic relationship but, rather, is based on summation of micro-economic relations. The price level is built up as an average of individual prices, and then price inflation is the rate of change of that price level. Further, price changes in one sector depend on wage and cost changes, and some of those cost changes reflect price changes in other sectors.

4.1. Price Setting

Firms set prices seeking to achieve their profit, growth and market share objectives. The target price of a firm can be portrayed as a mark-up over unit costs, with the specific formulation dependent on the objectives of the firm. As a general formulation, the target price at the level of the firm that would aid the firm to achieve its objectives is portrayed as a mark-up of price over unit costs. Formulations of this form can arise from profit maximisation under different industrial structures through to average cost pricing.

The general production relationship at the firm level is viewed in terms of output depending on labour inputs, intermediate domestic inputs, imported inputs and scale of capital stock. A general formulation for what may be termed the target price of firm i is:

$$p_i = m\left(\frac{q_i}{q_i^*}, dm_i\right).[w_i.l_i + c_i.d_i + f_i.z_i] \quad (1)$$

where q_i is output of firm, l_i labour input; d_i is intermediate domestic inputs with price c_i; z_i is imported inputs with price f_i and m mark-up over costs, where the mark-up depends on the measure of capacity utilisation; and dm_i is degree of monopoly/market power. The mark-up may decline with higher capacity utilisation initially, then be broadly constant and then rise with capacity utilisation.

Viewed at the firm/sector level, the following (obvious) points arise. A rise in demand facing that sector could well raise profit margin. Price–price spirals may occur whereby one sector's output price becomes another sector's input price.

Allowing for different types of labour and input, and recognising that prices of domestic inputs are similarly based, the price equations are expressed in matrix notation:

$$\text{p} = \text{A.p} + \text{B.w} + \text{C.f} \quad (2)$$

where p is vector of prices; elements of A refer to the domestic inputs plus mark-up (i.e., corresponding to the term *dm* in equation (1)); w is vector of wage rates and B is matrix of labour inputs plus mark-up (corresponding to $m_{i..}l_{i.}$); f is vector of foreign input prices and C is matrix of foreign input requirements plus mark-up ($m_{i}f_{i.}$ in the above). This provides:

$$\text{p} = (\text{I}-\text{A})^{-1}.[\text{B.w} + \text{C.f}] \quad (3)$$

In general, the elements of the matrices are dependent on output in the relevant sector. This would imply that an expansion of demand would have effects on relative prices, and that the effects would also depend on changes in the composition of demand. This equation clearly refers to price levels. Changes in price result from adjustments of actual prices towards the 'target' prices, and also from changes in profit margins, wages and foreign input prices. The rate of change over a given period (i.e., what is calculated as the rate of inflation) depends on the speed of adjustment. From the **p** vector, price of consumption goods could be highlighted and a consumer price index derived therefrom. The price of investment goods could be treated similarly.

An equation such as (3) should serve as a reminder of the interrelationships between prices and that the feed-through of wages and foreign prices into prices is likely to be subject to lags. More significantly, however, changes in foreign prices will have differential effects on relative prices. A change in relative prices can be significant in terms of income distribution; consider the effects of energy and food prices in the recent inflationary episode.

Expectations (of future costs and prices) may not play significant role. Price here is that at which the product concerned is offered, and can be readily changed. Expectations can be seen to be relevant when price is contracted for a significant period ahead, and the producer (and also the purchaser) pays some attention to the prices expected to appertain during the contracted period. When prices can be adjusted frequently, then expectations regarding the future course of prices are downgraded in significance, and prices respond to actual cost changes.

The relationships involved in equation (3) are complex and do not afford simple aggregate representation. I postulate that a relationship of the general form exists between *rp* (retail prices) and wages (index); *rp*/*w* is a U-shaped function of level of output and is dependent on the ratio of foreign input prices to wages.[2] In turn, level of output is treated as linearly related with total employment:

$$rp = m\left(\frac{Q}{Q}*\right).\left[w.\frac{L}{Q}+f.z\right] \tag{4}$$

where *rp* is index of retail prices, *Q* is aggregate output, Q^* is capacity output, *w* is wage index, *L* is employment, *f* is index of imported prices and *z* is imported inputs. Equation (4) can be re-arranged to express *w*/*rp* in terms of employment and ratio of imported prices to wages. This is illustrated in Figure 1 and labelled price determination.

At any point in time, firms would be some way off their target price, and would be adjusting towards the target price. In terms of the price determination curve, when the wage–price ratio is relatively high and hence the price–wage ratio is relatively low, firms would be adjusting their prices upwards, that is, faster than wages are increasing. In a similar vein, a relatively low wage–price ratio would be associated with prices.

The *rp*–*w* ratio will be higher for a higher market power reflected in a higher mark-up, *m*. The position of the price determination curve depends on the number of enterprises, and the scale of the capital stock. A higher price of imported materials, *F*, leads to higher prices and the ‘paradox of costs’ is in operation under which the profit share rises with imported prices to the detriment of wages.

Price equations such as (4) clearly relate to price level, and do not directly inform us of price changes and the rate of price inflation. It can readily be observed that, if any element of the right-hand side of eqation (4) is higher, then the target price will be higher. This would include wages and input prices and also profit margins. Lerner (1958) called this

[2]For a similar derivation, see Sawyer (2002).

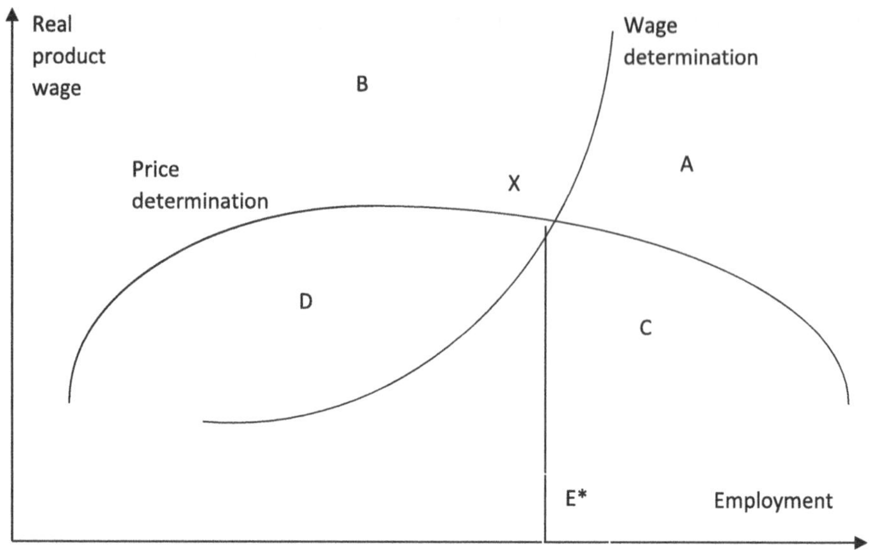

Figure 1. Price determination and wage determination curves.
In zone A: $\dot{w} > \dot{p}(-1)$; $\dot{p} \dot{>} \dot{w}(-1)$;
in zone B: $\dot{w} < \dot{p}(-1)$; $\dot{p} \dot{>} \dot{w}(-1)$;
in zone C: $\dot{w} > \dot{p}(-1)$; $\dot{p} \dot{<} \dot{w}(-1)$; and
in zone D: $\dot{w} < \dot{p}(-1)$; $\dot{p} \dot{<} \dot{w}(-1)$.

situation 'seller-induced inflation' driven by firms' pricing decisions. Lerner observed that, '[t]here is … no essential asymmetry between the wage element and the profit element in the price asked for the product.' A sellers' inflation can just as well be triggered by firms trying to protect or increase their profits as by rising wages. Thus, '[p]rices may rise not because of the pressure of buyers who are finding it difficult to buy all they want to buy at the current prices' but 'because of pressures by sellers who insist on raising their prices' (p. 258; quoted in Weber and Wasner 2023). Prices are 'administered' in the sense that firms make conscious decisions about them, and there can be a degree of 'stickiness' on prices resulting from factors such as information collection and decision-making times, etc. A firm facing oligopolistic or monopolistic competition needs to be aware of decisions taken by its competitors when making a decision on price changes. A complaint frequently made about firms' pricing behaviour (e.g., over oil and gas prices, over loan and deposit interest rates) is that firms are quicker to raise prices in the face of a cost increase than they are to lower prices in the face of a cost decrease. When faced with a substantial increase in costs, a firm may raise its price quickly in the belief that other firms faced with the same increase in costs will also raise theirs. Cost increases may then be passed on quickly and the rate of price increases will match the rate of cost increases. And contrary to the administered price and new Keynesian 'menu costs' literature, firms have the capacity to raise prices (and also lower prices) rapidly, though in practice the speed of the process would depend on the contractual arrangements, that is, long-term contracts governing price of supplies and price of output. The degree of monopoly and oligopolistic independence would be expected to impact on the mark-up of prices over costs; however, in an inflationary climate the effects on the speed of adjustment to cost changes may well be more substantial. It could also be noted that prices are often adjusted on a much more frequent basis than wages (and, indeed, on income sources such as pensions and benefits).

4.2. Wage Determination

In terms of the algebraic representation of the equilibrium relationship between real wages and employment, many of the approaches that are compatible with ours lead to similar outcomes — for example, trade union bargaining models and efficiency wage models (for more details, see Layard, Nickell and Jackman [1991] 2005, especially Chapters 8 and 9, and Sawyer 2002). The key elements of this approach are that real wages and employment are positively related, and money wages adjust to the experience of inflation as well as contain elements of seeking to adjust the real wage.

From their large empirical study across a range of countries, Blanchflower and Oswald (1994) concluded that,

> *A worker who is employed in an area of high unemployment earns less than an identical worker in a region with low joblessness.* ... The nature of the relationship appears to be the same in different countries. ... As a crude characterization of the data ... the wage curve is described by the formula:
>
> $\ln w = -0.1 \ln U + \text{other terms},$
>
> where $\ln w$ is the log of the wage [and] $\ln U$ is the log of unemployment in the worker's area .... A hypothetical doubling of unemployment is then associated with a drop in pay of 10 per cent (that is, a fall of one tenth). (p. 5, emphasis in original)

They postulate three ways of interpreting these results: 'First, the relationship might be the equation of a contract curve. Second, it might be a no-shirking condition. Third, it might be a kind of bargaining-power locus' (p. 93).

All of these interpretations would fit with the general ideas lying behind the wage determination curve.

Nominal wages are settled in a wide range of institutional settings through various forms of negotiation and bargaining. The specific formula used here is based on the idea of a target real wage on the part of workers, the achievement of which is related to the bargaining strength of workers, including the state of demand and unemployment. This is expressed as:

$$\dot{w} = a_1 + a_2 \dot{p}_{-1} + a_3 U + a_4(lnw_{-1} - lnrp_{-1} - lnT) \quad (5)$$

where w is money wage, p is retail price level, T is target real wage and U is unemployment rate. A dot over a variable indicates the proportionate rate of change of that variable.

The real wage would be constant when:

$$a_1 + a_3 U + a_4(lnw - lnp - lnT) = 0 \quad (6)$$

with $a_2 = 1$ assumed for convenience.[3] Equation (6) is interpreted as the wage determination curve in Figure 1 as a relationship between real wage and employment level

[3]The use of $a_2 = 1$ is a convenient simplification: without that assumption the inflation barrier level of employment developed later would also be a function of the rate of inflation.

(under the assumption that employment and unemployment are closely and negatively related).

For positions of the economy above the wage determination curve in terms of demand (as reflected in level of employment) and income distribution (represented by the wage–price ratio), wages tend to rise at a slower rate than prices. For positions of the economy below the wage determination curve, wages tend to rise at a faster rate that prices.

The institutional arrangements for wage determination vary widely from close to a spot market through to collective bargaining. The mechanisms in operation differ across sectors of the economy. In the analysis below I represent wage determination in terms of equations (4) to (6) above but recognise that it is not possible to provide an aggregation for the different forces at work into a single equation.

5. Inflationary Barriers and Inflation Dynamics

These ideas on price and wage determination are now brought together. In doing so, there is a position of the economy (in terms of real product wage and employment) at which wage and price inflation would be constant. Here, this is labelled the constant inflation rate of employment (CIRE), although it also involves a constant real product wage. The CIRE represents a combination of employment and income shares (represented in terms of the price–wage ratio), which is a form of balance in that prices and wages would be rising at the same rate (in a zero-productivity growth world) and inflation would be constant. It represents a position in which the competing claims regarding income are mutually compatible (or rather the abilities of each side to secure their competing claims are).

This position of balance may not be unique — the shape of the p and wage determination curve in Figure 1 is the simplest imaginable and the processes of aggregation could well lead to more complexity. Further, the composition of demand across sectors would influence the price determination curve as the price–output relationship differs across sectors. The CIRE may not operate as an attractor for the economy. For example, above the CIRE, there would be something of a wage–price spiral, and the wage–price ratio can vary. The change in the distribution of income could have effects on the level of demand, but there is no unambiguous movement of the level of demand towards that equivalent to the CIRE. The more general point would be that there is no particular reason to believe that the level of demand would be compatible with the CIRE. In other words, the level of aggregate demand based on the real product wage and the resulting distribution of income may well not be compatible with the CIRE. Fiscal and monetary policies may well be used to bring the level of demand in line with CIRE in pursuit of constraining inflation.

The CIRE evolves over time, particularly through investment and shifts in capacity, which would be reflected in Figure 1 as a shift rightwards on the price determination curve (see Sawyer 2002). The ability of the economy to produce non-inflationary full employment depends, *inter alia*, on there being sufficient productive capacity. In terms of Figure 1, the question is how does the CIRE compare with the notion of full employment (of labour). Higher levels of productive capacity would shift the price determination curve to the right, and could have the potential to enable CIRE to reach full employment.

At lower levels of employment, lower output and lower demand, each side is sufficiently weakened that it is difficult to maintain their income share. At higher levels of employment, higher output and higher demand, each side is emboldened to seek a higher income share.

5.1. Aggregate Demand and Price–Wage Inflation

In Figure 1, four zones, A, B, C and D, are identified that exhibit different patterns of price and wage increases. The economy can be operating in each of the zones depending on the level of aggregate demand (taken to be setting the level of economic activity) and the distribution of income (as reflected in the wage to retail price ratio).

In zone A, there is a price–wage–price spiral: price-setting behaviour results in prices rising faster than wages and wage-setting behaviour results in wages rising faster than prices. From the wage side, wages would tend to rise faster than prices, according to equation (4) seeking to attain the target real wage. From the price side, since price is lower (relative to wage) than is the firms' target, then firms would seek to raise prices faster than wages. In zone A, there would be a price–wage spiral, with workers seeking to raise money wages faster than prices, and firms to raise prices faster than wages. This general analysis does not tell us the speed at which inflation would be rising. This would depend on the speed of adjustments in the wage- and price-setting arrangements. Insofar as prices and wages can be changed on, say, a daily basis, the rise in inflation could be rather rapid. On the other hand, if the adjustments are more on an annual basis and adjustment on each round incomplete, the rise in inflation would be rather modest. Insofar as prices can be adjusted more frequently than wages, a higher level of demand could well see prices rising more rapidly than wages. Prices are, in many cases, in the hands of the producers whereas wages involve joint negotiations.

In response to a significant shock (say, a rise in global prices), prices may well adjust more quickly than wages, resulting in declining real wages, at least in the initial phase.

While the economy remains in zone A, price and wage inflation could be anticipated to continue to rise. There are no automatic market forces that would tend to move the economy towards the CIRE. Even if the economy were to reach CIRE, a level of price and wage inflation would be locked into the system. The rate of inflation that would be attained would be path-dependent.

In zone D, there is a reverse price–wage–price spiral: from price-setting behaviour there is downward pressure on prices, which rise more slowly that wages; but, from wage-setting behaviour, there is also a downward pressure on wages. There would likely be a lower limit on price and wage changes such that declines in nominal prices and wages would be rather small. In zone D, there would be a tendency for the pace of wage and price increases to decline, in something of a downward spiral. At low levels of wage and price increases, there may be little further fall, especially if decreases in wages or prices are involved.

In zone B, there would be movement in the wage–price ratio, with the rate of wage increases tending to be less than the rate of price increases from the wage determination perspective, and the rate of price increases tending to be faster than the rate of wage increases from a pricing perspective. In zone C, there would also be a movement in the wage–price ratio and the relationships between wage and price increases are the reversed of those in zone B.

5.2. Shifts in Pressures and Income Shares

Some moves in conflicts regarding income distribution and implications for inflationary pressure are initiated in an effort to reconcile claims when the economy is at the CIRE, with a corresponding level of demand. Shifts in the price determination curve and/or the wage determination curve, for whatever reason, would disturb an existing 'equilibrium' position, and can lead to a different pattern of wage and price changes.

Let us start our story with an economy operating close to CIRE. It can be 'disturbed' in a range of ways: a sharp increase in demand, reduction in supply potential, push for higher profits, push for higher wages or global price inflation. A rise in inflation may be relatively small or large, and there is a need to examine speed of response to such a rise. There may also be a need to enquire into patterns of the previous two decades and the shifts from wages to profits and the slow growth of real earnings: these proceeded without in general much effect on inflation.

A push for higher prices (relative to wages) would be represented by a downward shift in the price determination curve. This could result from an enhanced degree of market power in general (in the case of prices). A push for higher wages (relative to prices) would be represented by an upward shift in the wage determination curve and may result from strengthened trade unions (in the case of wages).

The shift in the price determination curve is illustrated in Figure 2 (and a similar discussion could be made for a shift in the wage determination curve). If the economy had been operating at point X, the immediate effect of the portrayed shift is that the economy would now be in a zone A situation, with prices and wages tending to rise faster than hitherto. But what the general observation does not tell us is how much inflation

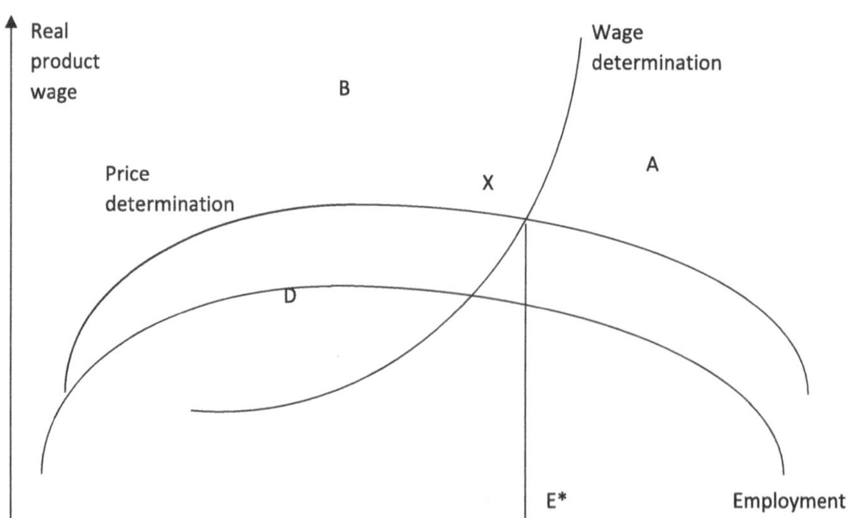

Figure 2. Shift in the price determination curve.

would rise by or over what period. The idea of price and wage changes to adjust price-wage ratios to their 'desired' levels has been mooted. But little is said, directly, on the speed of those adjustments. Rapid adjustments would show up as high rates of price and wage inflation.

5.3. Government

In the 'target real wage' approach, the target could be seen as the post-tax real wage. A rise in tax on wages and/or tax on goods and services would lower the post-tax real wage. Government taxation can be introduced in a simple manner by including taxes on wages (t_w) and prices (t_p). Equation (6) would then be replaced by:

$$a_1 + a_3U + a_4(\ln(1 - t_w)w - \ln(1 + t_p)p - lnT) = 0 \tag{7}$$

In terms of the pre-tax real wage, the wage determination curve in Figure 1 shifts upwards for a rise in tax rates, and the pre-tax real product wage rises and employment declines. Insofar as the rise in tax rates is matched by increases in public expenditure, how do workers value those increases in public expenditure? Although the term has somewhat fallen out of use, the idea of a 'social wage' was used to suggest benefits from public expenditure.

5.4. Foreign Prices

Higher foreign prices (relative to domestic wages) would lead to a downward shift of the price determination curve. At one level, the role of the foreign sector is straightforward. Variations in global prices feed through into domestic prices.[4] Commodity prices have been particularly volatile as a result a combination of shifts in supply/demand situation, the exercise of market power by producers (especially oil) and speculative activities. One noteworthy aspect here is the 'paradox of cost' effects. Import prices, together with wages, are marked-up in pricing equations and higher import prices lead to a rise in prices relative to wages and a rise in profits.

5.5. Loss of Productive Capacity

A major diminution of productive capacity (say, resulting from a natural disaster or the aftermath of war) would shift the price determination curve to the left. Insofar as the level of demand does not parallel the fall in supply potential, there would be inflationary consequences. The onset of high inflation (say, above 50 per cent per annum) and moves toward hyperinflation could be viewed in terms of a substantial loss of productive capacity together with the maintenance of a relatively high level of demand. The private sector and/or the public sector can account for the continuing level of demand. Each episode of high inflation must be examined to determine the sources explaining the effective collapse of capacity and the forces maintaining demand in order to understand these inflationary tendencies. This line of approach is consistent with that remarked upon by

[4]See, for example, Morlin (2023) for a theoretical exploration of inflation and conflict in an open economy. See Wildauer et al. (2023) for an empirical investigation into recent energy price shocks and inflation.

Åslund (2012): 'it is striking how few the causes of hyperinflation were. They were connected with either war/revolution/collapse of a state or utter irresponsibility' (p. 4).

6. Concluding Comments

'All happy families are alike; each unhappy family is unhappy in its own way' (Leo Tolstoy, *Anna Karenina*). The mainstream approach is based on an 'all inflations are alike' focus on a general movement in prices that is demand-driven and can be dampened by interest rate policy. Changes in relative prices and wages are viewed as insignificant features of inflation (and any changes in relative prices and wages reflecting shifts in relative demand and supply). A policy response involving raising interest rates to dampen demand is bizarre. Interest rates have little effect on inflation. In so far as they do have an effect on prices, it will not be on prices in areas of shortage of supply but on other prices and wages. It would be intended to depress wages and address the income inequality effects of the disruptions to supply.

The conflictual shares approach to inflation recognises that different trigger and transmission mechanisms explain inflationary episodes. The experience of inflation in 2022/23 is a clear example of supply disruptions generating rising prices in a key area, which may accompany supply shortages and can have a dramatic income distribution effect. Other experiences of rising inflation across industrialised countries have involved a large upswing in global demand (e.g., the armaments build-up during the Korean War). Policy responses should take into account the causes and mechanisms that have led to the inflationary episode, which is, of course, much easier said than done, not least because differing causes will be identified depending on the perspectives of policymakers. Further, policy responses and their implementation must be developed for the specifics of the inflationary episode. In some situations, addressing the underlying cause of a rapid rise in prices may be rather difficult. Take, for example, a major failure in domestic food supply: appropriate policy responses are alleviating suffering using price controls and rationing, and securing foreign supplies. To address global price rises, there may be little that domestic governments can do other than appearing to constrain the mark-up applied by domestic firms to imported costs, and raising domestic wages to limit the damaging effects of higher global prices on real wages.

Conflictual shares inflation theory does not provide a 'one size fits all' approach to inflation like that of the monetarist approach ('inflation is always and everywhere a monetary phenomenon') or the Phillips curve (always demand, though the term Phillips curve is defined in numerous ways and covers different mechanisms). The conflict inflation approach is (as most approaches to inflation are) located with an endogenous money approach, and the drivers of inflation and price and wage decisions.

The conflictual approach is consistent with a broadly constant rate of inflation provided that unemployment and distribution of income are consistent with the CIRE. Competing claims regarding the distribution of income are then 'reconciled'. An upswing in inflation can then be seen as arising from several possible sources. Some changes may proceed rather slowly — for example, the tendency of industrial concentration and market power to rise (summarised in Sawyer 2022) has been associated with a rise in profit share and a decline in wage share. This process has, however, occurred over a number of decades, and to what extent it has contributed to inflation is debatable, even though it appears to have raised profit share. In a similar vein, trade union power has been depleted over a number of decades. The impact of shifts such as these may well be evident to a greater extent on the wage–price ratio and income shares than on the rate of inflation. Major imbalances occurring via destruction of productive capacity or payments for unproductive employment, for example, can readily lead to major upswings in inflation. For industrialised countries (and others), the more significant upswings (and downswings) in inflation appear to result from global prices (as in the most recent episodes). Movements in global prices are transmitted through the domestic price and wage determination systems, which have consequences for the distribution of income.

Acknowledgements

I would like to thank reviewers for their comments on the initial draft.

Disclosure Statement

No potential conflict of interest was reported by the author.

ORCID

Malcolm Sawyer http://orcid.org/0000-0002-4565-5276

References

Åslund, A. 2012. 'Hyperinflations are Rare, But a Breakup of the Euro Area could Prompt One.' *Peterson Institute for International Economics Working Paper PB12-22.*

Beckerman, W., and T. Jenkinson. 1986. 'What Stopped the Inflation? Unemployment or Commodity Prices?' *Economic Journal* 96 (381): 39–54.

Blanchard, O., A. Amighini, and F. Giavazzi. 2021. *Macroeconomics: A European Perspective.* Harlow, England; New York: Pearson.

Blanchflower, D. G., and A. J. Oswald. 1994. *The Wage Curve.* Cambridge, Mass.: M.I.T. Press.

Friedman, M. 1968. 'The Role of Monetary Policy.' *American Economic Review* 58 (1): 1–17.

Galí, J. 2015. *Monetary Policy, Inflation and the Business Cycle. An Introduction to the New Keynesian Framework.* Second edition. Princeton, NJ: Princeton University Press.

Harrod, R. 1972. 'The Issues: Five Views.' In *Inflation as a Global Problem*, edited by R. Hinshaw. London: Johns Hopkins Press.

Hasan, S. 1999. 'New Evidence on Causal Relationships Between Money Supply, Prices and Wages in the UK.' *Economic Issues* 4 (2): 75–87.

Henry, S. G. B., M. Sawyer, and P. Smith. 1976. 'Models of Inflation in the United Kingdom.' *National Institute Economic Review* 77: 60–71.

Hoover, K. D. 1991. 'The Causal Direction Between Money and Prices: Al Alternative Approach.' *Journal of Monetary Economics* 27: 381–423.

Laidler, D., and M. Parkin. 1975. 'Inflation: A Survey.' *Economic Journal* 85 (340): 741–809.

Layard, P. R. G., S. J. Nickell, and R. Jackman. (1991) 2005. *Unemployment: Macroeconomic Performance and the Labour Market.* Oxford: Oxford University Press.

Lee, F. S. 1998. *Post Keynesian Price Theory.* Cambridge, New York: Cambridge University Press.

Lerner, A. P. 1958. 'Inflationary Depression and the Regulation of Administered Prices.' In *The Relationship of Prices to Economic Stability and Growth: Compendium of Papers Submitted by Panelists Appearing Before the Joint Economic Committee*, 257–268. Washington, D.C.: Government Printing Office.

Lipsey, R. 1960. 'The Relation Between Unemployment and the Rate of Change of Money Wage Rates in the United Kingdom, 1861–1957: A Further Analysis.' *Economica* 27 (105): 1–31.
Morlin, G. S. 2023. 'Inflation and Conflicting Claims in the Open Economy.' *Review of Political Economy* 35 (3): 762–790.
Pasinetti, L. 1974. *Growth and Income Distribution*. Cambridge: Cambridge University Press.
Rowthorn, R. E. 1977a. 'Conflict, Inflation and Money.' *Cambridge Journal of Economics* 1 (3): 215–239.
Rowthorn, R. E. 1977b. *Capitalism, Conflict and Inflation*. London: Lawrence and Wishart.
Sargan, J. D. 1964. 'Wages and Prices in the United Kingdom: A Study in Econometric Methodology.' In *Econometric Analysis for National Economic Planning*, edited by P. E. Hart, G. Mills, and J. K. Whitaker, 25–63. London: Butterworths.
Sawyer, M. 1982. 'Collective Bargaining, Oligopoly and Macro-Economics.' *Oxford Economic Papers* 34 (4): 428–448.
Sawyer, M. 2002. 'The NAIRU, Aggregate Demand and Investment.' *Metroeconomica* 53 (1): 66–94.
Sawyer, M. 2022. 'Monopoly Capitalism in the Past Four Decades.' *Cambridge Journal of Economics* 46 (6): 1225–1241.
Sawyer, M., S. Aaronovitch, and P. Samson. 1982. 'The Influence of Cost and Demand Conditions on the Rate of Change of Prices.' *Applied Economics* 14 (2): 195–209.
Sawyer, M., with S. Aaronovitch, and P. Samson. 1983. *Business Pricing and Inflation*. London: Macmillan and New York: St. Martin's Press, ix + 118.
Weber, I. M., and E. Wasner. 2023. 'Sellers' Inflation, Profits and Conflict: Why Can Large Firms Hike Prices in an Emergency?' *Review of Keynesian Economics* 11 (2): 183–213.
Wildauer, R., K. Kohler, A. Aboobaker, and A. Guschanski. 2023. 'Energy Price Shocks, Conflict Inflation, and Income Distribution in a Three-Sector Model.' *Energy Economics* 127: 106982. doi:10.1016/j.eneco.2023.106982.

Sellers' Inflation and Distributive Conflict: Lessons from the Post-COVID Recovery

Ettore Gallo and Louis-Philippe Rochon

ABSTRACT
The paper offers a post-Keynesian explanation of the soaring inflation experienced during the post-COVID recovery, coherent both at the microeconomic and macroeconomic levels. The microeconomic argument is rooted on the premise that price-making firms consider both their costs and their desired share of profits when setting prices. To defend profit margins in the aftermath of the pandemic, the initial cost-push shock was passed to consumers through higher prices; in a second phase, some firms, particularly in more highly concentrated and systemically significant sectors, benefited from the post-pandemic permissive pricing environment to increase their price mark-ups, leading to temporary profit-fueled inflation following the cost-push shock. This microeconomic explanation is compatible with the macroeconomic notion of a stable inflation barrier. For a given quantity of real output, it is shown that if profit earners defend their share of income following a cost-push, this will produce a one-time price increase, with inflation becoming more persistent if the target adapts endogenously — i.e., if the aggregate mark-up changes. The paper contrasts the notion of a wage-price spiral with that of a profit-price sink, arguing that sellers' inflation is a real — albeit temporary phenomenon.

1. Introduction

After almost three decades of relatively tame inflation, an unprecedented wave of price surges after the COVID-19 pandemic and the war in Ukraine has put our economies' recovery and social cohesion at risk. Indeed, starting in April 2021, inflation quickly rose and peaked at 9.1 per cent on an annual basis in July 2022 in the United States, although it has receded considerably at the time of writing (November 2023).

Ascertaining the nature of rising inflation, whether permanent or transitory, is key for determining appropriate policy responses both in terms of the fiscal/monetary policy mix as well as for income policies aimed at reducing inequality. Over the last years, in an era of unprecedented global challenges such as the post-COVID economic recovery and geopolitical conflicts, the dynamics of inflation have taken center stage in economic discourse. This research paper delves into the intricacies of these inflationary trends, aiming to shed light on their underlying mechanisms and implications. Through a comprehensive analysis rooted in the post-Keynesian perspective, this study seeks to construct a cohesive micro-macro framework that elucidates the current wave of inflation.

The motivation for this inquiry stems from the confluence of factors that have marked recent economic landscapes. Recent price surges in high-income economies have triggered debates surrounding the nature and drivers of post-pandemic inflation and has revealed both consensus and disagreements over its causes and implications. Indeed, within the post-Keynesian community, scholars like Lavoie (2023a, 2023b), Storm (2023), and Nikiforos and Grothe (2023) — in a series of blog posts for the @monetaryblog and of the Institute for New Economic Thinking (INET) — have been engaged in discussions about the fundamental nature of this inflation wave. At the heart of this debate is whether inflation — or some of it — is profit-led, cost-pushed, and/or conflict-driven. As discussed by Lavoie and Rochon (2023) in a response to Blanchard, theories once considered dormant such as conflict-driven inflation have experienced a resurgence, even within mainstream economics (see e.g., the contribution by Lorenzoni and Werning 2023).

The mainstream's 'rediscovery' of the topic has culminated in the revival of the concept of wage-price spiral, with economists and central bankers warning against the potential risks associated with the fact that workers' claims — if satisfied — would lead to further inflationary pressures. In turn, this has led some central bankers to warn against the threat posed by workers' demands. This was certainly the warning put forth by Andrew Bailey, the Governor of the Bank of England, in February 2022, by asking workers to 'show quite clear restraint' in the annual wage-bargaining process,[1] or similarly by the governor of the Bank of Italy (Visco 2023), who warned against wage-price spiral risks following the de-anchoring of inflation expectations.

However, as noted by Bivens (2022), there is very little evidence that a wage-price spiral might be in sight; as argued by the author, the observed inflationary trends as of July 2022 are closely tied to the dynamics of rising profits. The lack of evidence about the risk of a wage-price spiral has also been stressed by former Federal Reserve Governor Vice-Chair, Lael (Brainard 2023), who in a speech in January 2023, argued that 'despite constrained supply, wages do not appear to be driving inflation in a 1970s-style wage-price spiral'. Additionally, studies by Andler and Kovner (2022) and Weber and Wasner (2023), among more recent studies, have highlighted a positive correlation between gross profit margins and inflation rates, further contributing to the understanding of the phenomenon. While focusing on modeling the effect of energy price shocks, Wildauer et al. (2023, p. 2) provide evidence of the distributional impacts of the inflation episode in favor of profit earners, highlighting 'the fact that periods of high inflation do not only generate losers, but also winners'. Furthermore, Konczal and Lusiani (2022) have documented a notable increase in markups, particularly among companies situated in the higher echelons of the markup distribution prior to the pandemic. Further evidence of mark-up inflation in high-income countries is provided by Matamoros (2023), in which the author controls for changes in capacity utilization over time.

[1] https://www.theguardian.com/business/2022/feb/04/bank-of-england-boss-calls-for-wage-restraint-to-help-control-inflation

More recently, Nikiforos, Grothe, and Weber (2024) provide four estimates of the sales-weighted aggregate mark-up, showing that 'the average markup is — under any measure — above its pre-pandemic level', in line with other estimates by Glover, Mustre-Del Río, and von Ende-Becker (2023) and Conlon et al. (2023). In particular, the authors show that the sales-weighted average mark-up excluding firms significantly increased after the pandemic, reaching a plateau in 2022 and 2023.[2] This is consistent with the facts discussed by Rowthorn (2024, p. 10), who concludes that 'the evidence suggests that the burden of higher world prices was borne largely by wage and salary earners. Private firms were able to maintain their profit margins by passing on their higher costs to consumers'.

Once dismissed as a fringe theory, the very concept of sellers' (or profit-led) inflation has now been recognized by many international institutions. For instance, the IMF, under Christine Lagarde, argued that corporate profits — as of June 2023 — accounted for two-thirds of inflation: 'unit profits contributed around two-thirds to domestic inflation whereas, in the previous 20 years, the average contribution was one-third'.[3] More recently, Tiff Macklem, Governor of the Bank of Canada, was forced to admit that 'when input prices have gone up [...] those are getting passed through much more quickly to final goods prices. So households are bearing the full inflationary impact much more: that's what we can see pretty clearly in the data'.[4]

This debate therefore resolves one of the greatest asymmetries in economic theory: wages vs. profits in the determination of inflation. Theory, even among some heterodox economists, tends to blame workers for inflation, triggering the infamous wage-price spiral. Conversely, in this article we argue that price changes can be triggered just as well by profits, leading to a stable process that we label profit-price sink. This is the same position taken recently by Hein (2023a, pp. 2-3):

> Inflation may thus be triggered by an increase in claims of one or more of these groups of actors, which is not matched by a decline of the claims of any other group of actors. Inflation may hence be generated (1) by an increase in capitalists' real profits or profit share claims, triggered by excess demand, changes in the degree of price competition, or higher interest or dividend claims, which will generate profit-driven conflict inflation.

To a large extent, much of the debate around the relation between price surges and distribution seems to boil down to a sort of semantic controversy. A great deal of fuss revolves around the definitions of 'profit-led inflation' and the multifaceted notion of 'conflict'. In the context of profit-led inflation, scholars hold divergent views, sometimes identifying profit inflation as a persistent process driven by *greediness*, some others linking it with temporary price level increases resulting from cost-push shocks and mark-up/profit share targeting. Similarly, the term 'conflict' holds nuanced interpretations. On one hand, wages are perceived as the exclusive source of conflict, while on the other hand, the actions of profit earners defending and seeking to increase their margins could also be regarded as instances of conflict.

Against this backdrop, the primary objective of this research paper is to examine the current wave of inflation through the lens of post-Keynesian economics, aiming to

---

[2]This evidence will be modelled in Sections Three and Four.

[3]https://www.ecb.europa.eu/press/key/date/2023/html/ecb.sp230627 b8694e47c8.en.html.

[4]https://www.cbc.ca/news/business/inflation-profit-analysis-1.6909878.

construct a comprehensive micro-macro framework that explicates the underlying dynamics. Moreover, this investigation intends to contrast the revived yet contentious notion of the wage-price spiral with the concept of the profit-price sink, defined as a stable price level increase driven by a rise in the profit margin, permanently affecting the functional distribution of income but not inflation rates. By pursuing these goals, this research seeks to contribute to an understanding of the mechanisms driving contemporary inflation, hopefully enriching economic discourse with insights that bridge theoretical and empirical perspectives.

The paper proceeds as follows. Section Two summarizes the ongoing inflation debate. Section Three presents our microeconomic framework, modeling cost-push shock and upward flexibility in sectoral mark-ups in a simple Kaleckian pricing procedure. Section Four discusses the relevance of Joan Robinson's inflation barrier and connects it with the microeconomic analysis. By adapting her idea to account for a stable mechanism of price increase, it also discusses how the barrier might come from the resistance of profit earners rather than that workers. Last, Section Five concludes, summarizing our discussion.

2. The Great Inflation Debate

It is generally accepted that the causes of inflation can be classified as essentially 'demand-pull', 'cost-push' or 'conflict-driven'. What precisely drives inflation is important as it informs us subsequently as to what policies are best suited to address the problem. In other words, some austerity policies may be required if inflation is demand-driven, in an effort to calm the demand-fueled surge in prices. However, such policies may be ineffective and may indeed cause more harm if applied, for instance, to cost-push inflation (Stiglitz and Regmi 2023).

After having been dormant for many years, post-pandemic inflation has returned and has caught many economists, including heterodox and post-Keynesian, by surprise, and led to considerable confusion over the proper nature of the surge in prices. Clearly, there is no consensus and much research is still needed. Yet, this has not prevented central banks around the world from treating inflation as demand-driven, and adopting one of the most aggressive monetary policy austerity stand in history, increasing interest rates 11 times, since March 2022, in an 18-month span, in the United States, and 14 times in the UK.

Indeed, it is safe to argue that mainstream theory sees all inflation as being essentially demand-driven, and as such monetary policy is the only credible policy to bring it down closer to the central bank's chosen target. In other words, only austerity policies work, either of the monetary nature or indeed through fiscal austerity. Yet, what if inflation was not mostly demand-driven? In a recent study, Cerrato and Gitti (2022, p. 2) estimate that post-COVID inflation is only about 25 percentage demand-pull, thereby leaving the vast majority of inflation explained by non-demand-pull sources, finding that 'demand-driven economic recovery explains about one-fourth of the post-COVID increase in all-items inflation'. More importantly, the authors seem to argue that in normal, i.e., non-COVID, times, demand would have played an insignificant part: 'Had the slope of the Phillips curve not steepened after COVID, the demand contribution to the rise in inflation would have been small and statistically insignificant' (*ibid.*).

Whether the Phillips curve has steepened post-COVID is a matter of debate, yet we can draw two immediate conclusions. First, what precisely accounts for the rest, i.e., 75 percentage, of inflation? Second, if demand indeed explains but 25 percentage of overall inflation, how appropriate was monetary austerity as a policy response?

Olivier Blanchard contributed to an intense debate when, in December 2022, he wrote on Twitter — now X — that inflation was conflict-driven.[5] Indeed, he wrote 'Inflation is fundamentally the outcome of the distributional conflict, between firms, workers, and taxpayers.' This partly vindicated the view defended by many heterodox economists since Rowthorn first wrote about it in the *Cambridge Journal of Economics* — see Rowthorn (1977) and its recent reappraisal in the *Review of Political Economy* (Rowthorn 2024). Indeed, for post-Keynesians, inflation is driven by distributional conflicts. In other words, *inflation is always and everywhere a conflict phenomenon*, as recently restated by Galbraith (2023) and Hein (2023a). Hence, post-Keynesians reject the idea that inflation is necessarily related to economic activity or to unemployment, unless these impact directly the target real wage of either firms or workers, for instance through higher labor power.

Yet, there is one aspect of the conflict that is receiving increasing attention and indeed rewriting many of the previous post-Keynesian models of conflict inflation: seller's inflation — also known as profit inflation. Later in the paper, we discuss the relevance of sellers' inflation through post-Keynesian lenses, investigating its present relevance and whether it is permanent or transitory in nature.

3. Microeconomic Explanation

According to Joan Robinson (1979, p. 41), every theory of inflation has to start, by definition, with a theory of the price level:

> Inflation usually means a continuing rise of the general price level. But the general level of prices is an abstraction. Different prices behave differently and goods and services being sold alter their character as time goes by. [...] To see how inflation occurs we have first to inquire how prices are formed.

To do so, let us start from a standard pricing procedure rooted in the Kaleckian theory of mark-up pricing.[6] We consider the pricing procedure for the *i*th firm in the *j*th sector, so that the price (p_i) for the good produced by firm *i* is given by:

$$p_i = (1 + m_i)[w_j a_i + p_j^m \mu_i] + \epsilon_{i,-1} \tag{1}$$

where:

- m_i represents the firm's markup ($m_i > 0$);
- w_j is the uniform nominal wage in sector *j*;
- a_i stands for the labor-output ratio;
- p_j^m denotes the unit price of energy, raw materials, and intermediate products in sector *j*;

[5]https://twitter.com/ojblanchard1/status/1608967176232525824.

[6]In order to make the analysis as tractable as possible, we abstain from the consideration of intra- and inter-sectoral relations. Rather, we merely deal with the pricing behavior of a single firm, without modeling the feedback it has on other firms' cost and pricing structures. As we shall see in the remainder of the paper, the rationale for this choice — beyond its easier tractability — lies in the idea that price changes for few firms in a handful of key sectors produced cascade price increases in the overall economy and thus an increase in the general price level (Weber and Wasner 2023).

- μ_i refers to raw materials per unit of final output;
- $\epsilon_{i,-1}$ represents an error term reflecting unanticipated shocks from the previous period, similar to Setterfield (2023).

On the basis of equation 2, we might identify three main candidates to explain price increases at the firm and sectoral levels: (i) unanticipated shocks (as captured by $\epsilon_{i,-1}$); (ii) increase in the price of energy, raw material, and intermediate products p_j^m; (iii) increase in the mark-up (m_i).[7]

The first factor constitutes the only way through which our Kaleckian pricing procedure might capture the role of inflation expectations.[8] Similar to argument advanced by Setterfield (2023) — that however introduces an error term in the inflation rate rather than in the price level — the role of expectations is assumed to be negligible as a driver of post-COVID inflation. Furthermore, this is consistent with the view recently put forward by Rudd (2022). For the sake of simplicity, this channel is shut down in the remainder of the analysis, thus assuming $\epsilon_{i,-1} = 0$.

The second plausible channel is through a cost-push effect caused by an increase in the sectoral price of energy, raw materials, and intermediate products (p_j^m). *Ceteris paribus* the mark-up m_i, any cost-increase will be passed to prices, causing an increase in unit prices for the ith firm and, as we shall later see, allowing firms to maintain their profit margins. This direct channel is shown in Figure 1.[9]

At this stage, it is worth recalling that there exists a direct relation between cost-plus pricing procedures as the one presented in equation 2 and the functional distribution of income, as first recognized by Kalecki (1954).[10] More specifically, the profit share (π_i) of the ith firm can be expressed as follows:

$$\pi_{i,t} = \frac{m_{i,t}[w_j a_i + p_j^m \mu_i]}{m_{i,t}[w_j a_i + p_j^m \mu_i] + w_j a_i} \tag{2}$$

It can be readily shown that an increase in the price of energy, raw materials and intermediate products always leads, for a given mark-up, to a shift in the functional distribution of income from wage to profit earners:

$$\frac{d\pi_{i,t}}{dp_j^m} = \frac{m_{i,t}\mu_i w_j a_i}{\left\{m_{i,t}[w_j a_i + p_j^m \mu_i] + w_j a_i\right\}^2} > 0 \tag{3}$$

This change in the distribution of income generated within the firm is shown in Figure 2;

---

[7]It is worth stressing that there might be a fourth channel, i.e., a cost-push through wage increases (w_j). While it is undeniable that some sectors (mostly services) in the US experienced a significant increase in wages, it is unlikely that such sectors might have been significant for aggregate inflation (Bivens 2022; Weber et al. 2022; Weber and Wasner 2023). For this reason, we abstain from considerations of changes in the sectoral nominal wage by assuming it constant. Similarly, we abstain from other two potential channels which could play a role in the longer run, i.e., changes in labor productivity (affecting a_i) and in intermediate costs structures (e.g., improvements in energy efficiency, affecting μ_i).

[8]Unlike its mainstream counterparts, the post-Keynesian cost-plus pricing procedure presented here only allows for a one-time effect of expectations on prices, on the basis of the idea that the inability to predict market outcomes result in inventory rather than price changes (Gallo and Serra 2024).

[9]This is the line of argument put forward (Lavoie 2023c). The idea that profit shares can increase even though markups remain constant has also been recently discussed — using Cobb-Douglas and CES production functions — by Colonna, Torrini, and Viviano (2023).

[10]For further discussion, see Hein (2014, 2023b).

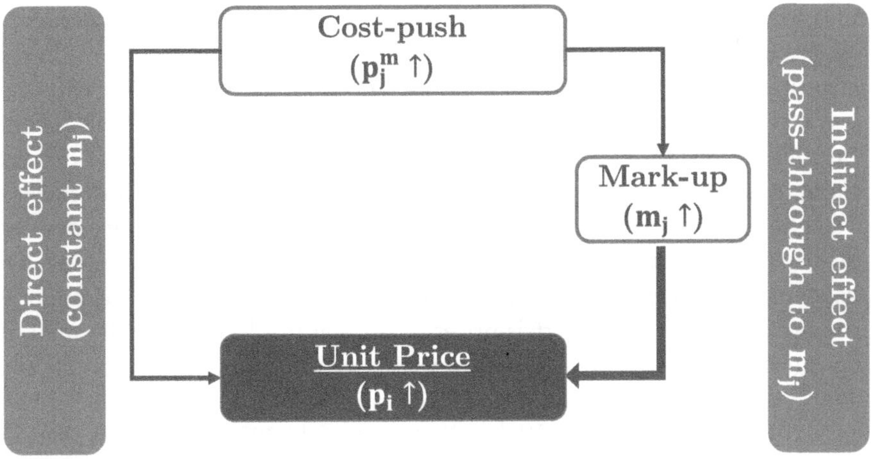

Figure 1. Drivers of price increases at the firm level. Source: authors' representation.

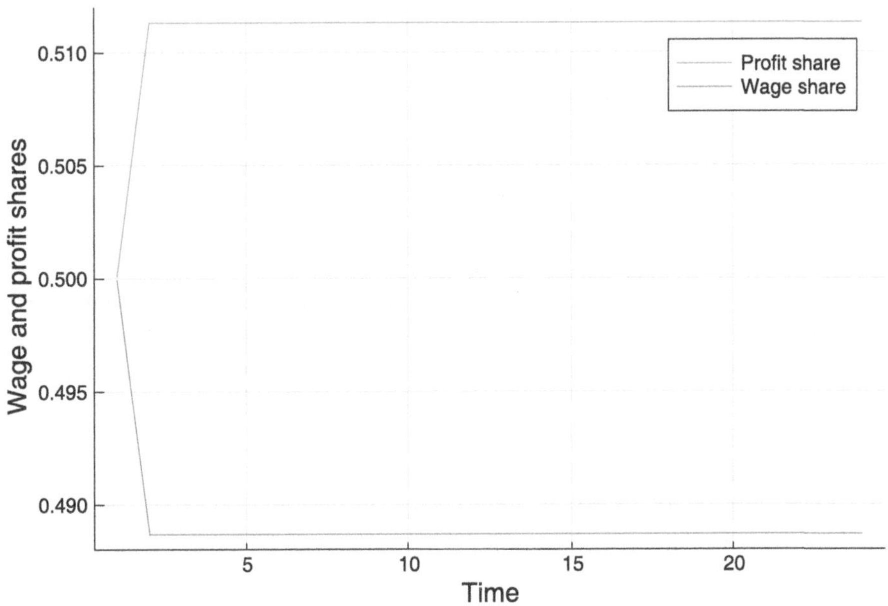

Figure 2. Effect of an increase in p_j^m on the functional distribution of income.

a cost-push shock caused by an increase in p_j^m has the effect of producing a one-time increase in the profit share and a symmetric decrease in the wage share (assuming zero rents).[11] In other terms, an increase in the price of energy, raw materials and intermediate products increases the price p_i and tilts the functional distribution of income in favor of profit earners *even* with a constant mark-up, as also discussed by Storm (2023).

[11]For the sake of the argument, henceforth we assume that aggregate income is evenly split between wages and profits, i.e., both the wage and profit shares are 50 percentage at time $t = 0$. For further discussion, see Appendix .

The last channel, which will be the main focus of the analysis in the remainder of the section, lies in the idea that the mark-up can endogenously adjust to exploit changes in cost structures and sellers' market conditions. This does not imply that mark-ups can increase at the will of the firm and regardless of sector- or industry-specific conditions. On the contrary, firms' mark-up ought to be seen as strongly dependent on sectoral mark-ups, in turn, affected by competition, concentration, and profitability constraints. Accordingly, it could be argued that mark-ups adjusted upwards following a drastic shift in cost structures and market conditions caused, first, by the Covid-19 pandemic (with the realignment of supply chains) and, second, by geopolitical tensions (leading to an increase in energy and raw materials prices). This upward flexibility in the mark-up in the US during the post-pandemic recovery has been documented by several authors (Conlon et al. 2023; Glover, Mustre-Del Río, and von Ende-Becker 2023; Matamoros 2023; Nikiforos, Grothe, and Weber 2024; Setterfield 2023), with firms that during this period were able to exploit increased corporate concentration and raise prices above 'the pass-through effects associated with rising costs' Setterfield (2023, p. 602).

At this stage, one might wonder why prices did not increase with mark-ups before the pandemic, given the substantial evidence of rising corporate concentration over the last 30 years.[12] The answer could be found in what (Setterfield 2023) calls the 'permissive pricing environment' that characterized the post-pandemic recovery. Albeit not always acknowledged in Kaleckian contributions, the theory of administered pricing initially formulated by Hall and Hitch (1939) regards pricing decisions as also regulated by a dynamic game between sellers and buyers around what they consider 'fair'. As argued by Setterfield (2023, p. 602), the unprecedented shocks in costs relaxed this fairness constraint and allowed firms to exploit the effects of rising concentration built up in the previous years; this created 'sources of cost-based price increases that provide "camouflage" for firms, allowing them to increase markups (and hence prices)'. Along with this effect, the structural fall in the labor share may have contributed to tame inflationary pressures by reducing workers' bargaining power (Cauvel and Pacitti 2022), while firms were able to increase their profit margins and achieve a higher profit share with mild price increases, along the lines of the model of Rochon and Setterfield (2007).

Albeit treated as parametric by the vast majority of post-Keynesian economists, there is no *a priori* reason to believe that mark ups are stable over time. Conversely, they might adapt over time as costs, market conditions, and trade patterns change. Bearing this in mind, we might formalize the idea in simple terms the notion of upward flexibility in sectoral mark-ups, that enables firms to adjust prices while considering consumer demand within the sector.[13]

The mark-up of each firm would thus gradually adapt as discrepancies between the mark-up of the individual firm ($m_{i,t}$) and the maximum one attainable within the sector ($m_{j,\max}$) emerge. More specifically, to account for the gradualness of the adjustment, we could model the process as following a logistic trajectory:

$$m_{i,t} = m_{i,0} + \frac{m_{\mathrm{j},\max} - m_{i,0}}{[1 + \exp(g_j \cdot (t_{\mathrm{mid}} - t))]^S} \tag{4}$$

[12]For the relation between market power and mark-ups before the pandemic, see De Loecker, Eeckhout, and Unger (2020).

[13]For empirical evidence of mark-up inflation after 2021, see Matamoros (2023).

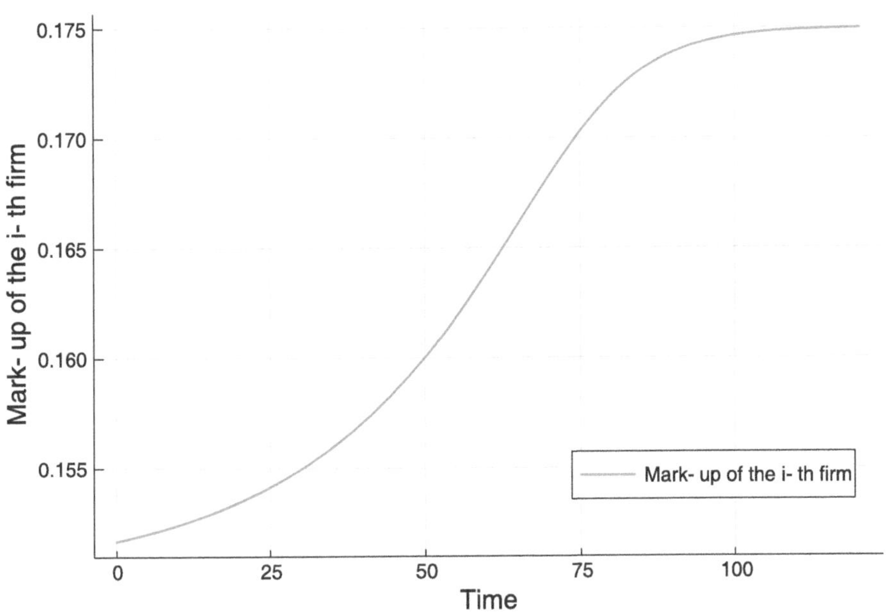

Figure 3. Endogenous evolution of the mark-up in the *i*th firm.

where $m_{i,0}$ represents the initial mark-up, g_j captures the pass-through effect, t_{mid} is the midpoint of the sigmoid, and S allows for shape control. The evolution of the mark-up of the *i*th firm in the *j*th sector is shown in Figure 3. Equation (4) implies that firms' mark-ups — at least in strategically significant sectors — gradually adapted to the higher sectoral mark-up, rapidly increasing up to t_{mid} and then stabilizing as the initial source of cost-push price increases started to fade. To this extend, it is worth noting that the limit to the logistic process, i.e., the maximum attainable sectoral mark-up $m_{j,\max}$ could be interpreted as an insurmountable limit, a constraint associated either with the maximum rate of profit in the sector[14] — in line with the Classical-Keynesian tradition — or with the boundary after which price increases start to be regarded as 'unfair' by buyers — as per (Hall and Hitch 1939). In both cases, a firm trying to sell their products with a mark-up above $m_{j,\max}$ would loose customers and hence market shares, at the benefit of other competitors in the sector.

In line with equation 2 discussed above, an increase in the mark-up will necessarily produce an increase in the firms' share of profits:

$$\frac{d\pi_{i,t}}{dm_{i,t}} = \frac{[w_j a_i + p_j^m \mu_i] w_j a_i}{\left\{m_{i,t}[w_j a_i + p_j^m \mu_i] + w_j a_i\right\}^2} < 0 \tag{5}$$

[14]In this sense, it should be noted that the maximum profit share achievable at $m_{j,\max}$ also corresponds to the maximum rate of profit, in line with Weisskopf's 1979 decomposition of the profit rate, i.e., $r = \pi u/v$. More specifically, given that we are abstaining from the analysis of quantity adjustments ($\Delta u = 0$) and under the conventional assumption of constant capital-capacity ratio, a change in the mark-up that raises the profit share will translate in a variation of the rate of profit equal to $\Delta r = \frac{u}{v}\Delta\pi$.

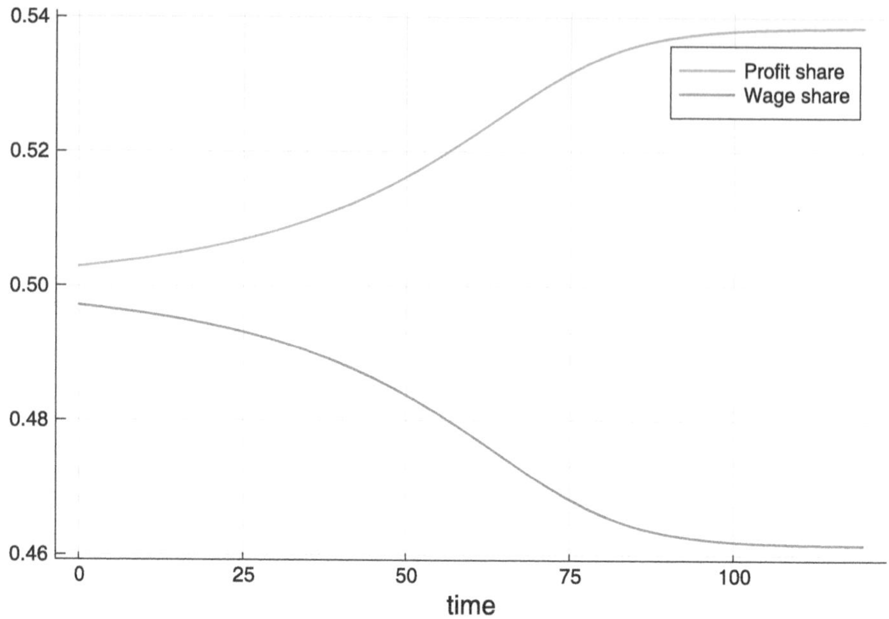

Figure 4. Effect of the upward flexibility in the mark-up on firm's income shares.

Unlike the case of the direct price effect of an increase in the cost of energy, raw materials, and intermediate products, the gradual adjustment in mark-up will gradually impact the distribution of income within the firm, as shown in Figure 4.

When translated to prices, the assumed behavior of mark-ups would produce a gradual increase in the price level, temporarily leading to accelerating rates of inflation up to a peak (associated with t_{mid}), with inflation rates gradually decreasing as firms mark-ups approach their sectoral maximum (Figure 5).

Summing up, this section was motivated by the idea that 'prices of manufacturers are quite insensitive to swings of demand, but react quickly to changes in costs' (Robinson 1979, p. 42). Therefore, firms' pricing behavior is affected both directly by cost increases (even with a constant mark-up) and indirectly — through rising mark-ups, when possible. In both cases, cost-based price surges create winners and losers. More specifically, both the direct and indirect channels through which higher costs pass on to prices imply an increase in the share of profits in income generated by the individual firm. In the direct case, firms would limit themselves to defend their profit margins passing the higher costs to prices. In the second case, when mark-ups increase, firms will try — and possibly succeed — to exploit the situation to increase their profit margins. While both channels lead to a relative redistribution from wages to profits within the firm, only in the latter case it is correct to talk about 'profit inflation' or 'sellers' inflation' (Weber and Wasner 2023), as price increases are caused by an increase in profit margins. Last, it is worth stressing that in our framework profit inflation emerges as a consequence of the gradual mark-up adjustment, with the process being stable, i.e., mark-ups increase only up to a plateau. In other terms, in this scenario profit inflation is only a temporary outcome.

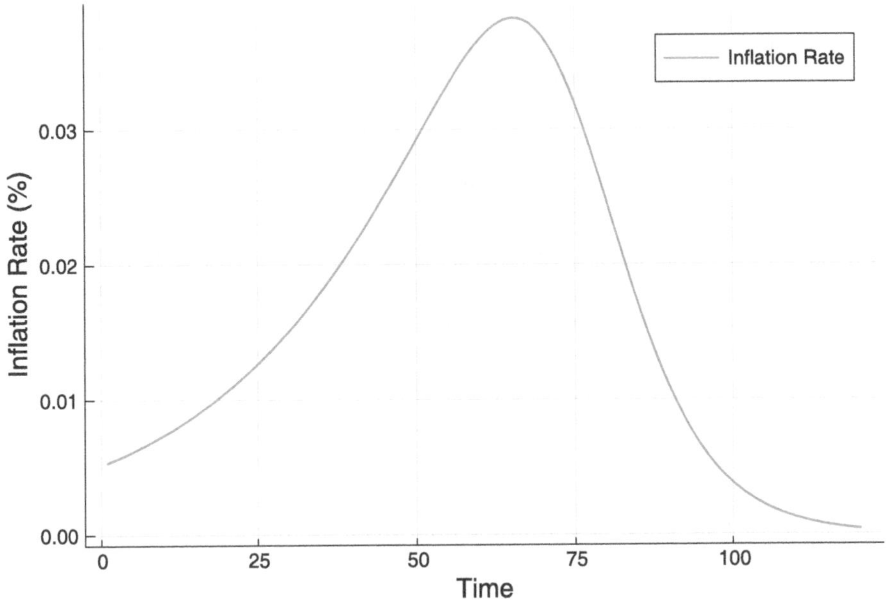

Figure 5. Effect of the upward flexibility in the mark-up on the inflation rate in the *i*th firm.

Let us now look at how the effect of the assumed mechanisms at the macroeconomic level.

4. Macroeconomic Explanation

Joan Robinson first introduced the concept of the 'inflation barrier' in her early work *Essays in the Theory of Employment* in 1937; in the vicinity of full employment, there will be:

> [...] a progressive rise in wages. [...] prices and profits will rise with money wages and all the circumstances which led to a first rise in wages will remain in force and lead to a second. (Robinson 1937, p. 5)

The more well-known contributions date to the post-war period, in particular her seminal contributions *The Accumulation of Capital* (Robinson 1956, pp. 48-50) and *Essays in the Theory of Economic Growth* (Robinson 1962, pp. 58-59), in which the inflation barrier is defined in connection to the Cambridge model (or Kaldor-Robinson model). In all these works, it is rather clear Robinson's focus on the inflation barrier as a problem of inherent wage resistance, in line with the historical experience at the time. With few exceptions,[15] the subsequent post-Keynesian tradition followed Robinson's steps.

While the notion of the 'inflation barrier' is useful as a conceptual framework mediating the relation between costs, distributive conflict, and prices, it needs to be re-adapted to be relevant in the current scenario. The story ought to be reversed from wage to profit

[15]See for instance, the discussion in Hein (2014, pp. 128-129).

resistance. As shown in the previous section, entrepreneurs too can resist increases in costs — defending or even trying to increase their profit margins. When profit earners resist a reduction in the profit share in the face of rising costs, it can lead to conflict-driven price surges, even in the absence of strong workers' resistance. The process, however, is unlikely to be explosive. As there are no strong evidence of the historical relevance of wage price spirals in high-income countries (Alvarez et al. 2022), it is equally unlikely that profit inflation may be a permanent phenomenon. Particularly in the absence of self-reinforcing feedback between profits, wages, and prices, profit-led price surges are likely to conform to a non-explosive process. In other terms, our interpretation of the inflation barrier differs from the common understanding of a cumulative (explosive) inflationary pressure stemming from unresolved distributive conflict (Hein 2014, 2023b). Rather, the cumulative process will take place only as long as — paraphrasing Robinson's words — *the circumstances which led to a first rise* in profits are in force. As we shall see, this implies that the inflation rate will remain positive only until the profit share target has been achieved, leading to a permanently higher price level rather than permanent inflation, in line with the interpretation of Holzman (1950). The inflationary process discussed above can be shown in a very simple accounting framework that draws upon an amended version of the one proposed by Holzman (1950) himself.

Coherently with the discussion presented in Section Three, we assume rents to be zero, so that nominal national income (Y_t) is divided between aggregate wages (W_t) and profits (Π_t). For the sake of simplicity, we also assume real income to be constant, assuming away the possibility that inflation can be the consequence of excessive aggregate demand. Accordingly, any change in nominal national income will be given by a change in prices, not in quantities:

$$Y_t = W_t + \Pi_t \tag{6}$$

Furthermore, let us assume that wage increases occur one period after an increase in nominal income (i.e., in the aggregate price level):

$$W_t = \omega_0 \eta Y_{t-1} \tag{7}$$

where ω_0 corresponds to the wage share at time $t = 0$ ($\omega_0 = W_0/Y_0$) and η is a parameter measuring the ability of workers to defend their real income. When $\eta = 1$, a change in nominal GDP entirely translated into a change in wages, keeping workers' real income constant. Conversely, with $\eta < 1$ ($\eta > 1$), workers' standard of living will decrease (increase) as nominal income increases, given that the pass-through from prices to wages is smaller (bigger) than one. For the sake of the discussion, in the numerical simulations we will assume $\eta = 1$ to show that profit-driven price surges may occur independently of workers' behavior.

While wage earners try to adjust ex-post nominal wages, profit earners set a profit share target (π_T), thus implicitly targeting the wage share ($1 - \pi_T$) as well. In other terms, profit earners will try to maintain their profits at a given percentage of total wage costs:[16]

$$\Pi_t = \frac{\pi_T}{1 - \pi_T} W_t \tag{8}$$

[16] It is worth noting that equation 8 implies that the ratio between the target profit and wage shares set by profit earners must be equal to the ratio of actual factor shares, i.e., $\frac{\pi_T}{1-\pi_T} = \frac{\Pi_t/Y_t}{W_t/Y_t} = \frac{\pi_t}{1-\pi_t}$.

Plugging equations 7 and 8 into 6 and rearranging, we can obtain the growth factor of nominal income, and thus of prices (Y_t/Y_{t-1}):

$$\frac{Y_t}{Y_{t-1}} = \frac{1}{1-\pi_T}\omega_0\eta \tag{9}$$

From equation 9, it is clear that if profit earners maintain a profit share target, any change in such target would have positive effects on nominal income and hence, given that real income is constant, on prices:

$$\frac{d(Y_t/Y_{t-1})}{d\pi_T} = \frac{\omega_0\eta}{(1-\pi_T)^2} > 0 \tag{10}$$

The target may be stable or evolve over time. In the remainder of the section, we will consider two scenarios. In the first scenario, profit earners set a target aimed at maintaining profits at the percentage of aggregate output observed soon after the shock:

$$\pi_T = \frac{\Pi_0 + \epsilon}{Y_0 + \epsilon} \tag{11}$$

where ε is a random shock, which could be interpreted as the cost-push effect discussed in Section Three.[17]

In this case, the profit share target increases in correspondence of the cost-push shock, producing a one-time increase in the actual profit share and a symmetric reduction in the wage share — in the absence of rents — as shown in Figure 6.[18]

What this implies at the macroeconomic level, with profit earners being able to defend their aggregate target, is that total profits will increase after the cost shock, with the wage bill remaining constant and subsequently increasing following increases in nominal income (Figure 7).

In the second scenario, the aggregate profit share target depends on the actual profit share of those firms that were able to exploit the shock in cost structures to increase their profit margins.[19] In this case, the target profit share would evolve endogenously, being a function of the profit share of those firms that are 'systemically significant' for inflation in the economy (equation 2):[20]

$$\pi_T = f(\underset{+}{\pi_{i,t}}) \tag{12}$$

If the target profit share increases so as to reflect the increase in the mark-up — and profit

[17]Intuitively, given that profits are by definition smaller than aggregate output, a positive cost-push shock will always produce an increase in the target. This could be shown formally as well. Given that $Y_0 = W_0 + \Pi_0$, it could be readily show that $d\pi_T/d\epsilon = W_0/(W_0 + \Pi_0 + \epsilon)^2 > 0$.

[18]This situation is similar to the first case discussed at the microeconomic level, in which the individual firm raises prices as a consequence of a cost-push shock caused by the increase in the price of energy, raw materials, and intermediate products.

[19]It is important to note that this scenario corresponds to one in which the *aggregate* mark-up increases, driven by the mark-ups of firms in strategically significant sectors. The empirical evidence that the aggregate mark-up has indeed increased in the US is not conclusive; the magnitude of the increase is still unclear, with some authors arguing that, despite sectoral shifts, the aggregate mark-up has remained roughly constant (Davis 2023).

[20]We avoid providing a specific functional form for the sake of generality. However, it is important to note that doing that would require weighting either the profit share or mark-up of systemically significant firms to account for their relative importance in the macroeconomy. For the sake of simplicity, in the simulation shown in Figure 7 we merely assume that π_T follows the same sigmoid behavior observed for *i*th firm.

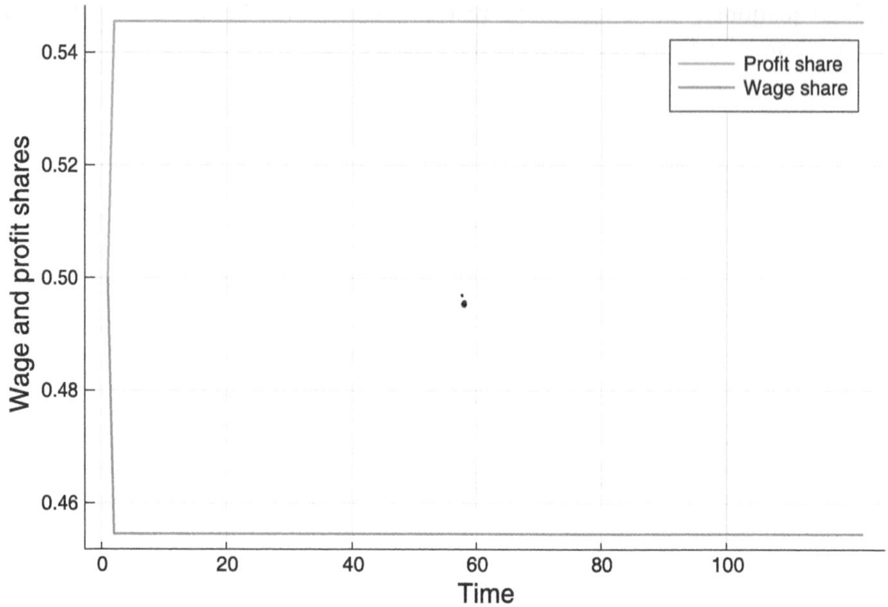

Figure 6. Effect of profit share targeting without an adjustment in the mark up.

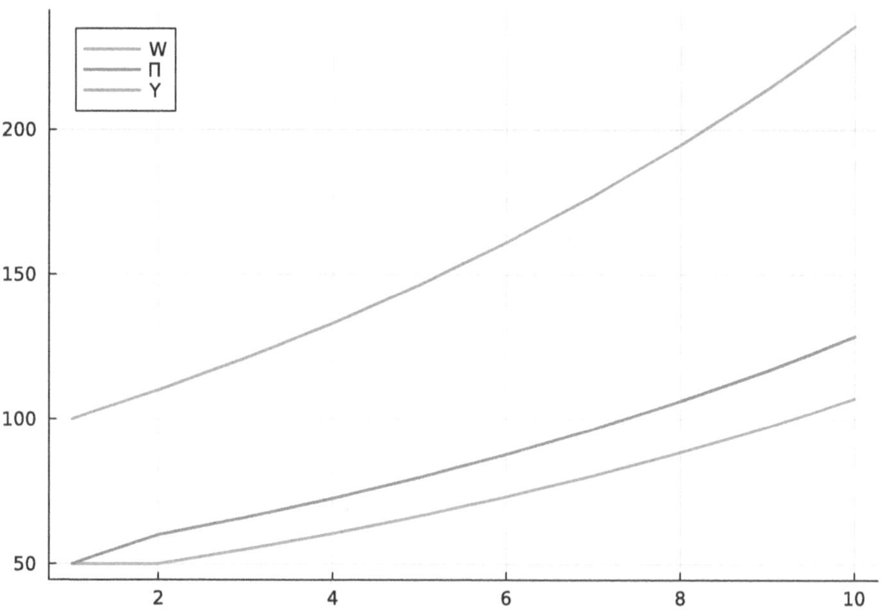

Figure 7. Effect of profit share targeting without an adjustment in the mark up.

earners are able to defend the target — it follows that after the initial rise in the profit share caused by the cost-push shock, there would be further increases as long as mark-ups endogenously adjust upwards. For illustrative purposes, this is shown in Figure 8.

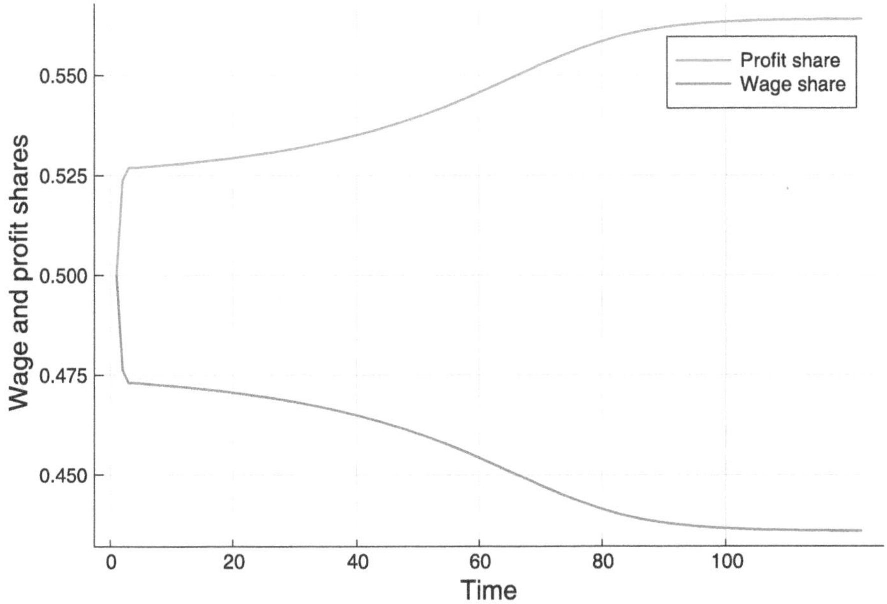

Figure 8. Effect of profit share targeting with an adjustment in the mark up.

We have now the full reflection of the microeconomic framework of endogenously evolving mark-ups at work at the macroeconomic level. If sellers are able to set and defend a target in the wake of rising mark-ups, this will foster increases in aggregate prices, until the process gets stabilized when mark-ups settle down at their higher levels. The aggregate action of sellers thus leads to positive inflation rates, but only for a certain amount of time. Profit (or sellers') inflation is real, but temporary. Conversely, the effects on the functional distribution of income — and particularly the perverse redistribution from wages to profits — is permanent, calling for greater policy attention.

Before concluding, it is important to note that the described mechanisms are assumed to be at work *independently* of changes in the conduct of both fiscal and monetary policy. This choice was motivated by our interest of looking specifically at the inflation-distribution nexus that emerges regardless of policy intervention. However, it is worth noting that these mechanisms can be deeply affected by economic policies such as the ones conducted in the US. First, by sustaining consumers' purchasing power, expansionary fiscal policies might have fostered the post-pandemic permissive pricing environment, stimulating demand and thus allowing firms to more easily raise mark-ups (and in turn prices). With constant real income but a falling labor share, firms would face lower demand for their products, making it difficult to further increase mark-ups. At the same time, the distributive effects to the detriment of workers could be exacerbated in an environment of rising interest rates. In situations where profit earners are capable of preserving, or even enhancing, their profit margins despite rising costs, increases in interest rates can intensify the shifts in income shares towards profits. This is due to the fact that interest rate hikes result in higher costs for firms, as discussed by Hein and Schoder (2011), Lima and Setterfield (2014), and Cucciniello, Deleidi, and Levrero (2022).[21]

5. Concluding Remarks

The paper has provided a post-Keynesian framework which coherently combines microeconomic and macroeconomic aspects of pricing theory, mark-up adjustments and profit share targeting to explain the surge in inflation observed during the post-pandemic recovery. It is argued that, particularly in some sectors, the surge in prices was caused by two factors. First, firms succeeded in protecting their profit margins in the wake of rising costs by passing on the cost increase to prices, thus unloading the relative weight of the adjustment on the backs of workers. In a second phase, the post-pandemic permissive pricing environment allowed some sectors to exploit years of increasing market concentration, with firms within these sectors being able to temporarily increase their mark-ups, leading in turn to transient profit-fueled inflation following the cost-push shock. Particularly in more concentrated sectors — or strategically significant in the terminology of Weber and Wasner (2023) — rising mark-ups have led to a permanent increase in the price level for the goods produced within the sector, with inflation rates transiently increasing and then steadily going down. In other terms, while we recognize that sellers' inflation might emerge from firms' pricing decision, it can only be temporary.

This microeconomic explanation of conflict inflation could be coupled at the macro level with Joan Robinson's notion of the 'inflation barrier' (Robinson 1937, 1956, 1962), where the latter is interpreted as a stable rather than explosive process. For a given quantity of real output, it is shown that if profit earners defend their share of income following a cost-push shock, this will produce a one-time price increase — with inflation becoming more persistent if the target adapts endogenously. In the latter case, if the aggregate mark-up changes in line with the mark-ups of those sectors systemically significant for inflation, transient sellers' inflation would become a macroeconomic phenomenon.

Our contribution yields few implications for conflict-driven inflation theory, reinforcing and generalizing the post-Keynesian claim that *inflation is always and everywhere a conflict phenomenon*. More specifically, it is argued that the traditional notion of workers being the sole agents responsible for explaining conflict inflation does not hold true in all cases. Instead, we have shown that following a cost-push shock, the increase in administered price can be solely attributed to the behavior of profit earners, that either maintain a certain mark-up to defend their profit margins from higher costs, or even try to increase it if the conditions allow. By anchoring our explanation in this framework, we also aim at bridging the gap between microeconomic and macroeconomic aspects in inflation theory, offering a coherent narrative at the firm, sectoral and aggregate levels.

Summing up, the paper contrasts the notion of a wage-price spiral with that of a profit-price sink, arguing that sellers' inflation is a real — albeit temporary phenomenon — leading to a higher price level but not persistently higher inflation rates. At the same time, temporary sellers' inflation produces a permanent shift in the functional distribution of income, tilting it in favor of profit earners and to the detriment of workers. To

[21]For more in-depth empirical analyses, see Deleidi and Levrero (2020) and Barbieri Góes (2023).

avoid the potential negative effects for macroeconomic and social stability of a decreased wage share, policy intervention through incomes policies would be required.

Acknowledgements

We are most grateful to Maria Cristina Barbieri Góes, Marc Lavoie, Achilleas Mantes, Franklin Serrano, Antonella Stirati, Isabella Weber, and two anonymous referees for their helpful comments and fruitful discussion. We would also like to thank the participants of the STOREP 2023 Conference (Bari, June 15-17, 2023), the 4th International Workshop on Demand-led Growth: "Money and Finance" (Rio de Janeiro, July 26-27, 2023), and the Workshop on Monetary Policy and Income Distribution at the Fields Institute (Toronto, November 16 - 17, 2023). All remaining errors are, of course, our own.

Disclosure Statement

No potential conflict of interest was reported by the author(s).

ORCID

Ettore Gallo https://orcid.org/0000-0002-4642-4779
Louis-Philippe Rochon http://orcid.org/0000-0002-8542-7497

References

Alvarez, J., J. Bluedorn, M. J. C. Bluedorn, M. N.-J. H. Hansen, N.-J. Hansen, Y. Huang, E. Pugacheva, and A. Sollaci. 2022. 'Wage-Price Spirals: What is the Historical Evidence?' IMF, Working Paper 2022/221.

Andler, M., and A. Kovner. 2022. 'Do Corporate Profits Increase When Inflation Increases?' Federal Reserve Bank of New York – Liberty Street Economics. Accessed September 27, 2023. https://libertystreeteconomics.newyorkfed.org/2022/07/do-corporate-profits-increase-when-inflation-increases/.

Barbieri Góes, M. C. 2023. 'A Tale of Three Prices: Monetary Policy and Autonomous Consumption in the US.' Structural Change and Economic Dynamics 67: 115–127.

Bivens, J. 2022. 'Corporate Profits Have Contributed Disproportionately to Inflation. How Should Policymakers Respond?' Economic Policy Institute Working Economics Blog. Accessed September 27, 2023. https://www.epi.org/blog/corporate-profits-have-contributed-disproportionately-to-inflation-how-should-policymakers-respond/.

Brainard, L. 2023. 'Staying the Course to Bring Inflation Down — Speech by Vice Chair Brainard on the Economic Outlook.' Accessed September 27, 2023. https://www.federalreserve.gov/newsevents/speech/brainard20230119a.htm.

Cauvel, M., and A. Pacitti. 2022. 'Bargaining Power, Structural Change, and the Falling Us Labor Share.' Structural Change and Economic Dynamics 60: 512–530.

Cerrato, A., and G. Gitti. 2022. "Inflation Since COVID: Demand or Supply.' *Available at SSRN 4193594.*

Colonna, F., R. Torrini, and E. Viviano. 2023. 'The Profit Share and Firm Markup: How to Interpret Them?' Bank of Italy, Occasional Paper (770).

Conlon, C., N. H. Miller, T. Otgon, and Y. Yao. 2023. 'Rising Markups, Rising Prices?' In *AEA Papers and Proceedings*. Vol. 113. American Economic Association, Nashville, TN.

Cucciniello, M. C., M. Deleidi, and E. S. Levrero. 2022. 'The Cost Channel of Monetary Policy: The Case of the United States in the Period 1959–2018.' Structural Change and Economic Dynamics 61: 409–433.

Davis, L. 2023. 'Profits and Markups During the Post-Covid Inflation Shock in the US Economy: A Firm-Level Lens.' In *Plenary Session — 27th FMM Conference 2023: Inflation, Distributional Conflict and Just Transition.*

Deleidi, M., and E. S. Levrero. 2020. 'The Price Puzzle and the Hysteresis Hypothesis: SVEC Analysis for the US Economy.' Review of Political Economy 32 (1): 22–29.

De Loecker, J., J. Eeckhout, and G. Unger. 2020. 'The Rise of Market Power and the Macroeconomic Implications.' The Quarterly Journal of Economics 135 (2): 561–644.

Galbraith, J. K. 2023. 'Convergence on Conflict? Blanchard, Krugman, Summers and Inflation?' Accessed September 27, 2023. https://medium.com/@monetarypolicyinstitute/convergence-on-conflict-inflation-in-the-21st-century-7bccb7b6479.

Gallo, E., and G. P. Serra. 2024. 'A Stock-Flow Consistent Model of Inventories, Debt Financing and Investment Decisions.' Structural Change and Economic Dynamics 68: 17–29.

Glover, A., J. Mustre-Del Río, and A. von Ende-Becker. 2023. 'How Much Have Record Corporate Profits Contributed to Recent Inflation?' Federal Reserve Bank of Kansas City Economic Review 108 (1): 1–13.

Hall, R. L., and C. J. Hitch. 1939. 'Price Theory and Business Behaviour.' Oxford Economic Papers 2 (1): 12–45. https://doi.org/10.1093/oxepap/os-2.1.12.

Hein, E. 2014. Distribution and Growth After Keynes: A Post-Keynesian Guide. Cheltenam: Edward Elgar.

Hein, E. 2023a. 'Inflation is Always and Everywhere ...a Conflict Phenomenon: Post-Keynesian Inflation Theory and Energy Price Driven Conflict Inflation.' IPE, Working Paper 224/2023.

Hein, E. 2023b. Macroeconomics After Kalecki and Keynes: Post-Keynesian Foundations. Cheltenham: Edward Elgar Publishing.

Hein, E., and C. Schoder. 2011. 'Interest Rates, Distribution and Capital Accumulation–A Post-Kaleckian Perspective on the US and Germany.' International Review of Applied Economics 25 (6): 693–723.

Holzman, F. D. 1950. 'Income Determination in Open Inflation.' The Review of Economics and Statistics 32 (2): 150–158.

Kalecki, M. 1954. Theory of Economic Dynamics: An Essay on Cyclical and Long-Run Changes in Capitalist Economy. New York: Rinehart & Company.

Konczal, M., and N. Lusiani. 2022. 'Prices, Profits and Power: An Analysis of 2021 Firm-Level Markups.' Roosevelt Institute, Working Paper.

Lavoie, M. 2023a. 'Profit Inflation and Markups Once Again.' INET. Accessed September 27, 2023. https://www.ineteconomics.org/perspectives/blog/profit-inflation-and-markups-once-again.

Lavoie, M. 2023b. 'Profit-Led Inflation Redefined: Response to Nikiforos and Grothe.' INET. Accessed September 27, 2023. https://www.ineteconomics.org/perspectives/blog/profit-led-inflation-redefined-response-to-nikiforos-and-grothe.

Lavoie, M. 2023c. 'Some Controversies in the Causes of the Post-Pandemic Inflation.' Monetary Policy Institute Blog. Accessed September 27, 2023. https://medium.com/@monetarypolicyinstitute/some-controversies-in-the-causes-of-the-post-pandemic-inflation-1480a7a08eb7.

Lavoie, M., and L.-P. Rochon. 2023. 'Olivier Blanchard and Inflation.' Monetary Policy Institute. Accessed September 27, 2023. https://medium.com/@monetarypolicyinstitute/olivier-blanchard-and-inflation-219f195125fe.

Lima, G. T., and M. Setterfield. 2014. 'The Cost Channel of Monetary Transmission and Stabilization Policy in a Post-Keynesian Macrodynamic Model.' Review of Political Economy 26 (2): 258–281.

Lorenzoni, G., and I. Werning. 2023. 'Inflation is Conflict.' National Bureau of Economic Research, Working Paper w31099.

Matamoros, G. 2023. 'Are Firm Markups Boosting Inflation? A Post-Keynesian Institutionalist Approach to Markup Inflation in Select Industrialized Countries.' Review of Political Economy 1–22.

Nikiforos, M., and S. Grothe. 2023. 'Markups, Profit Shares, and Cost-Push-Profit-Led Inflation.' INET. Accessed September 27, 2023. https://www.ineteconomics.org/perspectives/blog/markups-profit-shares-and-cost-push-profit-led-inflation.

Nikiforos, M., S. Grothe, and J. D. Weber. 2024. 'Markups, Profit Shares, and Cost-Push-profit-Led Inflation.' Industrial and Corporate Change 33 (2): 342–362.

Robinson, J. V. 1937. Essays in the Theory of Employment. London: Macmillan.

Robinson, J. V. 1956. The Accumulation of Capital. London: Macmillan.

Robinson, J. V. 1962. Essays in the Theory of Economic Growth. London and Basingstoke: Macmillan

Robinson, J. V. 1979. 'Solving the Stagflation Puzzle.' Challenge 22 (5): 40–46.

Rochon, L.-P., and M. Setterfield. 2007. 'Interest Rates, Income Distribution, and Monetary Policy Dominance: Post Keynesians and the "fair Rate" of Interest.' Journal of Post Keynesian Economics 30 (1): 13–42.

Rowthorn, R. 1977. 'Conflict, Inflation and Money.' Cambridge Journal of Economics 1 (3): 215–239.

Rowthorn, R. 2024. 'The Conflict Theory of Inflation Revisited.' Review of Political Economy 1–12.

Rudd, J. B. 2022. 'Why Do We Think that Inflation Expectations Matter for Inflation? (and Should We?).' Review of Keynesian Economics 10 (1): 25–45.

Setterfield, M. 2023. 'Inflation and Distribution During the Post-COVID Recovery: A Kaleckian Approach.' Journal of Post Keynesian Economics 46 (4): 587–611.

Stiglitz, J. E., and I. Regmi. 2023. 'The Causes of and Responses to Today's Inflation.' Industrial and Corporate Change 32 (2): 336–385.

Storm, S. 2023. 'Profit Inflation Is Real.' INET. Accessed September 27, 2023. https://www.ineteconomics.org/perspectives/blog/profit-inflation-is-real.

Visco, I. 2023. 'Monetary Policy and the Return of Inflation: Questions, Charts and Tentative Answers.' *CEPR Policy Insight*, 122.

Weber, I. M., J. L. Jauregui, L. Teixeira, and L. N. Pires. 2022. 'Inflation in Times of Overlapping Emergencies: Systemically Significant Prices from an Input-Output Perspective.' University of Massachusetts Amherst, Economics Department, Working Paper Series, (340).

Weber, I. M., and E. Wasner. 2023. 'Sellers' Inflation, Profits and Conflict: Why Can Large Firms Hike Prices in An Emergency?' Review of Keynesian Economics 11 (2): 183–213.

Weisskopf, T. E. 1979. 'Marxian Crisis Theory and the Rate of Profit in the Postwar US Economy.' Cambridge Journal of Economics 3 (4): 341–378.

Wildauer, R., K. Kohler, A. Aboobaker, and A. Guschanski. 2023. 'Energy Price Shocks, Conflict Inflation, and Income Distribution in a Three-Sector Model.' Energy Economics 127:106982.

Appendix: Parameter Values

The simulation exercise conducted in Sections Three and Four is purely illustrative and is meant to show the compatibility of the model with the stylized evidence of an S-shaped movement in the trend of unit prices in the US,[22] — thus capturing the permanent increase in the price level with temporarily rising inflation rates — as well as the observed decrease in the US wage share.[23]

Parameter values and initial conditions are reported in Table A1.

Table A1. Parameter values and initial conditions.

m_0	Initial mark-up	0.15
m_{max}	Maximum mark-up	0.175
t_{mid}	Midpoint of the sigmoid	75
g_j	Pass-through effect	0.12
S	Shape control parameter	0.3
Y_0	Initial value of aggregate output	100
W_0	Initial value of aggregate wages	50
Π_0	Initial value of aggregate profits	50
ε	Cost-push shock	10
η	Workers' bargaining power	1
ω_0	Initial wage share	0.5

[22]See data: Price per unit of real gross value added of nonfinancial corporate business, Quarterly, Seasonally Adjusted, A455RD3Q052SBEA, https://fred.stlouisfed.org/series/A455RD3Q052SBEA [Accessed October 1st, 2023].

[23]See data: share of corporate-sector income received by workers over recent business cycles, 1979–2023, https://www.epi.org/nominal-wage-tracker/ [Accessed October 1st, 2023].

Cost-Push and Conflict Inflation: A Discussion of the Italian Case

Davide Romaniello and Antonella Stirati

ABSTRACT

This study contributes to the ongoing discussion surrounding the recent surge in inflation. It presents an analytical framework and empirically examines inflation trends in Italy. The primary aim is to identify the underlying causes, distributive repercussions, and mechanisms through which inflation is propagated. We adopt a cost-push and distributive conflict perspective on current inflation. Within this perspective, some contributions argue for profit-driven inflation, while others dispute this interpretation, emphasizing that increases in the profit share, amid rising import costs do not necessarily imply heightened overall profitability. To clarify these issues, the paper puts forth an analytical framework that shows how escalating import costs can affect profit shares and set in motion a period of inflation propagation, even in the absence of a wage-price spiral. Turning attention to the Italian context, the study utilizes descriptive statistics, sectoral data, and simple simulations to gain insights into the drivers of inflation and its distributive consequences. Additionally, a local projections analysis is deployed to uncover the nature and timing of the propagation process. The paper concludes with some policy implications based on the findings.

1. Introduction

The main purpose of this paper is to contribute to the current debates on the nature and drivers of the recent inflation surge by proposing a theoretical framework and by means of an empirical analysis of inflation in Italy, looking at its causes, distributive effects, and propagation mechanisms. The case of Italy can be of interest, given the country's strong reliance on gas as the main source of energy, and at the same time a very subdued nominal wage growth in a labour market that is definitely far from full employment conditions.

The sudden re-emergence of high inflation has given rise to a lively debate on its causes that involves questions about the appropriate analytical framework and the empirical inquiry into the main determinants of inflation. In this context, the statement by Blanchard (2022) that inflation has its source in conflicting claims over income has elicited reactions from Post-Keynesian economists who claimed that they first proposed and elaborated this interpretation of inflation processes. As noted by Lavoie and Rochon

Supplemental data for this article can be accessed online at https://doi.org/10.1080/09538259.2024.2373738.

(2023), however, Blanchard had indeed already proposed a conflicting claims interpretation of inflation in an article published in 1986. But is everyone talking of the same conflicting claims theory?

Albeit at the cost of some simplification, we can distinguish two approaches to conflicting claims inflation. The first is the one proposed by Blanchard in his 1986 article and shared by most New-Keynesian models and textbooks. Its distinguishing features are that (i) conflict inflation does not affect income distribution, which remains unaltered at least in the medium run; (ii) there is an equilibrium unemployment rate (the NAIRU) that is a *de facto* attractor either through spontaneous market mechanisms or through monetary policy. The inflation process exhibits the 'accelerationist' property that out-of-equilibrium inflation or deflation will increase over time. Since the NAIRU is the unemployment level necessary to discipline the workers into accepting a real wage consistent with the *given real* mark-up, as such it attracts some consensus also among non-mainstream economists that regard this modelling as an acceptable representation of the notion that a certain 'reserve army' is necessary in a capitalist economy to keep real wages in check and profitability in line with firms' aspirations (Stockhammer 2008). The condition that the mark-up (and hence the profit rate that it must comprise) is *given in real terms* (that is, firms can continuously and completely pass through the increases in costs) is a necessary assumption underlying the accelerationist features of inflationary processes. The accelerationist view also requires that workers can always aim at, and obtain that nominal wages completely adjust to price inflation (although real wages never manage to grow, other things given, since firms can fix the real mark-up). In this perspective, inflation is generally regarded as the consequence of excess demand bringing the actual unemployment rate below the NAIRU (Lavoie 2022, p. 594).

There is, however, a second approach to conflict inflation, which is shared by many non-mainstream economists. Its main feature is the view that the conflict that underlies inflation can indeed alter income distribution persistently, depending on the bargaining strength of the parties involved, which in turn may depend on several circumstances concerning the labour market and its regulation, as well as macroeconomic conditions and constraints (see Hein 2023 and Serrano et al. 2024 for a systematic discussion and clarification of these approaches). Accordingly, there is neither a *given* mark-up in real terms nor a NAIRU; the unemployment rate depends on aggregate demand and hence, to a large extent, on fiscal policies. Changes in the unemployment rate may affect the inflation *rate*, but acceleration is regarded as a rare phenomenon, as confirmed by empirical evidence (Alvarez et al. 2022), most often triggered by repeated exogenous shocks to terms of trade. This view is based on an analytical framework in which income distribution is always, even in conditions of free competition, the result of power relations, along with social norms and institutions, and inflation is not only the manifestation of a conflict over income distribution but may also be the channel that brings about changes in income distribution that reflect those power relations. Within this framework, inflation is regarded as usually initiated by cost-push from a worsening of terms of trade or sustained nominal wage dynamics. The latter may be the consequence of persistently low unemployment or institutional and political factors, but is not necessarily or generally the result of excess demand for labour or products (Braga and Serrano 2023; Summa and Braga 2020). Similarly, sustained and persistent growth in world demand tends to cause increases in primary commodity prices, which, however, may not be connected with an excess demand as such, but with enhanced negotiating power of suppliers, or the need to resort to more costly sources of energy or other primary commodities. These cost-push factors then set in motion processes of price-wage or wage-price spirals as parties attempt to preserve, or enhance, their real earnings, but with both parties, workers and firms, normally unable to fully and immediately index them to cost and price changes.

We wish to locate our contribution within this second way of looking at the inflation process. However, we also note that the recent resurgence of inflation, for the moment, does not completely fit the description above: while a terms of trade shock is clearly detected and has been very large in Europe, little 'conflict' seems to be taking place on the part of wage earners. Real wages are falling everywhere and (for the moment) nominal wage growth remains moderate. In the Eurozone (Arce et al. 2023, chart 1, p. 2, and Hansen et al. 2023, p. 13) and in Italy (our case study), nominal wage growth has been, on average in the 2021–23 period, around 2 per cent per year, thus actually in line with the ECB inflation target. Perhaps as a consequence of what we have just described, several contributions interpret the current inflation as profit-driven, but other scholars have objected to this view, and among other things have noted that increases in the profit share or operating surplus, in a context of increasing import costs, are not necessarily evidence of an increase in profitability.

In the next section (Section Two), we survey different interpretations of the current inflation; subsequently (Section Three) we describe the main features of the Italian case. In Section Four, we propose a framework for analyzing the propagation of an increase in import prices and its impact on distribution, and in Section Five we discuss the data with a view to verifying the role, if any, of increases in profitability. In Section Six, we carry out an econometric analysis aimed at assessing the persistence and distributional impact of import prices in the period 1995–2023.

2. Controversies on the Interpretations of the Current Inflation

In the US, where inflation has been high but energy costs have not increased as much as in Europe, important economists such as Blanchard (2021, 2022) and Summers (2021) suggest that excess aggregate demand, caused by excessive fiscal stimulus, triggered a conflict over income distribution in the form of a wage-price spiral. Blanchard (2022) suggests that several routes are available to keep inflation under check (such as subsidies, or centralized negotiations), and it is better to avoid recessions induced by monetary tightening. But the fiscal stance, following this view, should be much more prudent than in the recent past.

Several critiques have emerged regarding this initial interpretation of US inflation. Blanchard and Bernanke (2023) argue that inflation during the COVID-19 era stemmed from higher commodity prices and increased demand for goods with inelastic supply or bottlenecks created during the pandemic, rather than primarily from labour market tightening. However, they continue to assert that excess labour demand would foster inflation due to increasing wages after the supply shock is reabsorbed. Building on the Bernanke and Blanchard model, Arce et al. (2024) find that supply shocks were also the main driver of inflation in the Euro area, with an even greater impact than in the US due to the region's higher exposure to the effects of the Russia-Ukraine war. Other criticism has been raised on empirical grounds by Ferguson and Storm (2023), who show that the timing of fiscal expansion and inflation surge are not consistent with the initial interpretation by Blanchard or that by Summers. In addition, real wages are losing ground, thus casting doubt on wage dynamics as the underlying factor in the surge of inflation, as suggested for example by Summers in an interview (Klein 2022). By contrast, Ferguson and Storm argue that there has been a price-price spiral whereby firms have been able to increase their margins (mark-ups); in other words, a 'profit' inflation is at play as manifested by the increase in the ratio of the (gross) operating surplus on value added. The same conclusion is supported by Storm (2023), who finds evidence of the role of increasing firm mark-ups in fostering inflation and causing growth in the profit share both in the US and in the Netherlands. In addition to rising corporate profitability, Breman and Storm (2023) find that a high degree of speculation in the crude oil market is responsible for two key effects. First, it directly contributed to the sharp increase in West Texas Intermediate (WTI) crude oil prices. Second, it indirectly contributed to an increase in energy price inflation between 0.75 and 1.5 per cent points (Breman and Storm 2023, p. 154). This, in turn, fostered an increase in the aggregate profit share and consumer price inflation.

Claims of and evidence for 'profit inflation' have also been advanced by other contributions. Weber and Wasner (2023) argue that price fixing by firms is such that an increase in costs can give rise to a coordinated increase in prices that allows a complete pass-through of costs but also, particularly in instances of supply shortages and disruptions, to price increases that allow an increase in profitability. They use data from company budgets to provide empirical support for their interpretation. Arce et al. (2023) and Panetta (2023) for the Eurozone, and Bivens (2022) for the US economy, follow a similar view, primarily based on a historically high ratio of operating surplus to real value added. Cucignatto and Garbellini (2023) using input-output data for the largest European economies, including Italy, argue that between 2018 and 2022 the increased direct and indirect costs due to a five-fold increase in gas prices on the Dutch gas market would have caused, other things equal, an increase in price indexes that was much lower (between 3.5 and 4 per cent in the Italian case), than their actual cumulative increase (about 11 per cent in the Italian case). Hence, they also support an interpretation of the current inflation as profit-driven. If these interpretations are correct, we would witness a cost-push plus conflicting-claims inflation where the increasing claims are one-sided and come from firms who see an opportunity to increase profit margins, taking advantage of an exogenous increase in costs, while nominal wages can barely recover even a fraction of those price increases. Inflation, therefore, would be effecting a (further) redistribution of income away from labour and in favour of profits.

Some non-mainstream authors have objected to the view that profit increases are major drivers of the current inflation. Lavoie (2023), based on Canadian data, argues that the increase in the operating surplus share in value added is in line with the cyclical behaviour of the latter; it therefore does not necessarily reflect an increase in profitability due to pricing behaviour but is a common feature during a recovery. The profit share on GDP typically exhibits a pro-cyclical behaviour owing to overhead labour costs, labour hoarding and so on, such that productivity increases rapidly in recoveries, and more rapidly than real wages. In addition to this, the profit share can increase owing to the impact of the increased costs of the material (imported) intermediate inputs. Some doubts concerning 'profit inflation' are raised also by Vernengo and Caldentey (2023), who show, based on US data, that energy prices and the consumer price index have tended historically to move closely together, in a way very similar to what was going on in 2021–22. They also predict, given the subdued nominal wage growth and the temporary nature of the energy price increase, that inflation will continue to slow down, as indeed it did slow down to a considerable extent at the end of 2022/beginning of 2023. A much-cited paper by IMF researchers (Hansen et al. 2023) looking at data for several mature economies, including the Eurozone, does not detect clear evidence of a generalized increase in profitability or margins over variable costs, despite the increase in the profit share and the contribution of unit profits (defined as profits per unit of real GDP) to the increase in the GDP deflator and consumer price index. The authors argue that in some industries in the Euro area the increase in unit profits may be due to increasing variable costs as well as to the ability of firms to (partly or fully) pass through the increases in costs. They also suggest, however, that the reduction in productive capacity during the pandemic and/or fast demand growth might have provided firms with pricing power (Hansen et al. 2023, pp. 15–16).

In addition to these empirical objections, profit inflation is also not so easily accepted, from an analytical point of view, even by non-mainstream economists, since it seems to violate the notion that competition is a disciplining force in the economy. Even when elements of monopoly, oligopoly, or product differentiation give some firms market power, the threat of entry into the industry by new competitors, as well as competition in product markets, should keep extra-profits in check. Finally, this interpretation of inflation raises the question of why, if firms can increase prices to satisfy their greed for higher profits, they did not do it before? On the other hand, it may not *a priori* be ruled out that, in the context of a general increase in costs at the global level and some supply disruptions, firms could try to take advantage of price increases elsewhere to increase their own prices above what is justified by actual cost increases, in an implicitly coordinated way. We will discuss Italian data below as a case study of the inflation surge, which can be of interest given its features concerning price and nominal wage dynamics. In Italy, the impact of the price increase of gas was substantial, given the relatively large dependence of the country on this source of energy, along with a still relatively large manufacturing sector (which is more 'energy-consuming' than the service sector). Among European countries, indeed, Italy reached the highest value of inflation rate (measured by the HICP) in November 2022 (12.6 per cent) followed by Germany (11.3 per cent), while the EU-27 average was 11.1 per cent. However, while the inflationary surge has been sizeable, nominal wage growth has remained, up to now, subdued. The European Commission (2023, p. 46) and OECD (2024, p. 6) also support this evidence, reporting that nominal wage growth in Italy has been one of the lowest in Europe. This has caused negative consequences for real wages throughout 2023. Several factors contribute to this trend including (a) Italy's use of forward-looking inflation measures, which exclude energy prices and have been on a downward trend, as a basis for sectoral wage negotiations, (b) infrequent and delayed collective bargaining rounds, (c) the absence of automatic indexation to inflation, and (d) the relative bargaining power of employers and unions. In fact, when examining the employee compensation data, the Italian year-on-year percentage change (with quarterly data) is the lowest among the largest economies of the European Union in almost all quarters of 2023.[1]

3. Descriptive Evidence on Cost-Push and Distributive Impact in Italy

In this section, we conduct a descriptive analysis of the Italian inflation surge from a sectoral perspective, looking at some distributive consequences. In Section Five below, we return to aggregate and sectoral data in order to dwell in a more detailed manner on the trends in profitability and the sources of inflation. Our data sources encompass a variety of datasets obtained from the Istituto Nazionale di Statistica (ISTAT), with the timing of data usage dependent on availability. As a result, we use monthly data to illustrate price and inflation trends, while in Section Five we use quarterly data to assess changes in mark-ups, and annual data for examining distribution and the ex-post rate of profits. Our econometric analysis (Section Six) is conducted using quarterly data. Additional details regarding data sources and methodology are reported in the online Appendix.

3.1. Descriptive Analysis of Sectoral Prices and the Inflationary Process: The Role of Energy and Imported Goods

As noted, Italy experienced an unprecedented surge in inflation in the 2021–23 period, after a long-lasting period of stagnant inflation rates. Figure 1 illustrates that the surge in the consumer price index began in July 2021 and reached its peak in November 2022, with an annual inflation rate of 12.6 per cent. After this date, inflation began to decrease, reaching 6.7 per cent (on an annual basis) by June 2023, and 0.9 per cent in February 2024. A small and temporary uptick in inflation occurred in the last months of 2023 on account of upward effects from energy prices (ECB 2023).

It is important to highlight that the surge was primarily triggered by the rocketing energy prices. Figure 2 provides evidence of this, showing that the price index of energy goods (right graph) nearly tripled compared to its 2019 value, thus becoming the main driver of the upward trajectory of the HICP index. This is further illustrated in the graph on the left, which compares the general HICP index (solid line) with the index excluding energy, food, alcohol and tobacco (dashed line).[2]

Despite a decline in energy prices after October 2022, the general index continued to rise, albeit at a slower pace, throughout 2023. It peaked at 122 in October 2022 and stabilized around 120 in early 2024 (January 2019 = 100). To gain deeper insights into the factors driving this inflationary process, we turn our attention to industrial producer prices for the domestic market, as illustrated in Figure 3. Again, the price dynamics observed here are primarily associated with the energy sector.[3] After a slight decrease between 2019 and 2020, energy prices exhibited a consistent upward trajectory. The

[1] According to Eurostat data, in Q3 2023, the percentage change in nominal wage per employee on a year-on-year basis was 3.53 per cent in Italy, 3.89 per cent in France, 6.04 per cent in Germany, and 6.54 per cent in the EU (27 countries). This ranking remained consistent throughout all quarters of 2023, except for Q2 2023, when the change in wage was 4.46 per cent in France and 4.52 per cent in Italy.

[2] This last index is the one used to calculate the so-called 'core' inflation.

[3] The industry labelled 'Energy' includes the domestic extractive industry of energy raw materials (oil, natural gas, lignite), the refining industry, the production of electricity, gas and water, steam, and the collection, purification and distribution of water.

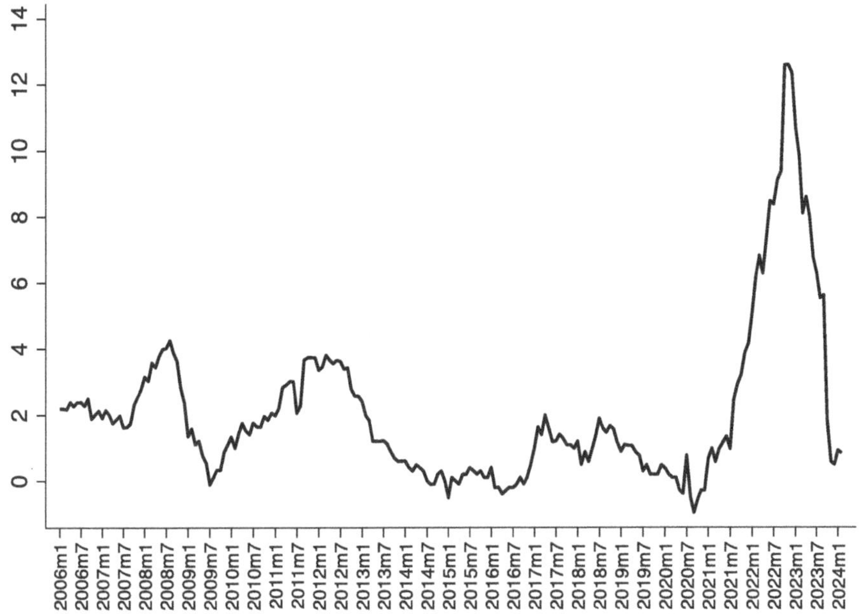

Figure 1. Harmonized index of consumer prices. Percentage change from the same period of the previous year. Source: ISTAT.

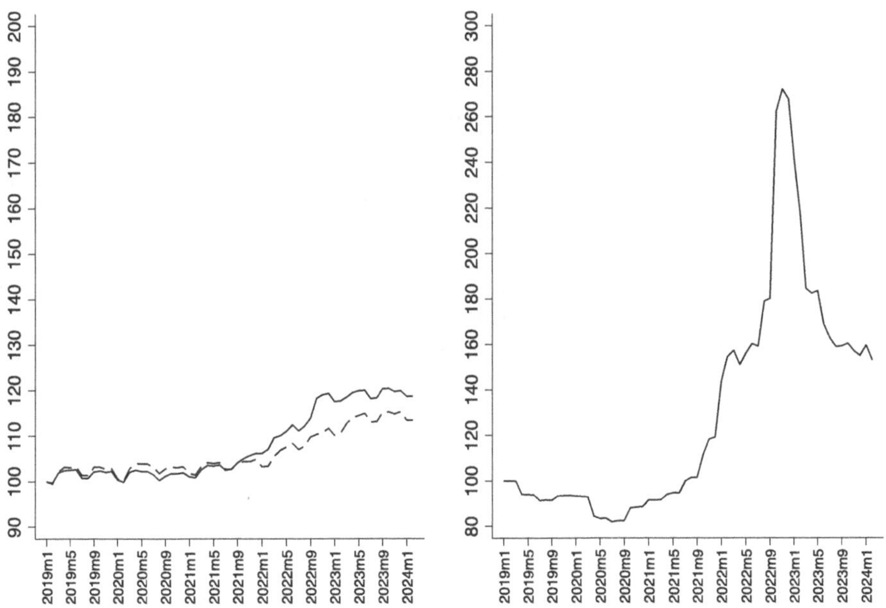

Figure 2. Harmonized index of consumer prices, for energy goods and for 'core' goods. Source: ISTAT. Base year 2019M1.

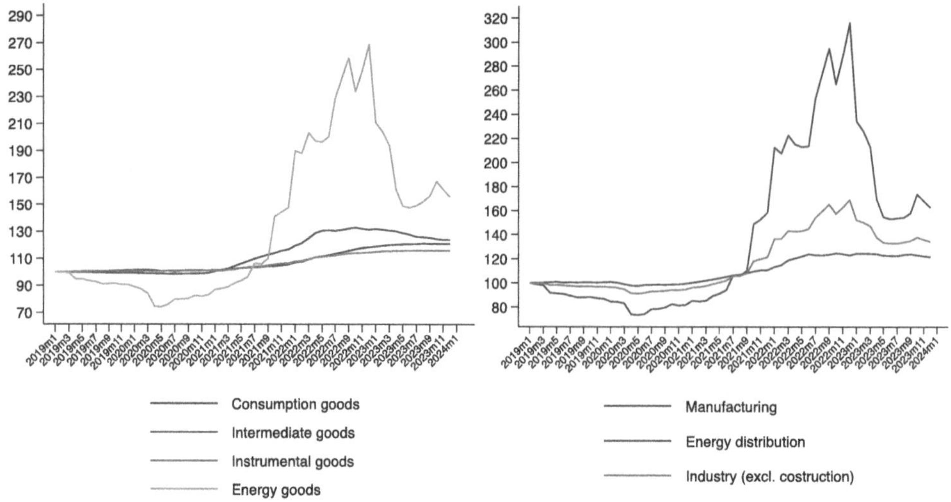

Figure 3. Industrial producer prices for the internal market, by COICOP 2018 classification (left graph) and by economic sector (NACE rev. 2, right graph). Source: ISTAT Base year 1–2019.

rate of increase gained momentum from the summer to the fall of 2021, and continued until December 2022. As shown in Figure 3, energy prices nearly tripled in under two years, surging from 106 in July 2021 to 270 in December 2022; after that they have declined, but remain substantially higher (by about 50 per cent) than in 2019. In 2021, the price of production for all categories of goods began to ascend. However, the prices of intermediate goods (indicated by the red line) exhibited a relatively more pronounced increase when compared to consumer goods (represented by the blue line) and capital goods (represented by the green line).

Furthermore, the same producer price indexes, this time categorized by economic sector, show that the price surge in energy distribution (the red line on the right-side of Figure 3) outpaced that of energy goods production (the yellow line on the right-side of Figure 3). In December 2022, the former reached a peak of 316, much higher than the latter, with a peak of 270 (base year 2019). Lastly, when we differentiate between the price of *manufacturing* and the price of *industry* excluding *construction* (the sector labelled 'industry', when *construction* is excluded, is comprised of manufacturing and energy production and distribution, with the latter representing about 15 per cent of this sector, and the former 85 per cent), we can discern that *industry* exhibits steeper price dynamics than *manufacturing*. This observation further confirms the pivotal role of energy prices in driving the overall increase in the price level.

Figure 4 illustrates the evolution of import prices. Among the various imported goods, energy prices exhibit the highest level of volatility and follow a similar trajectory to that described earlier for the prices of domestically produced and distributed energy goods. Between May 2020 and September 2022, the price of imported energy more than tripled, rising from 103.27 to 364. Additionally, starting in January 2021, there is a noticeable upward trend in the prices of instrumental, intermediate, and consumption imported goods. However, among these categories, the price of

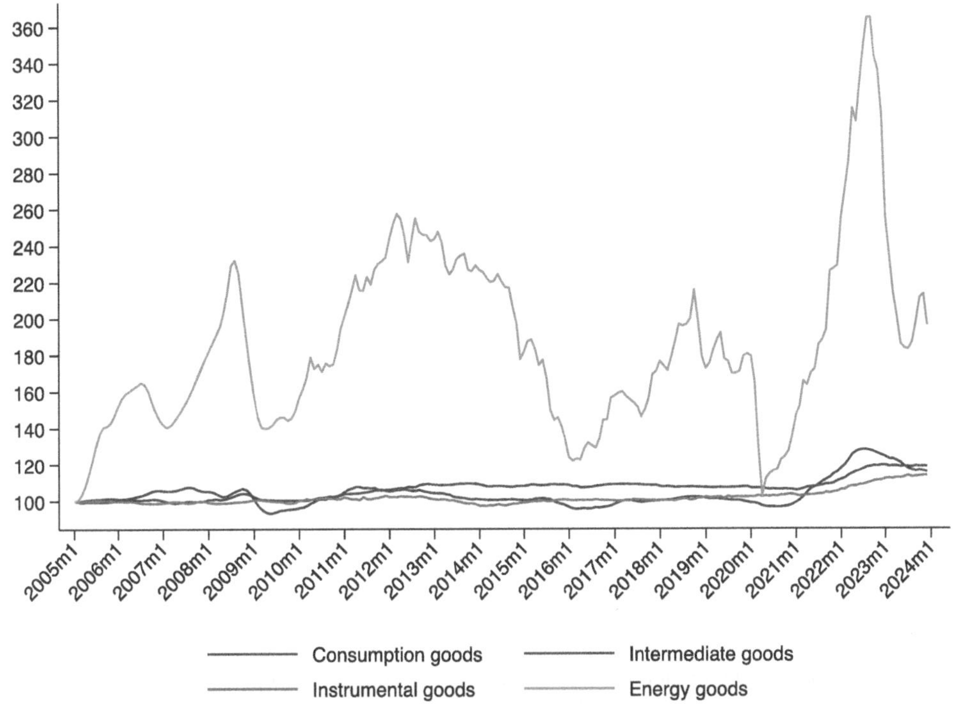

Figure 4. Import prices, COICOP 2018 classification. Source: ISTAT, Base year 1–2005.

intermediate goods experienced a more significant increase, climbing from 100 in January 2021 to 127 in July 2022. A general observation is that both import and production prices of energy began to decrease as of December 2022. A temporary upsurge in the price of imported energy occurred in the last months of 2023 but began declining again in December 2023.

3.2. The Distributive Effects of Inflation: Wages

The increase in inflation has raised concerns regarding wage dynamics, with some arguing against adjusting money wages to avoid a price-wage spiral (Schnabel 2023; Visco 2023). Figure 5 (left graph) provides an illustration of the path of nominal compensation. Since 2018, nominal compensation per hour worked has consistently shown a positive and increasing percentage change. It should be noted that the 2020 figure reflects the unique situation created by the pandemic: the sharp reduction in employment within some low-wage service industries heavily distorts the data. In 2023, hourly nominal wages in the entire economy were 7 percentage points higher than in 2019, resulting in an average annual growth rate over the period of about 1.58 per cent, lower than the 2 per cent that represents the ECB inflation target. The dynamics of nominal wages are somewhat stronger in the private sector than in the total economy, but still do not exceed the 2 per cent annual average growth.

When examining real compensation and accounting for the interplay between price dynamics and wage dynamics (Figure 5, right-side), it becomes evident that a substantial

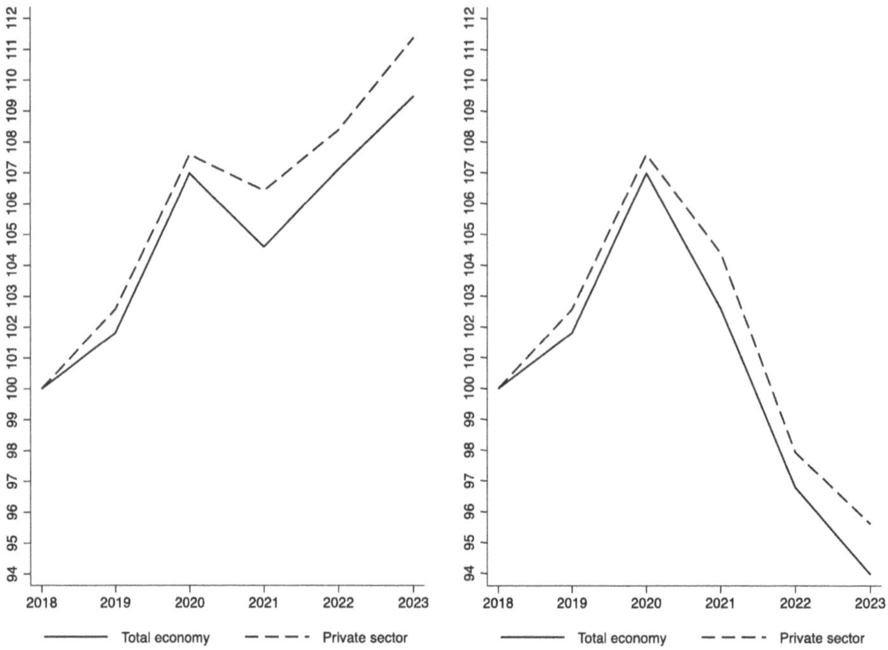

Figure 5. Nominal compensation per hour worked (left graph); real compensation per hour worked (right graph), base year 2018. Source: ISTAT.

decline in the level of real wages occurred after the COVID-19 pandemic. The very moderate growth of nominal wages combined with the resurgence in inflation, resulted in a significant decrease in real wages per hour worked. By 2023, the level of hourly real wages was about 6 percentage points lower than in 2019.[4] This highlights the challenging nature of the inflationary environment and its detrimental effect, in the current situation, on the purchasing power of wage earners.

Additionally, the trajectory of the adjusted wage share, presented in Figure 6, further confirms the extent of the reduction in real wage per employee that occurred in 2022 and 2023 and the deterioration of income distribution. Starting from 2022, the share of wages in relation to value-added rediscovered a long-term negative trend that had developed from the late 1970s until 2000.[5]

[4]It is important to note that while the HICP is used to assess overall real wage trends, it does not fully capture the disproportionate impact of inflation on different income groups. According to ISTAT (2022, pp. 246–249), when considering equivalent household consumption expenditure levels, families with the lowest expenditures—often those reliant on wages—have experienced an inflation rate nearly double that of wealthier families. This disparity arises because essential goods—particularly energy and food, which have seen the most significant price increases—constitute a larger proportion of the consumption baskets of those with middle to lower incomes.

[5]Note that the 1995–2023 period considered here includes the modest rise in Italy's adjusted wage share that occurred between 2001 and 2013. However, this recovery was modest and temporary compared to the significant decline in wage share witnessed in the preceding decades. If looked at from a long-run perspective, the wage share in Italy shows a clear and persistent negative trend from a level close to 75 per cent during the 1960s to 58 per cent in 2023. The increase in the early 2000s was largely due to the particularly negative trend of Italian labour productivity rather than to an increase in real wages. For a detailed analysis of the Italian case, see Levrero and Stirati 2005, and for more recent periods, Paternesi Meloni and Stirati 2023.

Figure 6. Adjusted wage share by sectors (NACE rev. 2). Authors' own calculation based on ISTAT data.
Note: Private sector refers to the difference between total economic activity and public administration and defense; compulsory social security (O 84) sector.

4. Some Analytical Pointers

Before we delve further into the empirical evidence, particularly regarding the evolution of profitability, we propose, in this section, a framework for the analysis of the inflationary process. We believe this can provide a contribution in two ways. It can clarify the transmission process from imports to domestic prices, and the persistence of inflation even when the increase in import prices is reversed, despite the subdued nominal wage growth. In addition, it can help clarify the different sources of the increase in the profit share.

Following Stirati (2001), we can represent various inflation scenarios according to circumstances, starting from nominal price equations of the type:

$$P_t = P_{t-1} A (1 + i_0 + \rho_0) + F_{t-1}(1 + i_0 + \rho_0) + lw_0 \tag{1}$$

where P is the nominal price vector, A is the matrix of domestically produced intermediate inputs per unit of output, i is the nominal interest rate that represents the pure remuneration of capital and minimum benchmark return that has to be earned on the historical cost of capital inputs (e.g., interest rate earned on long term bonds), and ρ is the rate of business profit in addition to the pure remuneration of capital, which may reflect elements of extra-profit due to market power as well as risk and illiquidity. In fact, business profits may differ across industries, but here we treat ρ as a scalar for simplicity. F is the cost in national currency of imports per unit of output, w is the nominal (uniform) wage, and l is the vector of labour inputs per unit of output. We assume for the moment a given and constant nominal profit rate and nominal wages, and we ignore fixed capital inputs. In what follows, we are interested in focusing on the effects of shocks to the costs of intermediate inputs and the inflationary impact these have when we consider the transmission process through interindustry exchanges. This is an aspect that in our view is often neglected in the debates on inflation. After clarifying this, we describe in a more intuitive way possible scenarios determined by changes in nominal wages and the profit rate (based on the more analytical account provided in Stirati 2001).

It is important to note that, while the nominal interest rate plus business profit on *historic* capital costs coincides with the *real* profit rate $(i + \rho)$ in a situation of null inflation, this is not the case when there is inflation. In this case, while competition tends to impose the nominal interest rate on *historic* capital cost as a benchmark, the real profit rate must be calculated based on the *replacement costs* of capital. In other words, a given constant nominal interest rate and/or a given nominal business profit rate earned on the actual historic cost of capital implies, if there is inflation, a decrease in the *real* profit rate, approximately equal to nominal profit rate minus inflation or, more precisely, minus the price inflation of the capital inputs specific to the industry.

Although the representation in equation (1) is less simple and intuitive than the usual aggregate variable costs and mark-up representation of price formation, it may improve the understanding of the propagation of the inflationary process. We can see why this is the case by looking at the usual mark-up representation of price formation (Lavoie 2024, 17) using symbols with the same meaning as above:

$$P = (1 + m)(wl + F) \tag{2}$$

where m is the mark-up, wl are unit labour costs (i.e., nominal wage times labour per unit of output), and F are the imported inputs costs in national currency per unit of output. In this representation of price formation, the economy is represented as if it was a vertically integrated industry, thus omitting an explicit representation of the exchanges among firms and sectors. In terms of equation (1) above, the mark-up in equation (2) must cover for the replacement of capital inputs, and for the profits (interest plus business profits) on the value per unit of output of *domestically* produced inputs along with imported capital inputs. In some cases it may be useful to look at the aggregate economy as a vertically integrated sector and ignore intra-industry exchanges within the domestic economy, as in equation 2, but when analyzing inflationary processes this may lead to neglecting some important features of the propagation process. It may also lead to neglecting the fact that with a given nominal profit rate and constant nominal wages, the mark-up over wage and foreign inputs costs as represented in equation (2) would have to increase owing to the increased prices of domestically produced inputs. Equation (1) above shows how an increase in imported inputs costs (which is definitely a major factor in the current burst of inflation) — even under the assumption of a constant nominal profit rate and nominal wage — will give rise to a succession of price increases, as the increase in the cost of imported inputs gradually enters into the prices of domestically produced intermediate inputs and hence causes several 'rounds' of increases in costs and prices. On the one hand, this would affect 'core' inflation, that is, net of imported energy costs, and on the other hand it would be reflected in an increased gross and net operating surplus over value-added (that is, an increase in the profit share), and an increase in the mark-up over labour and import unit costs as represented in equation (2).

Since the increase of (gross) operating surplus over value added (the 'profit share') is very often used in empirical analyses of current inflation as an indication of increases in profitability, it should be noted from equation (1) that, for given *nominal* interest and business profit rates, both the term $\boldsymbol{F}_{t-1}(\boldsymbol{i}+\boldsymbol{\rho})$ and the term $\boldsymbol{P}_{t-1}\boldsymbol{A}(\boldsymbol{i}+\boldsymbol{\rho})$ — that is, total remuneration of capital — would tend to increase relative to total value added along with the increases in the relative prices of imported inputs and, gradually, of domestically produced inputs. In the case of gross operating surplus, there would also be (with a lag) an increase in the historical costs of circulating (and fixed) capital that would be reflected in the component of gross operating surplus meant to cover for depreciation and turnover of capital, that is, in our simplified example with circulating capital only, the terms $\boldsymbol{F}_{t-1}$ and $\boldsymbol{P}_{t-1}\boldsymbol{A}$.[6]

To express this in formal terms, suppose we have an increase in the cost of imported inputs of m, which for simplicity we assume to be a scalar, while nominal interest rate and nominal wages remain unchanged. The price level *before* the change in the terms of trade in $t = 0$ is:

$$\boldsymbol{P}_0\boldsymbol{Q}_0 = \alpha + \beta + \gamma = 1 \tag{3}$$

where α, β, γ are, respectively, the weight of the (historical) value of domestically produced inputs plus the nominal profit rate on it, the weight of the value of imported inputs plus profits, and the weight of labour cost on the value of output in the initial period, and the left-hand side is the price index in the base year $t = 0$.

After the deterioration in the terms of trade by the rate m, the ratio of the 'final' price level to the initial price level converges to a finite value:

$$\boldsymbol{P}'\boldsymbol{Q}/\boldsymbol{P}_0\boldsymbol{Q}_0 = 1 + [\beta m \,/\, (1 - \alpha)] \tag{4}$$

where $[\beta m \,/\, (1 - \alpha)] < m$.

What should be noted here is that the impact on cumulated inflation (the total price increase) in equation (4) depends not only on the size of the increase in import prices (m) and on the weight of imports in production costs (β) but also on the term $1/(1\text{-}\alpha)$, with α representing the weight on total costs of domestically produced inputs. The propagation through the costs of domestically produced inputs thus represents a 'multiplier' of the impact on inflation of terms of trade shocks.

Demonstration: The difference between price levels at any time t after the change in the terms of trade is given by:

$$\boldsymbol{P}_t\boldsymbol{Q} - \boldsymbol{P}_{t-1}\,\boldsymbol{Q} = \alpha^{t-1}\,\beta m \tag{5}$$

Since $a < 1$ the term on the right-hand side tends to zero for t tending to infinity. The overall increase in the price level at any time t is given by:

$$\boldsymbol{P}_t\boldsymbol{Q}/\boldsymbol{P}_0\boldsymbol{Q} = 1 + \sum_t \alpha^{t-1}\,\beta m \tag{6}$$

The limit for t tending to infinity of the second term on the right-hand side is $\beta m/(1 - \alpha)$.

[6] A similar point is raised in Lavoie (2023) and Colonna et al. (2023).

What is of interest for the present analysis, among other things, is that, even under the assumption that domestic nominal distributive variables do not at all adjust to inflation and are assumed to remain constant (which of course is not quite realistic), the initial impulse coming from import costs will give rise for some time to a process of inflation involving the costs and prices of domestically produced inputs. This process will gradually subside, and the inflation rate will tend to zero until the new higher but constant price level is reached. Although this is a rather abstract picture, it sheds light on some of the processes of propagation that can be at work in feeding so-called 'core' inflation after a shock in imported energy prices.

Based on this apparatus and using results in Stirati (2001), we can consider different possible inflation scenarios depending on the behaviour of the terms of trade and nominal domestic variables:

(1) Suppose the increase in the price level of imported inputs is a lasting one. Although the increase in energy prices is now declining, it is reasonable to suppose that — due to the geopolitical situation and the shift to more expensive sources of gas, along with the costs of the green transition — there will be a persistent increase in the price level of energy inputs in Italy and other Eurozone countries, albeit significantly lower than what was witnessed in 2022. However, if the increase is *a once-and-for-all nominal level increase*, the ensuing inflationary process will gradually subside. As we have seen above, this will happen in the case in which nominal distributive variables remain constant but also (though more slowly) in the case in which both firms and workers attempt to keep real wages and real profits constant by passing through the increased costs. Inflation will subside because as the domestic price level increases, this represents a reduction in the worsening of the terms of trade, that is, in the change in relative prices between imported inputs and domestic output. As a result, the real income loss of the country due to terms of trade diminishes, and so does the degree of inconsistency between the conflicting claims on income.

(2) It is, however, reasonable to expect that the worsening of the terms of trade is a persistent one, i.e., that the relative price of imported energy inputs will be persistently higher *vis à vis* the domestic price level. This should be expected to occur to the extent that the higher price of energy inputs is caused by structurally higher costs of transportation of gas or production of energy from alternative sources. If so, then the evolution of inflation very much depends on the reaction of domestic nominal variables, since some, or all, parties will have to accept a reduction in their real incomes. In this case, on the assumption of only partial and lagged adjustment of nominal interest, business profits and wages to inflation, the latter will eventually stabilize, albeit at a rate higher than before the change in the terms of trade.

(3) Let us now consider an autonomous increase in the rate of business profits. In this case too there would be several 'rounds' of price and cost increases as the impact of increased prices affects costs of production through interindustry exchanges.[7] This, if

[7] Suppose that the addition to business profit rates or interest rates is λ, such that (i + ρ) becomes $(i + \rho + \lambda)$; in this case, the increase in the price level at any time t would be: $P_tQ - P_0Q = [1 + \sum_t (\alpha + \lambda\alpha)^{t-1} \lambda (\alpha + \beta)$ which converges to a finite total increase in the price level equal to: $\lambda(\alpha + \beta) / [1 - (\alpha + \lambda\alpha)]$.

nominal wages remain constant, would give rise to a *transitory* inflation process, until the new price level is reached. Should the increase in profit rates be confirmed by the data, this would *add* to the contribution to inflation of the changes in the terms of trade.

The above results are qualitatively similar to those presented by Lavoie (2022) in his chapter on inflation as a general case, when there is no full indexation of earnings and there are lags in the adjustment of prices and wages. In such circumstances, inflation itself establishes a 'compromise' between conflicting claims (Lavoie 2022, pp. 605–606 and 623–624). What we believe can be gained from the representation proposed here is that it provides an explicit recognition of the role of interindustry (and intrafirm) exchanges in the process of cost-push transmission and determination of the cumulative impact on the price level. One take-home message is that some time-lag between the increase in import costs and the increase in prices is inherent in the input-output characteristic of the production process. One of the factors influencing the lags in the transmission, along with the staggering of intrafirm and labour contracts, is likely to be the turn-over of circulating capital, which differs across industries, thus contributing to a staggered process.

Of course, if a certain rate of growth of productivity is introduced into the picture, these scenarios become more likely to exhibit a reduction in inflation and to exhibit it to a higher degree than would otherwise be the case. In addition, the increase in energy costs that can be expected as a structural, lasting one, is definitely of an order of magnitude much lower than the increase witnessed between 2021 and 2022.

5. Investigating Profitability Dynamics and the Drivers of Inflation in Italy

As discussed in Section Three, a growing body of literature is endorsing the idea that the increase in profits is at the root of the current inflation surge, or at least contributed significantly to it. In the light of what was discussed in the previous section, we shall now try to understand whether empirical evidence in the Italian case is supportive of the view that inflation can actually be regarded as (at least in part) profit driven.

As aptly noted in Hansen et al. (2023), it is not easy to capture the changes in profitability understood as the rate of return on capital, so it is appropriate to use a variety of measures or proxies. To deal with this, we analyze the profit share, the mark-up, the ex-post profit rate at aggregate and sectoral levels, and simple calculations based on the equations in Section Four.

One notable piece of evidence pertains to the evolution of the profit share.[8] Figure 7 illustrates that, over recent decades, the profit share has increased across all economic sectors.[9] This increase has been particularly pronounced in the energy sector, where we observe a continuous rise since 1995 with a sharp acceleration since 2021, followed by a partial, modest decline in 2023. In the construction sector, the profit share had

[8] We define profit share as 1 minus the adjusted wage share. Details on the data used in this calculation are reported in the online Appendix.

[9] While not directly related to inflation, there is evidence of a sustained increase in profitability in the Italian banking system since 2021 (Zolea, 2024). For an analysis of how monetary policy and the role of EU institutions might explain this phenomenon, see Cesaratto (2023).

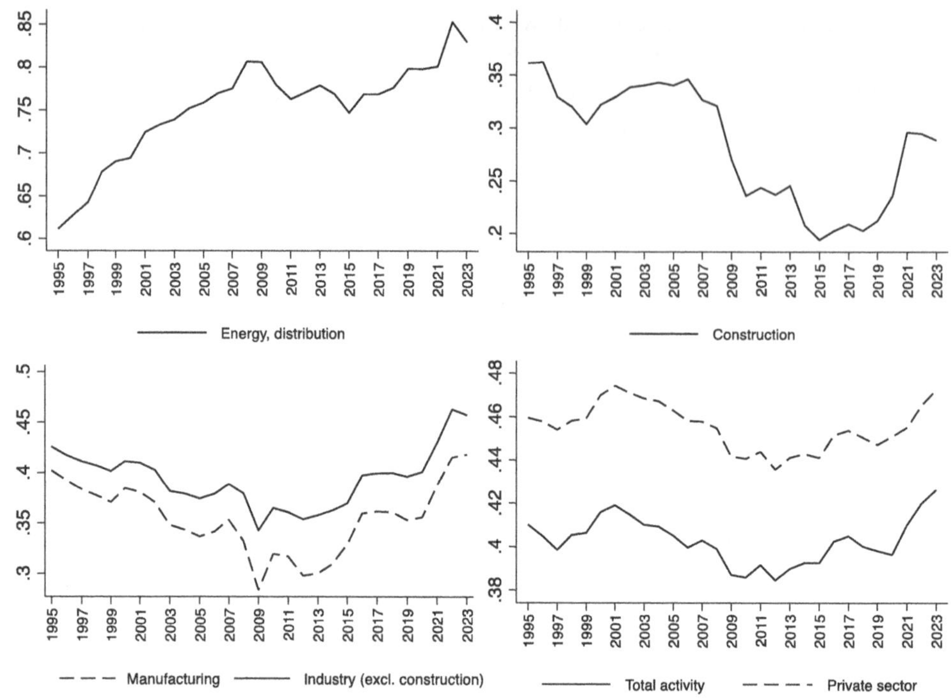

Figure 7. Profit share by sectors (NACE rev. 2). Authors' own calculation based on ISTAT data.

been decreasing after 2008 but experienced a significant recovery between 2019 and 2021, most probably driven by targeted government intervention (the so-called 'superbonus' — a strong tax credit for energy-efficient renovation of residential buildings). Furthermore, the trend of an increasing profit share after 2021 extends to all remaining sectors, including the aggregate measure of total economic activity. It is important to note, however, as discussed in the previous section, that this alone does not serve as conclusive proof that the rate of profit has increased.

Figure 8 illustrates the evolution of the mark-up, which is defined by ISTAT as the ratio of the GDP deflator to the value of unit variable costs — that is, labour costs and *all* intermediate inputs, including both domestically produced and imported inputs, per unit of output.[10] The trajectory of the mark-up in the broader macroeconomic context is intricately shaped by a multitude of trends in sector-specific mark-ups. Figure 8 shows that in *agriculture* and *construction* the increase in the mark-up with respect to the pre-pandemic years was significant, about 4 per cent. In the total economy, *industry* (excluding *construction*) and *manufacturing* mark-up increased moderately, between 0.5 and 1 per cent. In all sectors, except *construction*, the peak was reached in the first quarter of 2023, that is, after the decline in energy prices was already taking place, with a slight decline in mark-ups afterwards. Thus, it would seem that the increase in the mark-ups was caused by downward price inertia in the face of

[10]Recalling equation (2) (Section Four), the ISTAT measure would capture the $(1+m)$ term in the equation $P = (1+m)(pa + F + wl)$ where the unit costs of domestically produced inputs (pa) are included, at a price which, being an average, is likely to be an intermediate value between the historic and the replacement cost.

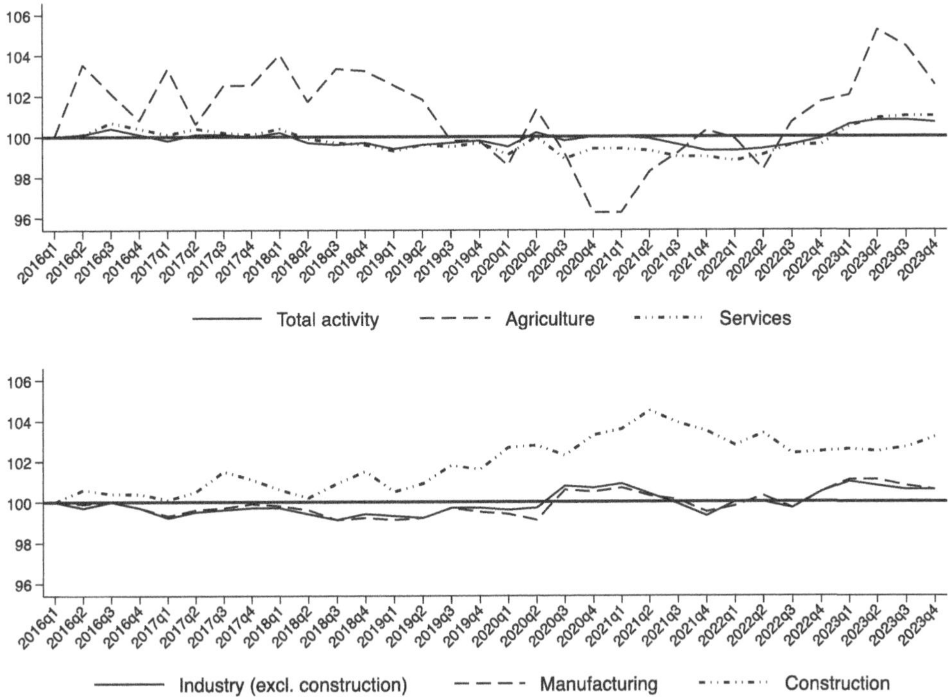

Figure 8. Firms' mark-up by sectors. (NACE rev. 2). Source: ISTAT.

the declining costs of energy, rather than being itself a driver of the inflation burst. The specific timing of the peak in *construction* is consistent with the sudden increase in demand in this sector caused by the public incentive mentioned above (i.e., the superbonus). Overall, mark-up increases and their timing are not consistent with their having a role in fuelling inflation; however, the costs of the worsening in the terms of trade have definitely been distributed to workers to a much larger extent than to firms.

To improve our understanding, we proceed with other measures of profitability. Figure 9 provides further empirical evidence, limited to 2021 for the energy sector. We have computed an ex-post actual rate of profit[11] by calculating the ratio of the gross operating surplus (GOS) (which includes gross mixed incomes exceeding average employee compensation)[12] to the value of net capital stock evaluated at the prevailing price of substitution. Across all the sectors examined, there has been a substantial stagnation in this actual rate of profit since 2009. An exception emerges in the *energy* and *construction* sectors; here, however, the increase in profitability started in 2015, well before the inflationary upsurge. The *energy distribution* sector witnessed a significant growth in the profit rate from 2018 to 2019. This growth continued in 2020, albeit at a slower pace, followed by a modest decline in 2021. By contrast, the construction industry's 2020

[11]For some considerations related to this measure, see the work of Levrero and Stirati (2005). They provide valuable insights and caveats that should be taken into account when interpreting and analyzing this particular measure of profit.

[12]We obtain a time series for the gross operating surplus by deducting the sectoral wage bill from the nominal value added. Following the methodology used to construct the adjusted wage share, the wage bill is calculated by applying the average wage of employees to the self-employed.

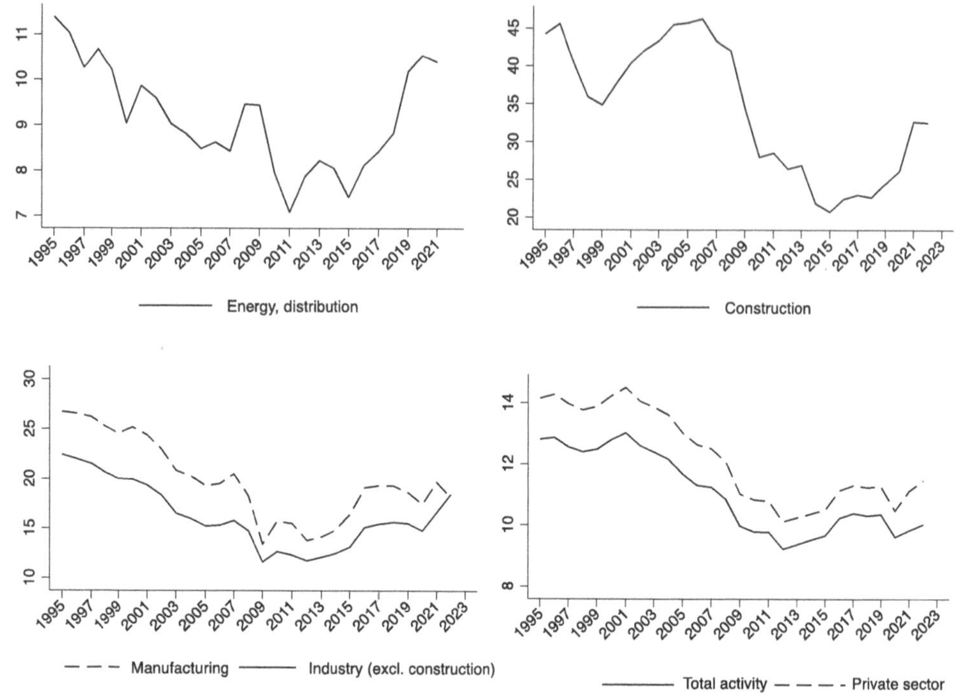

Figure 9. Ex-post rate of profits as GOS on net capital stock at current price of substitution, by sectors (NACE rev. 2). Authors' own calculation based on ISTAT data.

surge can be primarily attributed to the specific stimulus mentioned above; profitability, however, remains subpar with respect to the period preceding 2008. Regrettably, data for the *energy distribution* sector is unavailable for 2022. However, as before, we can gain insights by comparing the trend of this measure of profitability in the *industry* sector, which includes energy, with the *manufacturing* one: while the profit rate in the *manufacturing* sector (a subset representing 85 per cent of the overall *industry* category) experienced substantial stability, with minor fluctuations, the overall *industry* sector (including the energy sector with a 15 per cent weight) demonstrated continued growth. This indicates an upsurge in profitability within the energy distribution sector during this period, which is consistent with the previously discussed data.

Figure 10 shows the path of the ex-post rate of profit once circulating capital and capital depreciation are considered.[13] As it is possible to observe, there are some differences from Figure 9 in the sectoral patterns of profitability, although the overall trend remains largely unchanged. Notably, the profit rate for the entire economy exhibits an upward trajectory, increasing from 11.9 per cent in 2020 to 13.7 per cent in 2022. While data for the energy sector is unavailable after 2021, it is plausible that the rise

[13]We approximate the circulating capital by estimating it as the difference between the value of production and the value added. Following the approach outlined by Levrero and Stirati (2005), we calculate the ex-post rate of profit using the following formula: $r = (Qk - Dep/Y)/[(Kf + Kc)/Y]$, where Qk represents the profit share (which, as mentioned earlier, is 1 minus the adjusted wage share), Dep denotes capital depreciation at a current price of substitution, Kf represents the value of net capital stock at a current price of substitution, Kc is the estimated value of circulating capital, and Y represents the nominal value of production.

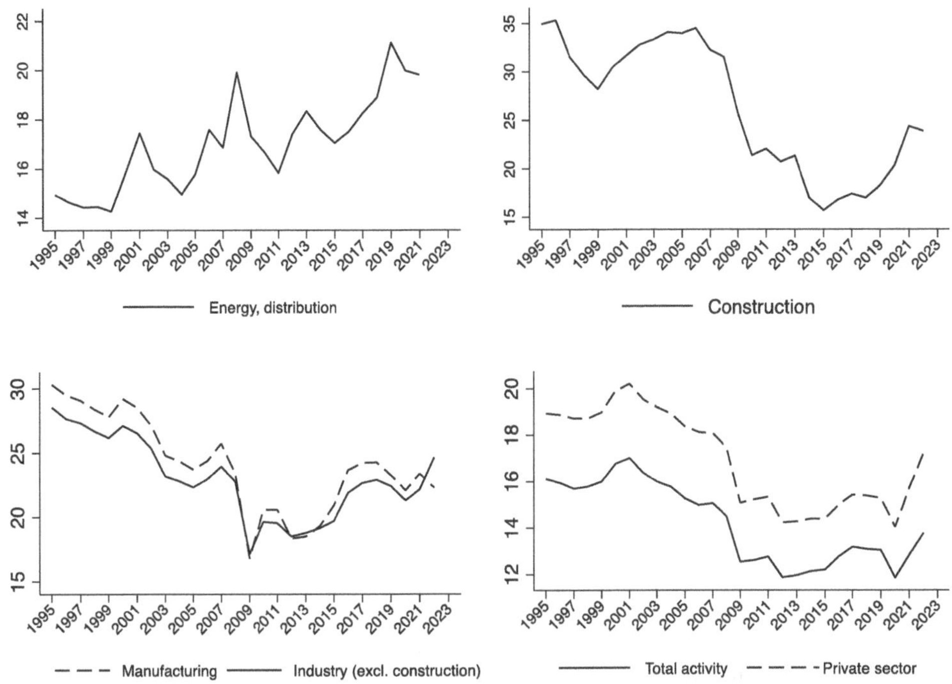

Figure 10. Ex-post rate of profits considering circulating capital and depreciation of capital, by sectors (NACE rev. 2). Authors' own calculation based on ISTAT data.

in the *total activity* profit rate is linked to economic recovery and to an increase in *energy* sector profits. This inference is drawn once again from the contrasting evidence emerging between the trend within the *industry* sector (including energy) and that within the *manufacturing* one. The latter shows substantial stability in this measure of the profit rate too, while, despite this, the broader industrial sector displays a significant upswing from 22.13 per cent to 24.63 per cent.

So far, the data suggest that while an increase in profits and margins is taking place in the *energy* sector, to a lesser extent in agriculture, and perhaps (with mixed evidence) in the construction industry, in all other sectors there are no indications of an increase in profitability, which appears to be relatively stable.[14]

5.1. Simple Calculations based on Price Equations

Back of the envelope calculations based on Italian data[15] and equations (4 and 5) in Section Four seem to fit actual trends well. Intermediate import (excluding energy)

[14]In almost all cases, profits and profit share are below the 1995 levels; however, the decline in the profit share during 2000–2008 is at least in part due to a decline in productivity that appears to be the consequence of statistical/ accounting artifacts related to the emergence of irregular employment in the early 2000s and to the growth of low-income self-employment favored by changes in legislation in those years (see Paternesi Meloni and Stirati 2023).

[15]The data source for this information is ISTAT, obtained from the national accounts and international trade and import price dataset. Moreover, data related to imported energy is derived from the input-output tables provided by ISTAT. In the exercise, we assume a 1 per cent pure remuneration of capital (the rate of return on long-term Italian bonds in 2021) and *completely abstract from profits of enterprise*. Of course, the latter are also proportional to capital and hence consideration of them would increase the weight and impact of the increases in costs that we consider in the text. All weights of labor, domestic and imported inputs and energy costs in total production refer to the year 2019.

prices peaked in the fourth quarter of 2021 with a 22 per cent increase *vis à vis* the first quarter of 2021 Then they fluctuated around that level, thus providing a contribution to inflation on impact — taking into account the weight of imported intermediate inputs relative to total production (4 per cent in 2019) — equal to 0.9 per cent, and an overall cumulated effect of 1.7 per cent. (with α equal to 0.49). During 2022, the price of gas on the Dutch market was on average 5 times higher than its price before the pandemic (Cucignatto and Garbellini 2023, p. 4), with a peak of a more than tenfold increase in the summer of that year. Since many prices, including domestic consumer prices of energy and electricity, are linked to that market, we consider a first scenario with such an increase (following Cucignatto and Garbellini 2023). Given the weight in total production of imported intermediate energy inputs (0.009 per cent), this should contribute on impact to 4.4 percentage points of inflation, while its overall effect is 8.6 per cent. If we add the nominal wage change of 2 per cent over 2022, given the weight of wage costs in total production (15 per cent), and assuming constant productivity,[16] the labour cost contribution to price increase would be 0.3 percentage points on impact and 0.6 overall. Thus, we reach a predicted 11 per cent total increase in GDP deflator after the whole impact of cost increases has been calculated.

In the alternative scenario, in which we assume a threefold increase in imported energy prices, in line with average actual imported energy costs in 2022 (see Figure 4), the predicted overall impact on inflation of all cost components would be 9 per cent. The actual GDP deflator changes from 110 to 120 between 2021-Q4 and 2023-Q1 with an increase of precisely 9 per cent. Thus, inflation, measured by the GDP deflator, is in line with what would be predicted by our equations, considering the actual increase in imported energy prices, and assuming no changes in the *nominal* remuneration of capital. The results of these simple calculations appear to be consistent with the data presented in the previous paragraph: an increase in profits in the energy sector, while in the other sectors *real* profitability — that is, taking into account the (largely transitory) increase in the replacement costs of capital — is roughly stable. Considering our simplifying assumptions, in particular the abstraction in the calculations from the profits of enterprise (see footnote 15) and from the increase in interest rates, it is likely that the propagation process from increases in costs had not yet fully developed in the first quarter of 2023. However, in light of the transitory nature of much of the shock in energy prices, it need not ever fully develop — the losses for firms would be only windfall losses, or would be compensated by downward price inertia as the input costs decline. In fact, recent ISTAT data indicate that in the remaining part of 2023 and the beginning of 2024 the GDP deflator stabilized at a value of 118, i.e., two points below its peak.

6. Econometric Analysis of the Inflation Propagation Process

6.1. Methodology

While several studies have identified rising mark-ups as a significant contribution to the inflationary surge (Section Two above), our analytical framework (described in Section Four) shows that an increase in the profit share can occur, even without a modification

[16] Productivity has actually declined somewhat, but this should be attributed to cyclical factors, which normally do not affect price formation.

of the (nominal) profit rate, in cases of rising intermediate costs, and also that such an increase would lead to a gradual propagation process acting through the consequent increase in domestically produced inputs. In addition, Section Three provides evidence of the size of the increase in the cost of imported intermediate goods and energy in Italy, while Section Four shows there is no clear evidence of an upsurge in real profitability within the Italian domestic sector, except for the *energy* sector. However, the inflationary surge has had a highly detrimental effect on real wages and the wage share. Therefore, the aim of this section is to estimate the effect of a shock to the price of intermediate imported goods on inflation and on the profit share, while controlling for changes in the mark-up.[17] Additionally, we explicitly examine the evolution of nominal wages and firms' mark-up, drawing conclusions on the distributional effects of the shock. We apply the Local Projections (LP) method (Jordà 2005) to a time series of quarterly data from Q1 2005 to Q4 2023.[18] All our variables are at log level except for the interest rate. Details on sources and definitions are reported in the online Appendix. Note that the price of imported intermediate goods refers to the inputs of the *industry* sector, excluding *construction*, while all the other variables refer to the *total activity*. This represents a conservative hypothesis in our analysis because we observe a sectoral shock's impact on *total activity*.

The LP[19] approach involves estimating individual single regressions for each horizon where the variable of interest is assessed following the occurrence of the shock. In this methodology, impulse response functions (IRFs) are generated using β coefficients obtained from regressions conducted over different time horizons (h). In practical terms, we perform regressions for the variable of interest at each period ($t + h$), taking the shocked variable at time t into account. This approach allows us to compute the average response of the dependent variable following the shock after h time periods have passed. Essentially, β coefficients indicate the impact in year $t + h$ resulting from an episode of innovation in the price of the imported intermediate goods that occurred at time t. Each coefficient is plotted through our IRFs. Thus, we estimate Equation 7:

$$y_{t+h} = \beta^h S_t + \sum_{j=1}^{p} \psi_j^h y_{t-j} + \sum_{j=1}^{p} \xi_j^h PIMP_{t-j} + \sum_{j=1}^{p} \varrho_j^h X_{t-j} + d_{2021} + \varepsilon_{t+h} \tag{7}$$

where t index represents time, h the time horizon, and j the time-lag. Δy_{t+h} is the level of the price index (HICP) or the level of profit share (PS)[20] between $t-1$ and $t+h$; S_t is the shock to the price of imported intermediate goods. We also consider the lagged value of both dependent variables (y_{t-j}) and the lagged value of the price of imported

[17]As reported in Section Five, the mark-up we use here, provided by ISTAT, is defined as the ratio of the GDP deflator to the value of labor costs and *all* intermediate inputs, including both domestically produced and imported inputs, per unit of output.

[18]According to Auerbach and Gorodnichenko (2017) and Plagborg-Møller and Wolf (2021), the LP approach represents an alternative to VAR models for obtaining the impulse response functions (IRFs). Furthermore, Jordà (2005) highlights the fact that LPs have various advantages because they are robust to different sources of misspecifications.

[19]LPs have recently found utility in evaluating medium-term effects of macroeconomic shocks, as evident in the works of Auerbach and Gorodnichenko 2012; Deleidi et al. 2023; Girardi et al. 2020; Paternesi Meloni et al. 2022.

[20]In contrast to the previous section, the profit share data used in this analysis is based on quarterly intervals rather than yearly ones. To derive this quarterly data, we had to rely on value added at market prices since factor price information is not accessible at the quarterly level.

intermediate goods ($PIMP_{t-j}$). In addition, the vector X_{t-j} refers to the lagged value of hourly nominal wage, short-run interest rate, and the mark-up of total industry (excluding construction). We add these three control variables to consider them only before the shock happened. d_{2021} is a dummy variable assuming a value equal to 1 in the first quarter of 2021, when the inflation upsurge started, and 0 otherwise.

However, the initial step involves identifying an exogenous shock to the price of the imported intermediate goods (S_t). To achieve this, we employ a recursive identification strategy within a VAR model. Following this approach, we have imposed restrictions on the matrix of contemporaneous relationships among variables, applying a standard Cholesky decomposition. This allows us to establish an ordering of variables from the most exogenous to the least, considering both theoretical relevance and data quality (Kilian and Lütkepohl 2017). Therefore, in this VAR model, the level of price of imported intermediate goods (*PIMP*) is ordered first as it is considered the most exogenous variable, while the second variable ordered is the level of the internal price (*HICP*). The final ordered variable is the profit share (*PS*). Additionally, we introduce an extension of our baseline model by modifying the identification strategy. Specifically, we incorporate the variables used as controls, such as the firms' mark-up, into the identification strategy. This extension aims to create a comprehensive model able to capture explicitly the role of mark-up in influencing the evolution of price level and distribution.

While *PIMP* and *HICP* remain as the first-ordered variables, we have designated the short-run interest rate (i) as the third variable, reflecting the typical response of the central bank to an inflationary surge. The nominal wage (w) is the fourth-ordered variable in our sequence — a choice based on empirical observations indicating that negotiated nominal wages respond to changes in consumer prices with a certain delay due to the wage formation mechanism and its evolution in the last decades in Italy (Gaddi 2023a, 2023b). The firms' mark-up is our fifth variable in the order as it is inherently influenced by both output prices and input costs. Finally, *PS* is the last variable in our sequence. Detailed equations for the estimation strategy (Equations 5.2 and 5.3) are reported in online Appendix 1.

6.2. Impulse Response Functions

In this section, we present our findings through impulse response functions (IRFs) for both the baseline model and the comprehensive one.

Figure 11 depicts the IRFs of our baseline model, illustrating the effect of a shock to *PIMP* on the evolution of internal price (*HICP*) and profit share (*PS*) over a time span of 16 quarters (equivalent to 4 years). These graphs reveal that, upon impact, the price of imported intermediate goods undergoes a 1 per cent increase. However, its trajectory evolves over time, gradually dissipating after 6 quarters. By contrast, the impact on the overall price level is less pronounced (by about 0.5 per cent at its peak) but highly persistent, remaining significant for up to 10 quarters, which is one year longer than the initial shock.[21] Additionally, the profit share displays a positive trend starting from the

[21] It is important to bear in mind that the present model is linear. Therefore, the return to the initial price level results from the dissipation of the shock. In other words, we have observed that when import prices increase, internal prices also rise. However, in this model, the reverse holds true as well. It is important to emphasize that we have noticed a

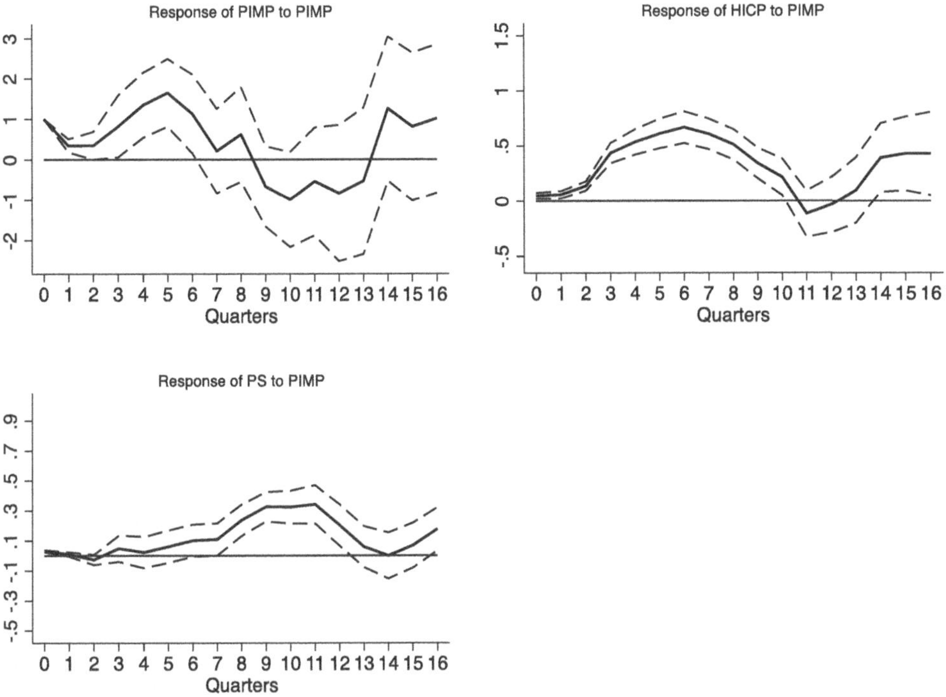

Figure 11. Impulse response function, Equation 7. 2005Q1–2023Q4. Dotted lines denote 68 per cent confidence bands.

5th quarter and tends to persist at a higher level until the end of the period. Furthermore, it indicates that, in the absence of changes in nominal wages, a shift in functional income distribution that increases the profit share can occur without changes in the mark-up, which we treat as a control variable.

Figure 12 displays the IRFs of the comprehensive model that explicitly deals with mark-up innovation. As it is possible to note, the results are consistent with our baseline model. An innovation in the price of imported intermediate goods produces a significant and relatively more persistent increase in the overall internal price index. The impact on profit share, and consequently on the functional income distribution, exhibits a delayed onset, similar to that in our baseline model, and becomes significant at the 7th quarter and persists through all the subsequent periods. This occurs without any significant innovation in the mark-up. Real wages fall, since we observe a relatively higher increase in HICP compared to the nominal wage, which displays a lower and relatively stagnant trajectory.

6.3. Robustness Check

At this stage, we enhance the robustness of our results through a two-step process. Firstly, we assess the impact of our shock on the HICP index excluding energy, food, alcohol, and

significant degree of persistence both in the shock and in the internal price response. The fact that the latter displays a more protracted persistence is the finding that we want to underline.

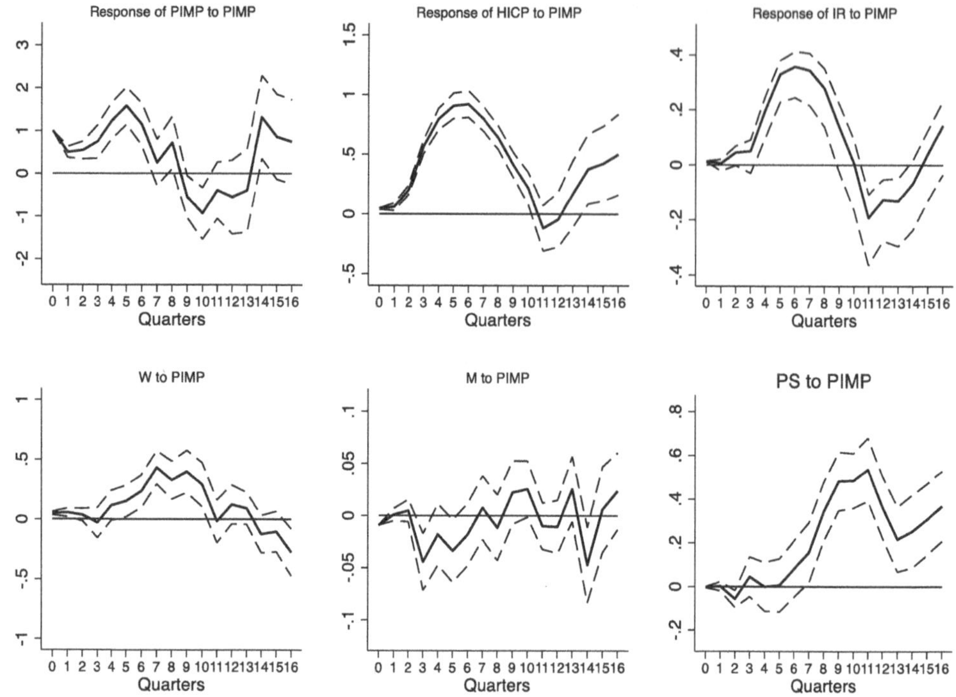

Figure 12. Comprehensive model. Equation 5.3. 2005Q1–2023Q4. Dotted lines denote 68 per cent confidence bands.

tobacco prices (hereafter HICP core), which is used to calculate core inflation. Then, we investigate the effects of shocks to alternative variables related to imported prices, specifically energy prices and the overall price of imported goods. Finally, we propose a comprehensive structural model that takes into account both past and contemporaneous relationships for all the variables in our model, including the control variables. The figures representing the impulse response functions are reported in the online Appendix.

6.4.1. The Effect of an Innovation in the Price of Imported Intermediate Goods on Core Inflation

To corroborate our findings, we conducted tests by analyzing the impact of the shock to PIMP on the core HICP, instead of on the general HICP. For this purpose, equation 7 and equation 5.2 (see online Appendix for 5.2) were modified, replacing the new price index (HICP core) to the old one (HICP). The baseline results — reported in Figure A1 — are reaffirmed as we observe a positive and enduring effect of the shock. Interestingly, while the elasticity is lower compared to HICP (here we find an elasticity of about 0.2 at 6 quarters compared to 0.6 in the previous model), the behaviour of core inflation is noteworthy: the shock appears to propagate to this variable with a slight delay of approximately 2 quarters, and it persists for up to 10 quarters.

6.4.2. Shock to the Imported Energy Price

At this point, we assess the impact of a shock to the price of imported energy (PIE), which is not included in the basket of goods used to calculate the index of imported intermediate goods, on HICP and PS (Figure A2). To do this, we replace PIMP with PIE in equation 7 and equation 5.2 (see online Appendix for 5.2). Our baseline findings are validated. The shock to PIE exhibits less persistence compared to the effect on HICP, lagging by about 6 quarters. This indicates that an increase in imported energy prices has a more extended impact on the overall internal price level. Similar to the previous results, the effect on functional income distribution is significant, with some delays, from quarter 8 until the end of the period, also controlling for mark-up in the period before the shock.

6.4.3. Shock to the Price of Total Imported Goods

Next, we examine the impact of a shock to the price of total imported goods (PITOT), which encompasses both intermediate and consumer imported goods, on HICP and PS (Figure A3). To do this, we replace PIMP with PITOT in equations 7 and equation 5.2 (see online Appendix for 5.2). Once again, our baseline findings are affirmed. The shock to PITOT demonstrates less persistence compared to the effect on HICP, lagging by approximately 3 quarters. This indicates that an upsurge in imported goods prices has a prolonged impact on the overall internal price level, which tends to remain significant even after the initial shock has dissipated. Similar to the previous results, the effect on profit share is significant with some delays, commencing at quarter 3 and remaining highly persistent, and significant until the end of the period, even when controlling for mark-up in the period preceding the shock.

7. Conclusions and Policy Implications

We have described different views concerning cost-push and conflict inflation and the interpretation of current inflation. Many studies dismiss the role of excess demand or excess liquidity at the origin of current inflation in the US. Such a role is most unlikely in the Eurozone, where fiscal stimulus has been less important and nominal wage dynamics have been very moderate on average. Several scholars have instead argued for, and empirically supported, a profit-driven inflation made possible by an initial push deriving from imported inputs, mostly energy inputs, and some supply disruptions, which provided an opportunity for price increases that went far beyond the increases in costs. According to this interpretation we would witness a peculiar, one-sided form of conflicting-claims inflation, in which firms are able to reap higher profits owing to the difficulty of keeping nominal wages up with inflation. In a way, it is ironic that the theory of conflict inflation is gaining increasing consensus on an analytical level (e.g., Lorenzoni and Werning 2023; Ratner and Sim 2022) at a time when conflicting claims seem to play very little role in driving actual inflation, at least as far as wage claims are concerned.

We have looked at Italian data as a case study for current inflation. The evidence we have analyzed suggests that there has not been, for the moment, a generalized increase in profitability and mark-ups on variable costs, with the notable exception of the sector of energy distribution (distribution of gas, and electricity). In the latter case, it is likely that a major role was played by the way in which prices are regulated, particularly their link to the gas prices established in the Dutch gas market. In fact, the price of gas for domestic customers (both firms and households) has been perfectly aligned with the the Dutch Title Transfer Facility (TTF) (Confindustria 2023), where futures contracts on gas are predominantly traded. This exposes the market to speculation, as the price is influenced not solely by the actual demand and supply of gas, but also by expectations on future price trends. Since, in addition, purely financial actors are allowed to operate in that market, such expectations are likely to cause 'overshooting' in price changes, with large and short-lived speculative bubbles. In other words, price volatility is likely to be higher than is justified by actual market conditions. Furthermore, the price of energy on the wholesale European market is determined based on the system marginal price (SMT). When setting the price of energy, the source from which it is produced (whether renewable, gas, coal, or nuclear) is not taken into account. Instead, at the end of the auction, all intermediaries pay the marginal price, which is the last price accepted, typically the highest among the offered prices.

The evidence we discussed suggests that the increase in 'core' inflation reflects propagation mechanisms of inflation that depend on intrafirm exchanges and the price increases of domestically produced intermediate goods. Nominal wage growth up to now has been far below inflation and, on average, almost in line with the ECB target inflation rate of 2 per cent, thus causing a very large decline in real wages.

As noted in Hansen et al. (2023), it is very difficult to have fully appropriate measures of profitability. We use several indicators, including ex-post profit rates. Evidence indicates that in domestic industries, excluding energy, profitability has on average remained roughly unchanged, while the losses from the terms of trade worsening have clearly impacted real wages to a large extent.

Our econometric findings align closely with this body of evidence. We find that the consumer price index exhibits a relatively persistent response to shocks in the prices of imported intermediate goods and energy. This is also consistent with the findings of Bijnens et al. (2023), who highlight the crucial role of imported intermediate goods in price inflation in Belgium. Furthermore, this persistence leads to a deterioration in income distribution due to the limited or absent reaction in nominal wages, with no evidence of increases in the mark-up.

In the near future, this situation may give rise to further propagation mechanisms deriving from the attempt of wage earners to adjust their real incomes. It is, however, unlikely that the adjustment will be complete: the average wage pass-through of inflation has generally been less than 1, historically, and about one-third in the 1985–2018 period (Paternesi Meloni and Stirati 2018; Romaniello 2023). In the case of Italy, however, substantial wage recovery is to be *hoped for* since real wages are already extremely low. Even in a scenario in which all parties are attempting to recover previous real incomes, the decreasing cost-push pressure from imported inputs, along with some increases in productivity, should bring about a decline in the inflation rate and its stabilization at a low rate. This aligns with the actual situation in 2024, when inflation in Italy fell below the European Central Bank's (ECB) target of 2 per cent (it was 0.9 per cent in February and 1.2 per cent in March 2024). Furthermore, according to the latest ISTAT data on contractual hourly nominal wages, March 2024 saw a year-over-year increase of 3 per cent. Despite the current deceleration in inflation, however, the cumulative increase both in contractual and actual hourly nominal wages since January 2021 still lags behind. In such circumstances, monetary and fiscal tightening aimed at creating unemployment and thus keeping nominal wages in check is likely to be extremely disruptive for Italy and most Eurozone countries. Some price controls and compensations for low-income households aimed at avoiding price-price and price-wage spiraling as a consequence of a largely *transitory* cost push seem to represent a better policy to counter inflation and prevent social and economic damage. Restrictive monetary policy may not only have a negative impact on aggregate demand and financial stability — for example, owing to increases in households' payments for interest on mortgages, or to the impact on the market value of bonds held by banks (as already happened in the US in the case of the Silicon Valley Bank) — but can also make inflation worse by raising the benchmark return on capital, the so-called cost-channel of monetary policy (see Cucciniello et al. 2022 for a discussion and empirical evidence; and Ginzburg and Simonazzi 1999, who also discuss the impact of interest rates on commodity markets). Accordingly, it is extremely important to look for alternative tools to contain inflation when triggered largely by the volatility of energy (and food) prices. The current surge in inflation should also lead to a general reconsideration of the rules concerning domestic energy price-fixing in Italy, as well as the regulation of the Dutch gas market in Europe. Concerning the latter, should access to it be reserved to actors that physically trade gas, with the exclusion, that is, of merely financial operators, the volatility of prices might be contained. Concerning the domestic price of energy, the large increases in the profit share and the increases in the mark-up and ex-post profit rates in the domestic energy distribution industry, suggest that there was, and probably still is, scope for a carefully designed policy of capping domestic energy prices, a policy that has proven successful in Spain. The ability to keep energy (and food) prices under control during a period of high volatility, thus avoiding cumulative price rises, would be extremely important for the Italian economy since, on the one hand, it is structurally very exposed to the impact of energy prices and, on the other hand, a higher inflation than trade partners would exacerbate a pre-existing problem of real exchange rate overvaluation for manufacturing products, with its negative impact on net exports. This is a particularly serious problem since exports are the only autonomous component of aggregate demand that could possibly drive GDP growth, given the constraints on public spending and the impact of inflation and interest rates on consumption. At the same time, the increase in the level of consumer prices significantly aggravates an already existing problem of low wages and in-work poverty, with consequences not only for domestic demand but also for social stability.

Acknowledgements

We would like to use this opportunity to acknowledge and thank the reviewers who reviewed this article and aided in its publication. Preliminary versions of this research have been presented at the following academic events: 20th STOREP Conference (June 2023); 27th FMM Annual Conference (October 2023); 7th International ASTRIL Conference (January 2024). We thank all the participants for fruitful discussion. The research benefited also from discussion with Gabriel Brondino, Giovanna Ciaffi, Giacomo Cucignatto, Matteo Deleidi, Antonino Lofaro. The usual disclaimer applies.

Disclosure Statement

No potential conflict of interest was reported by the author(s).

ORCID

Davide Romaniello http://orcid.org/0000-0001-9960-3036
Antonella Stirati http://orcid.org/0000-0002-4195-9416

References

Alvarez, J., J. Bluedorn, M. J. C. Bluedorn, M. N. J. H. Hansen, N. J. Hansen, Y. Huang, and A. Sollaci. 2022. 'Wage-Price Spirals: What is the Historical Evidence?' International Monetary Fund Working Paper 2022/221. https://www.imf.org/en/Publications/WP/Issues/2022/11/11/Wage-Price-Spirals-What-is-the-Historical-Evidence-525073.

Arce, Ó, M. Ciccarelli, A. Kornprobst, and C. Montes-Galdón. 2024. 'What Caused the Euro Area Post-Pandemic Inflation?' European Central Bank Occasional Paper 2024/343. https://www.ecb.europa.eu/pub/pdf/scpops/ecb.op343~ab3e870d21.fr.pdf.

Arce, Ó, E. Hahn, and G. Koester. 2023. 'How Tit-for-Tat Inflation Can Make Everyone Poorer.' *The ECB Blog*, March 30. https://www.ecb.europa.eu/press/blog/date/2023/html/ecb.blog.230330~00e522ecb5.en.html.

Auerbach, A. J., and Y. Gorodnichenko. 2012. 'Measuring the Output Responses to Fiscal Policy.' *American Economic Journal: Economic Policy* 4 (2): 1–27.

Auerbach, A. J., and Y. Gorodnichenko. 2017. 'Fiscal Stimulus and Fiscal Sustainability.' NBER Working Paper 23789. https://www.nber.org/system/files/working_papers/w23789/w23789.pdf.

Bijnens, G., C. Duprez, and J. Jonckheere. 2023. 'Have Greed and Rapidly Rising Wages Triggered a Profit-Wage-Price Spiral? Firm-Level Evidence for Belgium.' *Economics Letters* 232 (November): 111342.

Bivens, J. 2022. 'Corporate Profits Have Contributed Disproportionately to Inflation. How Should Policymakers Respond?' *Economic Policy Institute. Working Economics Blog*, April 21. https://www.epi.org/blog/corporate-profits-have-contributed-disproportionately-to-inflation-how-should-policymakers-respond/.

Blanchard, O. J. 1986. 'The Wage Price Spiral.' *The Quarterly Journal of Economics* 101 (3): 543–566.

Blanchard, O. J. 2021. 'In Defense of Concerns over the $1.9 Trillion Relief Plan.' *Peterson Institute for International Economics. Realtime Economics Blog*, February 18. https://www.piie.com/blogs/realtime-economics/defense-concerns-over-19-trillion-relief-plan.

Blanchard, O. J. 2022. *Twitter*, December 30. https://twitter.com/ojblanchard1/status/1608967176232525824?s=20&t=iBULYrau3zfh.

Blanchard, O. J., and B. S. Bernanke. 2023. 'What Caused the US Pandemic-Era Inflation?' NBER Working Paper 31417. https://www.nber.org/system/files/working_papers/w31417/w31417.pdf.

Braga, J., and F. Serrano. 2023. 'Post-Keynesian Economics: New Foundations by Marc Lavoie. Chapter 8: Inflation Theory.' *Review of Political Economy* 35 (4): 1096–1108.

Breman, C., and S. Storm. 2023. 'Betting on Black Gold: Oil Speculation and US Inflation (2020–2022).' *International Journal of Political Economy* 52 (2): 153–180.

Cesaratto, S. 2023. 'Annotazioni sull'implementazione della politica monetaria: ieri, oggi, domani.' (No. 904). University of Siena. Department of Political Economy and Statistics Working Paper 904. https://www.deps.unisi.it/sites/st02/files/allegatiparagrafo/16-01-2024/904.pdf.

Colonna, F., R. Torrini R, and E. Viviano. 2023. 'La quota dei profitti e il mark up: come interpretarli?' Banca d'Italia. Questioni di Economia e Finanza (Occasional Papers) N. 770. https://www.bancaditalia.it/pubblicazioni/qef/2023-0770/.

Confindustria. 2023. *Focus Energia e Sostenibilità*, n. 26, maggio. https://www.un-industria.it/DwnVer/117430/64746/focus-energia-e-sostenibilita-di-maggio-2023.

Cucciniello, M. C., M. Deleidi, and E. S. Levrero. 2022. 'The Cost Channel of Monetary Policy: The Case of the United States in the Period 1959–2018.' *Structural Change and Economic Dynamics* 61: 409–433.

Cucignatto, G., and N. Garbellini. 2023. 'Inflazione da costi o da profitti?' In *L'inflazione. Falsi miti e conflitto distributivo*. Milan: Punto Rosso.

Deleidi, M., F. Iafrate, and E. S. Levrero. 2023. 'Government Investment Fiscal Multipliers: Evidence from Euro-Area Countries.' *Macroeconomic Dynamics* 27 (2): 331–349.

European Central Bank. 2023. *ECB Economic Bulletin*. Issue 8/2023.

European Commission. 2023. *Labour Market and Wage Developments in Europe: Annual Review 2023*. Luxembourg: Publications Office of the European Union. https://data.europa.eu/doi/10.27671277.

Ferguson, T., and S. Storm. 2023. 'Myth and Reality in the Great Inflation Debate: Supply Shocks and Wealth Effects in a Multipolar World Economy.' *International Journal of Political Economy* 52 (1): 1–44.

Gaddi, M. 2023a. 'I meccanismi di indicizzazione dei salari.' In *L'inflazione. Falsi miti e conflitto distributivo*. Milan: Punto Rosso.

Gaddi, M. 2023b. 'Dall'inflazione programmata all'IPCA depurato.' In *L'inflazione. Falsi miti e conflitto distributivo*. Milan: Punto Rosso.

Ginzburg, A., and A. Simonazzi. 1999. *Foreign Debt Cycles and the 'Gibson Paradox': An Interpretative Hypothesis*. Materiali di discussione, Università degli studi di Modena- Dipartimento di economia politica (259).

Girardi, D., W. Paternesi Meloni, and A. Stirati. 2020. 'Reverse Hysteresis? Persistent Effects of Autonomous Demand Expansions.' *Cambridge Journal of Economics* 44 (4): 835–869.

Hansen, N. J., F. Toscani, and J. Zhou. 2023. 'Euro Area Inflation after the Pandemic and Energy Shock: Import Prices, Profits and Wages.' International Monetary Fund Working Paper 2023/131. https://www.imf.org/en/Publications/WP/Issues/2023/06/23/Euro-Area-Inflation-after-the-Pandemic-and-Energy-Shock-Import-Prices-Profits-and-Wages-534837.

Hein, E. 2023. 'Inflation is Always and Everywhere … a Conflict Phenomenon: Post-Keynesian Inflation Theory and Energy Price Driven Conflict Inflation, Distribution, Demand and Employment.' IPE Working Paper 224/2023. https://www.ipe-berlin.org/fileadmin/institut-ipe/Dokumente/Working_Papers/ipe_working_paper_224.pdf.

ISTAT. 2022. *Rapporto Annuale 2022. La situazione del paese*. Roma: Istituto Nazionale di Statistica.

Jordà, O. 2005. 'Estimation and Inference of Impulse Responses by Local Projections.' *American Economic Review* 95 (1): 161–182.

Kilian, L., and H. Lütkepohl. 2017. *Structural Vector Autoregressive Analysis*. Cambridge, UK: Cambridge University Press.

Klein, E. 2022. 'Transcript: Ezra Klein Interviews Larry Summers.' *New York Times*, March 29. https://www.nytimes.com/2022/03/29/podcasts/transcript-ezra-klein-interviews-larry-summers.html.

Lavoie, M. 2022. *Post-Keynesian Economics: New Foundations*. Cheltenham: Edward Elgar Publishing.

Lavoie, M. 2023. 'Some Controversies in the Causes of the Post-Pandemic Inflation.' *Monetary Policy Institute Blog*, May 15. https://medium.com/@monetarypolicyinstitute/some-controversies-in-the-causes-of-the-post-pandemic-inflation-1480a7a08eb7.

Lavoie, M. 2024. 'Conflictual Inflation and the Phillips Curve.' *Review of Political Economy*, 1–23.

Lavoie, M., and L. P. Rochon. 2023. 'Olivier Blanchard and Inflation.' *Monetary Policy Institute Blog*, January 3. https://medium.com/@monetarypolicyinstitute/olivier-blanchard-and-inflation-219f195125fe.

Levrero, E. S., and A. Stirati. 2005. 'Distribuzione del reddito e prezzi relativi in Italia 1970–2002.' *Politica economica* 21 (3): 401–434.

Lorenzoni, G., and I. Werning. 2023. 'Inflation is Conflict.' NBER Working Paper 31099.

OECD. 2024. 'Real Wages Regaining Some of the Lost Ground.' OECD Policy brief, March. https://www.oecd.org/employment/Policy-Brief-Real-wages-regaining-some-of-the-lost-ground.pdf.

Panetta, F. 2023. '*'Everything Everywhere All at Once: Responding to Multiple Global Shocks.' Speech at a Panel on 'Global Shocks.'* Policy spillovers and geo-strategic risks: how to coordinate policies' at The ECB and its Watchers XXIII Conference, Frankfurt am Main, March 22. https://www.ecb.europa.eu/press/key/date/2023/html/ecb.sp230322_2~af38beedf3.en.html.

Paternesi Meloni, W., and A. Stirati. 2018. 'A Short Story of the Phillips Curve: From Phillips to Friedman … and Back?' *Review of Keynesian Economics* 6 (4): 493–516.

Paternesi Meloni, W., and A. Stirati. 2023. 'Wages, Productivity, and the Evolution of the Labour Share in Italy: A Sectoral Analysis Through National Accounts.' *Economia & Lavoro* 10 (2): 9–42.

Paternesi Meloni, W., D. Romaniello, and A. Stirati. 2022. 'Inflation and the NAIRU: Assessing the Role of Long-Term Unemployment as a Cause of Hysteresis.' *Economic Modelling* 113: 105900.

Plagborg-Møller, M., and C. K. Wolf. 2021. 'Local Projections and VARs Estimate the Same Impulse Responses.' *Econometrica* 89 (2): 955–980.

Ratner, D., and J. Sim. 2022. 'Who Killed the Phillips Curve? A Murder Mystery.' Finance and Economics Discussion Series 2022-028. Washington: Board of Governors of the Federal Reserve System.

Romaniello, D. 2023. 'The Longer, the Weaker? Considering the Role of Long-Term Unemployment in an "Original" Phillips Curve.' *Review of Political Economy*, 1–34. https://doi.org/10.1080/09538259.2023.2286460

Schnabel, I. 2023. 'The Risks of Stubborn Inflation.' Speech at the Euro50 Group conference on 'New challenges for the Economic and Monetary Union in the post-crisis environment,' Luxembourg, June 19. https://www.bis.org/review/r230619e.pdf.

Serrano, F., R. Summa, and G. S. Morlin. 2024. 'Conflict, Inertia, and Phillips Curve from a Sraffian Standpoint.' *Review of Political Economy*, 1–26. https://doi.org/10.1080/09538259.2024.2336510

Stirati, A. 2001. 'Inflation, Unemployment and Hysteresis: An Alternative View.' *Review of Political Economy* 13 (4): 427–451.

Stockhammer, E. 2008. 'Is the NAIRU Theory a Monetarist, New Keynesian, Post Keynesian or a Marxist Theory?' *Metroeconomica* 59 (3): 479–510.

Storm, S. 2023. 'Profit Inflation is Real.' *PSL Quarterly Review* 76 (306): 243–259.

Summa, R., and J. Braga. 2020. 'Two Routes Back to the Old Phillips Curve: The Amended Mainstream Model and the Conflict-Augmented Alternative.' *Bulletin of Political Economy* 14: 81–115.

Summers, L. 2021. 'The Biden Stimulus is Admirably Ambitious. But It Brings Some Big Risks, Too.' *Washington Post*, February 4. https://www.washingtonpost.com/opinions/2021/02/04/larry-summers-biden-covidstimulus/.

Vernengo, M., and E. P. Caldentey. 2023. 'Price and Prejudice: Reflections on the Return of Inflation and Ideology.' *Review of Keynesian Economics* 11 (2): 129–146.

Visco, I. 2023. *Relazione annuale Anno 2022. Considerazioni finali del Governatore*. Roma: Banca d'Italia. https://www.bancaditalia.it/pubblicazioni/interventi-governatore/integov2023/cf_2022.pdf.

Weber, I. M., and E. Wasner. 2023. "Sellers' Inflation, Profits and Conflict: Why Can Large Firms Hike Prices in an Emergency?' *Review of Keynesian Economics* 11 (2): 183–213.

Zolea, R. 2024. 'An Estimation of the Italian Banking Sector Profit Rate in a Crisis Period.' *Journal of Post Keynesian Economics*, 1–21. https://doi.org/10.1080/01603477.2024.2309373

OPEN ACCESS

Inflation, Unemployment, and Inequality: Beyond the Traditional Phillips Curve

Lilian Rolim

ABSTRACT

This article undertakes a theoretical post-Keynesian analysis to explore the relationship between inflation, unemployment, and inequality. Firstly, we show the compatibility of the inequality-augmented Phillips curve, which first appeared in Rolim, Carvalho, and Lang (2023), with the post-Keynesian macroeconomic theory. The curve combines the Phillips curve, which relates unemployment and inflation and can be derived from the conflicting-claims inflation model, with the positive relation between unemployment and inequality due to the heterogeneous impact of unemployment on workers. The unemployment rate thus connects the inflation rate to income inequality in a three-dimensional relationship described by the inequality-augmented Phillips curve, which indicates a possible trade-off between low inflation and low inequality. Secondly, we consider the profits inflation case: when inflation is simultaneous with markup increases. Increases in the *ex-ante* markup rate shift the curve upwards, thus increasing the inflation rate and inequality. In this context, if monetary policy aims to control inflation by increasing unemployment, it will operate along the inequality-augmented Phillips curve and will further increase inequality.

1. Introduction

The Phillips curve is a guiding concept for monetary policy in many countries. The 'old' version of the curve, for which there is more empirical support in recent years, establishes a negative relationship between the level of the inflation rate and the level of the unemployment rate.[1] The theoretical explanation provided by mainstream authors to such a relationship is based on the idea that higher demand creates a tight labor market and, consequently, this results in wage inflation. Thus, in this view, inflation rates are a

[1]Conversely, the 'accelerationist' Phillips curve assumes a relationship between the level of unemployment (relative to its natural rate) and the rate of change of the inflation rate. Recent data does not support the 'accelerationist' Phillips curve (Blanchard 2016; Blanchard, Cerutti, and Summers 2015; Summa and Braga 2020). For more details for the United States and a discussion about the changing format of its Phillips curve, see Setterfield and Blecker (2022). In this article, 'Phillips curve' always refers to the 'old' Phillips curve.

demand-pull phenomenon and are explained by scarcity in the labor market (Summa and Braga 2020).

Conversely, in the post-Keynesian approach, inflation is predominantly a cost-push phenomenon. More precisely, inflation results from a disagreement between firms and workers concerning the distribution of income (Dutt 1987; Lavoie 2022; Rowthorn 1977). These conflicting-claims are made consistent through changes in nominal wages and prices - and workers and firms may be only partially successful in obtaining their desired real incomes. In this approach, the negative relationship between unemployment and inflation, which is captured by the Phillips curve, can only be explained through the dynamics of the class struggle and the evolution in the bargaining power of firms and workers. Accordingly, one should interpret nominal wage increases associated with lower unemployment rates not as a result of scarcity in the labor market, but rather as a result of higher bargaining power of workers (Serrano 2019; Summa and Braga 2020).

Regardless of the explanation for the Phillips curve, it is clear that a monetary policy tightening aiming to control the inflation rate may be associated with higher unemployment rates. This poses a trade-off to monetary policy authorities in terms of prioritizing low inflation rates or low unemployment rates. In the absence of strong inflationary pressures, there is some policy space for stimulating economic activity and reducing unemployment. However, when inflation rates accelerate, the debate over this trade-off intensifies, since strong recessions and substantial increases in unemployment may be required to reduce inflation. In such contexts, many authors raise concerns over the possible impacts of restrictive monetary policies on other economic dimensions and the adequacy of fighting inflation by increasing unemployment when inflation is generated by other factors.

This article aims to contribute to this debate in theoretical terms by considering two aspects that are relevant for a broad understanding of the relationship between inflation rates and other macroeconomic variables. Firstly, we explore the distributive dimension of the Phillips curve in order to expand the understanding of the trade-offs faced by policymakers. More precisely, we derive a macroeconomic version of the inequality-augmented Phillips curve (hereafter IAPC), which was first presented by Rolim, Carvalho, and Lang (2023) and indicate the possibility of a trade-off between low inflation and low inequality, in addition to the widely-discussed trade-off between low inflation and low unemployment. Our aim is to demonstrate that the curve is compatible with the post-Keynesian approach, in particular with the conflicting-claims inflation theory. In order to do so, we expand the conflict-augmented Phillips curve (Serrano 2019; Summa and Braga 2020) to a three-dimensional relationship by incorporating the positive relationship between unemployment rates and inequality (da Silva et al. 2022; Hoover, Giedeman, and Dibooglu 2009; Maestri and Roventini 2012; Mocan 1999).

Secondly, we analyze the dynamics of unemployment, inflation, and inequality when inflation is not explained by labor market conditions. This is important because inflation in emergent market economies in general (Rolim and Marins 2022, 2024) and in the current inflationary context in the center of the capitalist world (Glover, Mustre-del-Río, and Von Ende-Becker 2023; Konczal and Lusiani 2022; Lavoie 2023; Storm 2023; Weber and Wasner 2023) may occur simultaneously to increases in the profit share. Such inflationary process cannot be explained by movements along the IAPC. Yet, by investigating the case of profits inflation, we contend that the IAPC is still a useful framework for understanding the dynamics of unemployment, inflation, and inequality and the implications of monetary policy.

The remaining of this article is organized as follows. In Section Two, we formalize the macroeconomic version of the IAPC. In Section Three, we make use of the IAPC to analyze the case of profits inflation and the implications for monetary policy. Finally, Section Four presents the concluding remarks.

2. The Inequality-Augmented Phillips Curve

The IAPC was first presented by Rolim, Carvalho, and Lang (2023) as an emergent property obtained in an agent-based macroeconomic model. It is based on two empirical regularities that are reproduced by the model through a decentralized labor market and heterogeneous firms and workers. In this section, we explore the emergence of this curve in a closed economy macroeconomic (aggregate) framework based on those two empirical regularities: the Phillips curve and the unemployment-inequality curve. Our aim is to show that the IAPC is compatible with the post-Keynesian approach and its view of cost-push inflation arising from the class conflict over the income distribution. Given this compatibility, the curve can be a useful tool for analyzing the relationship between inflation and inequality in different contexts following a post-Keynesian approach - an analysis that we undertake in Section Three.

Due to the nature of our analysis, the unemployment rate is considered to be insensitive to changes in inequality and inflation. This allows us to focus on the key relationship underlying the Phillips curve (from unemployment to inflation), expanding it to emphasize inequality as a third dimension. We should also note that our analysis captures the dynamics of economies wherein domestic factors tend to be the most important sources of inflation, thus neglecting the case of economies with significant pass-through from the exchange rate or foreign prices to domestic prices, such as economies in the periphery (Rolim and Marins 2024). Therefore, we provide insights into the dynamics of inflation, inequality, and unemployment that may be more adequate for economies in the center of the capitalist world. Nevertheless, there is some parallel between the inflation dynamics in economies in the periphery and the profits inflation case to be explored in Section Three.

2.1. The Phillips Curve

The first empirical regularity is the inverse relationship between the level of the inflation rate and the level of the unemployment rate, which is known as the Phillips curve. As mentioned in the introduction, in a post-Keynesian approach this empirical regularity can be explained by the conflict over income distribution and the power dynamics associated with fluctuations in the unemployment rate in a cost-push inflation framework. A decrease in the unemployment rate is assumed to increase the bargaining power of workers, who are able to obtain higher nominal wages. However, there is only a partial increase in real wages (if any), since firms try to protect their profit margins by passing on the cost increases to prices, thus generating inflation. Moreover, nominal wage adjustments can be a response to firms' efforts to increase their profit margins through higher prices when costs are constant. In this case, workers try to protect their real wages by increasing nominal wages, which will trigger new price adjustments.

In short, inflation results from a disagreement over income distribution between workers and firms (Dutt 1987; Rowthorn 1977).

The relationship between inflation, unemployment, and the bargaining power of workers can be captured by the conflict-augmented Phillips curve (Serrano 2019; Summa and Braga 2020). This curve is fully compatible with the post-Keynesian framework outlined above, capturing cost-push inflation driven by conflicting-claims over the income distribution. Following Summa and Braga (2020), we can obtain an equation formalizing the conflict-augmented Phillips curve, which will be expanded to include the possibility of changes in the markup rate.

As shown in Equation 1, the *ex-post* proximate causes of inflation are the difference between nominal wage growth and productivity growth and the increase in the markup factor (Lavoie 2022, ch. 8). The latter factor captures the possibility of profits inflation (Davidson 1978), which is not expected to drive inflation rates in the long run but is considered an important factor in the recent inflationary dynamics, as we shall discuss in Section Three.

$$\hat{p} = \hat{w} - \hat{y} + \hat{k} \tag{1}$$

where $\hat{p}$ is the inflation rate, $\hat{w}$ is the growth rate of nominal wages, $\hat{y}$ is the growth rate of labor productivity, and $\hat{k}$ is the growth rate of the markup factor. Note that the markup factor is equal to $k = 1 + \theta$, where θ is the markup rate over unit costs. In our analysis, both $\hat{y}$ and $\hat{k}$ are assumed to be constant variables that are exogenously given.

Following Summa and Braga (2020), nominal wage adjustments depend on the expected inflation rate and on workers' desired increase in real wages, as well as on their capacity to adjust nominal wages, as follows:

$$\hat{w} = \alpha(\hat{p}^e + c) \tag{2}$$

where $\alpha > 0$ is the capacity of adjustments in nominal wages, $\hat{p}^e$ is the expected inflation rate, and c is the desired increase in real wages by workers. The latter variable is assumed to depend on autonomous claims and on the unemployment rate, as follows:

$$c = c_0 - \psi u \tag{3}$$

where $c_0 > 0$ is the autonomous claims, $\psi > 0$ is a parameter capturing the sensitivity of workers' claims to the unemployment rate, and u is the unemployment rate.

Assuming that the expected inflation rate is equal to the actual inflation rate (Palley 2019; Summa and Braga 2020),[2] the conflict-augmented Phillips curve is obtained by combining Equations 1 to 3, as follows:

$$\hat{p} = \left(\frac{1}{1-\alpha}\right)(\alpha c_0 + \hat{k} - \hat{y}) - \left(\frac{\alpha}{1-\alpha}\right)\psi u \tag{4}$$

As argued by Summa and Braga (2020), as long as workers are unable to fully incorporate their aspirations into nominal wages ($\alpha < 1$), the 'old' Phillips curve is valid. In this case, Equation 4 captures a negative relationship between the inflation rate and the unemployment rate in levels.

[2]This assumption guarantees that the *'inflation-unemployment trade-off that exists is not due to misperceptions'* (Palley 2019, p. 21).

For simplicity, we can assume that $(\frac{1}{1-\alpha})(\alpha c_0 - \hat{y}) = \eta$, $\hat{k} = 0$, and $(\frac{\alpha\psi}{1-\alpha}) = \rho$, so that the Phillips curve is described as follows:

$$\hat{p} = \eta - \rho u \tag{5}$$

Accordingly, the trade-off between inflation and unemployment increases with ρ.[3]

2.2. The Unemployment-Inequality Curve

The unemployment-inequality curve is the second stylized fact needed to derive the IAPC. It captures a positive relationship between unemployment and inequality found in the literature (da Silva et al. 2022; Mocan 1999), which is consistent with the empirically verified countercyclical Gini coefficient (Hoover, Giedeman, and Dibooglu 2009; Maestri and Roventini 2012). As argued by Rolim, Carvalho, and Lang (2023), this relationship results (at least partially) from the heterogeneous impact of the business cycle on workers. Indeed, numerous authors find that low-wage workers, unskilled workers, young workers, and less educated workers face larger fluctuations in their unemployment rates (Clark and Summers 1980; Kydland 1984; Mitchell, Wallace, and Warner 1985; Okun, Fellner, and Greenspan 1973; Solon, Barsky, and Parker 1994). This means that when unemployment increases, workers at the bottom of the income distribution tend to face a stronger decrease in their bargaining power, thus facing more significant reductions in their nominal wage adjustments than other workers. As a consequence, there is an increase in within-wage inequality, which tends to increase income inequality.

Moreover, if the low-wage workers are being dismissed in a higher proportion during recessions, there is an additional factor that increases income inequality. When a worker becomes unemployed, his/her gross income becomes zero and his/her net income becomes equal to the unemployment dole (if any) — excluding here other types of incomes (e.g., interest payments, profit dividends, and so on). Therefore, a recession is accompanied by a larger share of low-wage workers observing a significant decrease in their gross and net incomes relative to high-wage worker, which further increases the income disparities.

Interestingly, this empirical regularity is observed regardless of another empirical regularity that goes on the opposite direction: the counteryclical wage share (Giovannoni 2010). The cyclical behavior of the wage share is related to the presence of overhead labor (Lavoie 2022, ch. 5) and labor hoarding. These factors mean that aggregate profits tend to increase proportionally more than aggregate wages in the expansion phase of the cycle as firms can increase employment less than proportionally to the increase in economic activity. Given that the wage share tends to be negatively related to income inequality, this channel could lead to an increase in income inequality in the expansion phase of the cycle since a higher profit share redistributes income to

[3]The value of ρ can change through time, thereby reducing or increasing the slope of the Phillips curve. For instance, the flattening of the Phillips curve in the United States has been associated with a decrease in the bargaining power of workers due to labor market flexibilization and the decline in unionization. This type of argument has appeared both in the mainstream literature (Ratner and Sim 2022; Stansbury and Summers 2020) and in the heterodox literature (Palley 2019; Setterfield 2005; Setterfield and Blecker 2022; Setterfield and Lovejoy 2006; Summa and Braga 2020, among others). A flatter Phillips curve implies that a reduction in the inflation rate requires a larger increase in unemployment.

upper classes, whose incomes are also less equally distributed than wage income (Daudey and García-Peñalosa 2007; Wolff and Zacharias 2013). However, the effect of lower unemployment rates on within-wage (or within-workers) inequality counterbalances the inequality-inducing effect of a higher profit share during expansions, as suggested by the empirical literature (da Silva et al. 2022; Hoover, Giedeman, and Dibooglu 2009; Maestri and Roventini 2012; Mocan 1999).

We can formalize the dynamics of income inequality by considering both the direct effects of the unemployment rate and of the markup rate described above. For mathematical reasons, we consider the markup factor instead of the markup rate and assume a linear relationship. Accordingly, the income inequality variable G can be described by Equation 6:

$$G = \mu + \beta u + \gamma k \tag{6}$$

where $\mu > 0$ is the structural inequality level (independent of the unemployment rate or the markup rate), $\beta > 0$ is a parameter capturing the sensitivity of inequality to unemployment, and $\gamma > 0$ is a parameter capturing the effect of the markup factor on inequality. This latter relation reflects the relationship between the profit share and the personal income distribution that has been described above.

Also in this case we can simplify the equation since the markup is assumed to be fixed ($\hat{\kappa} = 0$). Therefore, assuming that $\mu + \gamma k = \lambda$, Equation 6 can be expressed by Equation 7:

$$G = \lambda + \beta u \tag{7}$$

2.3. Formalizing the Inequality-Augmented Phillips Curve

Sections 2.1 and 2.2 highlight the key role of the unemployment rate in a post-Keynesian framework. Through the Phillips curve, the unemployment rate appears as a key variable determining the level of the inflation rate. Moreover, through the unemployment-inequality curve, the unemployment rate appears as an important determinant of income inequality. These relations suggest that the unemployment rate is a key variable for the relationship between the inflation rate and income inequality.

Indeed, this is the information provided by the IAPC presented by Rolim, Carvalho, and Lang (2023), which is derived here based on Equations 5 and 6.[4] After a few manipulations, these equations form the system of linearly independent equations below:

$$\begin{cases} \hat{p} + \rho u - 0G = \eta \\ 0\hat{p} - \beta u + G = \lambda \end{cases} \tag{8}$$

Solving the system given by three variables and two equations provides a straight line in a three-dimensional space, which is the IAPC. To do so, we set $u = \iota$ and obtain

[4]The relations described by Equations 5 and 6 reflect the stylized facts that are reproduced by Rolim, Carvalho, and Lang (2023) and combined to form the IAPC. Differently from their work, here we take the macroeconomic relationships as the starting point (without presenting microfoundations and micro-level interactions that lead to these aggregate behaviors in agent-based models).

the resulting line described by Equation 9:

$$\begin{pmatrix} \hat{p} \\ u \\ G \end{pmatrix} = \begin{pmatrix} \eta \\ 0 \\ \lambda \end{pmatrix} + \iota \begin{pmatrix} -\rho \\ 1 \\ \beta \end{pmatrix} \tag{9}$$

where $\iota > 0$ is the constant of proportionality.

The IAPC obtained from Equation 9 is plotted in Figure 1. It is equivalent to the IAPC in Rolim, Carvalho, and Lang (2023), but we have derived it directly from the macroeconomic stylized facts discussed above. The curve is plotted in a three-dimensional space composed of our three key variables: unemployment, inflation, and inequality. Each point in the curve indicates the level of inequality and inflation for that specific unemployment rate. As the unemployment rate increases, we observe an increase in inequality and a decrease in inflation. Thus, the curve suggests a possible trade-off between low inequality and low inflation, in addition to the widely discussed trade-off between low unemployment and low inflation.

It is also possible to analyze the relationship between the pairs of variables that is underlying the IAPC. In Figure 2, we do so for the Phillips curve and unemployment-inequality curve, which are our two key stylized facts discussed above. These curves are obtained by taking a two-dimensional view of the three-dimensional space in Figure 1: from the left side (removing the inequality axis) and from above (removing the inflation axis) respectively. Figure 2(a) reports the traditional Phillips curve, which is characterized by a negative relationship between the unemployment rate and inflation rate. As discussed in Section 2.1, this relationship is consistent with the conflicting-claims inflation model if one assumes that the bargaining power

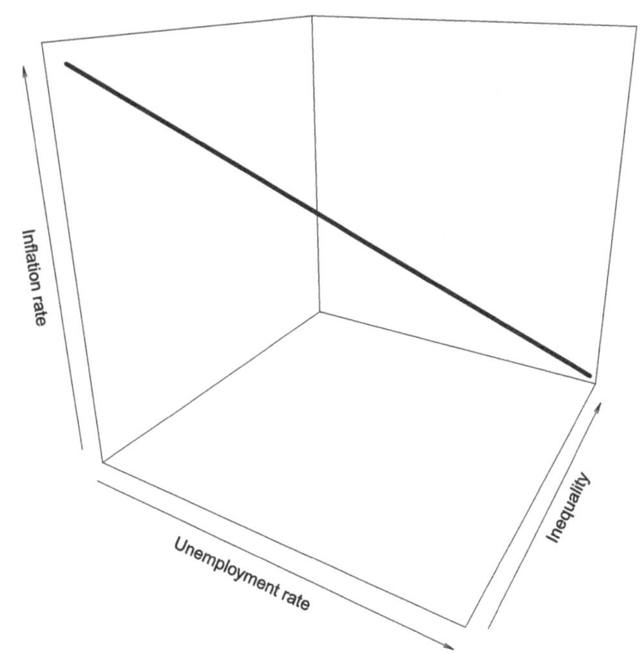

Figure 1. Inequality-augmented Phillips curve.

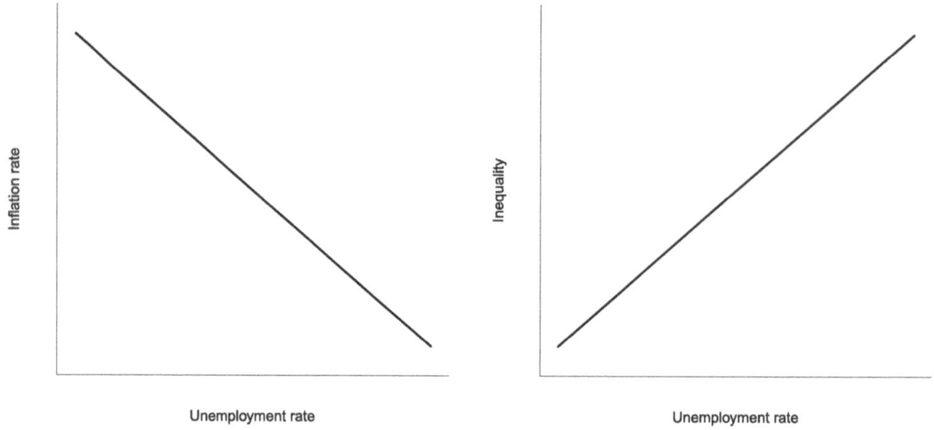

(a) Phillips curve (b) Unemployment-inequality curve

Figure 2. Inequality-augmented Phillips curve: 2D relationships. (a) Phillips curve and (b) Unemployment-inequality curve.

of workers tends to increase with reductions in the unemployment rate. In addition, Figure 2(b) presents the unemployment-inequality curve, indicating a positive relationship between unemployment and inequality that can be explained by the direct effect of unemployment on income inequality and its indirect effect through wage inequality (Section 2.2).[5]

3. Alternative Inflation Drivers

In the previous section, we have established a relation between our three key variables that suggests that higher inflation rates are associated with lower unemployment rates and lower income inequality. This relationship resulted from the labor market dynamics driving the inflation dynamics. One may reasonably question whether this relationship is always valid since numerous examples of these variables behaving in a different manner can be raised. Indeed, inflation in the periphery is strongly associated with the foreign sector (Rolim and Marins 2022, 2024) and the high inflation rates experienced recently by numerous countries at the center do not seem to be driven by nominal wage increases and were accompanied by a worsening in income distribution (Glover, Mustre-del-Río, and Von Ende-Becker 2023; Konczal and Lusiani 2022; Lavoie 2023; Storm 2023; Weber and Wasner 2023). In this section, we tackle this issue by verifying whether the IAPC is still a useful concept for post-Keynesian analyses when considering alternative inflation drivers, in particular, profits inflation.[6]

[5]Note that a possible counteracting force to the relationships captured by the IAPC could be that high wage earners may be better positioned to negotiate nominal wages, thus being able to better protect themselves against higher inflation. This could result in an increase in wage inequality in a context of high inflation and low unemployment. We thank an anonymous referee for pointing this out.

[6]The analysis presented in this section is in line with Setterfield's (2022) analysis, which is also based on the conflicting-claims inflation model and explores the relationship between inflation and wage share during the post-pandemic recovery.

3.1. Inequality-Inducing Inflationary Processes

In this section, we discuss three theoretical explanations for inflationary processes that are not driven by the labor market dynamics. They characterize processes in which prices go up simultaneously to an increase in the amount of profits per unit, but not necessarily higher markup rates.[7] There is still a relevant dimension of conflict over the income distribution since firms are able to either increase or protect their share of income, transferring the burden of cost increases to consumers. As usual, '[a]*t the heart of the inflationary process is the question of relative income distribution*' (Eichner and Kregel 1975, p. 1308).

The first case would be the case of constant markup rates ($\hat{k} = 0$ in Equation 1),[8] when firms know in advanced their unit labor and material costs and act as price-markers. Thus, the trigger of inflation in this case could be a foreign price shock. As suggested by Lavoie (2023), when firms observe an increase in unit imported material costs (and energy), they add a markup over those costs that leads to an increase in prices and in their profits.[9] While the markup over total unit costs remains the same, the relationship between profits and wages changes: firms obtain higher profits while wages are constant and there is an increase in the profit share (Rolim and Marins 2024). By passing on cost increases to prices, firms are solely protecting their profit margins, but it should be noted that the ability to do so is also expressing their significant strength; otherwise, they could decide to reduce profit margins to avoid price increases that could jeopardize their competitiveness. Moreover, there is a collective dimension to the issue, since firms are more likely to pass-on sector-wide cost increases to prices if their competitors are expected to do the same (Weber and Wasner 2023). Yet, in this case, rising profit shares do not mean that profits are causing the inflationary process - they result from such inflationary process.

A second possibility would be the *ex-post* varying markup case. Similarly to the third possibility and in contrast to the first case, it allows for changes in (real) markup rates.[10] It captures the dynamics of price-taker sectors, in which prices are determined in world markets and markup rates are endogenously determined by prices and costs. This is the case of commodities such as energy and food, wherein either a supply or demand shock may provoke changes in prices that are not related to firms' production costs. For instance, in the current context, supply bottlenecks related to the post-pandemic recovery and to the Ukraine war have triggered increases in prices of energy and food, leading to windfall profits in those sectors. Similarly, countries at the periphery are strongly

[7]As testified by the numerous discussions published by the Monetary Policy Institute blog (https://medium.com/@monetarypolicyinstitute) and the Institute for New Economic Thinking blog (https://www.ineteconomics.org/perspectives/blog), these theoretical explanations have been strongly associated with the debate over the causes of the high inflation rates experienced recently by numerous countries at the center.

[8]We are implying constant real markups. See Serrano (2010) for a distinction between nominal and real markup rates.

[9]See Lavoie (2022, ch. 8) and Storm (2023) for a detailed explanation of the effect of imported material costs on prices. Lavoie (2023) and Vernengo and Caldentey (2023) consider that the mechanism associated with unit imported material costs, in particular commodities such as energy and food, is the main explanation for the current inflationary phenomenon.

[10]Note that the distinction between *ex-ante* and *ex-post* markup rates developed in this section is, to some extent, related to the distinction between real and nominal markup rates discussed by Serrano (2010). However, an important difference is that the author considers real and nominal markup rates in the context of cost-determined prices, which is not the case here. Indeed, following the author's classification, we are implicitly assuming that cost-determined prices have fixed real markup rates. On the other hand, we restrict the *ex-ante* markup rates case solely to demand-determined prices.

exposed to this type of inflation through foreign price and exchange rate shocks (Rolim and Marins 2024). In such case, markup rates increase, but this is an *ex-post* increase, rather than being a deliberate strategy undertaken by price-makers. Arguably, there is an impact of these prices on imported inputs, but they also have a direct effect on domestic prices since energy and commodity goods form a relevant part of workers' consumption baskets. Commodity producers thus observed an increase in profits that is caused by higher prices (Vernengo and Caldentey 2023). Similarly to the previous case, it would be inappropriate to consider that $\hat{k} > 0$ *causes* higher inflation rates in the *ex-post* varying markup case, even if we do observe increases in the markup factor.

The third case refers to profits inflation (Davidson 1978). Because it is associated with an intentional effort by firms to increase their markup rates (Weber and Wasner 2023),[11] it can be defined as a case of *ex-ante* varying markup rates. Accordingly, it consists of a situation when $\hat{k} > 0$ is the primary cause of the price increases and, consequently, inflation rates. As argued by Dutt (1987), price dynamics associated with changes in the degree of monopoly, which would operate through markups, would not generate a Phillips curve.[12] Indeed, as discussed in the next section, profits inflation cannot be characterized by movements along the Phillips curve or the IAPC. Nonetheless, the IAPC is a useful concept for understanding the dynamics of inflation, unemployment, and inequality in such a context.

3.2. Inflation and Inequality Dynamics During Profits Inflation

In order to consider profits inflation, we must change solely one assumption in our model. While in Section Two, we had assumed that the markup factor is constant (so $\hat{k} = 0$), we now drop this assumption and allow for a positive increase in the markup rate.[13] This is still coherent with the post-Keynesian framework and its view that inflation in the long run hinges on the differential between nominal wage growth and productivity growth (Lavoie 2022, ch. 8) since we can interpret our model as capturing a specific time period in which markups are increasing, rather than describing the long-run dynamics.[14]

Considering the possibility of a varying markup factor implies that in each period the markup factor is a function of its initial value (k_0) and its growth rate, which is assumed

[11]In the current context, according to Weber and Wasner (2023), price-maker firms that would normally only increase prices when their competitors were expected to do the same interpreted the post-pandemic context as providing a positive sign for price increases. See also Matamoros (2023), Setterfield (2022), Storm (2023) for related analyses of the recent context.

[12]Note that in Dutt (1987, p. 81), the Phillips curve is understood as a positive association between price inflation and economic growth that is explained as follows: *'the desired (and ability) of workers to obtain faster increases in the wage raises the inflation rate and the real wage; this rise in the real wage redistributes income from capitalists to workers, raises aggregate demand and induces higher rates of growth'*. It is thus caused by a different mechanism relative to that in Section 2.1.

[13]Note that this adjustment may still capture the *ex-post* varying markup rate case if we reorganize Equation 1 to $\hat{k} = \hat{p} + \hat{y} - \hat{w}$ and consider exogenous shocks on $\hat{p}$. It can also reflect the constant markup case with rising unit material costs: in this case, even if the markup over total unit costs is constant, the markup over unit labor costs — which should cover profits and material costs — and the profit share are rising. Yet, since at the macroeconomic level, one has to assume that all material inputs are imported (Lavoie 2023), this case cannot be adequately captured by our closed economy model.

[14]In other words, we do not intend to model a permanent increase in the rate of growth of the markup, since it would generate an unrealistic trend for the profit share. We are thus solely capturing a short-run period while $\hat{k} > 0$ and describing the relationship between inflation, unemployment, and inequality during that specific period. This is why we consider only three periods in our analysis (two periods in which $\hat{k} > 0$).

to be fixed through our short-run analysis. Thus, the markup factor is expressed by Equation 10:

$$k_t = k_0(1+\hat{k})^t \quad (10)$$

Consequently, the inequality variable from Equation 6 is now time-dependent, as indicated by Equation 11:

$$G_t = \mu + \beta u + \gamma k_0(1+\hat{k})^t \quad (11)$$

The inflation rate is still constant during profits inflation. Based on Equation 4 and assuming that $(\frac{1}{1-\alpha}) = \tau$, it is now given by Equation 12:

$$\hat{p} = \eta + \tau\hat{k} - \rho u \quad (12)$$

The system of linearly independent equations describing the IAPC under profits inflation is given by Equation 13.

$$\begin{cases} \hat{p} + \rho u - 0G_t = \eta + \tau\hat{k} \\ 0\hat{p} - \beta u + G_t = \mu + \gamma k_0(1+\hat{k})^t \end{cases} \quad (13)$$

Solving the system provides the time-varying IAPC described by Equation 14, wherein we once again assume that $u = \iota$.

$$\begin{pmatrix} \hat{p} \\ u \\ G_t \end{pmatrix} = \begin{pmatrix} \eta + \tau\hat{k} \\ 0 \\ \mu + \gamma k_0(1+\hat{k})^t \end{pmatrix} + \iota \begin{pmatrix} -\rho \\ 1 \\ \beta \end{pmatrix} \quad (14)$$

Once again, the IAPC can be plotted in a three-dimensional space. To understand the effects of profits inflation, we consider three cases ($t = 0, 1, 2$) and explore the dynamics of inequality and inflation for a given unemployment rate (u^*), which is considered to be stable. Note that our model allows for increases in the nominal wage growth rate following an increase in the inflation rate due to the assumption that $\hat{p}^e = \hat{p}$ (Section Two). However, these adjustments are not enough to compensate the increase in the markup factor and are just an additional source of inflation that depends on the magnitude of α in Equation 2.

The case of profits inflation is illustrated in Figure 3. In $t = 0$ we have our baseline scenario from Section Two, wherein $\hat{k} = 0$. Point A in this figure represents the point equivalent to u^* at $t = 0$. Profits inflation starts in $t = 1$ with an increase in $\hat{k}$, which has two key implications for the shape of the IAPC that can also be analyzed through Equation 14: an increase in $\hat{k}$ leads to an increase in price inflation and in the inequality coefficient for the same level of the unemployment rate. This means that the IAPC shifts upward and rightward in the three-dimensional space, moving the economy from point A to point B. In $t = 2$, $\hat{k}$ is at the same level as in $t = 1$, so there is no further increase in the inflation rate. However, the markup factor is still increasing, thus leading to a more inequality for the same level of the unemployment rate (u^*). In terms of the three-dimensional space, this means that the IAPC shifts once again to the right and, still taking unemployment constant at u^*, the economy goes from point B to C.

Figure 4 provides the two-dimensional relations captured by the traditional Phillips curve and the unemployment-inequality curve. As in the previous case, they are

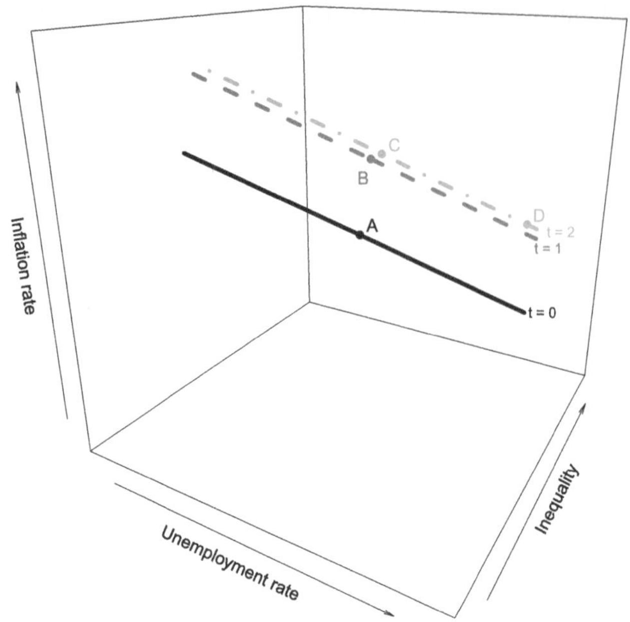

Figure 3. Inequality-augmented Phillips curves under profits inflation.

helpful to visualize the changes in the relationship between our key variables. Figure 4(a) reports the traditional Phillips curve. An increase in $\hat{k}$ represents a one-time-only upward shift in the Phillips curve: for the same level of unemployment u^* there is a higher inflation rate (from point A to points B and C). Since between $t = 1$ and $t = 2$ there is no further increase in $\hat{k}$, the Phillips curves for these scenarios overlap. Conversely, the unemployment-inequality shifts upward as long as $\hat{k} > 0$, as reported in Figure 4 (b). Therefore, we observe continuous increases in inequality even if the unemployment rate is kept constant, moving from point A to point B and, finally, to point C.

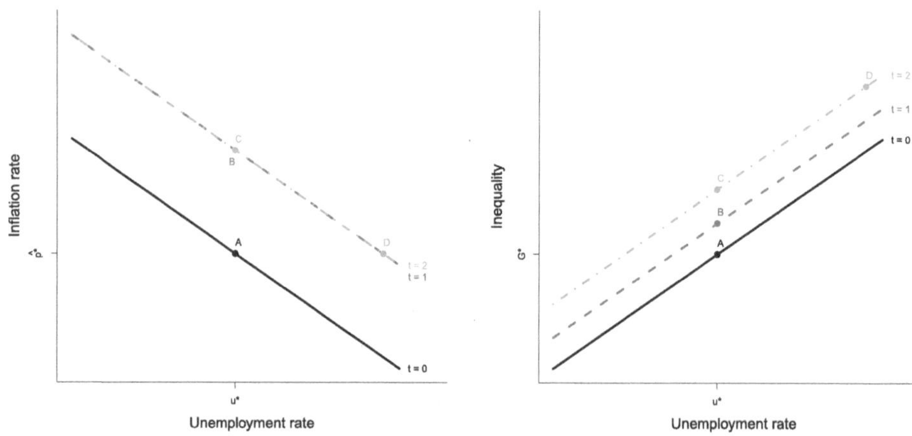

(a) Phillips curve (b) Unemployment-inequality curve

Figure 4. Inequality-augmented Phillips curves under profits inflation: 2D relationships. (a) Phillips curve and (b) Unemployment-inequality curve.

Overall, these results are consistent with the main findings in the literature exploring the implications of profits inflation, as discussed in Section 3.1. We observe that profits inflation causes an increase in the inflation rate that is not related to changes in the unemployment rate. While the Phillips curve may still be valid, inflation dynamics is not explained by movements along the Phillips curve, but by shifts of this curve that are caused by an exogenous factor ($\hat{k} > 0$). Moreover, profits inflation causes continuous upward shifts of the unemployment-inequality curve, leading to increases in inequality that are not related to the unemployment dynamics. In such a context, inequality will continuously increase until the increases in the markup factor cease and we are back to $\hat{k} = 0$.[15]

3.3. Monetary Policy During Profits Inflation

While it is clear that profits inflation is not related to labor market tightening, the public discourse is still very much attached to the idea of a stable Phillips curve. Thus, it is often argued that increasing unemployment rates is necessary for achieving price stability. Taking the case of the U.S. economy, for instance, references to an extremely tight labor market causing fast nominal wage growth have been made by the Federal Reserve Chair in order to justify promoting '*moderate demand growth*' (Powell 2022, p. 3). The reasoning is that a decrease in demand will increase unemployment and move the economy downwards along the Phillips curve, thus reducing inflation.

However, such policy prescription is rarely analyzed through its distributive implications. In this sense, the IAPC is once again a useful concept for understanding the implications of monetary tightening in such a context. Assuming that this policy is undertaken at $t = 2$ and that is able to induce higher unemployment rates — and, again, that this is the main channel of monetary policy —,[16] we would observe a downward movement along the IAPC from point C to point D in Figures 3 and 4. While this may be efficient to control inflation, which returns to the initial level ($\hat{p}^*$), it further accentuates the distributive dynamics induced by profits inflation. Indeed, bringing inflation back to its initial level in point A after the profits inflation shock requires more unemployment and, consequently, causes a further increase in inequality.[17]

Thus, under these conditions, monetary policy seems to exacerbate the distributive dynamics by transferring the burden to workers, who have already been affected the most by profits inflation.[18] Similarly to Rolim and Marins (2024), we find that fighting inflation through labor market tightening when it is caused by a factor other than labor market forces creates more inequality in the income distribution. Our results thus go in line with the view advocated by Storm (2022) and Weber and Wasner (2023), among others, that more adequate tools - going beyond monetary policy - are needed to fight inflationary pressures from different sources.

[15]In this case, the IAPC would shift downward.

[16]In the real world, there is often a lag between monetary tightening and its effect on the economy. We abstract from this lag due to the theoretical nature of this work, thus prioritizing a more qualitative analysis of the dynamics generated by such policy.

[17]Note that, even if inflation is controlled through an increase in unemployment, inequality will continue to increase as long as $\hat{k} > 0$.

[18]Another channel through which monetary policy reinforces the regressive distributive dynamics is through its adverse effect on debtors relative to creditors (Lavoie and Seccareccia 1999).

4. Conclusion

Inflation and inequality are intrinsically connected to each other due to their sensitivity to unemployment. This is explicitly captured by the IAPC, which first appeared in Rolim, Carvalho, and Lang (2023). In this article, we have derived this curve from macroeconomic equations describing the empirically verified relationship between unemployment and inflation (the traditional Phillips curve) and between unemployment and inequality. We have done so in a conflicting-claims inflation framework, thus obtaining a relationship that is closely related to the post-Keynesian view on inflation and which can be useful for exploring the relationship between inflation and inequality in this approach.

This is precisely what we have done next, focusing on the case of profits inflation. We have shown that the IAPC is still a useful concept to understand the implications of inflation rates resulting from higher markup rates: they are captured by shifts of the curve that lead to higher inflation and continuous increases in inequality for a constant unemployment rate. This provides important insights into empirical studies investigating the Phillips curve, since we may have time-varying Phillips curves depending on the inflationary source. However, when monetary policy is employed to fight this inflation dynamics by increasing unemployment, we move along the IAPC. This means that inflationary control causes more unemployment and inequality.

Therefore, our results provide some theoretical support for claims against rising interest rates to fight inflation that does not result from labor market pressures (Storm 2022; Weber and Wasner 2023, among others). If the unemployment rate is the main transmission mechanism of monetary policy, higher interest rates may achieve price stability not through its primary cause, but rather by a compensatory factor that deepens the distributive dynamics generated by profits inflation. However, as emphasized by Rolim and Marins (2024), one should avoid taking this conclusion too far, since the main monetary policy transmission mechanism may differ depending on the country, which has implications for the relationship between interest rates, inflation, and inequality.

Moreover, the IAPC provides some insights into rethinking central bank mandates. In the case of wage inflation (movements along the IAPC), a restrictive monetary policy could potentially address the primary cause of inflation, but this could possibly stop a welcomed redistributive process (associated with low unemployment rates). In the case of profits inflation, the monetary policy response would exacerbate a regressive distributive process. These issues could be prevented by an alternative central bank mandate that also includes income inequality as one of the concerns of monetary policy. This would be helpful in avoiding strong monetary policy responses that generate more inequality in order to control inflation rates.

Acknowledgments

The author thanks Hugo Rafacho and two anonymous referees for comments and suggestions. The author thanks Espaço da Escrita — Pró-Reitoria de Pesquisa — UNICAMP — for the language services provided.

Disclosure statement

No potential conflict of interest was reported by the author(s).

ORCID

Lilian Rolim http://orcid.org/0000-0002-9880-2823

References

Blanchard, O. 2016. 'The Phillips Curve: Back to the'60s?' *The American Economic Review* 106 (5): 31–34.

Blanchard, O., E. Cerutti, and L. Summers. 2015. 'Inflation and Activity - Two Explorations and Their Monetary Implications.' NBER Working Paper Series 21726.

Clark, K. B., and L. H. Summers. 1980. 'Demographic Differences in Cyclical Employment Variation.' NBER Working Paper Series 514:1–27.

da Silva, L. A. P, E. Kharroubi, E. Kohlscheen, M. Lombardi, and B. Mojon. 2022. *Inequality Hysteresis and the Effectiveness of Macroeconomic Stabilisation Policies*. Bank for International Settlements (BIS). https://www.bis.org/publ/othp50.pdf.

Daudey, E., and C. García-Peñalosa. 2007. 'The Personal and the Factor Distributions of Income in a Cross-Section of Countries.' *The Journal of Development Studies* 43 (5): 812–829.

Davidson, P. 1978. *Money and the Real World*. 2nd ed. London: Palgrave Macmillan UK.

Dutt, A. K. 1987. 'Alternative Closures Again: A Comment on 'Growth, Distribution, and Inflation'.' *Cambridge Journal of Economics* 11: 75–82.

Eichner, A. S., and J. A. Kregel. 1975. 'An Essay on Post-Keynesian Theory: A New Paradigm in Economics.' *Journal of Economic Literature* 13 (4): 1293–1314.

Giovannoni, O. 2010. 'Functional Distribution of Income, Inequality and the Incidence of Poverty: Stylized Facts and the Role of Macroeconomic Policy.' UTIP Working Paper 58.

Glover, A., J. Mustre-del-Río, and A. Von Ende-Becker. 2023. 'How Much Have Record Corporate Profits Contributed to Recent Inflation?' *The Federal Reserve Bank of Kansas City Economic Review*108 (1): 1–13.

Hoover, G. A., D. C. Giedeman, and S. Dibooglu. 2009. 'Income Inequality and the Business Cycle: A Threshold Cointegration Approach.' *Economic Systems* 33 (3): 278–292.

Konczal, M., and N. Lusiani. 2022. *Prices, Profits, and Power: An Analysis of 2021 Firm-Level Markups*. Roosevelt Institute Briefs. https://rooseveltinstitute.org/wp-content/uploads/2022/06/RI_PricesProfitsPower_202206.pdf.

Kydland, F. E. 1984. 'Labor-Force Heterogeneity and the Business Cycle.' *Carnegie-Rochester Conference Series on Public Policy* 21: 173–208.

Lavoie, M. 2022. *Post-Keynesian Economics: New Foundations*. 2nd ed. Cheltenham, UK: Edward Elgar.

Lavoie, M. 2023. 'Some Controversies in the Causes of the Post-Pandemic Inflation.' *Monetary Policy Institute Blog* 77: 14.

Lavoie, M., and M. Seccareccia. 1999. 'Interest Rate: Fair.' In *Encyclopedia of Political Economy*, edited by Phillip O'Hara, Vol. 1. London, UK: Routledge London.

Maestri, V., and A. Roventini. 2012. 'Inequality and Macroeconomic Factors: A Time-Series Analysis for a Set of OECD Countries.' Laboratory of Economics and Management Paper Series 2012/21.

Matamoros, G. 2023. 'Are Firm Markups Boosting Inflation? A Post-Keynesian Institutionalist Approach to Markup Inflation in Select Industrialized Countries.' *Review of Political Economy* 1–22. https://doi.org/10.1080/09538259.2023.2244440.

Mitchell, M. L., M. S. Wallace, and J. T. Warner. 1985. 'Real Wages Over the Business Cycle: Some Further Evidence.' *Southern Economic Journal* 51 (4): 1162–1173.

Mocan, H. N. 1999. 'Structural Unemployment, Cyclical Unemployment, and Income Inequality.' *Review of Economics and Statistics* 81 (1): 122–134.

Okun, A. M., W. Fellner, and A. Greenspan. 1973. 'Upward Mobility in a High-Pressure Economy.' *Brookings Papers on Economic Activity* 1973 (1): 207–261.

Palley, T. I. 2019. 'The Backward Bending Phillips Curves: Competing Micro-Foundations and the Role of Conflict.' *Investigación Económica* 68 (270): 13–36.

Powell, J. H. 2022. 'Restoring Price Stability.' Remarks at 'Policy Options for Sustainable and Inclusive Growth' 38th Annual Economic Policy Conference National Association for Business Economics.

Ratner, D., and J. Sim. 2022. 'Who Killed the Phillips Curve? A Murder Mystery.' *Finance and Economics Discussion Series* 2022 (028): 1–36.

Rolim, L., L. Carvalho, and D. Lang. 2024. 'Monetary policy rules and the inequality-augmented Phillips Curve.' *Economic Modelling.* https://doi.org/10.1016/j.econmod.2024.106780.

Rolim, L., and N. Marins. 2022. 'Inflation Targeting Regime and Income Distribution in Emerging Market Economies.' In *The Future of Central Banking*, edited by S. Kappes, L.P. Rochon, and G. Vallet. Cheltenham, UK: Edward Elgar Publishing.

Rolim, L., and N. Marins. 2024. 'Foreign Price Shocks and Inflation Targeting: Effects on Income and Inflation Inequality.' *Review of Political Economy.* https://doi.org/10.1080/09538259.2023.2301332.

Rowthorn, R. E. 1977. 'Conflict, Inflation and Money.' *Cambridge Journal of Economics* 1: 215–239.

Serrano, F. 2010. 'O Conflito Distributivo E a Teoria Da InflaÇão Inercial.' *Revista de Economia Contemporânea* 14 (2): 395–421.

Serrano, F. 2019. 'Mind the Gaps: The Conflict Augmented Phillips Curve and the Sraffian supermultiplier.' IE-UFRJ Working Paper 11.

Setterfield, M. 2005. 'Worker Insecurity and U.S. Macroeconomic Performance During the 1990s.' *Review of Radical Political Economics* 37 (2): 155–177.

Setterfield, M. 2022. 'Inflation and Distribution During the Post-COVID Recovery: A Kaleckian Approach.' *SSRN Electronic Journal.* https://ssrn.com/abstract=4250496.

Setterfield, M., and R. A. Blecker. 2022. 'Structural Change in the US Phillips Curve, 1948–2021: The Role of Power and Institutions.' The New School for Social Research - Department of Economics Working Paper 01/2022.

Setterfield, M., and T. Lovejoy. 2006. 'Aspirations, Bargaining Power, and Macroeconomic Performance.' *Journal of Post Keynesian Economics* 29 (1): 117–148.

Solon, G., R. Barsky, and J. A. Parker. 1994. 'Measuring the Cyclicality of Real Wages: How Important is Composition Bias?.' *The Quarterly Journal of Economics* 109 (1): 1–25.

Stansbury, A., and L. H. Summers. 2020. 'The Declining Worker Power Hypothesis: An Explanation for the Recent Evolution of the American Economy.' NBER Working Paper Series 27193.

Storm, S. 2022. 'Inflation in the Time of Corona and War.' Institute for New Economic Thinking Working Papers 185.

Storm, S. 2023. *Profit Inflation is Real.* Institute for New Economic Thinking Blog. https://www.ineteconomics.org/perspectives/blog/profit-inflation-is-real.

Summa, R., and J. Braga. 2020. 'Two Routes Back to the Old Phillips Curve: The Amended Mainstream Model and the Conflict- Augmented Alternative.' *Bulletin of Political Economy* 14 (1): 81–115.

Vernengo, M., and E. P. Caldentey. 2023. 'Price and Prejudice: Reflections on the Return of Inflation and Ideology.' *Review of Keynesian Economics* 11 (2): 129–146.

Weber, I. M., and E. Wasner. 2023. 'Sellers' Inflation, Profits and Conflict: Why Can Large Firms Hike Prices in An Emergency?.' *Review of Keynesian Economics* 11 (2): 1–21.

Wolff, E. N., and A. Zacharias. 2013. 'Class Structure and Economic Inequality.' *Cambridge Journal of Economics* 37 (6): 1381–1406.

Conflictual Inflation and the Phillips Curve

Marc Lavoie

ABSTRACT
This paper presents a pedagogical guide to conflictual inflation, showing the similarities and differences between the post-Keynesian analysis and the alternative mainstream WS-PS model. Among other things, it shows the difficulties that analysts meet when they try to justify the existence of a NAIRU. Productivity growth, wage-wage inflation and the possibility of a flat Phillips curve are considered within the framework of the post-Keynesian conflicting-claims model. The paper also deals with conflictual inflation within the context of an open economy that imports intermediate goods and raw materials.

1. Introduction

Olivier Blanchard (2022) created quite a stir just before the New Year when he argued in a tweet that inflation could be due to conflicting claims. He wrote:

> A point which is often lost in discussions of inflation and central bank policy. Inflation is fundamentally the outcome of the distributional conflict, between firms, workers, and taxpayers. It stops only when the various players are forced to accept the outcome. The source of the conflict may be too hot an economy: In the labor market, workers may be in a stronger position to bargain for higher wages given prices. But, in the goods market, firms may also be in a stronger position to increase prices given wages. And, on, it goes. The source of the conflict may be in too high prices of commodities, such as energy. Firms want to increase prices given wages, to reflect the higher cost of intermediate inputs. Workers want to resist the decrease in the real wage, and ask for higher wages. And on it goes.

There was a commotion both in mainstream circles that still believed that inflation is always and everywhere caused by an excess supply of money, but also among some heterodox economists who thought that the theme of conflictual inflation only belonged to the heterodox tradition (Lavoie and Rochon 2023). Indeed, a look at the large number of post-Keynesian textbooks of the 1970s, 1980s and 1990s shows that all important earlier post-Keynesian works emphasized conflictual inflation. The purpose of the present article is pedagogical: it purports to present the similarities and differences among the main presentations of conflictual inflation, both mainstream and heterodox.

Historically, conflictual inflation has been modelled for some time within heterodox economics, starting with the contribution of Robert Rowthorn (1977). Some form of the theory of conflictual inflation was present among the members of the Cambridge Economic Policy Group at the Department of Applied Economics of the University of Cambridge in the mid-1970s and early 1980s. A partial model of conflict inflation can be found in the description of the New Cambridge model by Francis Cripps and Wynne Godley (1976), while Roger Tarling and Frank Wilkinson (1982, p. 41) contended that 'periods of sustained wage inflation are caused by worsening inconsistency between workers' aspirations and the level of real wages which they actually receive'. Indeed, there is a long tradition in industrial relations and economic sociology that sets social conflicts and power relations at the heart of economic analysis. It is not surprising that distribution conflict over the split between profits and wages should play a role in the determination of inflation.

It may also be argued that Joan Robinson's (1956, p. 48) inflation barrier, where the needs of firms to finance investment through their profits clash with the minimum real wage deemed acceptable by workers, is part of that tradition. Her inflation barrier led Alfred Eichner and Jan Kregel (1975, p. 1308) to argue in their survey of post-Keynesian economics that 'at the heart of the inflationary process is the question of relative income distribution'. This had been previously ascertained by Paul Davidson (1972, p. 347) when he claimed that 'the distribution of income is both a cause and a consequence of inflationary processes'. Davidson (1972, pp. 348–349), without modelling it however, proposed the main features of the modern theory of conflictual inflation by arguing that inflation was the 'result of some economic groups attempting to increase their share in the total real income of the economy'. Thus firms, through what he called profits inflation, would attempt to increase their profit margins relative to wage costs. Symmetrically, labour would attempt to raise their share at the expense of profit margins. With the rival group refusing to accommodate, this will generate inflation. Davidson also underlined the possibility of wage-wage inflation as some workers try to improve their relative wages and move up the wage-earners' pecking order.

Earlier models of conflictual inflation by heterodox or post-Keynesian authors can be attributed to Lance Taylor (1985) and Paul Dalziel (1990). Taylor associates the notion of conflict inflation to the Latin American structuralist theory of inflation, partly inspired, he says, by Michał Kalecki following a 1955 visit to Mexico City.[1] These conflicting-claims theories of inflation, he continues, had a Latin flowering and were inspired by the dynamics of inflation in Brazil. Present post-Keynesian models of conflictual inflation, however, mostly arise from the neat specification provided by Amitava Dutt (1987) in a response to Stephen Marglin. Dutt (1990, pp. 83–85) later added partial indexation to his wage inflation equation. The complete model that will be considered here is to be found in Lavoie (1992, pp. 391–397) and was developed recently in the post-Keynesian textbooks of Blecker and Setterfield (2019) and Lavoie (2022). In the meantime, a variant of this conflictual inflation theory linked to a Phillips curve analysis was studied by Stockhammer (2008), Hein and Stockhammer (2010) and Hein (2023).

Amongst mainstream authors, besides Blanchard, James Tobin (1981, p. 28) also, at some point, underlined the role of conflictual inflation, as recalled by Richard Burdekin and Paul Burkett (1996, p. 1) in their book on this topic. They argued that:

[1] As pointed out by Peter Reynolds (1987, p. 114), the conflictual theory of inflation can be seen as a development of Kalecki's ideas, even though Kalecki himself did not produce a theory of inflation.

> Inflation is the symptom of deep-rooted social and economic contradiction and conflict. There is no real equilibrium path. The major economic groups are claiming pieces of pie that together exceed the whole pie. Inflation is the way that their claims, so far as they are expressed in nominal terms, are temporarily reconciled. But it will continue and indeed accelerate so long as the basic conflicts of real claims and real power continue.

The last sentence provides a clue as to what may distinguish the mainstream view of conflict inflation with the view advocated by post-Keynesians, or at least most of them. Tobin's last sentence introduces the acceleration thesis, associated with the so-called 'equilibrium rate of unemployment', also called the natural rate of unemployment, the non-accelerating inflation rate of unemployment (NAIRU) or in less fancy terms the steady-inflation rate of unemployment (SIRU). Indeed, the conflict inflation model provided by mainstream authors, based on the wage-setting and price-setting relations, the WS-PS model, was ultimately a model that determined this NAIRU. This WS-PS variant of conflict inflation was first developed in the book of Layard, Nickell, and Jackman (1991). The WS-PS model is at the heart of the textbook of Wendy Carlin and David Soskice (2015). Not surprisingly, it is also within the CORE textbook, since Carlin was heavily involved in this project. The WS-PS model is a long-time feature of Blanchard's textbooks in intermediate macroeconomics. For instance, it is to be found more than 20 years ago in the Canadian version of his textbook (Blanchard and Melino 1999), although we shall see that he argues in its 8th edition (Blanchard 2021) that the equilibrium rate of unemployment arising from it may not be a NAIRU.

Conflictual inflation is now being found among the mainstream, beyond their textbooks. Recently, some mainstream authors (Lorenzoni and Werning 2023; Ratner and Sim 2022) have produced fancy models inspired by the post-Keynesian approach to conflictual inflation based on aspiration gaps, rather than on the Wicksellian monetary approach, citing Kalecki, Rowthorn and Lavoie along the way. Indeed, in a debate with Emiliano Brancaccio, Blanchard himself has recognized the relevance of the post-Keynesian work on income distribution:

> Regarding Post-Keynesians: I must admit that I have not read all they have written. However, in general, the importance of the concept of income distribution seems to be quite an important topic for them, but less important for us. Hence, I think they have useful points to communicate on this front. I am in favor of drawing inspiration from their work. (Blanchard and Brancaccio 2019, p. 286)

The next section starts with a description of the WS-PS model of conflictual inflation and then imbeds into various specifications of the Phillips curve, including its acceleration incarnation. The third section is devoted to the post-Keynesian view of conflictual inflation and its alternative Phillips curves, including the variant with the acceleration hypothesis. It also deals with the implications of wage-wage inflation, productivity growth, imported inflation, and the possibility of a flat Phillips curve.

2. The Mainstream View

2.1. The WS-PS Model of Conflictual Inflation

The purpose of the WS-PS model, as it was first conceived, was to determine the non-accelerating inflation rate of unemployment — the NAIRU. Most of the action resides on the labour market. This mainstream model presumes that there exists a hypothetical economy with perfect competition but that real economies are embroiled with imperfections and rigidities, mostly in the labour market, but also possibly in the goods market. The greater these imperfections, the higher the rate of unemployment which will be needed to steady the inflation rate and achieve the real wage compatible with a non-accelerating inflation rate. The WS-PS model is an alternative to the standard way that identifies the NAIRU within the Phillips curve analysis. This NAIRU, often called an equilibrium rate of unemployment, is defined as the rate which equates the real wage needed by price setters (firms) and the real wage desired by wage setters (workers). When this equilibrium rate is reached, conflict is resolved, and the inflation rate does not change anymore.

Going back to Blanchard, and his concern regarding conflictual income distribution, here is what he was saying in his recent debate (Blanchard and Brancaccio 2019, p. 283):

> I have always seen the level of unemployment as reflecting in part a distributive struggle between workers and companies. Workers want wages to match what they need to spend and firms want to set prices based on the wages they have to pay. Everyone wants more. How can this conflict be resolved? My thesis is that, unfortunately, it is partly resolved through unemployment, which increases to the point where workers' wage demands match what companies are willing to pay.

The PS equation is derived from a standard markup pricing procedure, given by equation 1. Neoclassical theory usually relies on marginalism, in particular, the assumption that marginal costs are rising and hence that the marginal product of labour is decreasing as production increases. However, modern mainstream authors, in particular, New Keynesians, often assume a constant marginal cost, and hence suppose, as post-Keynesian authors usually do, that the price can be written under the form of markup pricing, with the price being dependent on the unit labour cost w/λ such that:

$$p = (1 + m)w/\lambda \tag{1}$$

where w is the nominal wage rate, λ is the constant labour productivity and m is the percentage markup over unit costs. The PS equation simply inverts equation 1 in terms of the real wage, and assumes that it yields the real wage pursued by firms:

$$\frac{w}{p} = \frac{\lambda}{(1 + m)} \tag{2}$$

While there is no ambiguity about the PS equation, the WS equation can give rise to several different specifications. Indeed, at least in the past, for instance in Blanchard and Melino (1999) and Carlin and Soskice (2015), the WS equation was only given in implicit form and with a curve showing a negative relationship between the real wage pursued by workers and the rate of unemployment. Blanchard (2021) however presents a linear version of the WS equation which tells us that workers wish to obtain a real wage which is some proportion of their average labour productivity λ, the proportion being given by the term in parentheses in equation 3; this share is somewhat reduced when the rate of unemployment U is higher, and it depends on a parameter z which we can interpret as some measure of the bargaining power of workers. This linear specification is thus given by:[2]

$$\frac{w}{p^e} = \lambda(z + 1 - \alpha U) \tag{3}$$

Combining equations 1 and 3 and assuming that eventually, price expectations will be right so that $p = p^e$, yields a measure of the NAIRU. We first obtain equation 4:

$$p = \frac{(1+m)}{\lambda} p^e \lambda(z + 1 - \alpha U) \tag{4}$$

Solving for U, we have:

$$U^* = \frac{z + m/(1+m)}{\alpha} = \frac{z + \pi}{\alpha} \tag{5}$$

where $\pi = m/(1+m)$ is the profit share (in a closed vertically-integrated economy).

The higher are m (or π) and z, which are proxies for the share of profits and wages that firms and workers wish to achieve, the higher will be the natural rate of unemployment. This is illustrated with the help of Figure 1.

An alternative, perhaps simpler, specification of the WS equation could be the following, given by equation 3A:

$$\frac{w}{p^e} = (z - \alpha U) \tag{3A}$$

where z now represents the target real wage of workers if the rate of unemployment were zero. Combining equations 2 and 3A, and solving for U while again assuming that $p = p^e$, we obtain an alternative measure of the NAIRU, equation 5A:

$$U^* = \frac{z - \lambda(1-m)}{\alpha} \tag{5A}$$

With specification 3A, the NAIRU depends on the discrepancy between the real wage z that workers would like to have if there were no unemployment and an approximation of the real wage $\lambda(1-m)$ that firms are willing to grant.[3] A higher labour productivity λ facilitates the equalization of the targets of workers and firms, without so much need for increases in the rate of unemployment. In both equations 5 and 5A, an increase in the markup m of firms and in z, the proxy standing for the real wage demands of workers, will both lead to an increase in the NAIRU.

For mainstream economists, the markup m will need to be higher the larger are the payroll taxes that firms are being forced to contribute to support social programmes. A lack of competition in the goods market will also be said to induce increases in the markup. Similarly, for mainstream economists, the z parameter affecting the WS relation will be larger the stronger are labour unions and various laws protecting workers, including unemployment insurance programmes, notably their generosity and duration, as well as the level of the minimum wage. The contributions that workers have to make to

---

[2]In Blanchard's textbooks, it is assumed for simplicity that $\lambda = 1$.

[3]For small enough values of m, $1/(1+m) \cong (1-m)$, as argued by Carlin and Soskice (2015, p. 59). Note that in equation 5, the equilibrium rate of unemployment depends on the sum of the two main parameters, whereas in equation 5A it depends on their difference.

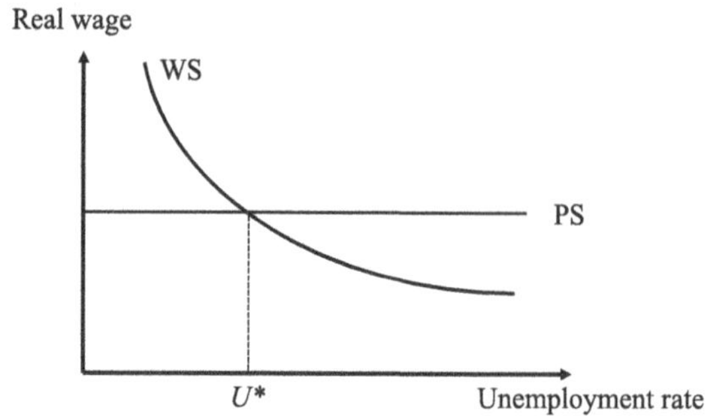

Figure 1. The determination of the NAIRU in the WS-PS model.

various compulsory schemes, including income taxes, will also contribute to a rise in z. The NAIRU according to this view, often associated in the past with the work of OECD economists, is thus entirely a supply-side affair, independent of aggregate demand.[4] The solution to reduce unemployment over the long run is fairly simple according to these economists: besides retraining workers, it suffices to introduce reforms that will make the labour market more flexible, by reducing the so-called tax wedge and by abolishing many programmes and regulations that are said to get in the way of a competitive labour market.[5]

2.2. The Phillips Curves

The previous section identified what the NAIRU would be within the framework of the conflictual relationship between wage-setters and price-setters when the prices expected by workers and their representatives are being actually realized. For some time now, Blanchard has been arguing that the equilibrium rate of unemployment arising from the WS-PS model may or may not be a NAIRU, depending on how the price expectations of wage-setters are being entertained. Starting from equation 4, Blanchard derives a relationship between the rate of inflation and the rate of unemployment:[6]

$$\hat{p} = \hat{p}^e + (\pi + z) - \alpha U \tag{6}$$

How exactly this relationship can be depicted depends on the behaviour of inflation expectations $\hat{p}^e$. As a general statement, inflation expectations may be written as a function of two variables, past inflation, $\hat{p}_{-1}$, and an anchored or given level of inflation, $\hat{\bar{p}}$. This gives rise to equation 7:

$$\hat{p}^e = \beta\hat{p}_{-1} + (1 - \beta)\hat{\bar{p}} \tag{7}$$

Blanchard then distinguishes three cases. The traditional downward-sloping Phillips

[4]It is well-known that the OECD have advocated for enhanced flexibility in labour markets to reduce unemployment rates, ever since the early 1980s, but more so in their famous 1994 strategic report (OECD 1994). See Evans and Spriggs (2022) for a detailed analysis of these OECD views and of their more recent recantation.

[5]Heterodox economists argue by contrast that in a recession, retraining won't be of much help. As the saying goes, training 100 dogs (workers) to better retrieve bones (jobs) won't make much of a difference in the aggregate if there are only 90 bones (jobs) out there.

[6]The equation is slightly different from the one that can be found in Blanchard (2021), because, once more, we do not assume here that $\lambda = 1$.

curve would correspond to the case, where $\beta = 0$, in which case equation 6 becomes equation 8:

$$\hat{p} = \hat{\bar{p}} + (\pi + z) - \alpha U = \hat{\bar{p}} + \alpha(U^* - U) \tag{8}$$

The equilibrium level of unemployment U^* which was defined by equation 5 through the WS-PS model now represents the rate of unemployment which is such that the actual rate of inflation is equal to the anchored level of inflation. Thus, $U^*$is not a NAIRU.

The second case is the general one, when $0 < \beta < 1$. Combining equations 6 and 7, and recalling the definition of the equilibrium rate of unemployment given by equation 5, we get:

$$\hat{p} = \beta\hat{p}_{-1} + (1 - \beta)\hat{\bar{p}} + \alpha(U^* - U) \tag{9}$$

An interesting specific case of this general case is when the rate of inflation gets stabilized, that is, when $\hat{p} = \hat{p}_{-1}$. This case is usually associated with a long-run Phillips curve. Here, however, we get once again a traditional downward-sloping Phillips curve, but a steeper one, as reflected by equation 10, when compared to equation 8. Once again, U^* is not a NAIRU.

$$\hat{p} = \hat{\bar{p}} + \alpha(U^* - U)/(1 - \beta) \tag{10}$$

The two curves illustrating equations 8 and 10 are shown in Figure 2. In both cases, the anchored expected level of inflation gets realized only when the rate of unemployment is equal to the equilibrium rate of unemployment identified through the WS-PS model.

Finally, we may consider the third case, the one where $\beta = 1$. Equation 9, then becomes:

$$\hat{p} - \hat{p}_{-1} = \Delta\hat{p} = \alpha(U^* - U) \tag{11}$$

Now we get the accelerationist Phillips curve, where the *change* in the rate of inflation depends on the level of the rate of unemployment, or more precisely on the discrepancy between the equilibrium rate of unemployment, as determined in the WS-PS model, and the actual rate of unemployment. This equilibrium rate of unemployment U^* is indeed a NAIRU. The inflation rate gets stabilized only when the actual rate of unemployment equates this NAIRU.

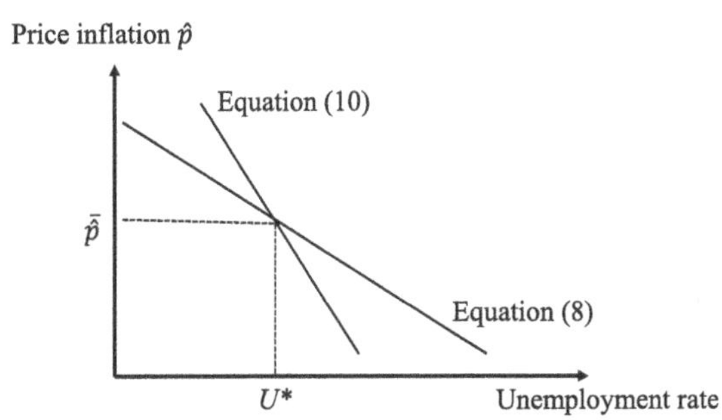

Figure 2. The Phillips curve with fully or partially anchored expectations.

Ever since the early 1990s, several central banks have announced an explicit inflation target $\hat{p}^T$ and have pursued interest rate targeting policies in order to achieve their targeted inflation rate. The top of Figure 3 represents the case when inflation expectations are totally unanchored, with the expected inflation rate for this period being equal to the inflation rate of the previous period. When the central bank announces an inflation target and sets its target (real) interest rate appropriately, the target inflation rate will eventually be achieved, once the actual rate of unemployment equates the NAIRU, as shown at the bottom of Figure 3. Carlin and Soskice (2015, pp. 90–91) provide a clear verbal and graphical explanation of how the economy will be brought back to the NAIRU, and back to the target inflation rate, by the interest rate policy of the central bank following an increase in aggregate demand.[7]

The accelerationist thesis, where the *change* in the inflation rate, instead of its *level*, depends on the rate of unemployment, transforms any attempt to lower the actual rate of unemployment below its natural rate into a futile exercise since it would only lead to an acceleration of the rate of inflation. Mainstream macroeconomic textbooks retain the accelerationist thesis, even those that do a good job in explaining how central banks set interest rates (Carlin and Soskice 2015; Milligan et al. 2023).

If expansionary policies are unable to reduce the NAIRU, what can be done to reduce permanently the rate of unemployment? The answer is implicitly imbedded in equations 5 and 5A. First, if the wage demands of workers react more strongly to an increase in the rate of unemployment, less of an increase in unemployment will be needed to bring the real wage target of workers towards that of firms and hence to bring the inflation rate towards the target of the central bank. This implies a lower α parameter. Second, if firms target a lower markup m or a lower profit share π, this will also help in generating a smaller NAIRU. This is an argument which is rarely heard, but which generated some attention in the case of the Covid inflation episode, associated with profit inflation. Third, as discussed in the previous section, a fall in the z parameter, associated with the imperfections and rigidities of the labour market, will also generate a lower NAIRU. Finally, an increase in labour productivity, following equation 5A, will achieve a reduction in the NAIRU. Central banks pretend that the best thing they can do is to make sure that inflation rates are low, because, so they claim, low inflation rates promote technical progress (Lavoie and Seccareccia 2021). There would thus be a virtuous circle: low inflation rates $\hat{p}$ generate high levels or high growth rates of productivity, which themselves lead to

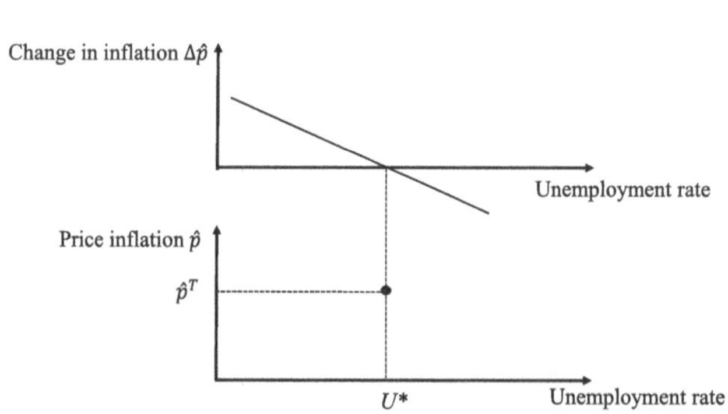

Figure 3. The accelerationist case with inflation targeting.

a lower natural rate of unemployment U^*. As is often the case in mainstream textbooks, this claim can be attributed to Milton Friedman (1977), and thus corresponds to a *positively-sloped* segment of the long-run Phillips curve, as still argued today by James Dorn (2020, p. 139)! The argument is that high inflation generates unpredictability and increased uncertainty, as the variability of price signals creates confusion in the minds of economic agents — an argument which is often associated with F.A. Hayek.[8]

3. The Heterodox Analysis of the Phillips Curve

3.1. Post-Keynesian Inflation Theory in a Nutshell

We now move towards a more specific heterodox view of the Phillips curve, based on post-Keynesian economics. Post-Keynesians believe that inflation is essentially the result of a conflict over income distribution. There are three main causes of inflation in post-Keynesian analysis. First, there is conflictual inflation arising from a conflict between workers and firms over the relative income shares. This part is very similar to the arguments of the WS-PS model, and several quotes have been provided in the introduction about this cause of inflation. There is real-wage resistance by workers (Hicks 1975), as labour unions find that the profit share is too high and unjust (Kaldor 1959). Within this framework, inflation can also be generated by the efforts of firms to raise their income share.[9]

Second, there is conflictual inflation arising from the comparison of wages relative to other wages: this is wage-wage inflation or relative wage inflation, tied to fairness relative to other workers and the desire to keep one's rank in the wage hierarchy. This can be found early on in the post-Keynesian literature, referring to Keynes (1936, p. 14), when he explained why workers were concerned with their nominal wage rate, arguing that it was rational for them to resist reductions in money wages, pointing out that 'the struggle about money-wages primarily affects the distribution of the aggregate real wage between different labour groups'. But it can also be found in Joan Robinson (1962, p. 70), when she says that 'the causes of movements in money wages are bound up with the competition of different groups of workers to maintain or improve their relative positions', as well as in Richard Kahn (1972, p. 142) who wrote that the main cause of inflation 'is the competitive struggle between trade unions and different sections of labour, exacerbated by the absence of an agreement about relative wages'. The salience of fairness in determining wage bargaining and its impact on wage inflation was long part of what we may refer to as the early industrial relations literature, with authors such as John Dunlop, Lloyds Reynold, Clark Kerr and Richard Lester, before the advent of the Phillips curve. It is at the heart of the book of Adrian Wood (1978).

---

[7]Post-Keynesians have long discussed within this framework the transition path back to the target inflation rate and the technical problems that may be encountered along the way (Lavoie 2004; Setterfield 2004).

[8]I have never understood why mainstream economists don't object to flexible exchange rates: one would have thought that fluctuations in import or export prices would also generate a lot of uncertainty in the minds of importers or producers of exports.

[9]There could be another source of conflict, that between rentiers and non-rentiers. Firms may raise their markup, and reduce real wages, to compensate, fully or in part, for higher (real) interest costs, as firms attempt to recover an entrepreneurial profit net of interest costs, as the Sraffians would put it. The pricing equation could then be:

$$p = (1 + m)(1 + i)(w/\lambda) \text{ or } p = (1 + m_0 + m_i i)(w/\lambda).$$

The implications for inflation and monetary policy are discussed in Hein and Stockhammer (2010).

Third, there is imported inflation, arising from the rise in the prices of raw materials, the prices of which are determined by supply and demand forces or by speculation on world markets. Imported inflation also arises from the depreciation of the domestic currency. So, what we have here is an international income share conflict. All in all, a trilateral conflict of interest exists between workers, industrialists, and raw materials producers (Reynolds 1987, p. 117).

Finally, leaving aside tax-push inflation, it should be emphasized that aggregate demand only plays a mitigated role in the current post-Keynesian analysis of inflation, at least compared to its role in mainstream economics. This is true regardless of how aggregate demand is being measured, whether it is its level, its rate of growth, the share of investment, the rate of capacity utilization or the rate of unemployment.[10] Thus, internal factors, besides changes in the value of the exchange rate, only have small effects on the domestic inflation rate. By contrast, aggregate demand at the world level may have substantial effects on the domestic inflation rate, because an increase in overall aggregate demand will increase the prices of raw materials and commodities on world markets. These price increases will then be transmitted to the various domestic economies through the cost channel. This was well explained by Kalecki when the made a distinction between demand-determined and cost-determined prices, a distinction which is at the heart of post-Keynesian economics.

> Generally speaking, changes in the prices of finished goods are 'cost-determined' while changes in the prices of raw materials inclusive of primary foodstuffs are 'demand-determined'. The prices of finished goods are affected, of course, by any 'demand-determined' changes in the prices of raw materials but it is through the channel of costs that this influence is transmitted ... The production of finished goods is elastic as a result of existing reserves of productive capacity. When demand increases it is met mainly by an increase in the volume of production while prices tend to remain stable ... The situation with respect to raw materials is different ... With supply inelastic in short periods, an increase in demand causes a diminution of stocks and a consequent increase in price. The initial price movement may be enhanced by the addition of a speculative element. The commodities in question are normally standardized and are subject to quotation at commodity exchanges. A primary rise in demand which causes an increase in prices is frequently accompanied by secondary speculative demand. (Kalecki 1971, pp. 43–44)

3.2. Conflictual Inflation in the Short Run

We shall now present a specification of the post-Keynesian conflicting-claims theory of inflation. The model that we are to present has some similarities with the preceding WS-PS model that was described in Section 2.1, most specifically when equations 3A and 5A are being used. In both the WS-PS model and the conflicting-claims inflation model, the real wage (or the wage share) is at the heart of the conflict between firms and employees.

The conflict arises because, on the one hand, workers would like to benefit from high real wages, while on the other hand, each firm would like to impose low real wages, thinking that this should lead to higher profits, even though, if all firms do the same, this is

[10]There is a small number of post-Keynesians, however, who have claimed in the past that if investment activity rose faster than consumption activity, this would lead to profit inflation in the consumption sector (Weintraub, Minsky, Graziani, and also Keynes's *Treatise on Money*). It was also said that a rise in the public deficit to GDP ratio would raise the price of consumption goods.

likely to lead to a fall in sales and employment in the aggregate, and hence possibly a fall in profits. The attempt by each of these two groups to increase its share of the cake can lead to wage and price increases. Inflation does not necessarily occur because of high economic activity or low unemployment; it results from a social conflict.

Here we present one of many possible formalizations of this view of inflation — a kind of generic representation of the post-Keynesian view. The representation obtained with the help of the following equations is thus a heterodox variant of the Phillips curve. The variables and parameters are the same as in the previous WS-PS model and its Phillips curve, with the explicit addition of the real wage, denoted by $\omega = (w/p)$, with ω_f and ω_w standing for the real wage targeted by firms and workers respectively, while ω is the actual real wage. As was the case with equation 3A, we assume that the rate of unemployment has a negative impact on the target real wage of workers (equation 12).[11] The μ and ψ_1 parameters represent the bargaining power of workers and firms respectively, that is, their ability to bring back the actual real wage towards their respective targeted real wage.

$$\omega_w = z - \alpha U \tag{12}$$

$$\hat{w} = \mu(\omega_w - \omega) + \beta \hat{p}_{-1} \tag{13A}$$

$$\hat{w} = \mu[(z - \alpha_1 U) - \omega] + \beta \hat{p}_{-1} \tag{13B}$$

$$\hat{p} = \psi_1(\omega - \omega_f) + \psi_2 \hat{w} \tag{14}$$

The main difference with the previous Phillips curve is that we have both a wage inflation equation and a price inflation equation, which depend on each other, and which respond to the discrepancies between the actual real wage and the targeted real wage. In addition, in contrast to the WS-PS model, there is no presumption that the actual real wage will adjust to the real wage targeted by firms. Another difference is that post-Keynesians prefer to argue that workers incorporate past inflation rates in their wage demands, rather than some hypothetical expected inflation rate, so that the variable $\hat{p}_{-1}$ is included in the wage inflation equation 13A. It is also assumed (temporarily) that price inflation only partially reflects wage inflation, through the term $\psi_2 \hat{w}$.[12] Both the positive $\psi_2 < 1$ and $\beta < 1$ parameters reflect the fact that neither firms nor workers have full indexation power, as wages and prices are changed at discrete intervals.[13] Indeed, whatever the specification, econometric studies show that the wage indexation parameter β is always much smaller than unity (Cunningham, Rai, and Hess 2019; Galí and Gambetti 2020). In order to keep the model simple despite the addition of the real wage, the growth rate of labour productivity has been omitted for now.

All else equal, if the realized real wage ω is lower than the targeted real wage of workers ω_w, this will lead to faster wage inflation. The parameter μ measures to what extent

[11] Hein (2023, p. 144) uses a form similar to equation 12, assuming that the target real wage of workers will be (positively) influenced by the rate employment.

[12] This implies that firms may face some constraints in setting prices, such as foreign competition. It may also arise from price lists that are published in advance, or from the heterogeneity in the unit costs of firms. (Tarling and Wilkinson 1985).

[13] See Taylor (1991, pp. 86–93), Godley and Cripps (1983, pp. 200–204) and Serrano (2019), who all emphasize that these indexation parameters depend on how often prices are being changed and how often wage contracts are being renegotiated.

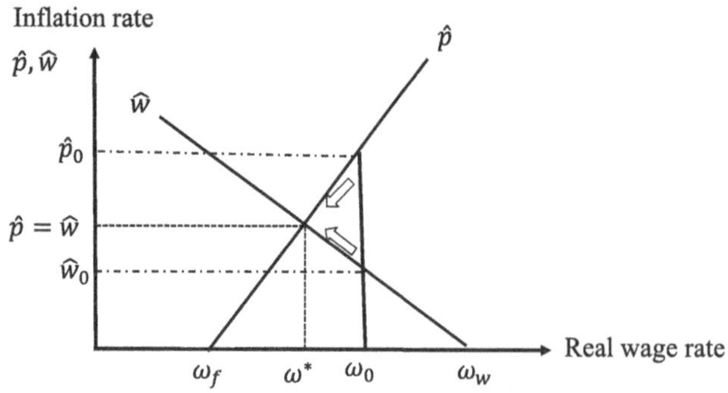

Figure 4. Conflictual inflation in the post-Keynesian approach.

workers dispose of sufficient bargaining power to obtain the increases in their nominal wage rate w which will get them closer to their real wage target. In a symmetric manner, equation 14 which describes price inflation also contains a target real wage for firms, denoted by ω_f. This target is equivalent to a targeted percentage markup or profit margin.[14] If the actual real wage turns out to be higher than their target, firms attempt to achieve their target by speeding up price inflation beyond wage inflation. If they succeed, this means that there is an increase in their profit margin.

Figure 4 above illustrates conflicting inflation in the general case. The wage inflation curve is downward sloping with respect to the actual real wage, while the price inflation curve is upward sloping. When the actual real wage is relatively high, price inflation will be higher than wage inflation, and vice-versa when the real wage is relatively low. In the case shown in the figure, with the starting real wage being ω_0, price inflation exceeds wage inflation and hence through time this will push down the real wage w/p. This process, all other things being equal, will eventually bring the wage inflation and price inflation rates equal to each other, with the real wage settling at $w/p = \omega^*$. After some manipulations, and assuming that $\hat{p} = \hat{p}_{-1}$ in the long run, we find that these two inflation rates will then be:

$$\hat{w} = \hat{p} = \frac{\mu\psi_1(\omega_w - \omega_f)}{\mu(1 - \psi_2) + \psi_1(1 - \beta)} \tag{15}$$

Obviously, in this setting, the inflation rate goes down to zero when the real wage target of workers is the same as the real wage target of firms. Thinking in terms of a Phillips curve, and thus combining equation 15 with equation 12, we find a downward-sloping Phillips curve, with a lower inflation rate being associated with a higher rate of unemployment.

3.3. Conflict Inflation with Firms Having the Upper Hand

We may consider some specific cases of conflict inflation. So far, we have assumed, realistically it seems, that firms only passthrough cost increases in a gradual way and not

[14]In other typical heterodox representations of conflictual inflation, the targets are sometimes expressed in terms of profit shares or wage shares.

instantaneously (Braga and Serrano 2023; Tarling and Wilkinson 1985). Let us now assume instead that firms have the ability to fully passthrough, or index, any wage increase, thus implying that the passthrough parameter ψ_2 in the equation 14 of price inflation is such that $\psi_2 = 1$.[15] What happens in the long run, with $\hat{p} = \hat{p}_{-1}$? Firms now have the last word when setting prices. As a consequence, in the long run, the realized real wage will become the real wage targeted by firms, so that $\omega = \omega_f$. This can be seen by recalling that in the long run $\hat{p} = \hat{w}$, so that the term $\psi_1(\omega - \omega_f)$ in the price inflation equation 14 needs to equal zero, thus implying that the actual real wage converges to the real wage target of firms. Substituting this value into equation 13A or 13B and still assuming that $\hat{p} = \hat{p}_{-1}$, we find that:

$$\hat{w} = \hat{p} = \frac{\mu(\omega_w - \omega_f)}{(1-\beta)} = \frac{\mu(z - \alpha U - \omega_f)}{(1-\beta)} \tag{16}$$

Alternatively, we can find equation 16 by starting from equation 15, and imbed the specific value $\psi_2 = 1$ into it. It is ever more obvious that inflation is the result of a conflict, which is proportional to the discrepancy between the target of firms and that of workers. We recover the standard downward-sloping Phillips curve, since the lower the rate of unemployment U, the higher the rate of inflation.

There is a second particular situation that should be of interest. Take the case where the central bank has a target inflation rate, which we denote by $\hat{p}^T$, and suppose that central bankers do everything to achieve it. Substituting this value for the price inflation rate on the left-hand side of equation 16, and solving for the rate of unemployment, we obtain the rate of unemployment that the central bank needs to impose in order to attain its inflation target:

$$U^T = \frac{\mu(z - \omega_f) - (1-\beta)\hat{p}^T}{\mu} \tag{17}$$

It follows that the lower the inflation target $\hat{p}^T$, the higher the actual rate of unemployment will need to be for the target to be achieved. In order to avoid such a bad result, one would need to hope that the austerity policies pursued by the central bank and possibly by the government would have induced workers to reduce the value of the z parameter, corresponding to the target real wage at zero unemployment, or the value of the indexation parameter β. A reduction in the bargaining power of workers is probably the situation since the 1990s, as a consequence of the high nominal and real interest rates that central banks imposed in the 1980s and 1990s and as a consequence of globalization. Or else, there would have to be a decrease in the profit margins of firms, as proxied by the ω_f parameter. The long-run situation when firms have the last word is illustrated with the help of Figure 5. An increase in the exogenous target of workers as given by z shifts the wage inflation curve upwards, while an increase in the rate of unemployment shifts this curve downwards, thus leading to a decrease in the equilibrium rate of inflation.

[15]This assumption is often found, implicitly or explicitly, in many models of conflictual inflation. Skott (2023, p. 8) also assumes that the actual real wage can be no different from the real wage target of firms. In his model, which he believes to be more plausible and consistent with new behavioural economics, workers gradually adjust their real wage target to the actual real wage, whatever the rate of unemployment. Blanchard (2023), in an online presentation, uses the same target adjustment process, as did Hein and Stockhammer (2010, p. 336) at some point.

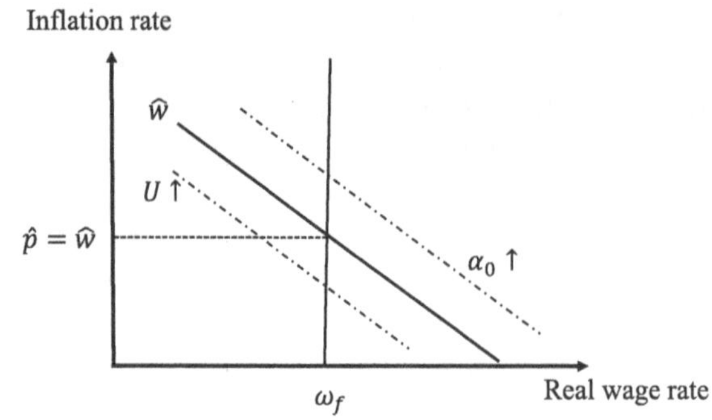

Figure 5. The conflicting-claims model of inflation when firms hold the upper-hand.

3.4. A Post-Keynesian NAIRU with Conflictual Inflation

While most post-Keynesians seem to adopt the specification of the inflation process presented in Sections 3.2 or 3.3, others, such as Hein (2006), propose an alternative specification of conflicting-claims inflation which generates a NAIRU, where a discrepancy between the actual rate of unemployment and this NAIRU generates unexpected inflation and changes in the actual rate of inflation, thus imbedding the acceleration thesis. Stockhammer (2008) argues that there does exist a NAIRU in post-Keynesian economics, pointing out, as we did here, the similarities between the WS-PS model of the New Keynesians and the income share targets found in the post-Keynesian theory of conflicting-claims inflation. This post-Keynesian NAIRU, however, from his standpoint and in contrast to the mainstream view, 'is neither exogenous nor is it a strong attractor for actual unemployment' (Stockhammer 2008, pp. 500–501). The mechanisms explaining why the NAIRU is more of an *attractee* than an attractor, and hence endogenous, modified by demand-side factors, are to be found in Hein and Stockhammer (2010) and Hein (2023).

Hein (2006) makes the clearest presentation of the post-Keynesian NAIRU. As was assumed in Section 3.3, Hein (2006) presumes that $\psi_2 = 1$ in the price inflation equation, and hence that firms have the power to achieve their target percentage markup and thus their target real wage. He assumes further that wages are fully indexed to past price inflation, so that the wage indexation parameter must be $\beta = 1$. This additional hypothesis implies that the inflation rate only gets stabilized when the triple equality $\omega_w = \omega_f = \omega$ is achieved, that is, when distributional conflict is eliminated. Stable inflation, with zero unexpected inflation, is achieved when the economy reaches a specific rate of unemployment — the dreaded NAIRU. Starting from equation 13B, since in the long run we need to have $\hat{w} = \hat{p}$, it implies that the first term of the equation needs to be zero, so that $\mu[(z - \alpha U) - \omega_f] = 0$. This heterodox NAIRU is thus equal to:

$$U^* = \frac{z - \omega_f}{\alpha} \tag{18}$$

Formally, it shows many similarities with the WS-PS model of Section Two, and this heterodox NAIRU is equivalent to the mainstream NAIRU defined by equation 5A. An equivalent NAIRU result is obtained by Hein (2023, p. 147), but in terms of a counterpart stable inflation rate of employment (SIRE).[16] As Braga and Serrano (2023, p. 1101) emphasize, Rowthorn (1977) or Hein (2006) can derive a conflictual inflation NAIRU because they assume that '(i) firms unilaterally have the power to fix the profit share on income; and at the same time (ii) workers always manage to incorporate the whole of expected inflation into their actual money increases'. Both extreme assumptions can be questioned, the first one because of the fact that firms set their prices on the basis of normal unit costs and rarely on actual unit costs, and the second one because while workers are likely to fully incorporate (past or expected) price inflation in their *desired* wage increases, they are in general unlikely to achieve the desired increases during the *actual* bargaining process (Summa and Braga 2020, p. 90). Furthermore, as argued earlier, there is much empirical evidence that the β parameter in the wage inflation equation is much smaller than unity.

3.5. Wage-Wage Inflation and Technical Progress

So far, for simplicity, we have left aside the possibility of wage-wage inflation and of productivity growth. Both of these issues are taken into account by Blecker and Setterfield (2019, pp. 215–218) and Lavoie (1992, pp. 414-417; 2022, pp. 616–618) in a conflictual inflation model. Targets must now be expressed in terms of wage shares or profit shares, because the increase in labour productivity implies changes in real wages.

The wage inflation equation must now take into account wage-wage inflation, which we shall denote by Ω_{ww}, whose value is higher when workers in different trades are more aware of their place in the wage hierarchy, as explained in Section 3.1. In addition, we assume that there is productivity-led inflation, meaning that workers incorporate within their wage demands a component related to the rate of growth of labour productivity, which we denote by $\hat{\lambda}$, with Ω_λ being the proportion of technical progress which is incorporated in the wage inflation equation. The notion of productivity-led inflation can also be related to Hicks (1955) but Amit Bhaduri has well explained its logic within the context of wage-wage inflation:

> Considerable empirical evidence now exists to suggest that higher money wage settlement may first take in those industries which are placed in particularly favourable economic circumstances. Thus, in industries with an exceptionally high growth in labour productivity… higher money wage settlements may take place first. Then comes into operation the 'propagation effect' of a *wage-wage spiral* which tries to restore the *relative* money wage structure. (Bhaduri 1986, p. 199)

The wage inflation equation may thus be written as:

$$\hat{w} = \mu(\omega_w - \omega) + \beta\hat{p}_{-1} + \Omega_{ww} + \Omega_\lambda\hat{\lambda} \tag{19}$$

where the ω now represent wage shares.

Similarly, we must take into account productivity growth in the price inflation equation. Firms may decline to pass on to prices part of the reduction in unit costs arising from productivity growth, so that only a proportion ψ_λ of the productivity gain will be

[16]There is what seems like an anomaly in the specification of the NAIRU found in Hein (2023). See the appendix.

passed on to consumers in the form of price reduction. The price inflation then becomes:

$$\hat{p} = \psi_1(\omega - \omega_f) + \psi_2\hat{w} - \psi_\lambda\hat{\lambda} \tag{20}$$

With technical progress, a constant wage share will require the equality $\hat{w} = \hat{p} + \hat{\lambda}$. Thus, in equilibrium, when in addition, $\hat{p} = \hat{p}_{-1}$, combining equations 19 and 20, we can find the equilibrium wage share:

$$\omega^* = \frac{(1-\psi_2)(\mu\omega_w + \Omega_{ww}) + (1-\beta)(\psi_1\omega_f) + \ [(1-\psi_2)(\Omega_\lambda - 1) + (1-\beta)(\psi_\lambda - \psi_2]\hat{\lambda}}{(1-\beta)\psi_1 + (1-\psi_2)\mu} \tag{21}$$

This is a rather awful-looking expression, hard to interpret. We can provide a simpler expression by omitting price and wage indexation, that is, by setting $\beta = \psi_2 = 0$. We then get a simpler equation yielding the equilibrium wage share:

$$\omega^* = \frac{(\mu\omega_w + \Omega_{ww}) + (\psi_1\omega_f) + \ [\Omega_\lambda - (1-\psi_\lambda)]\hat{\lambda}}{\psi_1 + \mu} \tag{21A}$$

The equilibrium wage share is a weighted average of the two wage share targets of firms and workers. Wage-wage inflation does have a positive impact on the wage share. In addition, we can see that the wage share is a positive function of the growth rate of labour productivity when workers manage to grab a higher proportion of productivity gains than the proportion of productivity gains that firms decline to pass on to consumers in the form of lower prices and hence wish to keep for themselves. This is what Robert Boyer (1988) calls a Fordist regime, presumably the regime that existed until the oil shocks of the 1970s. Otherwise, when the equilibrium wage share falls as a consequence of productivity gains, this is the anti-Fordist regime.

We can insert equation 21A into equation 20 (while still assuming $\Psi_2 = 0$) and find the impact of productivity gains on the long-run rate of price inflation. We get:

$$\hat{p}^* = \frac{\psi_1\mu(\omega_w - \omega_f) + \psi_1\Omega_{ww}) - \ [\mu\psi_\lambda + \psi_1(1-\Omega_\lambda)]\hat{\lambda}}{\psi_1 + \mu} \tag{22}$$

As before, the equilibrium level of price inflation depends on the discrepancy between the wage share targeted by workers and the wage share targeted by firms. It also depends on the extent of wage-wage inflation. And as one would expect, the negative effect of productivity growth on price inflation is a weighted sum of the proportion ψ_λ of the productivity gains that are passed on to consumers in the form of lower prices and of the proportion $(1 - \Omega_\lambda)$ of the productivity gains that are not incorporated in the wage demands of workers.[17] Figure 6 illustrates the equilibrium position of the economy when productivity growth is taken into consideration. As to the Phillips curve, not shown here, it would have its standard downward-sloping shape once we take into account in equation 22 the role of unemployment for the determination of the wage share targeted by workers, as shown in equation 12.

[17] There is a small mistake in equation (5.10) of Blecker and Setterfield (2019, p. 217), which pertains to measure the impact of productivity growth on price inflation.

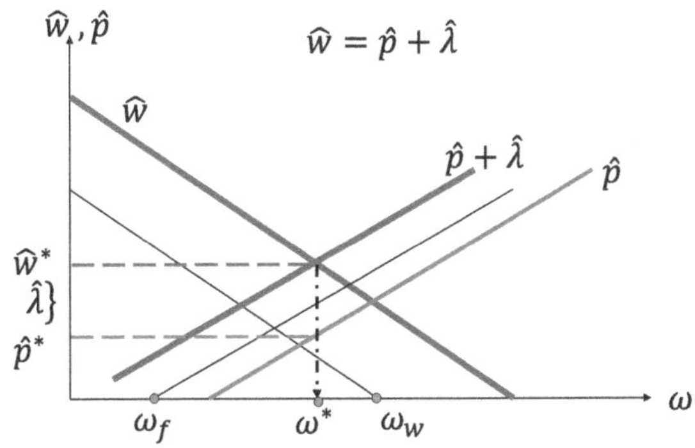

Figure 6. Inflation and productivity growth in the conflictual model.

3.6. Conflict Inflation in the Open Economy

So far, the discussion of conflictual inflation has been done implicitly within the context of a closed economy. Recent events, notably the Covid pandemic and the war in Ukraine, with their detrimental effects from lockdowns and bottlenecks in the supply chains of manufacturing and on agricultural and energy prices, with many of these commodities being imported, have reasserted the relevance of imported inflation.

This is consistent with the post-Keynesian view that the rate of inflation changes essentially for reasons that arise from the cost side, in particular, the prices of imported inputs and the world prices of commodities such as oil, and also when these are subjected to fluctuations in the exchange rate. As Philip Arestis and Malcolm Sawyer (2005, p. 959) point out for instance, 'inflationary pressures arise from, *inter alia*, conflict over income shares, and from cost elements, with the price of raw materials, especially oil, being the most important'. Conflictual inflation then also involves the evolution of the cost of imported goods, in particular imported materials, as Latin American economists know just too well.

How can we take into account the increase in unit costs caused by the breakdown in supply chains and the increase in the cost of imported inputs? We can rely on the formulation provided by Hein and Vogel (2008, p. 482) and inspired by Kalecki (1971, p. 62), writing out the price equation as:

$$p = (1 + m)(\frac{w}{\lambda} + ep_f v_m) \tag{23}$$

where e is the nominal exchange rate, p_f is the price of the imported goods in the foreign currency and v_m is the number of imported material inputs per unit of production. Calling j the aggregate cost of imported materials to the wage bill, so that:

$$j = \frac{ep_f v_m}{w/\lambda} \tag{24}$$

the price equation can be rewritten as:

$$p = (1 + m)(1 + j)\frac{w}{\lambda} \tag{25}$$

It follows that the real wage that firms would like to set would be equal to:

$$\frac{w}{p} = \omega_f = \frac{\lambda}{(1+m)(1+j)} \tag{26}$$

Thus, any increase in the cost of imported material cost beyond that of wages is bound to lead to a decrease in the target wage rate of firms and provoke, besides its direct effect on price inflation, an additional conflictual inflation. Workers will respond to their reduced real wages by attempting to catch up and raise wage inflation, along the lines of Section 3.1 and Figure 4. When the new equilibrium is being reached, the real wage (or the wage share) will be lower while inflation will be higher, all else being equal (that is, assuming no change in the rate of unemployment). Similar results can be achieved in a Sraffian open-economy two-sector model with conflicting claims (Morlin 2023).

3.7. A Flat Segment of the Phillips Curve

So far there has been no discussion of the values taken by the parameter α which represents the sensitivity of workers' demand for wage increases to changes in the rate of unemployment. The smaller the value of this parameter, the flatter will be the Phillips curve, whatever its specification. Ever since the 1990s, several authors of empirical studies have come to the conclusion that $\alpha \cong 0$, at least for a range of rates of unemployment. For instance, Peach, Rich, and Cororaton (2011) show in their empirical work that the Phillips curve has three segments: two exterior segments which have the standard negative (positive) relationship between inflation and unemployment (capacity utilization), and one interior segment where the Phillips curve is horizontal. As long as unemployment rates are neither very high or very low, they will have little or no effect on wage or price inflation. There is now a large number of empirical studies that show that the Phillips curve has considerably flattened out in several industrialized countries, as reported by Summa and Braga (2020).

While even some central bankers now consider the existence of a flat segment in the Phillips curve, from very early on post-Keynesian authors have considered or argued that there is a range of rates of unemployment or of rates of utilization such that the Phillips curve is flat (Hein (2006) and Kriesler and Lavoie (2007), among many others). Richard Lipsey (2016, p. 426), whose work in the early 1960s did so much to popularize the concept of the Phillips curve, also rejects the NAIRU and argues that there exists a flat segment, which he calls the non-inflationary band of unemployment, although he uses the acronym NAIBU.[18]

As James Forder (2014) shows in his book, until the 1960s, few economists believed in a stable relationship between inflation and unemployment. Indeed, several post-Keynesians denied the existence of any relationship between inflation and the level of economic activity, even at the pinnacle of monetarism. Cripps (1977, p. 110) wrote that 'the Phillips curve, whether in its original or its new form … [is] incomplete and misleading in modern conditions. Excess demand provides at most only a minor component of a comprehensive examination'. Similarly, Godley (1983, p. 170) affirmed that 'I do not accept

[18] Peter Skott (2023, p. 10) denies the relevance of a flat Phillips curve, claiming that empirical research shows otherwise.

that it is a foregone conclusion that inflation rates will be higher if unemployment is lower'. John Cornwall (1983, p. 74) argued that 'there are markets which never clear in the sense that situations of excess demand and supply do not generate wage and price changes of any kind .... This theory gives rise to horizontal short and long-run Phillips curves'.

How can one explain the horizontal segment? The most popular explanation, endorsed by heterodox economists and some mainstream ones, besides the fact that the unit direct cost of firms is constant over a large range of their rates of capacity utilization, is that the horizontal segment must be attributed to the institutional changes in the labour market, which arose from the fears generated by automation, free trade, liberalized capital movements and globalization (Setterfield 2007). These changes in behaviour gave rise to the missing deflation puzzle during the 2008 financial crisis and thereafter to the missing inflation puzzle when rates of unemployment plummeted.[19] As Ratner and Sim (2022, p. 2) put it, 'the "missing inflation" puzzle is due to a collapse of workers' bargaining power'.

4. Conclusion

The main purpose of the paper has been to respond to the present revival in the theory of conflictual inflation. It attempts to provide a pedagogical guide, showing the tight similarities between conflictual inflation as presented on the one hand by some mainstream authors within the framework of the WS-PS model and on the other hand the conflicting-claims approach of post-Keynesian analysis, while also acknowledging their differences. Among other things, the paper has shown the difficulties that analysts meet when they try to justify the existence of a NAIRU, in particular as shown in the appendix. The paper considers also the specific case when firms hold the upper hand in the bargaining process, and it discusses the impact of productivity growth on both the wage share and the rate of inflation. The paper also shows the implications for conflictual inflation of taking into account imported inflation due to the increase in the prices of imported raw materials and intermediate goods. This last issue has been of considerable interest over the last couple of years, with much talk about sellers' inflation or profit inflation.

Acknowledgements

The article benefitted from the very useful comments of the two referees of the journal, as well as those of Franklin Serrano. All possible controversial statements remain mine.

Disclosure Statement

No potential conflict of interest was reported by the author(s).

[19]A flatter Phillips curve also implies, unfortunately, that large increases in the rate of unemployment will be required before the central bank can succeed in reducing the inflation rate, if the above-target inflation rate is due to high economic activity.

ORCID

Marc Lavoie http://orcid.org/0000-0002-9942-1803

References

Arestis, P., and M. Sawyer. 2005. 'Aggregate Demand, Conflict and Capacity in the Inflationary Process.' *Cambridge Journal of Economics* 29 (6): 959–974.
Bhaduri, A. 1986. *Macroeconomics: The Dynamics of Commodity Production.* Armonk: M.E. Sharpe.
Blanchard, O. 2021. *Macroeconomics.* 8th ed. Upper Saddle River, NJ: Pearson.
Blanchard, O. 2022. https://twitter.com/ojblanchard1/status/1608967176232525824?lang=fr.
Blanchard, O. 2023. 'The inflation Burst: An (Anticipatory) Autopsy.' Paris School of Economics. https://www.youtube.com/watch?v=krV3uGBSbgc.
Blanchard, O., and E. Brancaccio. 2019. 'Crisis and Revolution in Economic Theory and Policy: A Debate.' *Review of Political Economy* 31 (2): 271–287.
Blanchard, O., and A. Melino. 1999. *Macroeconomics.* 1st Canadian ed. Scarborough: Prentice-Hall.
Blecker, R., and M. Setterfield. 2019. *Heterodox Macroeconomics: Models of Demand, Distribution and Growth.* Cheltenham: Edward Elgar.
Boyer, R. 1988. 'Formalizing Growth Regimes.' In *Technical Change and Economic Theory*, edited by G. Dosi, C. Freeman, R. Nelson, G. Silverberg, and L. Soete. New York: Pinter.
Braga, J., and F. Serrano. 2023. 'Post-Keynesian Economics: New Foundations by Marc Lavoie Chapter 8: Inflation Theory.' *Review of Political Economy* 35 (4): 1096–1108.
Burdekin, R. C. K., and P. Burkett. 1996. *Distributional Conflict and Inflation: Theoretical and Historical Perspectives.* London: Palgrave Macmillan.
Carlin, W., and D. Soskice. 2015. *Macroeconomics: Institutions, Instability, and the Financial System.* Oxford: Oxford University Press.
Cripps, F. 1977. 'The Money Supply, Wages and Inflation.' *Cambridge Journal of Economics* 1 (1): 101–112.
Cripps, F., and W. Godley. 1976. 'A Formal Analysis of the Cambridge Economic Policy Group Model.' *Economica* 43 (November): 335–348.
Cornwall, J. 1983. *The Conditions for Economics Recovery.* Oxford: Martin Robertson.
Cunningham, R., V. Rai, and K. Hess. 2019. 'Exploring Wage Phillips Curves in Advanced Economies.' Bank of Canada Staff Discussion Paper 2019-8.
Dalziel, P. C. 1990. 'Market Power, Inflation, and Incomes Policy.' *Journal of Post Keynesian Economics* 12 (3): 424–438.
Davidson, P. 1972. *Money and the Real World.* London: Macmillan.
Dorn, J. A. 2020. 'The Phillips Curve: A Poor Guide for Monetary Policy.' *Cato Journal* 40 (1): 133–150.
Dutt, A. K. 1987. 'Alternative Closures Again – A Comment on "Growth, Distribution and inflation".' *Cambridge Journal of Economics* 11 (1): 75–82.
Dutt, A. K. 1990. *Growth, Distribution and Uneven Development.* Cambridge: Cambridge University Press.
Eichner, A. S., and J. A. Kregel. 1975. 'An Essay on Post-Keynesian Theory: A New Paradigm in Economics.' *Journal of Economic Literature* 13 (4): 1293–1311.
Evans, J., and W. W. Spriggs. 2022. 'The Great Reversal.' Economic Policy Institute. https://www.epi.org/unequalpower/publications/workers-and-economists-oecd/.
Forder, J. 2014. *Macroeconomics and the Phillips Curve.* Oxford: Oxford University Press.
Friedman, M. 1977. 'Inflation and Unemployment.' *Journal of Political Economy* 85 (3): 451–472.
Galí, J., and L. Gambetti. 2020. 'Has the U.S. Wage Phillips Curve Flattened? A Semi-Structural Exploration.' In *Changing Inflation Dynamics, Evolving Monetary Policy*, edited by G. Castex, L. Galí, and D. Saravia. Santiago: Banco Central de Chile.
Godley, W. 1983. 'Keynes and the Management of Real National Income and Expenditure.' In *Keynes and the Modern World*, edited by D. Worswick and J. Trevithick. Cambridge: Cambridge University Press.

Godley, W., and F. Cripps. 1983. *Macroeconomics*. London: Fontana.

Hein, E. 2006. 'Wage Bargaining and Monetary Policy in a Kaleckian Monetary Distribution and Growth Model.' *Intervention: Journal of Economics* 3 (2): 305–330.

Hein, E. 2023. *Macroeconomics After Kalecki and Keynes: Post-Keynesian Foundations*. Cheltenham: Edward Elgar.

Hein, E., and E. Stockhammer. 2010. 'Macroeconomic Policy Mix, Employment and Inflation in a Post-Keynesian Alternative to the New Consensus Model.' *Review of Political Economy* 22 (3): 317–354.

Hein, E., and L. Vogel. 2008. 'Distribution and Growth Reconsidered: Empirical Results for Six OECD Countries.' *Cambridge Journal of Economics* 32 (3): 479–511.

Hicks, J. R. 1955. 'The Economic Foundations of Wage Policy.' *Economic Journal* 65 (259): 389–404.

Hicks, J. R. 1975. 'What Is Wrong with Monetarism?' *Lloyds Bank Review* (October): 1–13.

Kahn, R. F. 1972. 'Memorandum of Evidence Submitted to the Radcliffe Committee.' In *Selected Essays on Employment and Growth*, edited by R. F. Kahn. Cambridge: Cambridge University Press.

Kaldor, N. 1959. 'Economic Growth and the Problem of Inflation: Part 2.' *Economica* 26 (4): 287–298.

Kalecki, M. 1971. *Selected Essays on the Dynamics of the Capitalist Economy*. Cambridge: Cambridge University Press.

Keynes, J. M. 1936. *The General Theory of Employment, Interest, and Money*. London: Macmillan.

Kriesler, P., and M. Lavoie. 2007. 'The New View on Monetary Policy: The New Consensus and Its Post-Keynesian Critique.' *Review of Political Economics* 19 (3): 387–404.

Lavoie, M. 1992. *Foundations of Post-Keynesian Economic Analysis*. Aldershot: Edward Elgar.

Lavoie, M. 2004. 'The New Consensus on Monetary Policy Seen from a Post-Keynesian Perspective.' In *Central Banking in the Modern World: Alternative Perspectives*, edited by M. Lavoie and M. Seccareccia. Cheltenham: Edward Elgar.

Lavoie, M. 2022. *Post-Keynesian Economics: New Foundations*. 2nd ed. Cheltenham: Edward Elgar.

Lavoie, M., and L.-P. Rochon. 2023. 'Olivier Blanchard and Inflation.' https://medium.com/@monetarypolicyinstitute/olivier-blanchard-and-inflation-219f195125fe.

Lavoie, M., and M. Seccareccia. 2021. 'Going Beyond the Inflation Targeting Mantra: A Dual Mandate.' https://www.mcgill.ca/maxbellschool/files/maxbellschool/7_lavoie_0.pdf.

Layard, R., S. Nickell, and R. Jackman. 1991. *The Unemployment Crisis*. Oxford: Oxford University Press.

Lipsey, R. G. 2016. 'The Phillips Curve and an Assumed Unique Macroeconomic Equilibrium in Historical Context.' *Journal of the History of Economic Thought* 38 (4): 415–429.

Lorenzoni, G., and I. Werning. 2023. 'Conflict Inflation.' NBER, Working Paper 31099. http://www.nber.org/papers/w31099.

Milligan, K., P. Oreopoulos, B. Stevenson, and J. Wolfers. 2023. *Principles of Macroeconomics*. New York: Macmillan.

Morlin, G. S. 2023. 'Inflation and Conflicting Claims in the Open Economy.' *Review of Political Economy* 35 (3): 762–790.

OECD (Organization for Economic Cooperation and Development). 1994. 'The OECD Jobs Study: Facts, Analysis, and Strategy.' https://www.oecd.org/els/emp/1941679.pdf.

Peach, R., R. Rich, and A. Cororaton. 2011. 'How Does Slack Influence Inflation.' *Federal Reserve Bank of New York Current Issues in Economics and Finance* 17 (3): 1–7.

Ratner, D., and J. Sim. 2022. 'Who Killed the Phillips Curve? A Murder Mystery.' Federal Reserve Board, Finance and Economics Discussion Series 2022-028.

Reynolds, P. J. 1987. *Political Economy: A Synthesis of Kaleckian and Post Keynesian Economics*. Brighton: Wheatsheaf Books.

Robinson, J. 1956. *The Accumulation of Capital*. London: Macmillan.

Robinson, J. 1962. *Essays in the Theory of Economic Growth*. London: Macmillan.

Rowthorn, R. E. 1977. 'Conflict, Inflation and Money.' *Cambridge Journal of Economics* 1 (3): 215–239.

Serrano, F. 2019. 'Mind the Gaps: The Conflict Augmented Phillips Curve and the Sraffian Supermultiplier.' Discussion Paper 011/2019, Instituto de Economia, UFRJ.

Setterfield, M. 2004. 'Central banking, Stability and Macroeconomic Outcomes: A Comparison of New Consensus and Post-Keynesian Monetary Macroeconomics.' In *Central Banking in the Modern World: Alternative Perspectives*, edited by M. Lavoie and M. Seccareccia. Cheltenham: Edward Elgar.

Setterfield, M. 2007. 'The Rise, Decline and Rise of Income Policies in the US During the Post-War Era: Institutional-Analytical Explanation of Inflation and the Functional Distribution of Income.' *Journal of Institutional Economics* 3 (2): 127–146.

Skott, P. 2023. 'Phillips Curves, Behavioral Economics and Post-Keynesian Macroeconomics.' Working Paper 2/2023, Business School, Aalborg University.

Stockhammer, E. 2008. 'Is the NAIRU Theory a Monetarist, New Keynesian, Post Keynesian or a Marxist Theory?' *Metroeconomica* 59 (3): 479–510.

Summa, R., and J. Braga. 2020. 'Two routes Back to the Old Phillips Curve: The Amended Mainstream Model and the Conflict-Augmented Alternative.' *Bulletin of Political Economy* 14 (1): 81–115.

Tarling, R., and F. Wilkinson. 1982. 'Inflation and Unemployment – A Critique of Meade's Solutions.' *Economic Policy Review* 8 (2): 39–43.

Tarling, R., and F. Wilkinson. 1985. 'Mark-up Pricing, Inflation and Distributional Shares: A Note.' *Cambridge Journal of Economics* 9 (2): 179–185.

Taylor, L. 1985. 'A Stagnationist Model of Economic Growth.' *Cambridge Journal of Economics* 9 (4): 383–403.

Taylor, L. 1991. *Income Distribution, Inflation, and Growth: Lectures on Structuralist Macroeconomic Theory*. Cambridge, MA: MIT Press.

Tobin, J. 1981. 'Diagnosing Inflation: A Taxonomy.' In *Development in an Inflationary World*, edited by M. J. Flanders and A. Razin. Cambridge, MA: Academic Press.

Wood, A. 1978. *A Theory of Pay*. Cambridge: Cambridge University Press.

Appendix. Hein's (2023) wage and price equations[20]

In a section titled 'The Hein and Stockhammer approach', Hein (2023, p. 147) presents an alternative approach to the issue of conflictual inflation, which he contends to be based on 'plausible inflation expectations'. Using our own notations, but relying on the rate of employment e and his NAIRU-equivalent SIRE e^N, Hein starts with the wage inflation equation:

$$\hat{w} = \mu(e - e^N) + \hat{p}_{-1} \tag{A1}$$

Note that this implies that the indexation parameter is such that $\beta = 1$. He then contends that the price equation ought to be:

$$\hat{p} = \psi_2 \mu(e - e^N) + \hat{p}_{-1} \tag{A2}$$

This leads him to conclude that unexpected inflation $\hat{p}^u$, or the change in the inflation rate, is equal to the difference between actual employment and the SIRE, thus recovering the acceleration hypothesis:

$$\hat{p} - \hat{p}_{-1} = \hat{p}^u = \psi_2 \mu(e - e^N) \tag{A3}$$

But how does one move from A1 to A2? Normally, we would have $\hat{p} = \hat{w}$ if there is a full pass-through of unit wage costs to prices, or else $\hat{p} = \psi_2 \hat{w}$, but here we have neither. It is as if the partial

[20]This appendix is the result of an email exchange with Eckhard Hein and a longer email conversation with Franklin Serrano.

passthrough coefficient ψ_2 only concerns wage inflation arising from the current employment level and not increases in unit labour costs arising from historical factors (past inflation). Why would firms be able to fully incorporate into pricing wage increases when the increase is the same as those of the previous year, but not so when the increase in growth terms is bigger or smaller than in the previous year?

Assuming that $\hat{p} = \psi_2 \hat{w}$, we have instead of A2:

$$\hat{p} = \psi_2[\mu(e - e^N) + \hat{p}_{-1}] \tag{A4}$$

If the passthrough coefficient is such that $\psi_2 = 1$, we are back to a version of the accelerationist hypothesis, and e^N plays indeed a role equivalent to a NAIRU, since we then have:

$$\hat{p} - \hat{p}_{-1} = \hat{p}^u = \mu(e - e^N) \tag{A3'}$$

When the passthrough coefficient ψ_2 is smaller than unity, we get:

$$\hat{p} - \hat{p}_{-1} = \psi_2\mu(e - e^N) - (1 - \psi_2)\hat{p}_{-1} \tag{A4'}$$

And hence in the long run, where $\hat{p} = \hat{p}_{-1}$, this formalization produces a standard Phillips curve, where the *level* of inflation depends positively on the level of employment, as shown in the equation below and the accompanying figure.

$$\hat{p} = \frac{\psi_2\mu(e - e^N)}{1 - \psi_2}$$

There is no NAIRU or SIRE anymore. The variable e^N now only stands for the rate of employment that will generate zero inflation.

A curious feature of this specification of equation A4 with $0 < \psi_2 < 1$, as was pointed out to me by Serrano and Hein himself, is that wages grow faster than prices whenever the rate of employment e exceeds e^N (since $\hat{w} = \hat{p}/\psi_2$). With positive price inflation, real wages will keep rising; and reciprocally with price deflation, real wages will keep falling. Income distribution remains constant only with zero inflation. With this specification, e^N becomes instead a zero-inflation stable income distribution rate of employment, a ZISIDRE!

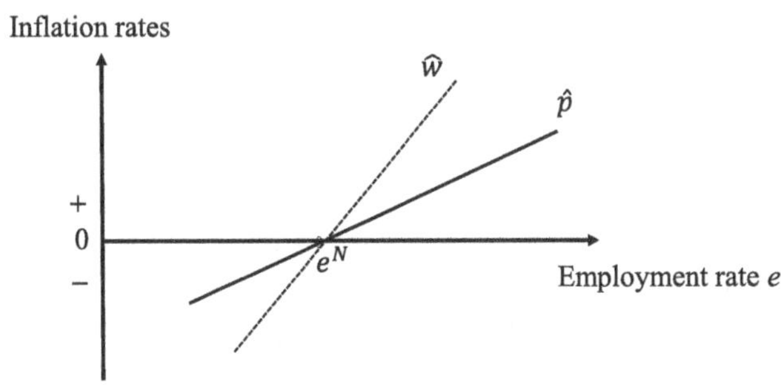

Figure A1. Hein's ZISIDRE.

Which Policies Against Inflation After Covid-19 and the War in Ukraine: The Italian Case

Luigi Salvati and Pasquale Tridico

ABSTRACT

The aftermath of the pandemic crisis and the war in Ukraine have revived the debate on the causes and consequences of inflation, as well as the policies needed to combat its effects. Despite the obvious absence of a role for monetary policy in triggering price rises, the response of monetary authorities, especially in the Eurozone, has been conventional: raising interest rates, with negative consequences for activity levels. In this paper we argue that the inflation episode we are witnessing is a consequence of the attempt by profit-makers to maintain the same (if not higher) levels of profitability as before. It is, therefore, a case of conflict inflation. The policies needed to avoid severe consequences for the weakest sections of the population should be aimed at compensating workers against the loss of purchasing power. In this context, Italy is a case study. It is one of the few advanced countries where there is no statutory minimum wage. Considering data from the main studies on the conditions of Italian workers and building our argument on the most recent economic theory, we stress the need for the introduction of a legal minimum wage in Italy and, in general, for upstream redistribution policies.

1. Introduction

The debate on inflation of the last few months, also thanks to the interventions of some world-renowned economists such as Blanchard, Stiglitz and Krugman, is dusting off some unorthodox interpretations in the explanation of the recent inflation dynamics.

Economic theory has long been divided on the origins of inflation, between those who defined it as a purely monetary phenomenon and those who define it as the result of a distributive conflict between firms, workers and, in some cases, the State itself, which, through the tax wedge affects wages and prices.

The evolution of economic theory over the last thirty years, as well as the definition of monetary policies and, in Europe, the behavior of the European Central Bank, seem to have essentially identified as possible only inflation as a monetary phenomenon, i.e., deriving from excess demand, linked to expansionary monetary policies, thus supporting the monetary origin of the wage-price inflationary spiral.

The idea of a wage-price spiral as one of the main causes of inflation, moreover, had been the main analysis in the 1980s in Italy and in other countries, where, with the indexation of wages to prices (the so-called 'Scala mobile'), the spiral was self-sustaining and inflation galloped, in some cases also favored by accommodating monetary policies.

The inflation rate in 2022 reached 11 per cent, both in Italy and in other EU countries, and in 2023 we are still around 6 per cent, but today the phenomenon seems to have different origins. First, during the Covid-19 pandemic, the various supply-side shocks accompanied by bottlenecks in different segments of the value chain and supply shortages caused temporary shortages that had an impact on the initial inflation increases. Subsequently, the energy crisis, following Russia's war of aggression in Ukraine, generated a significant increase in prices in the energy sector, which led to further increases in other productive sectors. And all this with monetary wages that have remained substantially unchanged, given the absence of automatic mechanisms for indexing wages to prices, especially as regards the energy component. This obviously triggers a distributive conflict, with rising prices and extra profits and stagnant wages.

In fact, the spiraling of inflation is determined, in this historical moment, by what we could call a 'price-price' factor, rather than by the wage-price spiral.

The energy sector, from which everything originated, in this new phase, is characterized by imperfect competition, in which companies mainly charge a mark-up on costs. In this sector, therefore, the increase in the cost of inputs in the initial phase was followed by a rise in prices which further increased prices in other sectors. The various regulatory interventions aimed at taxing extra profits started, in fact, from the observation that the profits of energy companies evidently operating in imperfect, monopolistic or oligopolistic competition, had increased beyond the levels considered normal. These increases in energy prices have determined the inflationary spiral and caused increases in other sectors that suffer direct or indirect consequences from the price of energy (transport, logistics, transformation, distribution chains, food sector, etc.).

In this article, we will focus on the economic policies necessary to contain inflation, with particular reference to the Italian case. We will summarize the main theories of inflation (Section Two). Subsequently (Section Three), we will analyze the most recent data on the behavior of inflation in Italy and we will underline that data, in our opinion, clearly highlight the unfoundedness of the vision of inflation as a monetary phenomenon or as a demand-led phenomenon. After focusing on the opportunity of the introduction of a statutory minimum wage in Italy and its consequences (Sections Four and Five), we conclude (Section Six) with suggestions for alternative policies compared to the indiscriminate increase in interest rates as a tool to fight inflation.

2. Explanations: monetary phenomenon or distributional conflict?

Among the theoretical tools used to explain the behavior of inflation, one of the most successful is undoubtedly the so-called Phillips curve. In its different incarnations, this theoretical apparatus is able to represent the different ways of depicting the relationship between inflation, unemployment and economic policies.

As is known, the Phillips curve describes the relationship between inflation and unemployment. Introduced by Phillips (1958), based on data from the United Kingdom for the period 1861–1957, the curve represents an empirical regularity describing a tradeoff between the unemployment rate and the rate of growth of money wages. Subsequently, Lipsey (1960), in an attempt to establish a theoretical model underlying the aforementioned relationship, suggested that the Phillips curve can be explained by the different bargaining positions of workers as unemployment varies: when the unemployment rate is low, workers are in a strong bargaining position to negotiate higher wages, which leads to an increase in prices and inflation. Samuelson and Solow (1960) confirm Phillips's conclusions using data from the United States and introduce what they call the 'modified Phillips curve' or 'price-level modification of the Phillips curve.' This refers to a decreasing relationship between the unemployment rate and the average annual increase in prices.

Friedman (1968) criticized the idea that there is a stable and long-term Phillips curve. He argued that inflation is primarily determined by monetary policy and that increases in inflation only result in a temporary increase in output and employment. To use his famous words (Friedman 1963), 'Inflation is always and everywhere a monetary phenomenon'. According to him, the expectations of workers and businesses adapt to monetary policies, nullifying the long-term tradeoff between inflation and unemployment.

As a result, in the presence of adaptive expectations (and, hence, of an 'expectations-augmented Phillips curve'), in the long run the Phillips curve can be described as a vertical line at the so-called natural unemployment rate. Phelps (1967) notoriously had reached similar conclusions.

In an even more extreme view, Lucas (1972, 1973) emphasized the importance of rational expectations in determining inflation and challenged the idea that economic policy can exploit a long-term Phillips curve. An expansionary monetary policy, even in the short term, will only increase inflation expectations and, therefore, will have no effect on the unemployment rate.

The verticalist view of the long-run Phillips curve has been prevalent for a long time. Until today, the textbook version states that in the long run, economic policy has no role in influencing the unemployment rate. Due to the operation of inflation expectations by economic agents, the unemployment rate cannot significantly deviate from the level defined by the NAIRU (Non-Accelerating Inflation Rate of Unemployment), a concept, introduced mainly by Modigliani and Papademos (1975) which gradually replaced the natural rate of unemployment, that can be defined as the rate of unemployment below which inflation is expected to rise. Monetary policy, therefore, can only affect the inflation rate. Inflation, in turn, is seen as primarily a monetary phenomenon.

The description of inflation as a symptom of distributive conflict has long been overlooked. Over time, several critical authors have emphasized the importance of distributive conflict in explaining inflation. For example, Rowthorn (1977) constructs a model in which inflation is nothing but the result of conflict between workers and capitalists. In his words (p. 224):

> The working class can shift distribution in its favour by fighting more vigorously for higher wages, although the cost of such militancy is a faster rate of inflation, as capitalists try, with only partial success, to protect themselves by raising prices. Likewise, capitalists can shift distribution in their favour by pursuing a more aggressive profits policy, but workers fight back, so that once again the rate of inflation rises. Thus wage militancy and an aggressive profits policy are both inflationary, but their effects on distribution are different. The former shifts distribution in favour of wages and the latter in favour of profits.[1]

[1] It should be emphasized that above a certain level of inflation, the NAIRU reappears in Rowthorn's model. In this case, expectations are fully met, but wage agreements take into full consideration future inflation. In other words, here inflation plays no role in determining distribution and, therefore, cannot be seen as genuine conflict-driven inflation.

Dutt (1992) also develops a model based on the idea of conflict inflation that takes into account the interactions between inflation, accumulation and distribution. In this model, workers demand a real wage that is an increasing function of the difference between their target real wage and the actual real wage. Firms, on the other hand, target a certain markup on prime costs and a certain ratio of desired investment to capital stock. The markup, in turn, abstracting from changes in technology, can be represented as an inverse function of the real wage, so that the variation in prices imposed by capitalists follows an opposite trend to the variation in real wages demanded by workers. Finally, the firm's target markup (and, therefore, their target real wage) is an increasing (decreasing, if one considers the real wage) function of the degree of capacity utilization.

On the same footing, Rosenberg and Weisskopf (1981), Stirati (2001) and Summa and Serrano (2018) present models which explain inflation as the result of inconsistent claims over the distribution of income between classes. Recently, Setterfield (2023) used a conflicting claims approach in order to disentangle the different effects of higher wages, supply shocks due to the pandemic crisis, and the price-setting behavior of firms. From a structuralist point of view, Kim (2023) also endorses conflict inflation. By using a dataset for 21 OECD countries over the past four decades, the author identifies a significant connection between inflation and structuralist variables, particularly labor share, and suggests that disinflation in the same period is primarily the result of less pronounced social conflict.

Although these authors can all be included in the post-Keynesian school of thought, it is important to note that interpretations of NAIRU are also diverse in the post-Keynesian world. The same NAIRU has also been used in contributions that see inflation as a class conflict, with NAIRU playing a decisive role. In this approach, NAIRU can be derived from the same assumptions underlying the conflict inflation theory (Lavoie 2022, chapter 8; Hein 2023, for example, supports such a compatibility). An idea that was already present in other contributions of the post-Keynesian school, such as, for example, in Stockhammer (2008), for whom 'the NAIRU model is consistent with the Post Keynesian theory of inflation in that inflation is caused by a real distributional conflict rather than by growth of the money supply'. This conclusion has been challenged by other members of the post-Keynesian school of thought (see, for example, Summa and Braga 2020; and Braga and Serrano 2023, who convincingly suggest that the existence of the NAIRU and the theory of inflation as the result of conflicting claims cannot be reconciled), but in our view, it has helped to bring the explanation of inflation as a phenomenon caused by distributional conflict back into the public debate.

The idea of inflation as a phenomenon arising from distributional conflict gained significant exposure on social media in late December 2022, when Olivier Blanchard, on Twitter, published a series of eight tweets, the first of which read: 'A point that is often lost in discussions of inflation and central bank policy. Inflation is fundamentally the outcome of the distributional conflict, between firms, workers, and taxpayers. It stops only when the various players are forced to accept the outcome'.[2]

As noted, however, by Galbraith (2023), while rejecting the explanation of inflation as a monetary phenomenon, Blanchard himself draws the conclusion that, in the absence of better tools, the task of taming inflation is left to central banks: 'But, in the end, forcing the players to accept the outcome, and thus stabilizing inflation, is typically left to the

[2]https://twitter.com/ojblanchard1/status/1608967176232525824.

central bank. By slowing down the economy, it can force firms to accept lower prices given wages, and workers to accept lower wages given prices'.[3]

Finally, it should be noted that within the post-Keynesian explanation of inflation as a consequence of distributional conflict, there are at least two different positions. The first is that the current inflation is a profit-led inflation (see, for example, Bivens 2022 and Weber and Wasner 2023). According to this view, although the pandemic and the war in Ukraine generated a first round of inflation, there would have been an additional effect arising from the fact that firms would have used their market power to increase mark-ups and, in this way, their profits, causing a temporary acceleration of inflation. The second position (supported, in particular, by Lavoie 2023; and Vernengo and Pérez Caldentey 2023) is that the increase in profits is not the cause of the acceleration of inflation, but that the economic recovery, thanks to the presence of overhead labor, and the increase in the price of intermediate goods, have led to an increase in the share of profits in income. The role of intermediate goods, combined with the dynamics of international trade and of the exchange rate, also plays a role in a recent contribution by Morlin (2023). Using open-economy price equations and adopting a classical-Keynesian theoretical framework, Morlin argues that an increase in the prices of imported intermediate goods (or a depreciation of the exchange rate) leads to higher costs and, consequently, higher prices. However, this is only part of the story. Indeed, there is also an increase in the prices of non-tradable goods. In the model, following a depreciation, there is a rise in the profit rate in the sector of tradable goods. Due to competition and, therefore, the tendency for profit rates to equalize across different sectors, the price of non-tradable goods also increases.

3. Inflation: Some Stylized Facts on the Origins of a Distributional Conflict. What Happened in Italy?

The chart in Figure 1 shows the trend of the HICP (Harmonized index of consumer prices) for the European Union, the Euro area and a few selected countries. Although with some differences in timing, it can be seen that as of the beginning of 2021, a substantial stability of consumer prices has given way to a sustained year-on-year increase. The increase in the index, originally due to the bottlenecks (Harding, Lindé, and Trabandt 2023; Schmitt-Grohé and Uribe 2022) that had been created in some sectors following the post-pandemic recovery, has been strengthened following the start of the Russian invasion of Ukraine, due to the pressures on energy raw materials. Between the end of 2022 and the beginning of 2023, the increase began to slow down and then give way to a reduction in the index, which, however, has not yet reached pre-Covid levels (except in Spain, where the decrease began earlier and was considerably faster).

The Phillips curve came back in several analysis, both in Europe and in US. For the Italian case, this is represented by Figure 2.

In an IMF paper that was widely reported in the media, Hansen, Toscani, and Zhou (2023) show that in the euro area, the decomposition of the consumption deflator reveals that in 2021–22, 45 per cent of price increases is due to profits, 40 per cent to import prices, 25 per cent to labor costs, while taxes had a negative impact, in reducing costs. Similar analyses and positions were also presented by the ECB.

[3]https://twitter.com/ojblanchard1/status/1608967186856701953.

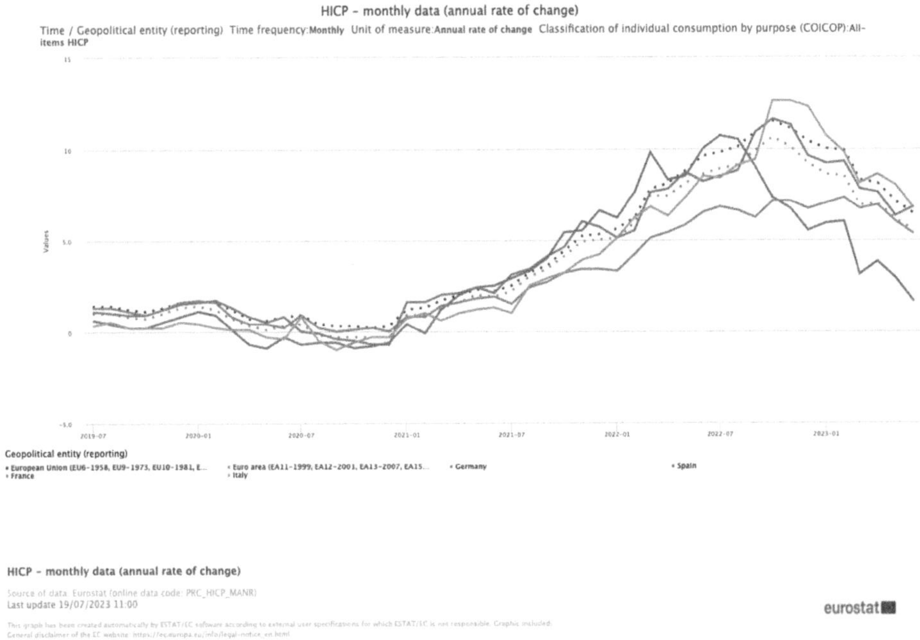

Figure 1. HICP — monthly data (annual rate of change) for EU, Eurozone and some selected European countries. Source: authors' elaboration based on eurostat data. Data for this figure can be retrieved at the following URL: https://ec.europa.eu/eurostat/databrowser/bookmark/1af4aa2b-c851-46ae-b238-91cb1e0f04fe?lang=en.

Inflation today is not only a result of increase of foreign energy prices: in fact, at domestic level, prices increase independently from energy, and is clear, for instance in the Italian case where the national statistical office (Istat) reports, once a year, also the increases of

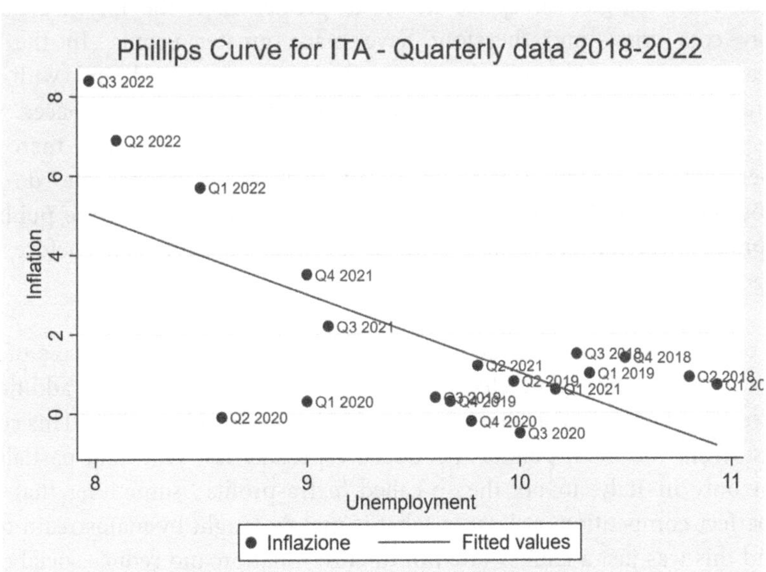

Figure 2. The Phillips curve for Italy. Source: authors' calculation on ISTAT data.

foreign energy prices and domestic energy prices. This case was evident when metalworking and firms' owners agreed on wage increases with the renewal of what is considered to be the best Italian national collective bargaining (metalworking agreement).

Inflation in May 2023 was 7.6 per cent. The incidence of energy prices was a minority, in fact inflation, net of them, was about one point less (6.2 per cent). While at the end of 2022 inflation had reached 11.6 per cent, achieving an average annual growth of 8.1 per cent, and energy prices accounted for more than 50 per cent.

Sitting at the table, all parties to the negotiation were surprised to register two phenomena.

(1) First, the inflation rate, calculated by Istat and used for the negotiations, i.e., the so-called IPCA-nei (the consumer price index excluding imported energy products), was equal to 6.6 per cent, only 1 point lower than the 'normal IPCA', which includes energy prices. This demonstrates that there is now in Italy as in other Eu countries a basic inflation that is not directly influenced by energy prices and means a loss of purchasing power on the part of workers, who are affected by decisions on prices, on all fundamental goods. Of course, energy goods are fundamental, but their increase found an explanation in the energy crisis following the war between Ukraine and Russia. On the other hand, the increase in prices, and not in money wages, resulting from the price-price spiral that has developed in the last two years, and which increased profit, is not consistent with a money-driven inflation. On the contrary conflict is prevailing, and since collective bargaining is weak (apart from the metalworking sector which managed to get an increase of +6.6 per cent, i.e., 123 euros per month on average) and wage indexation is not in place, profits increase.
(2) The second consideration which comes from the metalworking case is that Italian companies (as in other Eu countries according to the discourse of ECB) have had, unjustifiably, margins for price increases greater than the increase due to the energy cost crisis, and therefore have made greater profits. In the end, the increases made by the metalworkers, the most unionized and with the best contracts for workers, applies to around 1.5 million workers. Faced with this story, which ended in a positive way for the workers, however, there are over 70 per cent of workers, largely protected by worse contracts, who do not have ex-post safeguard clauses for the recovery of inflation, both in the public and in the private sectors, and remain with lower wages for 5/6 years before contracts being partially renewed.

It seems clear therefore that today inflation is not generated by an excess of demand. Instead, it is an inflation generated by a price-price factor, which, in addition to the initial coverage of energy costs, has caused profits to grow unjustifiably. This conclusion comes also from the main policy, introduced especially last year, and partially also in 2023, not only in Italy, to tax the so-called 'extra-profits', something that does not exist in perfect competition, at least in what is mainly taught by mainstream textbooks. At the end this was just a clumsy attempt to curb inflation and reduce social costs. The taxation of extra profits implies that prices have already increased, and an ('extra') taxation would be a further incentive for companies to increase prices and therefore pass taxation onto consumers, especially in the energy sector and in contiguous ones which often they are monopolistic in nature. On the contrary, an increase in prices should have been and could still be avoided through a cap-price on the goods of energy products for households.

In conclusion, the Italian case teaches us that continuing to keep money wages constant, in the face of rising prices, driven today only to a small extent by the cost of energy, and largely by a general increase in prices and therefore by profit, causes two problems: (1) a further impoverishment of workers, with an increase in inequalities between workers in protected sectors (few) and less protected (most) and (2) a depression of aggregate demand and therefore of economic growth, above all by virtue of increases interest rates by the ECB, evidently too much concerned about inflation and too little about the loss of purchasing power of workers and the recession. Also in this context, the minimum hourly wage, of which we will speak later, indexed to inflation, emerges as the decisive factor, as happens in other Eu countries such as Spain and Germany: not only as a protection against lower wages, but also, as a 'floor' for wage average growth above the minimum.

4. Would Italy Benefit from the Introduction of a Statutory Minimum Wage?

The extent of the phenomenon of in-work poverty in Italy is very large. In recent years there have been several attempts to develop policy instruments to reduce the incidence of such a phenomenon. In most cases, these have been income support instruments (especially in the form of minimum guaranteed income) accompanied by labor force activation mechanisms. These instruments, however, do not address what is one of the most evident features of the Italian labor market regulation: the absence of a legal minimum wage.

Of the 27 countries of the European Union, 22 have some form of legal minimum wage. Besides Italy, Austria, Denmark, Finland and Sweden do not have a statutory minimum wage. The amounts vary and reflect the conditions of the labor market, as well as the cost of living in different countries. For example, in Germany and the Netherlands, the gross monthly minimum wage (considering part-time and full-time workers) is approximately €2,000, while in France it is just under €1,750. In Spain and Slovenia, it is respectively €1,260 and approximately €1,200. The ratio to the median monthly gross amount of employee earnings is higher (between 60 and 70 per cent) in France, Portugal, Slovenia, and Romania. At lower levels (between 50 and 60 per cent) are countries such as Poland, Germany, Greece, Belgium, and the Netherlands. In Spain, the value is slightly below 45 per cent.[4]

In recent years, several bills for the introduction of a legal minimum wage have been tabled in the Italian Parliament. In some cases, they were proposed by political forces that were part of the parliamentary majority at the time. In others, by opposition parties. In no case, however, has the parliamentary discussion reached an advanced stage.

[4]These data were retrieved from the Eurostat website, in the "Statistics explained" section, page 'Minimum wage statistics' on September 18, 2023. URL of the page: https://ec.europa.eu/eurostat/statistics-explained/index.php?title=Minimum_wage_statistics.

The absence of a legal minimum wage implies that minimum wages are set, for the different sectors, through collective bargaining. This means that, as things stand, the introduction of a minimum wage law would affect two categories of workers. Firstly, workers not covered by collective bargaining. Secondly, those who, although covered by a collective agreement, are nevertheless (and by virtue of that agreement) paid less than a certain threshold value (which should be legally imposed).

The number of workers potentially affected by the introduction of a statutory minimum hourly wage, therefore, depends on two factors. The first is the amount of the minimum wage per hour worked. The second is the relevant definition of wage. More precisely, it is the set of wage components that, taken together, allow the statutory threshold to be reached. These include, for example, any additional monthly payments (such as 13th and 14th month), severance pay, and the employer's share of social security contributions.

The current political debate in Italy is focused on the need of a legal minimum wage. This is at least the proposal from the opposition to the Government, which fixes a legal minimum wage not below 9 euros (gross wage) per hour, and obviously leaves the trade unions free action to bargain collective agreements above that threshold.

In the last two years the wage issue in Italy has become particularly serious in light of inflation which came close to 12 per cent last year, and is around 6 per cent today, eroding around 15 per cent of the purchasing power of fixed income workers. This erosion comes in the aftermath of the pandemic crisis which had exacerbated inequalities and poverty. And it also comes after thirty years in which the average real wages of Italians decreased by 2.9 per cent between 1990 and 2020, a unique case in Europe (see Figure 3).

Over the last twenty years, however, the regulatory capacity of the National Collective bargain (CCNL in Italian) has been strongly weakened by both endogenous and exogenous factors. Not only has the 'anti-competitive' function of collective bargaining weakened, but in the worst cases, known as 'pirate bargaining', it has even been a harbinger of social dumping and law shopping, as highlighted by numerous economists and jurists (Garnero and Lucifora 2022). We increasingly observe a situation within which new trade unions and employers' organizations emerge with little or no representative capacity, signatories of downward collective bargaining agreements, the proliferation of pirate bargaining and the 'corporateisation' of employment relations. Today, in the absence of a law on union representation, INPS and CNEL register as many as more than 1000 CCNL in force, while 30 years ago were a little more less than 100. In light of this evolution, experts of labor market (and also some political parties) have rightly called for the need for a legal minimum wage, especially if integrated with collective bargaining.

As shown by the literature, the careful choice of the amount of the minimum wage is crucial for the success of the policy. A minimum wage that is too low would have negligible impacts on the labor market, but would risk not significantly improving the economic conditions of the weakest workers. On the contrary, an amount that is too high, although significantly improving the quality of life of the workers involved, risks having a negative impact on employment and the economic dynamics of companies. To consciously choose a minimum wage level, it is important to take advantage of the rich scientific literature on the subject, as well as European indications and comparisons.

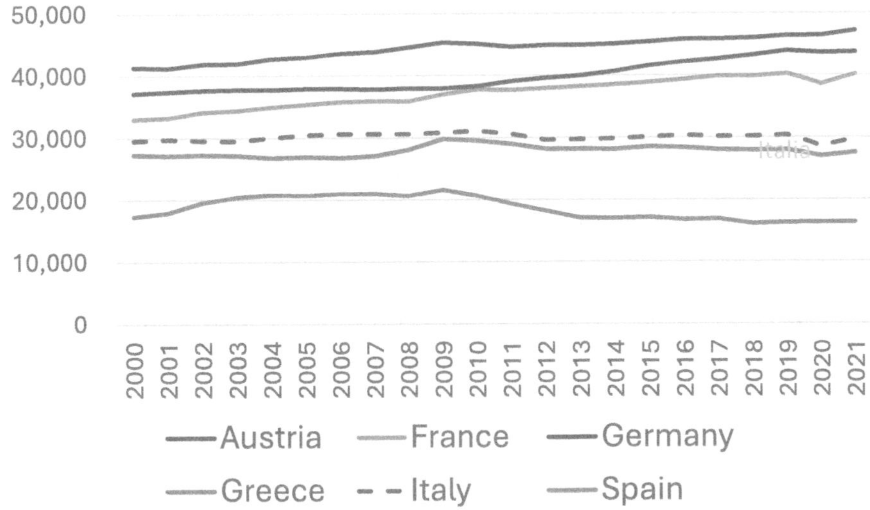

Figure 3. Average yearly wages, current prices 2000–2021. Source: OECD.

The proposal for a European directive on an adequate minimum wage was presented on 28 October last year, forming part of the initiatives planned under the 'European Pillar of Social Rights'. Among the reasons justifying the proposal there is certainly the European Union's desire to guarantee a wage that allows workers to live in dignity, as well as the fight against phenomena such as wage dumping and the promotion of gender equality.

At present, the minimum wage is decided by collective bargaining in 5 countries of the union, while in the remaining 22 it is provided for by law. However, many workers in the union do not benefit from this protection at the moment, and furthermore, the minimum level provided is often not adequate to guarantee a dignified lifestyle. International standards are used as objective evaluation criteria, which set the minimum level of adequacy as 60 per cent of the gross median salary or 50 per cent of the average gross salary.

However, the directive does not give direct indications on the method of quantifying the salary, but leaves individual states free to determine its value, taking into account their own socio-economic conditions.

Data on the hourly minimum wage amounts in force in Europe in July 2023 show an important separation between countries that record hourly minimum wage values around €10–12 (such as France, the Netherlands, Ireland, Belgium, Germany and the United Kingdom, and Luxembourg) and countries with low amounts, close to or less than €5, in Central and Eastern European countries, with Spain and Greece in the middle.[5]

In order to calculate the two adequacy parameters cited by the directive, if we consider for Italy the wages of the universe of full-time fixed-term workers (belonging to the non-agricultural private sector for the year 2022) it is determined that 50 per cent of median wages amount to €10.59, while 60 per cent of median wages amount to €7.65. These estimates are consistent with the proposals in the Italian Parliament for legal minimum wage values of €9.

[5]See https://ec.europa.eu/eurostat/statistics-explained/index.php?title=Minimum_wage_statistics#Minimum_wages_expressed_in_purchasing_power_standards for updated data. Data retrieved 13 Nov, 2023.

As regards the sectoral subdivision, there is a very wide variability of workers with hourly wages below 9 euro: starting from 1.8 per cent in the 'finance and insurance' sector and from 4.4 per cent in the 'information and communication' sector, 24.3 per cent for the 'accommodation and catering' sector and 35.5 per cent for 'other activities' in the services sector. The impact of the introduction of this rule would therefore have repercussions that will be very heterogeneous between the different sectors. However, considering the subdivision between the macro-regions, as regards employees, the incidence in percentage terms of the workers involved is higher in the south and in the islands (17.5 per cent), compared to the center (16.7 per cent) and the north (13.1 per cent). In total, 4.2 million workers would benefit from a legal minimum wage at 9 euros per hour, around 29 per cent of the Italian working force. Moreover, since the number of workers with hourly wage below 9 euro is higher in the South, the minimum wage could also become an instrument to reduce disparities among workers and among Italian regions.

Regarding demographic variables, the introduction of a minimum wage affects women more than men. Furthermore, if we compare part-time employees, who are often women, with full-time employees, we note that the incidence is much higher for the former (19.7 versus 12.7 per cent respectively). These data indicate that the instrument of introducing the minimum wage is effective for promoting gender equality, helping to close the pay and pension gap and helping women achieve economic independence. With reference to age groups, however, among private employees, the rule would have a greater impact on the young group (between 14 and 29 years) with 28.9 per cent, while the other groups show more limited effects, around 11–12 per cent.

Considering current high inflation pressure, the minimum wage, should be indexed to the inflation rate, at least to the one not including the energy price (HPCA). This would have also a positive effect on medium wages, which in the last 20 years, not only in Italy but widely speaking in the whole Eurozone, lost productivity gains, as the graph below shows. In the case of Italy, between 1995 and today productivity increased by 12 per cent on average, while wages did not increase at all (Figure 4).

Also to be considered positive are the impacts that that the introduction of a minimum wage would have on the increase in incomes of the workers involved (3.3 billion euro) and on public finances, (+1,5 billion),[6] in the case, for example, of a minimum wage of 9 euros, and with a significant increase in disposable income for families. For companies, net of dynamic effects, there would conversely be an increase in costs. In redistributive terms, a reduction in inequality would be achieved, calculated as the Gini index (−0.2 points), and a reduction in the frequency and intensity of poverty (−0.3 points and −1.4 points respectively).

Finally, the incidence of the share of workers that would be affected is inversely proportional to the size of the company itself. In fact, for small businesses, under fifteen employees, the incidence settles at around 20 per cent, and then gradually decreases as the number of employees increases, reaching the minimum incidence, around 10.2 per cent, for businesses with more of two hundred employees.

[6]These estimates are taken from the 19th INPS (INPS 2021, p. 242).

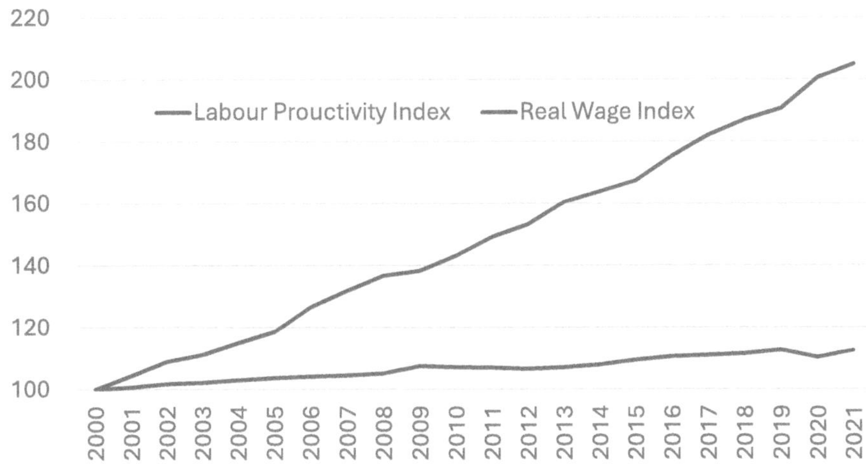

Figure 4. Wage and productivity in the Eurozone 2000–2021. Real wage index (2021 Constant prices and NCU) is a weighted average (by population) of the national index of the following countries: Austria, Belgium, Estonia, Finland, France, Germany, Greece, Ireland, Italy, Latvia, Lituania, Luxembourg, Netherlands, Portugal, Slovenia, Spain.

5. What Does the Economic Literature Suggest on the Impact of the Introduction of the Minimum Wage?

There is now a large literature on the effects of the minimum wage, since the first introduction of this economic policy instrument in the United States in 1938 by President Roosevelt, with the aim of ensuring that 'no economic activity that survives by paying wages below at the subsistence level has any right to continue to exist in this country. […] And by subsistence level I do not mean "mere" subsistence – I mean a wage adequate for a decent living' (1933, Statement on National Industrial Recovery Act). Several economists report a neutral or positive employment impact of the introduction and increases in the minimum wage in the USA (Card and Krueger 1994) and the United Kingdom (de Linde Leonard, Stanley, and Doucouliagos 2014; Dolton, Bondibene, and Wadsworth 2010; Stewart 2004). In Germany, which has a consolidated bargaining tradition, the introduction of the minimum wage in 2015 is added to the bargaining system and has had neither a crowding-out effect on union bargaining nor a negative employment impact. It had a positive effect on the incomes of around 20 per cent of the workers who were involved. Some economists have instead found a reallocation effect of workers, previously paid wages below the minimum wage threshold, towards high-wage companies, and jobs are not destroyed but upgraded. Finally, in China the introduction of the minimum wage in 2004 increased the labor costs of companies but at the same time raised their productivity, and in Hungary, in 2001, the increase in the minimum wage from 35 per cent to around 60 per cent of the median wage had minimal effects on employment, had an increase in prices (in sectors not open to international trade), and a limited reduction in profits.

Various works have shown how company prices represent one of the margins for adjustment, especially in sectors such as catering, logistics and commerce: around 80 per cent of the increase in the minimum wage was absorbed by an increase in prices.

Similar estimates are provided by the analysis accompanying the directive in question at a European level, where it is expected that approximately 75 per cent of the economic costs of the introduction of the minimum wage will be passed on to consumers. This suggests that the introduction of the minimum wage also entails a redistributive effect: while the increase in the minimum wage has an impact on the wages of low-income workers, and does not produce unemployment, the economic cost of such policies is borne by the whole of consumers, and not of businesses.

Another factor to consider is the impact on productivity dynamics. Several economists show an increase in hourly sales, with effects concentrated precisely on the contribution of low-productivity workers in the USA. Similarly, for firms in the UK, we find evidence of an increase in the firm's total factor productivity. Another element is the increase in the reallocation of workers towards large, high-wage companies, typically characterized by high productivity. On the other hand, as argued by an important Italian economist, Sylos Labini, low wages stimulate labor intensive investments, with low technological content and drivers of low productivity (Sylos Labini 1993; 1999). Conversely, higher wages can stimulate capital intensive investments, accelerate consumption dynamics and therefore restart aggregate demand and labor productivity. Furthermore, low wages are often accompanied by insecurity and poor incentives for employees, leading to a decrease in workers' commitment and therefore efficiency in the workplace.

The recent increases in inequality, both functional (between capital and labor) and interpersonal (captured by the Gini index), probably have their origins not only in the poor dynamics of productivity — heavily attributed to Italy in any comparison with other countries and economies — but also in a socially inefficient allocation of productivity advantages. The empirically detected trend, from the 1980s onwards, of a reduction in the wage share of GDP highlights a relatively new phenomenon that in the past many economists had excluded, instead affirming a certain constancy of the Capital/GDP and Wages/GDP ratios. This last ratio, the labor share, is decreasing not only in Italy but in all advanced countries. In this context, much economic evidence demonstrates that higher wages, and not lower wages, at least in the more advanced economies, would be functional to a positive productivity dynamic, because they would act as a stimulus for capital intensive investments and because they would trigger the distributive levers of growth through the expansion of aggregate demand.

6. Conclusions

Current inflation, as discussed in this paper, appears as a distributive conflict phenomenon rather than a monetary phenomenon. If restrictive monetary policy, wrongly, takes place, unemployment increases with further result to weaken the position of trade unions and workers and to reduce the bargained real wage to the level of the price-determined real wage, and a decrease of real wages occurs.

On the contrary, expansionary fiscal policies would support employment rate at higher level, and the possible costs of higher inflation, driven by wages, could be monitored with income policy and control prices along with tax wedge calibration. A minimum wage, in this context, indexed to inflation, appears even more necessary, to protect purchasing power of the lower part of income distribution, and to avoid further increases of poor workers.

In the case of Italy, the absence of a minimum wage, and the weakening of trade unions, allowed for a loss of purchasing power for 70 per cent of workers, mostly in the service sector, where bad collective contracts were not renewed in the last 5 years, and did not recover at all inflation increases. A different case took place in the metal working sector, where a better collective contract allows for an ex-post adjustment to inflation and a recover of purchasing power (for 1,5 million workers). The negotiations for this collective agreement also underlined the fact that increases in energy prices only explained a small part of the increase in inflation. Hence, if collective contracts are ineffective, not able to bargain wage increases, appropriate minimum levels and inflation recovery increases, as it is for most of workers in Italy, a minimum wage — indexed to inflation — appears to be a better policy. As highlighted by the literature, the introduction and increases of the minimum wage do not appear to have negative effects on employment. On the contrary, the minimum wage, serving as a tool to increase actual wages, helps support aggregate demand and reduce the incidence of the phenomenon of so-called working poor. Moreover, wage increases also have additional positive consequences for the economy: on one hand, they boost tax and contribution revenues, supporting the budgets of states and social security institutions; on the other hand, they encourage investments in new technologies, as described by the Sylos Labini effect.

Acknowledgements

(LS) This article was developed within the project funded by Next Generation EU — 'GRINS — Growing Resilient, INclusive and Sustainable' project (PE0000018), National Recovery and Resilience Plan (NRRP) — EP9 — Mission 4, C2, Intervention 1.3. The views and opinions expressed are only those of the authors and do not necessarily reflect those of the European Union or the European Commission. Neither the European Union nor the European Commission can be held responsible for them (LS and PT) The authors would like to thank the two anonymous referees who kindly reviewed the earlier version of this manuscript and provided valuable suggestions and comments.

Disclosure Statement

No potential conflict of interest was reported by the author(s).

References

Bivens, J. 2022. 'Corporate Profits Have Contributed Disproportionately to Inflation. How Should Policymakers Respond?' Economic Policy Institute, Working Economics Blog. https://www.epi.org/blog/corporate-profits-have-contributed-disproportionately-to-inflation-how-should-policymakers-respond/.

Braga, J., and F. Serrano. 2023. 'Post-Keynesian Economics: New Foundations by Marc Lavoie Chapter 8: Inflation Theory.' *Review of Political Economy*, 35 (4): 1–13.

Card, D., and A. B. Krueger. 1994. 'Minimum Wages and Employment: A Case Study of the Fast-Food Industry in New Jersey and Pennsylvania.' *American Economic Review* 84 (4): 772–793.

de Linde Leonard, M., T. D. Stanley, and H. Doucouliagos. 2014. 'Does the UK Minimum Wage Reduce Employment? A Meta-regression Analysis.' *British Journal of Industrial Relations* 52 (3): 499–520.

Dolton, P., C. R. Bondibene, and J. Wadsworth. 2010. 'The UK National Minimum Wage in Retrospect.' *Fiscal Studies* 31 (4): 509–534.

Dutt, A. K. 1992. 'Conflict Inflation, Distribution, Cyclical Accumulation and Crises.' *European Journal of Political Economy* 8 (4): 579–597.

Friedman, M. 1963. *Inflation: Causes and Consequences*. New York: Asia Publishing House.

Friedman, M. 1968. 'The Role of Monetary Policy.' *American Economic Review* 58 (1): 1–17.

Galbraith, J. 2023. 'Convergence on Conflict? Blanchard, Krugman, Summers and Inflation.' Monetary Policy Institute Blog, https://medium.com/@monetarypolicyinstitute/convergence-on-conflict-inflation-in-the-21st-century-7bccb7b6479.

Garnero, A., and C. Lucifora. 2022. 'Turning a "Blind Eye"? Compliance with Minimum Wage Standards and Employment.' *Economica*, 89 (356): 884–907.

Hansen, N., F. Toscani, and J. Zhou. 2023. 'The Role of Import Prices, Profits and Wages in the Current Inflation Episode in the Euro Area.' IMF Working Paper 23/131. International Monetary Fund.

Harding, M., J. Lindé, and M. Trabandt. 2023. 'Understanding Post-Covid Inflation Dynamics.' *Journal of Monetary Economics*. 140 (Supplement): S101–S118.

Hein, E. 2023. *Macroeconomics After Kalecki and Keynes: Post-Keynesian Foundations*. Cheltenham, UK, and Northampton, MA, USA: Edward Elgar Publishing.

INPS. 2021. 'XIX Rapporto Annuale.' https://www.inps.it/content/dam/inps-site/pdf/allegati/3415KEY-xix_rapporto_inps_31_10_2020_compressed.pdf.

Kim, H. 2023. 'Inflation in OECD Countries: An Empirical Assessment of a Structuralist Theory of Inflation.' *Review of Political Economy*, 1–25. https://doi.org/10.1080/09538259.2023.2171285

Lavoie, M. 2022. *Post-Keynesian Economics. New Foundations*. Cheltenham: Edward Elgar Publishing.

Lavoie, M. 2023. 'Some Controversies in the Causes of Post-Pandemic Inflation.' Monetary Policy Institute blog #77, May 14, https://medium.com/@monetarypolicyinstitute/some-controversies-in-the-causes-of-the-post-pandemic-inflation-1480a7a08eb7.

Lipsey, R. G. 1960. 'The Relation Between Unemployment and the Rate of Change of Money Wage Rates in the United Kingdom, 1862–1957: A Further Analysis.' *Economica* 27 (109): 1–19.

Lucas, R. E., Jr. 1972. 'Expectations and the Neutrality of Money.' *Journal of Economic Theory* 5 (2): 353–374.

Lucas, R. E., Jr. 1973. 'Some International Evidence on Output-Inflation Tradeoffs.' *The American Economic Review* 63 (3): 326–334.

Modigliani, F., and L. Papademos. 1975. 'Targets for Monetary Policy in the Coming Year.' *Brookings Papers on Economic Activity* 1975 (1): 141–165.

Morlin, G. S. 2023. 'Inflation and Conflicting Claims in the Open Economy.' *Review of Political Economy* 35 (3): 762–790.

Phelps, E. S. 1967. 'Phillips Curves, Expectations of Inflation and Optimal Unemployment Over Time.' *Economica* 34 (135): 254–281.

Phillips, A. W. 1958. 'The Relationship Between Unemployment and the Rate of Change of Money Wage Rates in the United Kingdom, 1861–1957.' *Economica* 25 (110): 283–299.

Rosenberg, S., and T. E. Weisskopf. 1981. 'A Conflict Theory Approach to Inflation in the Postwar U.S.' *Economy. American Economic Review* 71 (2): 42–47.

Rowthorn, R. E. 1977. 'Conflict, Inflation and Money.' *Cambdridge Journal of Economics* 3 (1): 215–239.

Samuelson, P. A., and R. M. Solow. 1960. 'Analytical Aspects of Anti-Inflation Policy.' *The American Economic Review* 50 (2): 177–194.

Schmitt-Grohé, S., and M. Uribe. 2022. 'What Do Long Data Tell Us About the Inflation Hike Post COVID-19 Pandemic?' (No. w30357). National Bureau of Economic Research.

Setterfield, M. 2023. 'Inflation and Distribution During the Post-COVID Recovery: A Kaleckian Approach.' *Journal of Post Keynesian Economics* 46 (4): 587–611.

Stewart, M. B. 2004. 'The Impact of the Introduction of the U.K. Minimum Wage on the Employment Probabilities of Low-Wage Workers.' *Journal of the European Economic Association* 2 (1): 67–97.

Stirati, A. 2001. 'Inflation, Unemployment and Hysteresis: An Alternative View.' *Review of Political Economy* 13 (4): 427–451.

Stockhammer, E. 2008. 'Is the NAIRU Theory a Monetarist, new Keynesian, Post Keynesian or a Marxist Theory?' *Metroeconomica* 59 (3): 479–510.

Summa, R., and J. Braga. 2020. 'Two Routes Back to the Old Phillips Curve: The Amended Mainstream Model and the Conflict-Augmented Alternative.' *Bulletin of Political Economy* 14 (1): 81–115.

Summa, R., and F. Serrano. 2018. 'Distribution and Conflict Inflation in Brazil Under Inflation Targeting, 1999–2014.' *Review of Radical Political Economics* 50 (2): 349–369.

Sylos Labini, P. 1993. *Progresso tecnico e sviluppo ciclico*. Roma-Bari: Laterza.

Sylos Labini, P. 1999. 'The Employment Issues: Investment, Flexibility and the Competition of Developing Countries.' *BNL Quarterly Review* 52 (210): 257–280.

Vernengo, M., and E. Pérez Caldentey. 2023. 'Price and Prejudice: Reflections on the Return of Inflation and Ideology.' *Review of Keynesian Economics* 11 (2): 129–146.

Weber, I. M., and E. Wasner. 2023. 'Sellers' Inflation, Profits and Conflict: Why Can Large Firms Hike Prices in an Emergency?' *Review of Keynesian Economics* 11 (2): 183–213.

Kaleckian Models of Conflict Inflation, Distribution and Employment: A Comparative Analysis

Eckhard Hein and Christoph Häusler

ABSTRACT

This paper conducts a systematic comparison of two main textbook variants within the Kaleckian tradition of post-Keynesian conflict inflation and distribution theory: the Blecker and Setterfield (2019) and Lavoie (1992; 2022) (BSL) model based on Dutt (1987), and the Hein (2023a) and Hein and Stockhammer (2011) (HS) model founded on Rowthorn (1977). Focusing on a basic closed economy framework sans government, we explore various iterations of each approach. Our analysis reveals that disparities chiefly centre around the treatment of price inflation expectations ('indexation') and the incorporation of bargaining power in wage- and price-inflation equations. BSL variants generally yield stable price Phillips curves, stable distribution and employment curves, and hence stable equilibria. Only the BSL-3 variant with complete indexation and complete pass-through generates shifting Phillips and employment curves, implying instability. It is thus similar to the HS-0 approach, which has bargaining power and complete indexation representing adaptive expectations in wage inflation and incomplete pass-through in price inflation. Introducing a workers' wage share target directly into the wage-inflation equation, but keeping full indexation/adaptive expectations in wage inflation and incomplete pass-through in price inflation, allows for stable and even flat Phillips curves, stable distribution and employment curves, and hence stable equilibria in the HS approach.

1. Introduction

In the post-Keynesian conflict theory of inflation, we can distinguish two basic traditions, the Keynes (1930 [1973]; 1936 [1973]), Kaldor (1955/56; 1957), Robinson (1956; 1962) and Marglin (1984) tradition, and the Kalecki (1954; 1971), Rowthorn (1977) and Dutt (1987) tradition. In each tradition, persistent inflation arises because of conflicting income claims, as Kaldor (1959) pointed out, and may then be modified by inflation expectations. In the basic closed economy model version, these conflicting claims are the capitalists' profit share claims and the workers' wage share claims. The first post-Keynesian inflation theory tradition assumes normal rates of capacity in long-run growth and flexible goods market prices.[1] Capitalists' profit share claims vary directly with excess demand in the goods market, while workers' wage share claims are determined by a constant conventional real wage, or they may vary with economic activity and capitalists' profits. The second tradition allows for variable rates of capacity utilisation beyond the short run; changes in demand thus cause changes in output and capacity utilisation.[2] Prices in oligopolistic or monopolistic industry and service sectors are set by firms following some cost-plus pricing strategy. Only in the primary sector with inelastic supply, changes in demand trigger changes in prices. Target profit shares of firms are thus mainly affected by those factors, which determine their cost-plus pricing in the goods market. In Kaleckian mark-up pricing on constant unit variable costs (Kalecki 1954, chs. 1–2; 1971, chs. 5–6), these are the degree of price competition, overhead costs and the bargaining power of trade unions. Furthermore, the ratio of unit raw material and semi-finished costs to unit direct wage costs and the sectoral composition of the economy matter for the economy-wide target profit share of firms.

In this Kalecki-Rowthorn-Dutt tradition, two prototype conflict inflation and distribution models for the closed economy without a government have been proposed.[3] The first is based on Dutt (1987), and can be found in the textbooks by Blecker and Setterfield (2019) and Lavoie (1992; 2022) (BSL). It derives stable upwards sloping wage and price Phillips curves and a stable profit-squeeze distribution curve. The second is based on Rowthorn (1977) and is incorporated in Hein and Stockhammer (2009; 2011) and Hein (2023a) (HS). Here, inflation and distribution are only constant at the employment rate providing consistent income claims, the stable inflation rate of employment (SIRE), while inconsistent claims generate changes in wage and price inflation, as well as in distribution, with potentially destabilising feedback effects on aggregate demand and employment.

Against the background of the increase in inflation since 2021, in the course of the recovery from the Covid-19 recession and the Russian war in Ukraine, post-Keynesian conflict approaches to explaining inflation have received some attention again.[4] On the one hand, several empirical/econometric papers have supported the conflict character of the rise in inflation, recently triggered by increasing energy prices and profit share claims of firms (i.e., Kim 2023; Matamaros 2023; Weber and Wasner 2023). On the other hand, several theoretical/conceptual contributions have applied post-Keynesian conflict theories in order to explain the simultaneous rise in inflation and profit shares observed since 2021. Lavoie (2024b), Matamaros (2023) and Setterfield (2023) have made use of some versions of the BSL approach for this purpose. Morlin (2023) has used a similar approach for an open economy applying a Classical-Keynesian two sector model.

---

[1]For presentations of the Kaldor-Robinson first generation post-Keynesian distribution and growth models, see Blecker and Setterfield (2019, ch. 3), Hein (2014, ch. 4), and Lavoie (2022, ch. 6), for example.

[2]For presentations of the Kalecki-Steindl post-Keynesian distribution and growth models, see Blecker and Setterfield (2019, ch. 4), Hein (2014, chs. 5–11), and Lavoie (2022, ch. 6).

[3]For open economy versions of the prototype models, see Lavoie (2022, ch. 8) and Hein (2023a, ch. 5). See also Bastian and Setterfield (2020), Blecker (2011), Sasaki et al. (2013), and Vera (2014).

[4]Also in some variants of orthodox economics, inflation has been modelled as conflict inflation. See, for example, the textbook presentations in Blanchard (2017) and Carlin and Soskice (2009, 2015), and recently Bernanke and Blanchard (2023) and Lorenzoni and Werning (2023). See Lavoie (2024a), Rowthorn (2024) and Summa and Braga (2020) for discussions and assessments.

Hein (2024) has provided a systematic comparison of the two traditions of post-Keynesian conflict inflation theory pointed out above, the Keynes-Kaldor-Robinson-Marglin and the Kalecki-Dutt-Rowthorn lines, and their implications for the analysis of the recent increase in inflation. For the latter tradition he has applied an open economy version of the HS model, because he finds the arguments in favour of incomplete indexation in particular in the wage inflation equation of the BSL approach, which is a condition for deriving stable Phillips and distribution curves in that approach, little convincing. He argues that in the BSL approach it remains unclear how power affects the different determinants in particular in the wage inflation equation in a coherent way.

Lavoie (2024a) has presented a comparison of mainstream and post-Keynesian models of conflict inflation and the Phillips curve. For the post-Keynesian approach, he is relying on different versions of the BSL model, and he is criticising the HS approach for presenting a special case in assuming complete indexation. Furthermore, he points out to an anomaly found in Hein (2023a, ch. 5).

Serrano et al. (2024) have agreed with Hein's (2023a) critique of the BSL approach regarding incomplete indexation in wage inflation, if understood as compensation for past losses in real wages or as representing inflation expectations. However, they are re-interpreting the indexation terms in wage and price inflation as referring to the frequencies of wage and price adjustment, in the tradition of Tarling and Wilkinson (1985), which are then taken to represent bargaining power. This allows them to generate different cases with stable wage and price Phillips curves, as well as distribution curves, as a rule, and inflation acceleration as a special case. However, also in their reformulation it remains unclear how targets are related to bargaining power, represented by the frequencies of wage and price setting, in a coherent way. How can workers' target real wages or wage shares exceed the prevailing values while the frequency of wage setting and hence bargaining power is low? Furthermore, uniquely relating bargaining power to the frequency of wage setting is difficult to apply to organised labour markets and wage bargaining systems, coordinated to different degrees, with longer-term collective wage contracts.

Therefore, although we see the merits of Serrano et al. (2024) in terms of clarifying some issues, we do not follow their approach but rather provide a systematic re-examination and comparison of BSL and HS approaches in the current paper. Similar to Serrano et al. (2024), we provide several variations starting from the two prototypes. But different from their approach, we assume for all cases that workers set nominal wages based on past period inflation, while firms then set prices based on current wage inflation. Furthermore, we will not only look at the inflation generating process, as in Serrano et al. (2024), but our model variants will also include the interaction with demand and thus employment generation. It will be seen that different results are based on the different ways income claims of capitalists and workers, as well as inflation expectations (indexation), are modelled in the wage- and price-inflation equations. Only slight variations in the specification of wage- and price-inflation equations can lead to different results regarding the Phillips curve, distribution curve, employment curve and the type of the respective (dis-)equilibria. The main contribution of this paper is thus didactic and pedagogic and should help to clarify the major differences between these approaches. Applying the different cases to historical situations is well beyond the scope of this exercise.

In what follows, in Section two, we present the foundations of each of the prototype approaches and the basic model assumptions for their comparison. Section three then presents the two prototypes, the BSL-0 and the HS-0 models. In Section four, we provide three variations of the BSL model, while Section five contains three variations of the HS model. Section six compares and assesses these variations, and it concludes.

2. Foundations of the Prototype Approaches and Basic Model Assumptions for Comparison

The BSL approach of modelling distribution conflict, inflation, distribution, and demand and employment in a post-Keynesian/Kaleckian framework is based on Dutt's (1987) critique of Marglin's (1984) model, which is in the Keynes, Kaldor and Robinson tradition. Dutt criticised Marglin's model for not allowing for variations in capacity utilisation and thus excluding the possibility of wage-led demand and growth by design. Dutt (1987) then provided the foundations for later, more elaborate work by Cassetti (2002; 2003), Dutt (1992), Palley (2007; 2012), Rochon and Setterfield (2007), Setterfield (2008; 2023), and others. The main features, distinguishing this approach from the alternative HS approach based on Rowthorn (1977), are that inflation expectations have no or only incomplete effects in the wage- and price-inflation equations of the models. Lavoie (1992, p. 393) calls this incomplete 'indexation'. Inconsistent claims generate constant inflation or deflation and constant functional distribution at any rate of employment. Consistent claims generate constant prices and hence zero inflation. Textbook versions of the BSL approach can be found in Blecker and Setterfield (2019, ch. 5) and Lavoie (1992, ch. 7, 2022, ch. 8).

The alternative HS approach of modelling inflation, distribution and employment is based on Rowthorn (1977). Similar approaches have then been used by Arestis and Sawyer (2005), Hein (2006), Hein and Stockhammer (2010), Lavoie (2006), Sawyer (2002), and Stockhammer (2008), for example. The main feature of this approach, as compared to the BSL variant, is the focus on adaptive inflation expectations of workers in the wage-inflation equation. Inconsistent distribution claims generate unexpected (or 'unanticipated' in Rowthorn 1977) (dis-)inflation and changes in distribution at any rate of employment.[5] Only with consistent claims, constant inflation and constant distribution are generated. There is hence always an inflation barrier, a 'non-accelerating inflation rate of unemployment' (NAIRU) or a 'stable inflation rate of employment' (SIRE). However, in this approach, although 'there is a NAIRU at any point in time, (...) it is neither exogenous nor is it a strong attractor for actual unemployment', as pointed out by Stockhammer (2008, pp. 500–501). The consistent claims equilibrium is endogenous to aggregate demand and to economic policies through various channels, endogenous aspirations, labour market persistence, capital stock, real interest rate, tax rate and real exchange rate and their effects on targets (Hein 2023a, ch. 5; Hein and Stockhammer 2010).

[5]Rowthorn (1977) distinguishes two regimes. In a very low inflation regime, inflation expectations do not matter for workers' nominal wage setting, and he obtains then the usual Phillips curve, as in the BSL variant. However, in a high(er) inflation regime, workers' inflation expectations matter, and Rowthorn then derives unanticipated inflation as a function of economic activity. The latter idea has been included into Hein (2023a, ch. 5), Hein and Stockhammer (2009, 2010, 2011) and Stockhammer (2008).

For the sake of comparing the two approaches and generating some variants, we assume a one good closed economy, in which, however, firms may be different and may operate with different technologies and labour productivities. This heterogeneity provides the grounds for nominal wage setting having an impact on income shares, as explained by Sylos-Labini (1979). With nominal wages rising, only firms with the highest productivity (growth) can fully pass wage increases to prices, while firms with lower productivity (growth) have to reduce the mark-up to remain price-competitive - the average industry mark-up thus falls. With nominal wages falling, the firms with lowest productivity (growth) have to fully pass this on to prices, while firms with higher productivity growth do not have to - the average industry mark-up rises. With heterogeneity in the firm sector, wage (dis-)inflation will thus only be partly passed through to price (dis-)inflation. A full pass-through (or indexation) would thus require a homogenous firm sector, ceteris paribus.

For all the model variants to be outlined below, we have workers' power determining their target wage share (Ω_W^T) depending on the structure of the labour market and the social benefit system (union density, wage bargaining coverage, wage bargaining co-ordination, employment protection legislation, minimum wages, unemployment benefits) and positively affected by the level of economic activity and hence the employment rate (e):[6]

$$\Omega_W^T = 1 - h_W^T = \Omega_0 + \Omega_1 e, \quad 1 > \Omega_0 > 0, \ \Omega_1 \geq 0 \tag{1}$$

with Ω_0 and Ω_1 representing the structural features of the labour market, the wage bargaining and the social benefits system.

The firms' target profit share (h_F^T) and thus their target wage share (Ω_F^T) is given by the constant mark-up in pricing, and thus, in a simple one good economy, by the structure of the goods market (degree of price competition) and the structural bargaining power of the trade unions, as well as by overhead costs, each affecting firms' power to set prices:

$$\Omega_F^T = 1 - h_F^T = 1 - h_0, \quad 1 > h_0 > 0 \tag{2}$$

For the wage and the price setting equations in each of the model variants, we assume that workers' current period nominal wage setting is affected by past period price inflation, indicating 'adaptive expectations' in the HS approach or 'indexation' in the BSL variant. Firms' price setting, however, will be affected by current period nominal wage inflation. It is thus assumed that workers set nominal wages at the beginning of the period, partly based on past period inflation, while firms then set prices partly based on current period wage inflation. This is different from what is assumed in Serrano et al. (2024) in their assessment of the BSL and HS approaches, where it is assumed that both workers and firms simultaneously set wages and prices based on price and wage inflation expected or indexed, and then the frequency of wage and price setting is viewed as an indicator of bargaining power.

[6]While Lavoie (1992, ch. 7, 2022, ch. 8) refrains from relating workers' target real wage rate or wage share to the employment rate and rather prefers the growth rate of the employment rate as a determinant, Blecker and Setterfield (2019, ch. 5.2.3) have the workers' targets affected by the level of economic activity. For the sake of comparability with the alternative approach, we follow their model in the short-run reformulation by Hein (2023a, ch. 5.2.1).

We also assume that there is neither coordination of wage bargaining among trade unions or employers nor coordination between wage setters and price setters in order to internalise macroeconomic externalities of wage and price setting. As shown in Hein and Stockhammer (2009; 2010; 2011) and Hein (2023a, ch. 6), for example, such wage bargaining coordination as part of post-Keynesian incomes policy could align workers' wage share targets with those of firms, make Phillips curves horizontal in some relevant range and prevent inflation rates from varying with employment rates.

We assume for all the model variants that a wage-led demand regime, as usually found in empirical research for domestic demand,[7] and, with constant labour productivity, therefore a wage-led employment regime prevails. Furthermore, in a monetary production economy with creditor–debtor relationships between rentiers and firms, real debt effects of unexpected inflation on aggregate demand and employment have to be taken into account. The effects will be expansionary if the 'normal case' conditions (Lavoie 1995) of real interest rate effects on aggregate demand and a 'debt burdened regime' prevail (Hein 2014, ch. 9), which we assume here. We can thus apply the following employment curve, with unexpected inflation being a determinant only in those model variants, which generate persistent unexpected inflation:

$$e = e(\Omega, \hat{p}^u), \quad \frac{\partial e}{\partial \Omega} > 0, \ \frac{\partial e}{\partial \hat{p}^u} > 0 \tag{3}$$

Based on these common elements, we can now distinguish the prototype BSL and HS models as we find them in the respective literature, as well as the respective modifications, according to the wage- and price-inflation equations applied, the inflation (Phillips) and distribution curves generated and the type of the derived (dis-)equilibria. We apply the same stepwise procedure for each model variant in this and the following sections. We start with wage- and price-inflation equations, derive the deviation of current period's wage and price inflation from past period's inflation, check whether these discrepancies will disappear and stable wage- and price-inflation curves emerge, discuss the changes in distribution and the feedbacks on the employment curve, and finally check whether stable equilibrium positions emerge. If unexpected inflation disappears, we will ignore the rightwards shifts of the employment curve caused by temporary unexpected inflation in order to keep the graphical presentations as simple as possible, because these shifts will not change the qualitative results.

3. The Two Prototype Textbook Models

3.1. The Prototype BSL Model: BSL-0

Following Blecker and Setterfield (2019, ch. 5.2.3) and Lavoie (1992, ch. 7; 2022, ch. 8), workers' current period's nominal wage inflation ($\hat{w}_t$) is determined by the deviation of past periods' wage share (Ω_{t-1}) from their target wage share and by past period inflation

[7]For empirical multi-country results on the distribution-led nature of demand and growth, making use of the structural or single equation estimation approach and finding wage-led demand results for domestic demand throughout, i.e., excluding the effect of distributional changes on net exports, see Hartwig (2014), Onaran and Galanis (2014) and Onaran and Obst (2016).

($\hat{p}_{t-1}$), which is assumed to be incompletely 'indexed' (Lavoie 2022, p. 601):

$$\begin{aligned}\hat{w}_t &= \varphi_1(\Omega_W^T - \Omega_{t-1}) + \varphi_2\hat{p}_{t-1}, \qquad \varphi_1 > 0, 1 > \varphi_2 \geq 0 \\ &= \varphi_1(\Omega_0 + \Omega_1 e - \Omega_{t-1}) + \varphi_2\hat{p}_{t-1}\end{aligned} \tag{4}$$

Short-run excess wage inflation ($\hat{w}_t^x$), the deviation of current wage inflation from expected and hence past period's price inflation, is given as.

$$\begin{aligned}w_t^x = \hat{w}_t - \hat{p}_{t-1} &= \varphi_1(\Omega_W^T - \Omega_{t-1}) - (1 - \varphi_2)\hat{p}_{t-1} \\ &= \varphi_1(\Omega_0 + \Omega_1 e - \Omega_{t-1}) - (1 - \varphi_2)\hat{p}_{t-1}\end{aligned} \tag{5}$$

Firms' price inflation is determined by the deviation of their target wage share from past period's wage share and by current wage inflation, which is assumed to be incompletely passed through to current price inflation, which would be in line with assuming heterogeneity in the firm sector, as explained above following Sylos Labini (1979):

$$\begin{aligned}\hat{p}_t &= \pi_1(\Omega_{t-1} - \Omega_F^T) + \pi_2\hat{w}_t, \qquad \pi_1 > 0, 1 > \pi_2 \geq 0 \\ &= \pi_1(\Omega_{t-1} - \Omega_F^T) + \pi_2[\varphi_1(\Omega_W^T - \Omega_{t-1}) + \varphi_2\hat{p}_{t-1}] \\ &= \pi_1(\Omega_{t-1} - 1 + h_0) + \pi_2[\varphi_1(\Omega_0 + \Omega_1 e - \Omega_{t-1}) + \varphi_2\hat{p}_{t-1}]\end{aligned} \tag{6}$$

The short-run change in inflation, which in an adaptive expectation framework can be called unexpected inflation ($\hat{p}_t^u$), is given as:

$$\begin{aligned}\hat{p}_t^u = \hat{p}_t - \hat{p}_{t-1} &= \pi_1(\Omega_{t-1} - \Omega_F^T) + \pi_2\varphi_1(\Omega_W^T - \Omega_{t-1}) - (1 - \pi_2\varphi_2)\hat{p}_{t-1} \\ &= \pi_1(\Omega_{t-1} - 1 + h_0) + \pi_2\varphi_1(\Omega_0 + \Omega_1 e - \Omega_{t-1}) - (1 - \pi_2\varphi_2)\hat{p}_{t-1}\end{aligned} \tag{7}$$

Since $\pi_2, \varphi_2 < 1$, short-run changes in inflation rates will disappear ($\hat{p}_t^u = \hat{p}_t - \hat{p}_{t-1} = 0$) after several periods, and from equations (4) and (6) we obtain for equilibrium price and wage inflation and the equilibrium wage share:

$$\hat{p}^* = \hat{w}^* = \frac{\varphi_1\pi_1(\Omega_0 + \Omega_1 e + h_0 - 1)}{\varphi_1(1 - \pi_2) + \pi_1(1 - \varphi_2)} \tag{8}$$

$$\Omega^* = \frac{\dfrac{\varphi_1}{1 - \varphi_2}(\Omega_0 + \Omega_1 e) + \dfrac{\pi_1}{1 - \pi_2}(1 - h_0)}{\dfrac{\varphi_1}{1 - \varphi_2} + \dfrac{\pi_1}{1 - \pi_2}} \tag{9}$$

The assumptions of incomplete or no 'indexation' and hence of constant or sticky inflation expectations of workers in the wage-inflation equation together with incomplete pass-through of wage inflation to price inflation thus generates a stable Phillips curve in equation (8) with $\frac{\partial \hat{p}^*}{\partial e} > 0$ and a stable profit-squeeze distribution curve in equation (9) with $\frac{\partial \Omega^*}{\partial e} > 0$.

As argued by Hein (2023a, ch. 5), it remains somewhat unclear why in the BSL-0 model workers should be powerful and aim at a higher wage share ($\Omega_W^T - \Omega_{t-1} > 0$) and hence raise wage inflation (equation 4) without fully taking into account expected price inflation, which, in a basic approach, could be assumed to follow adaptive expectations ($\hat{p}_t^e = \hat{p}_{t-1}$). Therefore, it remains unclear why $\varphi_2 < 1$. It implies that workers' power allows them to aim at a higher real wage rate and higher wage share, but workers systematically underestimate future inflation and have some kind of money illusion. A similar argument holds for the firm sector and the price-inflation equation (5). What exactly does a lower target wage share of firms then the previous period's actual wage share ($\Omega_{t-1} - \Omega_F^T > 0$) mean if they cannot even fully pass-through current wage inflation, which, of course, may be the case, as we have pointed out above? In our view, the BSL approach suffers from a lack of a clear distinction between power and expectations components in the wage- and price-inflation equations.

Lavoie (2022, p. 601) has argued that the inclusion of the last period's inflation into the wage inflation function should not be interpreted as workers' price inflation expectations. He argues that instead of anticipating future inflation, workers only demand a compensation for previous inflation. However, this effect is already taken into account in the aspiration gap, which increases with past period inflation, because it means a lower real wage rate and a lower wage share in the previous period. Consequently, in the BSL-0 model the price indexation parameter in the wage inflation function should be interpreted as workers' inflation expectations. However, if these are considered to be irrelevant, the indexation parameter in the BSL-0 approach should simply be left aside, because the aspiration gap sufficiently captures the workers' power and desire to receive a compensation for past period's inflation.

The full BSL-0 model is displayed in Figure 1. In the upper left quadrant, we have the wage- and price-inflation equations (4) and (6). In the upper right quadrant, the target wage shares of workers and firms from equations (1) and (2) are shown, as well as the profit-squeeze distribution curve from equation (9) and the wage-led employment curve from equation (3). For the latter, we ignore the effects of short-run changes in inflation (equation 7) and the related real debt effects on aggregate demand and employment, which would shift this curve to the right, because these changes in inflation finally disappear. The lower right quadrant shows the equilibrium Phillips curve from equation (8). As shown by Blecker and Setterfield (2019, p. ch. 5.3), the stability of the model equilibrium requires the employment curve in the upper right quadrant to be steeper than the distribution curve. Such an equilibrium, given by the intersection of the wage-led employment curve and the profit-squeeze distribution curve, is shown in e_1^*, $\Omega^*(e_1)$, $\widehat{p_1^*} = \widehat{w_1^*}$.

A structural improvement of workers' bargaining power, i.e., a rise in Ω_0 or Ω_1 in equation (1), will lead to an upwards shift/rotation of the workers' target wage share curve, the profit-squeeze distribution curve (9), the wage-inflation curve (4) and the Phillips curve (8). As a result, we will get higher equilibrium wage and price inflation, a higher equilibrium wage share and a higher equilibrium employment rate.

A higher target profit share of firms will shift their target wage share curve (2), the profit-squeeze distribution curve (9), and the price-inflation curve (6) down each, and the Phillips curve (8) will shift up. We will get a lower equilibrium wage share and a lower employment rate, and depending on the slope of the employment curve, we may get higher or lower inflation in the new equilibrium.[8]

[8]A very flat wage-led employment curve, i.e., a strong effect of the decline in the wage share on the employment rate, may over-compensate the upwards shift in the Phillips curve, such that we get a decline in equilibrium inflation in this case.

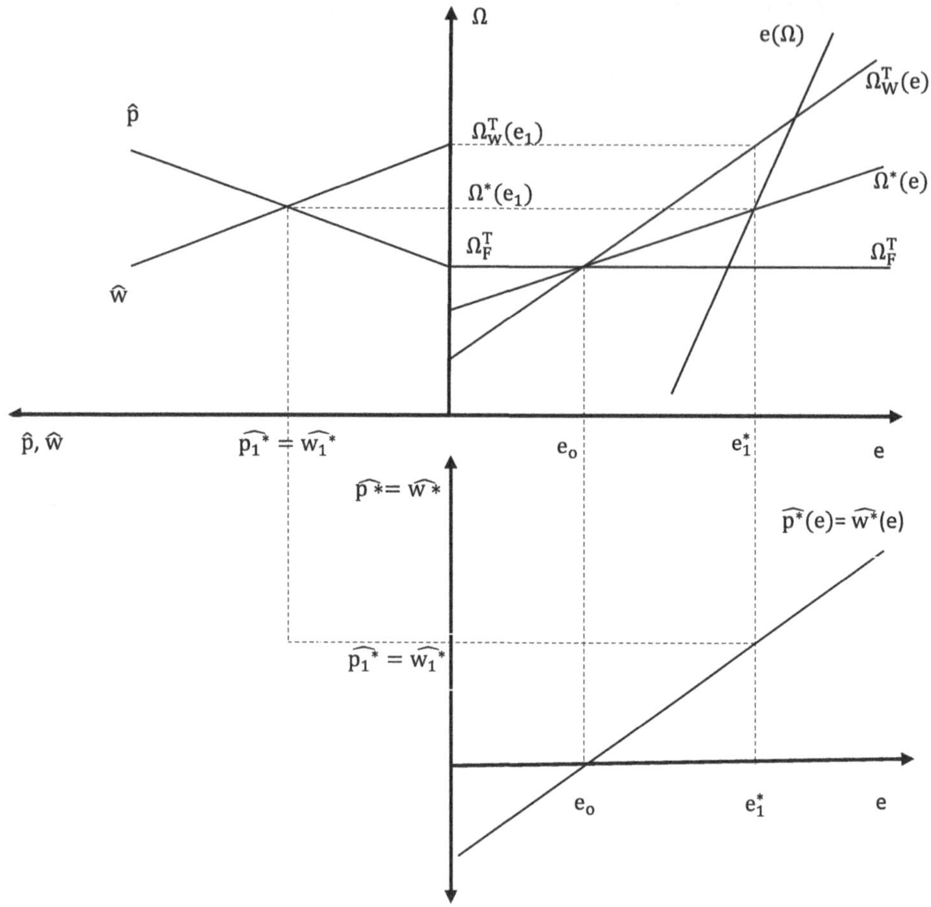

Figure 1. The prototype BSL model: BSL-0.

3.2. The Prototype HS Model: HS-0

Hein and Stockhammer (2009; 2011) have formulated an alternative to the BSL approach in a growth model framework and Hein (2023a, ch. 5.2.2) in a short-run level framework. Here we follow the latter. From the workers' and firms' target wage shares in equations (1) and (2), a consistent claims rate of employment, the SIRE (e^N), is derived:

$$e^N = \frac{1 - h_0 - \Omega_0}{\Omega_1} \tag{10}$$

With $e > e^N$, we have a positive aspiration gap, i.e., the workers' target wage share exceeds the firms' target, and workers try to improve the wage share, for given labour productivity, by raising nominal wage inflation above expected price inflation. For the latter, adaptive expectations are assumed, i.e., $\hat{p}_t^e = \hat{p}_{t-1}$. With $e < e^N$, we have a negative aspiration gap, i.e., the workers' target wage share falls short of the firms' target, and workers are too weak to keep wage inflation in line with expected price inflation. We thus get:

$$\hat{w}_t = \omega(e_t - e^N) + \hat{p}_{t-1}, \quad \omega > 0 \tag{11}$$

For the excess of wage inflation over expected price inflation we have:

$$\hat{w}_t^x = \hat{w}_t - \hat{p}_t^e = \hat{w}_t - \hat{p}_{t-1} = \omega(e_t - e^N) \tag{12}$$

Firms have a constant target wage share from equation (2), but for the reasons put forward by Sylos Labini (1979), firms' price inflation in the aggregate can only partially pass through wage inflation. Here, it is assumed that this incomplete pass-through is related to the excess of wage (dis-)inflation given by the (un-)favourable employment rate relative to the SIRE. It is thus assumed that, although firms are heterogenous, they raise prices according to expected inflation given by past price inflation, i.e., following a perceived stable trend, and then can only incompletely pass through excess wage (dis-)inflation, because of their heterogeneity, as explained above:

$$\hat{p}_t = \vartheta\omega(e_t - e^N) + \hat{p}_{t-1}, \quad 1 > \vartheta \geq 0 \tag{13}$$

Unexpected inflation in each period is thus given by:

$$\hat{p}_t^u = \hat{p}_t - \hat{p}_{t-1} = \vartheta\omega(e_t - e^N) \tag{14}$$

Excess wage inflation from equation (12) exceeds unexpected inflation in equation (14). Because of rising wage inflation with rising employment rates and incomplete pass-through to price inflation, we also obtain a profit-squeeze distribution curve:

$$\Omega = \Omega(e), \quad \frac{\partial\Omega}{\partial e} > 0 \tag{15}$$

In the HS-0 model, target wage shares are not directly included in the wage- and price-inflation equations (11) and (13). These equations are rather affected by the employment rate relative to the SIRE ($e_t - e^N$). For given structural determinants of workers' and firms' target wage shares determining the SIRE in equation (10), changes in the employment rate affecting workers' power directly impact wage and price inflation. Changes in the structural features, impacting the respective wage share targets, affect wage and price inflation through the effect on the SIRE. For example, a falling degree of competition in the goods market raises firms' target mark-up, lowers the SIRE, and, for a given employment rate, price and wage inflation increase, albeit not in step because of incomplete pass-through.

The full HS-0 model is shown in Figure 2. In the upper right quadrant, we have the workers' and the firms' target wages shares from equations (1) and (2), the profit-squeeze distribution curve from equation (15) and the wage-led employment curve from equation (3). The upper left quadrant and the lower right quadrant show the unexpected inflation curve from equation (14) and excess wage inflation from equation (12). The model does not generate a stable Phillips curve. Only at the SIRE (e^N) will wage and price inflation be equal and constant, and unexpected price inflation and excess wage inflation will be zero, generating constant functional distribution, too. Any employment rate $e \neq e^N$ will be associated with unexpected price (dis-)inflation and higher excess wage (dis-)inflation, and hence with rising or falling wage shares. This makes the

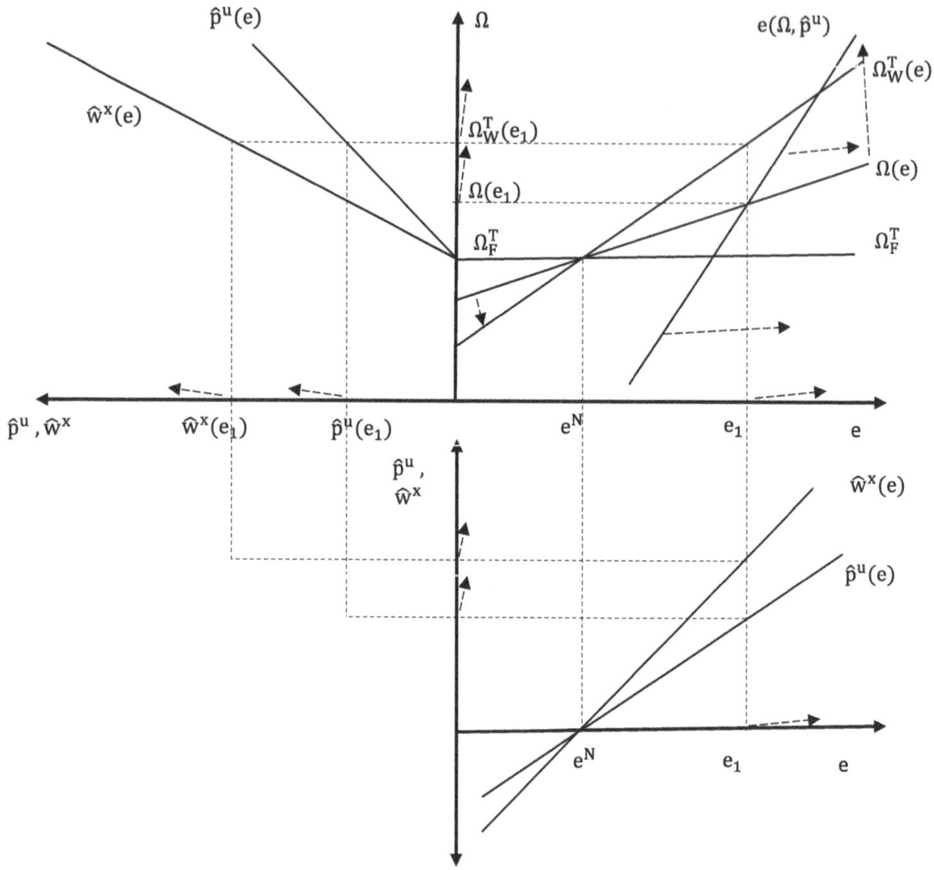

Figure 2. The prototype HS model: HS-0.

profit-squeeze distribution curve rotate towards the workers' target wage share curve. The intersection of profit-squeeze distribution and wage-led employment curve in e_1 thus does not generate a stable equilibrium, because the distribution curve will rotate counter-clockwise, since excess wage inflation will exceed unexpected price inflation, and the employment curve will shift to the right because of real debt effects of unexpected inflation on aggregate demand. The employment rate will rise beyond e_1 in this process, without reaching an equilibrium. It will thus move ever farther away from e^N. The SIRE/NAIRU is thus 'not a strong attractor' (Sawyer 2002), and any deviation will lead to a cumulatively unstable process, with rising (falling) employment rates, rising (falling) unexpected inflation and rising (falling) excess wage inflation, the latter exceeding the former, and hence rising (falling) wage shares, even exceeding (falling below) the workers' target wage share.

The results regarding accelerating wage and price inflation are thus similar to the Carlin and Soskice (2009; 2015) three equation model, as a version of new consensus macroeconomics (NCM). Carlin/Soskice, however, assume full pass-through of wage inflation to price inflation, hence $\vartheta = 1$, which means that the distribution curve is always equal to the firms' target wage share curve in their model. Furthermore, they do not consider any direct feedback effects of accelerating inflation on demand-determined employment via changes in distribution or real debt. In their model, the employment rate is then affected by interest rate variations introduced by inflation-targeting monetary policies, or also by real exchange rate variations induced by international inflation differentials in the open economy.

A structural improvement of workers' bargaining power in the HS-0 model, i.e., a rise in Ω_0 or Ω_1 in equation (1), will lead to an upwards shift/rotation of the workers' target wage share curve and of the profit-squeeze distribution curve (15). The wage-led employment curve (3) will shift to the right because of higher unexpected inflation. In the lower right quadrant, the unexpected inflation curve (14) and the excess wage-inflation curve (12) will shift up. As a result, we will get a lower SIRE, but a higher employment rate, higher unexpected inflation, higher excess wage inflation and a higher wage share in the new temporary position, with further upwards shifts, as indicated above.

A higher target profit share of firms will shift their target wage share curve (2) and the profit-squeeze distribution curve (15) down. The wage-led employment curve (3) will shift to the right because of higher unexpected inflation. In the lower right quadrant, the unexpected inflation curve (14) and the excess wage-inflation curve (12) will shift up. As a result, we will get a lower SIRE. The temporary effects on the other variables are undetermined. With a weak real debt effect on the shift of the employment curve, the employment rate will fall, and with a flat employment curve, also unexpected inflation and excess wage inflation may go down in the new temporary position. However, then the rotation of the distribution curve and the shift of the employment curve will raise the employment rate and drive up unexpected inflation and excess wage inflation again and thus shift the employment rate farther away from the new SIRE in a cumulative process.

4. Modifying the BSL-0 Model

If in the BSL model either wage inflation is fully indexed with respect to past price inflation ($\varphi_2 = 1$), indicating workers having adaptive expectations, or current price inflation fully passes through current wage inflation ($\pi_2 = 1$), equilibrium distribution as a function of the employment rate in equation (9) is no longer defined. If both wage inflation is fully indexed and price inflation fully passes through wage inflation, also equilibrium inflation as a function of the employment rate in equation (8) is not defined any more. Let us now examine three cases: First, we can assume that only wage inflation is fully indexed, but pass-through of wage inflation to price inflation is incomplete. Second, we will assume the reverse, i.e., partial indexation of wage inflation and full pass-through to price inflation, and, third, we can have full indexation of wage inflation and full pass-through to price inflation.

4.1. The BSL Model with Full Indexation/Adaptive Expectations in the Wage-Inflation Equation and Partial Pass-Through in the Price-Inflation Equation: BSL-1

With full indexation of wage inflation, or adaptive expectations of workers and trade unions while attempting to move the wage share up to their target, the wage-inflation equation in the BSL model, taking into account workers' target wage share equation (1), turns to:

$$\begin{aligned}\hat{w}_t &= \varphi_1(\Omega_W^T - \Omega_{t-1}) + \varphi_2\hat{p}_{t-1}, \quad \varphi_1 > 0, \varphi_2 = 1 \\ &= \varphi_1(\Omega_0 + \Omega_1 e - \Omega_{t-1}) + \hat{p}_{t-1}\end{aligned} \tag{16}$$

Excess wage inflation in the short run is thus given as:

$$\hat{w}_t^x = \hat{w}_t - \hat{p}_{t-1} = \varphi_1(\Omega_W^T - \Omega_{t-1}) = \varphi_1(\Omega_0 + \Omega_1 e - \Omega_{t-1}) \tag{17}$$

For price inflation we assume a partial pass-through of contemporary wage inflation as in equation (6), which we reproduce here:

$$\begin{aligned}\hat{p}_t &= \pi_1(\Omega_{t-1} - \Omega_F^T) + \pi_2\hat{w}_t, \quad \pi_1 > 0, 1 > \pi_2 \geq 0 \\ &= \pi_1(\Omega_{t-1} - 1 + h_0) + \pi_2\hat{w}_t\end{aligned} \tag{6}$$

Including wage inflation (16) into price inflation (6) yields for unexpected inflation in the short run:

$$\begin{aligned}\hat{p}_t^u = \hat{p}_t - \hat{p}_{t-1} &= \pi_1(\Omega_{t-1} - \Omega_F^T) + \pi_2\varphi_1(\Omega_W^T - \Omega_{t-1}) - (1 - \pi_2)\hat{p}_{t-1} \\ &= \pi_1(\Omega_{t-1} - 1 + h_0) + \pi_2\varphi_1(\Omega_0 + \Omega_1 e - \Omega_{t-1}) - (1 - \pi_2)\hat{p}_{t-1}.\end{aligned} \tag{18}$$

Since $\pi_2 < 1$, over several periods unexpected inflation will converge to zero, the economy will converge towards $\hat{p}_t = \hat{p}_{t-1}$, and we get:

$$\begin{aligned}\hat{p}_t &= \frac{\pi_1(\Omega_{t-1} - \Omega_F^T) + \pi_2\varphi_1(\Omega_W^T - \Omega_{t-1})}{1 - \pi_2} \\ &= \frac{\pi_1(\Omega_{t-1} - 1 + h_0) + \pi_2\varphi_1(\Omega_0 + \Omega_1 e - \Omega_{t-1})}{1 - \pi_2}\end{aligned} \tag{19}$$

For wage inflation this implies:

$$\begin{aligned}\hat{w}_t &= \frac{\pi_1(\Omega_{t-1} - \Omega_F^T) + [\varphi_1(1 - \pi_2) + \pi_2\varphi_1](\Omega_W^T - \Omega_{t-1})}{1 - \pi_2} \\ &= \frac{\pi_1(\Omega_{t-1} - 1 + h_0) + [\varphi_1(1 - \pi_2) + \pi_2\varphi_1](\Omega_0 + \Omega_1 e - \Omega_{t-1})}{1 - \pi_2}\end{aligned} \tag{20}$$

Wage inflation will thus exceed price inflation. This is why the profit-squeeze distribution curve will rotate towards the workers' target wage share curve. As soon as this is reached, wage inflation will be equal to price inflation, and the latter will be driven by the deviation of the firms' target wage share from the actual wage share, which is equal to the workers' target wage share, as can be derived from equations (19) and (20), or also from equation (8):

$$\hat{p}_t^* = \hat{w}_t^* = \frac{\pi_1(\Omega_W^T - \Omega_F^T)}{1 - \pi_2} = \frac{\pi_1(\Omega_0 + \Omega_1 e - 1 + h_0)}{1 - \pi_2} \tag{21}$$

with:

$$\Omega^* = \Omega_W^T = \Omega_0 + \Omega_1 e \tag{22}$$

The effects of full indexation of wage inflation to past price inflation, hence adaptive

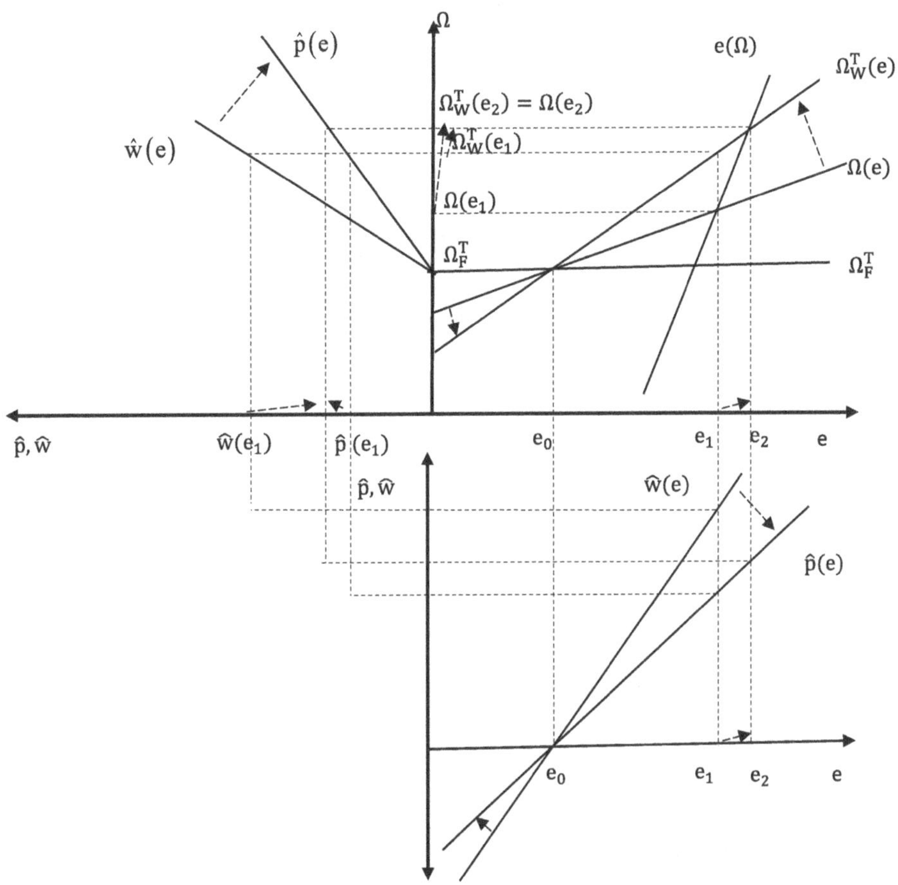

Figure 3. The BSL model with full indexation of wage inflation and incomplete pass-through to price inflation: BSL-1.

expectations, and an incomplete pass-through to price inflation in the BSL-1 model are shown in Figure 3. The upper left and lower right quadrants show the price and wage-inflation equations (19) and (20), with the former rotating towards the latter. In the upper right quadrant, the rotation of the distribution curve towards the workers' target wage share means that the economy will not remain at the temporary position at e_1, but that it will move to a higher stable equilibrium employment rate at e_2 with the workers' target wage share reached, provided the slope or the employment curve exceeds the slope of the workers' target wage share curve. In the final equilibrium, workers will reach their target wage share at a higher equilibrium employment rate, and inflation will only be driven by the firms' unsuccessful desire to lower the wage share towards their target wage share.

In this stylised presentation, we have ignored the effects of short-run unexpected inflation from equation (18) on the employment curve (3). Including these would also shift this curve to the right, but since unexpected inflation will peter out, we will still reach an equilibrium with a higher employment rate, a higher inflation rate and the wage share equal to the workers' target wage share.

The results regarding long-run distribution and inflation in the case of full indexation of past inflation in the wage-inflation equation and partial pass-through of wage inflation to price inflation are in line with Lavoie (2022, ch. 8). However, Lavoie neither has targets related to employment rates nor does he discuss the feedback effects on economic activity and the employment rate.

4.2. The BSL Model with Partial Indexation in the Wage-Inflation Equation and Full Pass-Through to Price Inflation: BSL-2

In the alternative case of incomplete indexation of wage inflation to past inflation, but complete pass-through of current wage inflation to current price inflation, we receive the opposite results, as can be shown as follows. We keep wage-inflation equation (4):

$$\begin{aligned}\hat{w}_t &= \varphi_1(\Omega_W^T - \Omega_{t-1}) + \varphi_2\hat{p}_{t-1}, \quad \varphi_1 > 0, 1 > \varphi_2 \geq 0 \\ &= \varphi_1(\Omega_0 + \Omega_1 e - \Omega_{t-1}) + \varphi_2\hat{p}_{t-1}\end{aligned} \tag{4}$$

Excess wage inflation is thus again given as:

$$\begin{aligned}w_t^x = \hat{w}_t - \hat{p}_{t-1} &= \varphi_1(\Omega_W^T - \Omega_{t-1}) - (1-\varphi_2)\hat{p}_{t-1} \\ &= \varphi_1(\Omega_0 + \Omega_1 e - \Omega_{t-1}) - (1-\varphi_2)\hat{p}_{t-1}\end{aligned} \tag{5}$$

For price inflation we now assume a homogenous firms sector with a full pass-through of wage inflation:

$$\begin{aligned}\hat{p}_t &= \pi_1(\Omega_{t-1} - \Omega_F^T) + \pi_2\hat{w}_t, \quad \pi_1 > 0,\ \pi_2 = 1 \\ &= \pi_1(\Omega_{t-1} - 1 + h_0) + \hat{w}_t\end{aligned} \tag{23}$$

Inserting wage inflation from equation (4) into the price equation (23) yields for unexpected inflation:

$$\begin{aligned}\hat{p}_t^u = \hat{p}_t - \hat{p}_{t-1} &= \pi_1(\Omega_{t-1} - \Omega_F^T) + \varphi_1(\Omega_W^T - \Omega_{t-1}) - (1-\varphi_2)\hat{p}_{t-1} \\ &= \pi_1(\Omega_{t-1} - 1 + h_0) + \varphi_1(\Omega_0 + \Omega_1 e - \Omega_{t-1}) - (1-\varphi_2)\hat{p}_{t-1}\end{aligned} \tag{24}$$

Unexpected price inflation will thus exceed unexpected wage inflation. Since $\varphi_2 < 1$, over several periods unexpected inflation will converge to zero, the economy will converge towards $\hat{p}_t = \hat{p}_{t-1}$, and we get:

$$\begin{aligned}\hat{p}_t &= \frac{\pi_1(\Omega_{t-1} - \Omega_F^T) + \varphi_1(\Omega_W^T - \Omega_{t-1})}{1-\varphi_2} \\ &= \frac{\pi_1(\Omega_{t-1} - 1 + h_0) + \varphi_1(\Omega_0 + \Omega_1 e - \Omega_{t-1})}{1-\varphi_2}\end{aligned} \tag{25}$$

Wage inflation will hence converge to:

$$\begin{aligned}\hat{w}_t &= \frac{\varphi_2\pi_1(\Omega_{t-1} - \Omega_F^T) + \varphi_1(\Omega_W^T - \Omega_{t-1})}{1-\varphi_2} \\ &= \frac{\varphi_2\pi_1(\Omega_{t-1} - 1 + h_0) + \varphi_1(\Omega_0 + \Omega_1 e - \Omega_{t-1})}{1-\varphi_2}\end{aligned} \tag{26}$$

Wage inflation thus falls short of price inflation, and the distribution curve will rotate

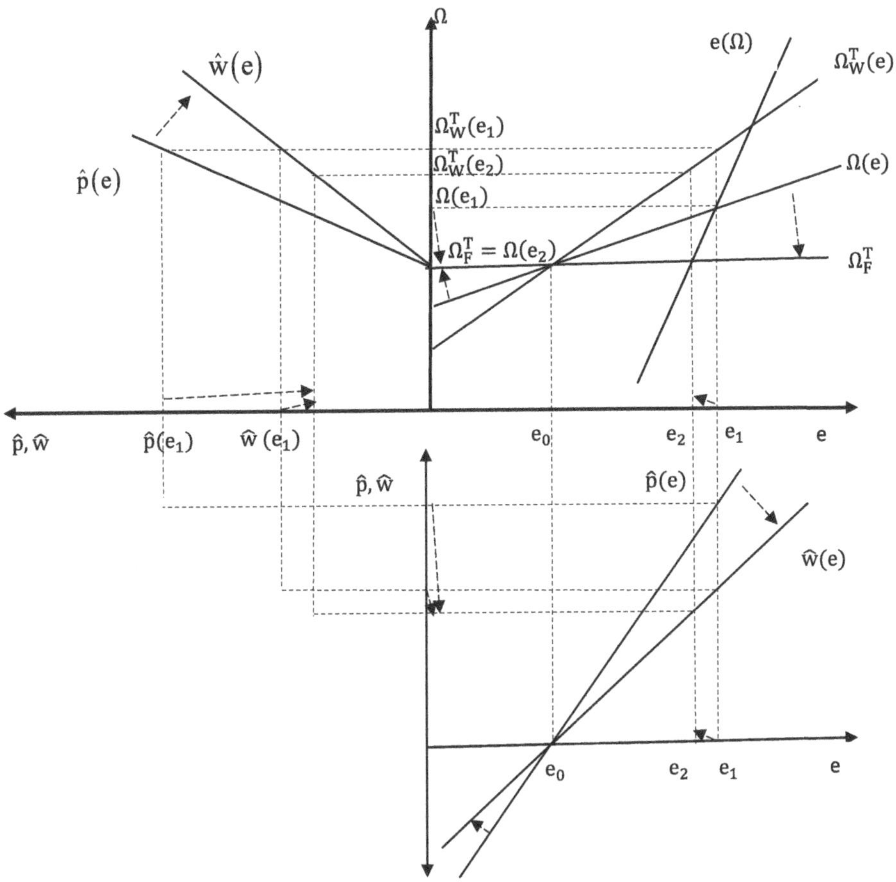

Figure 4. The BSL model with incomplete indexation of wage inflation and full pass-through to price inflation: BSL-2.

towards the firms' target wage share curve. Since this implies that firms will reach their target wage share, price inflation converges to wage inflation, and both are driven by the deviation of the actual wages, equal to the firms' target, from the workers' target wage share. From equations (25) and (26), as well as from equation (8), we get for the final equilibrium:

$$\hat{p}^* = \hat{w}^* = \frac{\varphi_1(\Omega_W^T - \Omega_F^T)}{1 - \varphi_2} = \frac{\varphi_1(\Omega_0 + \Omega_1 e - 1 + h_0)}{1 - \varphi_2} \tag{27}$$

with

$$\Omega^* = \Omega_F^T = 1 - h_0 \tag{28}$$

In Figure 4 these adjustments in the BSL-2 model are shown. The position at e_1 is not a stable equilibrium, since price inflation exceeds wage inflation because of incomplete indexation of the latter. The distribution curve rotates towards the firms' target wage share and the price-inflation curve adjusts to the wage-inflation curve. This leads to a new stable equilibrium at e_2 with a lower employment rate, a lower inflation rate, equal to and driven by wage inflation, and a lower wage share, equal to the firms' target.

In this stylised presentation, we have again ignored the effects of short-run unexpected inflation from equation (24) on the employment curve (3). Including these would also shift this curve to the right, but since unexpected inflation will peter out, we will still reach an equilibrium. Depending on the relevance and the strength of the real debt effects on aggregate demand, this equilibrium could even mean a higher employment rate, a higher inflation rate as compared to the initial positon at e_1, with the wage share equal to the firms' target wage share.

Again, our results regarding long-run distribution and inflation in the case of incomplete indexation of past inflation in the wage-inflation equation and complete pass-through of wage inflation to price inflation are in line with Lavoie (2022, ch. 8), who, however, does not relate them to the employment rate, as pointed out above.

4.3. The BSL Model with Full Indexation/Adaptive Expectations in Wage Inflation and Complete Pass-Through to Price Inflation: BSL-3

In the final variant of the BSL model, BSL-3, we assume simultaneous full indexation/adaptive expectations in wage inflation and complete pass-through in price inflation with a homogenous firms sector, as in equations (16) and (23):

$$\begin{aligned} \hat{w}_t &= \varphi_1(\Omega_W^T - \Omega_{t-1}) + \varphi_2 \hat{p}_{t-1}, \quad \varphi_1 > 0, \varphi_2 = 1 \\ &= \varphi_1(\Omega_0 + \Omega_1 e - \Omega_{t-1}) + \hat{p}_{t-1} \end{aligned} \tag{16}$$

$$\begin{aligned} \hat{p}_t &= \pi_1(\Omega_{t-1} - \Omega_F^T) + \pi_2 \hat{w}_t, \quad \pi_1 > 0, \pi_2 = 1 \\ &= \pi_1(\Omega_{t-1} - 1 + h_0) + \hat{w}_t \end{aligned} \tag{23}$$

Excess wage inflation is given by:

$$\begin{aligned} \hat{w}_t^x &= \hat{w}_t - \hat{p}_{t-1} \\ &= \varphi_1(\Omega_W^T - \Omega_{t-1}) \\ &= \varphi_1(\Omega_0 + \Omega_1 e - \Omega_{t-1}) \end{aligned} \tag{17}$$

Making use of equations (16) and (23), we receive for unexpected inflation:

$$\begin{aligned} \hat{p}_t^u &= \hat{p}_t - \hat{p}_{t-1} \\ &= \pi_1(\Omega_{t-1} - \Omega_F^T) + \varphi_1(\Omega_W^T - \Omega_{t-1}) \\ &= \pi_1(\Omega_{t-1} - 1 + h_0) + \varphi_1(\Omega_0 + \Omega_1 e - \Omega_{t-1}) \end{aligned} \tag{29}$$

Only if firms' and workers' targets are consistent, will excess wage inflation and unexpected price inflation be zero and wage and price inflation will be equal and constant. The model thus generates a SIRE at:

$$e^N = \frac{1 - h_0 - \Omega_0}{\Omega_1} \tag{10}$$

like the HS-0 model. However, different from that model, for $e \neq e^N$ in the BSL-3 model, unexpected inflation will exceed excess wage inflation, as can be seen in equations (17) and (29). Workers set nominal wages first and firms then set prices, completely passing through wage inflation and adding to it according to the deviation of the wage

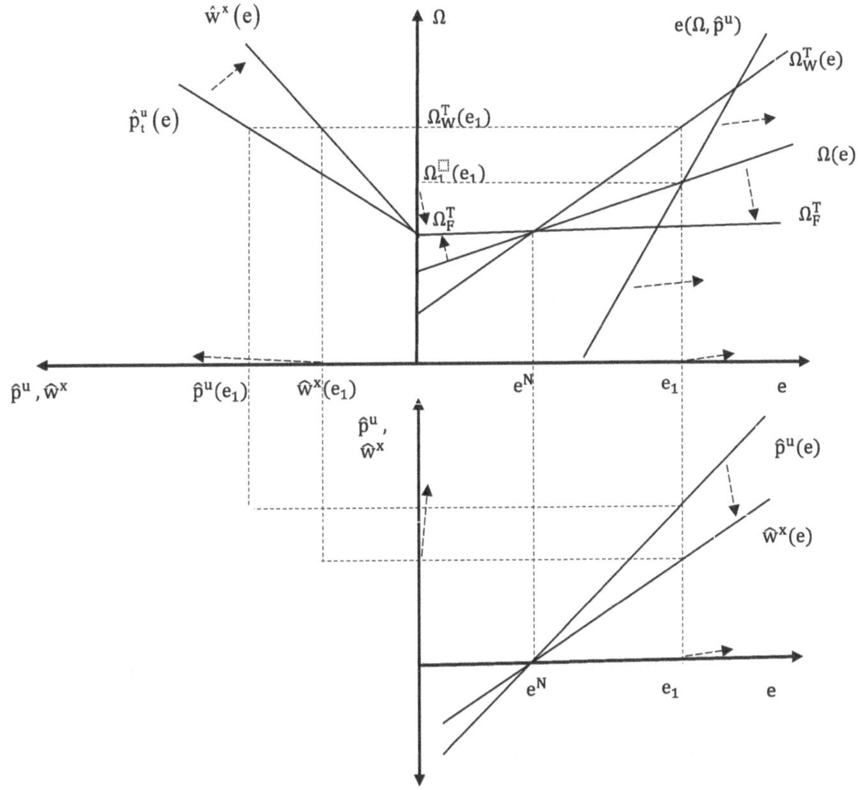

Figure 5. The BSL model with full indexation of wage inflation and complete pass-through to price inflation: BSL-3.

share from their target. The profit-squeeze distribution curve thus rotates towards the firms' target wage share and hence becomes horizontal. Since firms finally reach their distribution target, unexpected price inflation converges to excess wage inflation and is driven by the latter:

$$\hat{w}_t^x = \hat{w}_t - \hat{p}_{t-1} = \hat{p}_t^u = \hat{p}_t - \hat{p}_{t-1} = \varphi_1(\Omega_W^T - \Omega_{t-1}) = \varphi_1(\Omega_0 + \Omega_1 e - \Omega_{t-1}) \quad (30)$$

The results of the BSL-3 model are shown in Figure 5. The model does not generate a stable Phillips curve anymore, and we will have unexpected price (dis-)inflation and excess wage (dis-)inflation for any deviation from the SIRE ($e \neq e^N$). Since unexpected price (dis-)inflation exceeds excess wage (dis-)inflation, the distribution curve convergences towards the firms' target wage share curve, and the unexpected price-inflation curve converges towards the excess wage-inflation curve. The position at e_1 is thus highly unstable. For a given employment curve, the rotation of the distribution curve would move the employment rate towards the SIRE and would thus be stabilising around the latter. However, real debt effects (equation 3) of unexpected inflation shift the employment function to the right and destabilise employment around the SIRE. Starting with e_1, we will thus see rising employment rates together with rising unexpected inflation being equal to excess wage inflation and hence a constant wage share equal to the firms' target.

The results regarding accelerating wage and price inflation, as well as firms always reaching their target, are thus similar to the Carlin and Soskice (2009; 2015) NCM model. As pointed out above, however, Carlin/Soskice do not consider any direct feedbacks of accelerating inflation on demand-determined employment.

5. Modifying the HS-0 Model

From Sections 3 we have got that the HS-0 model differs from the BSL-0 model in two respects. First, target wage shares of firms and workers are not directly included into the wage- and price-inflation equations. Instead, these equations include, directly via the employment rate and indirectly via the SIRE, the relative powers of workers and firms. We will see in variants HS-2 and HS-3 what difference it makes to directly include the workers' target wage share relative to the actual wage share. Second, in the HS-0 model incomplete pass-through of wage inflation to price inflation has been assumed. More specifically, it was assumed that firms raise prices according to expected inflation given by past price inflation and only incompletely pass through excess wage (dis-)inflation. In the variant HS-1 and HS-2, we will see what differences arise, if we assume that incomplete pass-through is related to total wage inflation and not only to excess wage inflation.

5.1. The HS Model with Incomplete Pass-Through of Total Wage Inflation: HS-1

For the HS-1 version, we keep the wage-inflation equation (12) and hence the excess wage-inflation equation (13) from the HS-0 model:

$$\hat{w}_t = \omega(e_t - e^N) + \hat{p}_{t-1}, \quad \omega > 0 \tag{12}$$

$$\hat{w}_t^x = \hat{w}_t - \hat{p}_t^e = \hat{w}_t - \hat{p}_{t-1} = \omega(e_t - e^N) \tag{13}$$

However, instead of partial pass-through of excess wage inflation, we now assume partial pass-through of total wage inflation in the new price-inflation equation:

$$\hat{p}_t = \vartheta[\omega(e_t - e^N) + \hat{p}_{t-1}], \quad 1 > \vartheta \geq 0 \tag{31}$$

Unexpected inflation in the short run thus turns to:

$$\hat{p}_t^u = \hat{p}_t - \hat{p}_{t-1} = \vartheta\omega(e_t - e^N) - (1 - \vartheta)\hat{p}_{t-1} \tag{32}$$

Since $\vartheta < 1$, over several periods unexpected inflation will vanish ($\hat{p}_t - \hat{p}_{t-1} = 0$), and we obtain for price and wage inflation:

$$\hat{p}_t = \frac{\vartheta\omega(e_t - e^N)}{(1 - \vartheta)} \tag{33}$$

$$\hat{w}_t = \frac{\omega(e_t - e^N)}{(1 - \vartheta)} = \frac{1}{\vartheta}\hat{p}_t \tag{34}$$

The model thus generates a stable price Phillips curve. However, wage inflation will exceed price inflation at any employment rate. The profit-squeeze distribution curve is thus not stable, but will rotate towards the workers' target wage share curve and even beyond.

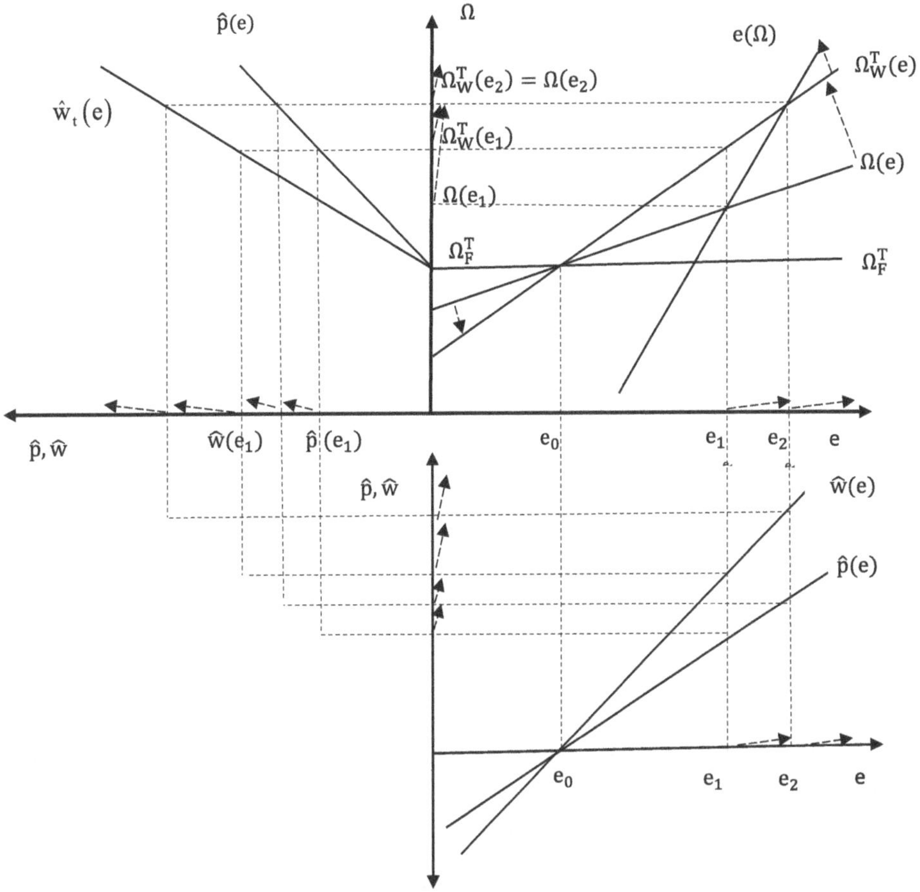

Figure 6. The HS model with incomplete pass-through of total wage inflation: HS-1.

The HS-1 model is shown in Figure 6. In the upper left and lower right quadrants we have the wage- and price-inflation equations (33) and (34), with a zero inflation rate at e_0, as in the BSL model variants. However, at $e \neq e_0$, wage (dis-)inflation exceeds price (dis-)inflation. This rotates the distribution curve in the upper right quadrant towards the workers' target wage share. The position at employment rate e_1 will thus move to the higher employment rate e_2, at which workers have reached their target wage share. Since unexpected inflation will peter out in the long run in this model variant, again we ignore short-run real debt effects of unexpected inflation on the wage-led employment curve, which would shift this curve and the employment rate e_2 farther to the right. But at e_2, wage inflation still exceeds price inflation, and the distribution curve would rotate beyond the workers' target, moving the employment rate further above e_2 and destabilising the economy. We would thus see rising employment rates, rising wage shares and rising price inflation falling short of wage inflation, and hence a cumulatively unstable process along stable wage- and price-Phillips curves. However, the inconsistency driving this process, namely wage shares rising above workers' target, can be taken care of by directly including the workers' target wage share into the wage-inflation equation. This is what we do in the next variant.

5.2. The HS Model with the Target Wage Share in the Wage Inflation Function and Partial Pass-Through of Total Wage Inflation: HS-2

In the HS-2 variant, we are using the wage-inflation equation (16) together with the excess wage-inflation equation (17) from the BSL-1 model, in which we have the deviation of last period's wage share from the workers' target and in in which we interpret full indexation as workers having adaptive expectations:

$$\begin{aligned}\hat{w}_t &= \varphi_1(\Omega_W^T - \Omega_{t-1}) + \varphi_2\hat{p}_{t-1}, \quad \varphi_1 > 0, \varphi_2 = 1 \\ &= \varphi_1(\Omega_0 + \Omega_1 e - \Omega_{t-1}) + \hat{p}_{t-1}\end{aligned} \tag{16}$$

$$\hat{w}_t^x = \hat{w}_t - \hat{p}_{t-1} = \varphi_1(\Omega_W^T - \Omega_{t-1}) = \varphi_1(\Omega_0 + \Omega_1 e - \Omega_{t-1}) \tag{17}$$

For price inflation, we assume partial pass-through of total wage inflation here, as in the HS-1 variant:

$$\begin{aligned}\hat{p}_t &= \vartheta[\varphi_1(\Omega_W^T - \Omega_{t-1}) + \varphi_2\hat{p}_{t-1}], \quad 1 > \vartheta \geq 0 \\ &= \vartheta[\varphi_1(\Omega_0 + \Omega_1 e - \Omega_{t-1}) + \hat{p}_{t-1}]\end{aligned} \tag{35}$$

Unexpected inflation in the short run turns to:

$$\begin{aligned}\hat{p}_t^u &= \hat{p}_t - \hat{p}_{t-1} = \vartheta\varphi_1(\Omega_W^T - \Omega_{t-1}) - (1-\vartheta)\hat{p}_{t-1} \\ &= \vartheta\varphi_1(\Omega_0 + \Omega_1 e - \Omega_{t-1}) - (1-\vartheta)\hat{p}_{t-1}\end{aligned} \tag{36}$$

Because of incomplete pass-through, unexpected price inflation in equation (36) will thus fall short of excess wage inflation in equation (16). Since $\vartheta < 1$, over several periods unexpected inflation will vanish ($\hat{p}_t - \hat{p}_{t-1} = 0$), and inflation turns constant, with wage inflation exceeding price inflation:

$$\hat{p}_t = \frac{\vartheta\varphi_1(\Omega_W^T - \Omega_{t-1})}{1-\vartheta} = \frac{\vartheta\varphi_1(\Omega_0 + \Omega_1 e - \Omega_{t-1})}{1-\vartheta} \tag{37}$$

$$\hat{w}_t = \frac{\varphi_1(\Omega_W^T - \Omega_{t-1})}{1-\vartheta} = \frac{\varphi_1(\Omega_0 + \Omega_1 e - \Omega_{t-1})}{1-\vartheta} = \frac{1}{\vartheta}\hat{p}_t \tag{38}$$

With wage inflation exceeding price inflation, the wage share will rise towards workers' target, and wage and price inflation will converge towards zero, which means we have in the long run:

$$\hat{p}_t^* = \hat{w}_t^* = 0 \tag{39}$$

with

$$\Omega^* = \Omega_W^T = \Omega_0 + \Omega_1 e \tag{40}$$

The HS-2 variant is shown in Figure 7. In the upper left and lower right quadrants we have the wage- and price-inflation curves from equations (37) and (38). Since wage (dis-)inflation exceeds price (dis-)inflation at any employment rate, the distribution curve in the upper right quadrant rotates towards the workers' target wage share curve. In the course of this process, wage- and price-inflation curves rotate to zero; we thus obtain a horizontal Phillips curve at zero inflation. Starting with the employment rate e_1, the economy will thus move to the employment rate e_2. Again, we ignore the rightward

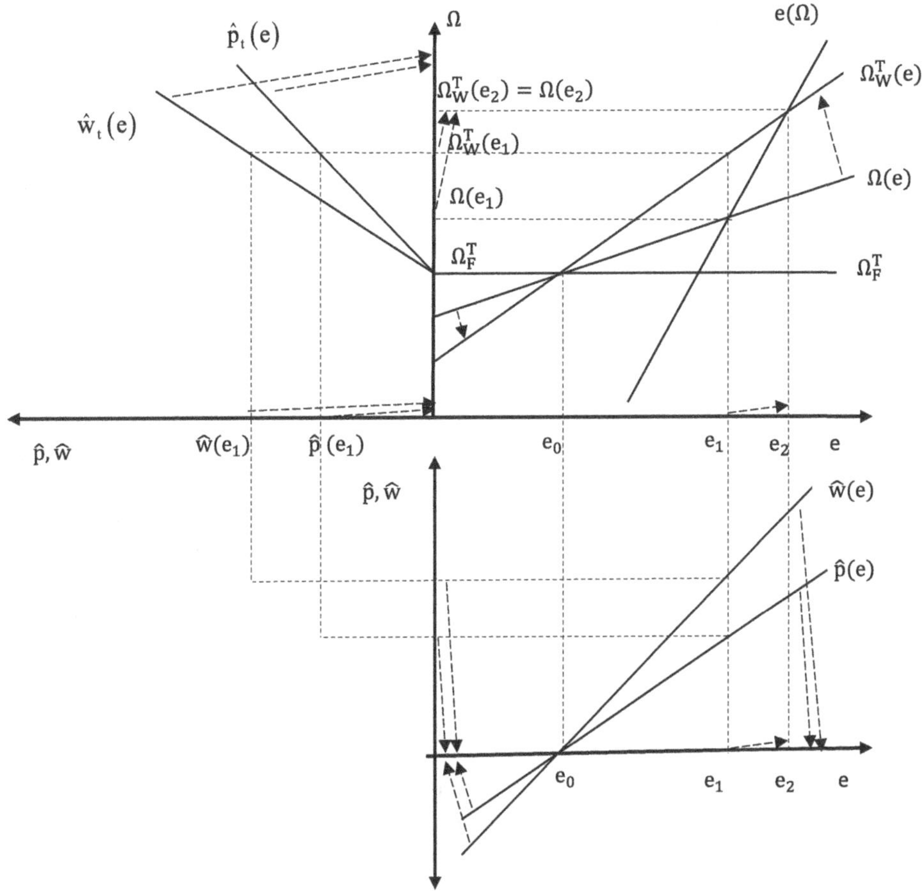

Figure 7. The HS model with the target wage share in the wage-inflation function and partial pass-through of total wage inflation: HS-2.

shifting effects of temporary unexpected inflation on the employment curve. At e_2, the model economy reaches a stable equilibrium with zero wage and price inflation, hence with constant prices, and the wage share equal to the workers' target wage share.

5.3. The HS Model with the Target Wage Share in the Wage Inflation Function and Partial Pass-Through of Excess Wage Inflation: HS-3

In the final model variant to be discussed, HS-3, we will explore whether it makes a difference to include the partial pass-through of excess instead of total wage inflation, as in the HS-0 model, in an HS model with the target wage share of workers in the wage-inflation equation. We start again with the wage inflation and the excess wage-inflation equations from the previous variant, the HS-2:

$$\begin{aligned} \hat{w}_t &= \varphi_1(\Omega_W^T - \Omega_{t-1}) + \varphi_2 \hat{p}_{t-1}, \quad \varphi_1 > 0, \varphi_2 = 1 \\ &= \varphi_1(\Omega_0 + \Omega_1 e - \Omega_{t-1}) + \hat{p}_{t-1} \end{aligned} \tag{16}$$

$$\hat{w}_t^x = \hat{w}_t - \hat{p}_{t-1} = \varphi_1(\Omega_W^T - \Omega_{t-1}) = \varphi_1(\Omega_0 + \Omega_1 e - \Omega_{t-1}) \tag{17}$$

For price inflation, we assume partial pass-through of excess wage inflation only, like in the HS-0 model:

$$\begin{aligned}\hat{p}_t &= \vartheta\varphi_1(\Omega_W^T - \Omega_{t-1}) + \varphi_1\hat{p}_{t-1}, \quad 1 > \vartheta \geq 0 \\ &= \vartheta\varphi_1(\Omega_0 + \Omega_1 e - \Omega_{t-1}) + \hat{p}_{t-1}\end{aligned} \tag{41}$$

Unexpected inflation is thus:

$$\begin{aligned}\hat{p}_t^u = \hat{p}_t - \hat{p}_{t-1} &= \vartheta\varphi_1(\Omega_W^T - \Omega_{t-1}) \\ &= \vartheta\varphi_1(\Omega_0 + \Omega_1 e - \Omega_{t-1})\end{aligned} \tag{42}$$

Because of incomplete pass-through, price inflation falls short of wage inflation at any employment rate, and unexpected inflation is lower than excess wage inflation. This means that the profit-squeeze distribution curve rotates towards the workers' target wage share curve. Since the workers finally reach their target, excess wage inflation and unexpected price inflation will each converge towards zero, and wage and price inflation will converge to some definite but path-dependent rate.

$$\hat{w}_t^x = \hat{w}_t - \hat{p}_{t-1} = \hat{p}_t^u = \hat{p}_t - \hat{p}_{t-1} = 0 \tag{43}$$

with

$$\Omega^* = \Omega_W^T = \Omega_0 + \Omega_1 e \tag{44}$$

The HS-3 model is shown in Figure 8. In the upper-left and lower-right quadrant we find the excess wage-inflation curve from equation (17) and the unexpected inflation curve from equation (42). Since wage inflation exceeds price inflation at employment rate e_1, the distribution curve will rotate towards the workers' target wage share curve in the upper-right quadrant, and excess wage and unexpected price inflation will converge towards zero. In this convergence process, the employment curve will shift to the right because of expansionary real debt effects on aggregate demand until the equilibrium is reached. When the distribution curve has turned equal to the workers' target wage share curve, excess wage and unexpected price inflation will turn to zero, and the model economy reaches an equilibrium at the employment rate e_2, with path-dependent constant inflation and the equilibrium wage share equal to the workers' target.

6. Comparison, Assessment and Conclusions

In this paper, we have systematically discussed two main post-Keynesian/Kaleckian textbook conflict inflation and distribution models, the BSL and HS prototype models and three variations each. In Table 1, the main characteristics of our eight model variants are summarised, according to the respective wage- and price-inflation equations used, the emanating Phillips, distribution and employment curves and the implications for (dis-)equilibria. Most of the BSL model variants generate stable Phillips, distribution and employment curves which lead to stable equilibria. Depending on the assumptions regarding indexation of wage inflation and pass-through in price inflation, equilibrium distribution will settle between workers' and firms' target wages shares (BSL-0), or we

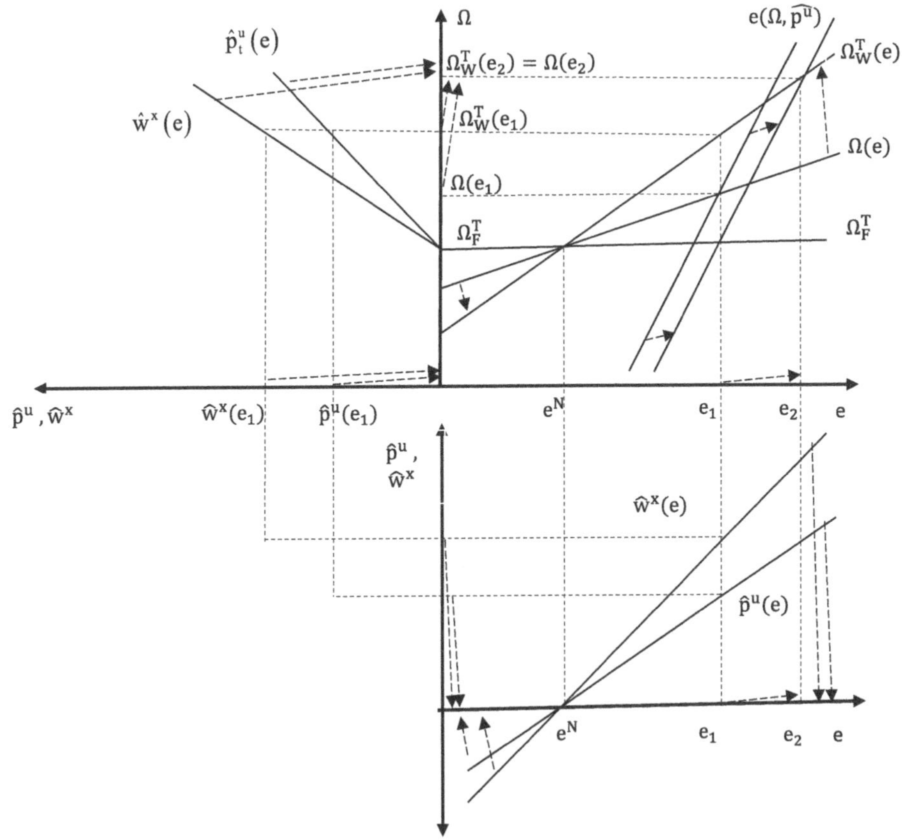

Figure 8. The HS model with the target wage share in the wage-inflation equation and partial pass-through of excess wage inflation: HS-3.

will see 'corner solutions', with the equilibrium wage share equal to the workers' target (BSL-1) or the firms' target (BSL-2). Only the BSL-3 variant with complete indexation in wage inflation and complete pass-through to price inflation does not generate stable Phillips, distribution and employment curves, and hence no stable equilibrium. Here, only at the SIRE will inflation, distribution and employment be constant. This variant is closest to the HS-0 model, which also has shifting Phillips, distribution and employment curves, and hence no stable equilibrium, whenever the employment rate deviates from the SIRE. The HS-1 model with incomplete pass-through of total wage inflation, instead of only excess wage inflation as in HS-0, also does not generate a stable equilibrium, although it has a stable upwards sloping Phillips curve, and hence no single SIRE anymore, like the BSL-0, BSL-1 and BSL-2 models. Here, the instability is generated by omitting the workers' target wage share from the wage-inflation equation, such that workers keep on raising nominal wage inflation above expected price inflation, although targets have been reached, because they have the power to do so. Remedying this problem in the HS-2 and HS-3 models, generates stable and flat Phillips curves, either at zero or at path-dependent constant inflation, hence no single SIRE anymore, and thus stable equilibria. Different from the BSL-0, BSL-2 and BSL-3 models, the HS models each have a

Table 1. BSL and HS model variants compared.

	Wage inflation	Price inflation	Phillips curve	Distribution curve	Employment curve	Equilibrium?
BSL-0	Incomplete indexation $\hat{w}_t = \varphi_1(\Omega_W^T - \Omega_{t-1}) + \varphi_2 \hat{p}_{t-1}$, $\varphi_1 > 0, 1 > \varphi_2 \geq 0$	Incomplete pass-through $\hat{p}_t = \pi_1(\Omega_{t-1} - \Omega_F^T) + \pi_2 \hat{w}_t$, $\pi_1 > 0, 1 > \pi_2 \geq 0$	Upwards sloping in e, stable	Profit-squeeze, stable $\Omega_W^T(e) > \Omega(e) > \Omega_F^T$	Wage-led, stable	Constant $e \neq e_0$, $\hat{p}^* = \hat{w}^*$, $\Omega_W^T > \Omega^* > \Omega_F^T$
BSL-1	Complete indexation $\hat{w}_t = \varphi_1(\Omega_W^T - \Omega_{t-1}) + \varphi_2 \hat{p}_{t-1}$, $\varphi_1 > 0, \varphi_2 = 1$	Incomplete pass-through $\hat{p}_t = \pi_1(\Omega_{t-1} - \Omega_F^T) + \pi_2 \hat{w}_t$, $\pi_1 > 0, 1 > \pi_2 \geq 0$	Upwards sloping in e, stable	Profit-squeeze, rotating towards $\Omega_W^T(e) = \Omega(e)$	Wage-led, stable	Constant $e \neq e_0$, $\hat{p}_t^* = \hat{w}_t^*$, $\Omega_W^T = \Omega^*$
BSL-2	Incomplete indexation $\hat{w}_t = \varphi_1(\Omega_W^T - \Omega_{t-1}) + \varphi_2 \hat{p}_{t-1}$, $\varphi_1 > 0, 1 > \varphi_2 \geq 0$	Complete pass-through $\hat{p}_t = \pi_1(\Omega_{t-1} - \Omega_F^T) + \pi_2 \hat{w}_t$, $\pi_1 > 0, \pi_2 = 1$	Upwards sloping in e, stable	Profit-squeeze, rotating towards $\Omega_F^T(e) = \Omega(e)$	Wage-led, stable	Constant $e \neq e_0$, $\hat{p}_t^* = \hat{w}_t^*$, $\Omega^* = \Omega_F^T$
BSL-3	Complete indexation $\hat{w}_t = \varphi_1(\Omega_W^T - \Omega_{t-1}) + \varphi_2 \hat{p}_{t-1}$, $\varphi_1 > 0, \varphi_2 = 1$	Complete pass-through $\hat{p}_t = \pi_1(\Omega_{t-1} - \Omega_F^T) + \pi_2 \hat{w}_t$, $\pi_1 > 0, \pi_2 = 1$	Upwards sloping in e, shifting for any $e \neq e^N$	Profit-squeeze, rotating towards $\Omega_F^T(e) = \Omega(e)$	Wage-led, shifting	Rising/falling $e \neq e^N$, rising/falling $\hat{w}$, $\hat{p}$, $\Omega^* = \Omega_F^T$
HS-0	Adaptive expectations, no explicit workers' target $\hat{w}_t = \omega(e_t - e^N) + \hat{p}_{t-1}$, $\omega > 0$	Incomplete pass-through of excess wage inflation $\hat{p}_t = \vartheta\omega(e_t - e^N) + \hat{p}_{t-1}$, $1 > \vartheta \geq 0$	Upwards sloping in e, shifting for any $e \neq e^N$	Profit-squeeze, rotating towards $\Omega_W^T(e) = \Omega(e)$ and beyond	Wage-led, shifting	Rising/falling $e \neq e^N$, rising/falling $\hat{w}$, $\hat{p}$, rising/falling Ω
HS-1	Adaptive expectations, no explicit workers' target $\hat{w}_t = \omega(e_t - e^N) + \hat{p}_{t-1}$, $\omega > 0$	Incomplete pass-through of total wage inflation $\hat{p}_t = \vartheta[\omega(e_t - e^N) + \hat{p}_{t-1}]$, $1 > \vartheta \geq 0$	Upwards sloping in e, stable	Profit-squeeze, rotating towards $\Omega_W^T(e) = \Omega(e)$ and beyond	Wage-led, shifting	Rising/falling $e \neq e_0$, rising/falling $\hat{w}$, $\hat{p}$, rising/falling Ω
HS-2	Adaptive expectations, explicit workers' target $\hat{w}_t = \varphi_1(\Omega_W^T - \Omega_{t-1}) + \varphi_2 \hat{p}_{t-1}$, $\varphi_1 > 0, \varphi_2 = 1$	Incomplete pass-through of total wage inflation $\hat{p}_t = \vartheta[\varphi_1(\Omega_W^T - \Omega_{t-1}) + \varphi_2 \hat{p}_{t-1}]$, $1 > \vartheta \geq 0$	Horizontal in eat $\hat{p} = 0$, stable	Profit-squeeze, rotating towards $\Omega_W^T(e) = \Omega(e)$	Wage-led, stable	Constant $e \neq e_0$, $\hat{p}_t^* = \hat{w}_t^* = 0$, $\Omega^* = \Omega_W^T$
HS-3	Adaptive expectations, explicit workers' target $\hat{w}_t = \varphi_1(\Omega_W^T - \Omega_{t-1}) + \varphi_2 \hat{p}_{t-1}$, $\varphi_1 > 0, \varphi_2 = 1$	Incomplete pass-through of excess wage inflation $\hat{p}_t = \vartheta\varphi_1(\Omega_W^T - \Omega_{t-1}) + \varphi_1 \hat{p}_{t-1}$, $1 > \vartheta \geq 0$	Horizontal in e at path-dependent $\hat{p}$, stable	Profit-squeeze, rotating towards $\Omega_W^T(e) = \Omega(e)$	Wage-led, stable	Constant $e \neq e_0$, $\hat{p}_t^* = \hat{w}_t^*$, $\Omega^* = \Omega_W^T$

tendency of distribution moving towards and finally achieving the workers' target wage share (or even to go beyond this in HS-0 and HS-1), because each of the models assume incomplete pass-through of (excess) wage inflation to price inflation.

This comparison is meant to clearly spell out the differences and implications of each of the basic post-Keynesian/Kaleckian textbook conflict inflation models and their variations in a transparent way. In this context, we have already pointed out some of the problems of each of the approaches. In the BSL approach in general, it remains unclear why workers, who feel strong enough to target a higher wage share by means of raising nominal wage inflation, do not fully take into account expected price inflation—in a simple model indicated in an adaptive way by past period's inflation. Similarly, it remains unclear why firms, if they feel sufficiently powerful to raise the profit share and thus lower their target wage share, cannot fully take into account current wage inflation while setting prices. In other words, in these models the relationship between targets and power to push for achieving the targets remains vague and does not seem to be fully consistent. In the HS approaches, in particular the HS-0 and HS-1 variants, power relationships, indicated by the deviation of the employment rate from the SIRE, are directly introduced into the wage- and price-inflation equations, generally assuming incomplete pass-through of wage (dis-)inflation to price (dis-)inflation. However, the omission of targets from the wage-inflation equation leads to implausible results, if the long-run implications are considered: Powerful workers may increase wage inflation above expected price inflation although they have already reached their targets. Directly including workers' targets into the wage-inflation equation and linking that with incomplete pass-through in price inflation may generate more plausible results, generating a tendency towards flat Phillips curves and wage shares tending towards workers' targets, with the latter directly related to workers' bargaining power.

But we refrain from drawing too broad conclusions from the exercises presented in this paper, in particular regarding real-world relevance or applicability. As pointed out, the model versions are simple textbook models for closed economies without a government, operating with constant technology. The latter has allowed us to identify the demand regime with the employment regime. However, allowing for technical change and productivity growth may question whether a wage-led demand regime also generates a wage-led employment regime (Storm and Naastepad 2013). And including the external sector may question whether the demand regime is always wage-led, as assumed here (Onaran and Galanis 2014; Onaran and Obst 2016). Including the possibility of profit-led demand and employment regimes would thus generate further model variants. We have also assumed that the demand regime is always debt-burdened, or that normal case conditions for changes in real interest payments of the firm sector hold. Also this may be questioned, and allowing for puzzling case conditions and debt-led demand regimes would provide further variations (Hein 2023b).

Furthermore, in the model versions we have assumed that there is no macroeconomic wage bargaining coordination taking inflation externalities of nominal wage setting into account, neither on the workers'/trade unions' side, nor on the firms'/employer associations' side, nor between trade unions and employer associations. As proposed in post-Keynesian macroeconomic policy models (Hein 2023a, ch. 6, Hein and Stockhammer 2010), wage bargaining coordination could align wage share targets of workers and firms and contribute to flatten the wage- and price-Phillips curves, at least in certain ranges. We have also not systematically discussed for each of the model versions the effects of changes in the structural and institutional conditions for nominal wage setting in the labour market and price setting in the goods market. Also this would have to be taken into account when applying the conflict inflation and distribution theories in order to explain real world trends.

Acknowledgements

We are grateful for helpful comments to Ryan Woodgate and two anonymous referees. For editing assistance we thank Samuel Küppers. Remaining errors are exclusively ours, of course.

Disclosure Statement

No potential conflict of interest was reported by the author(s).

ORCID

Eckhard Hein http://orcid.org/0000-0002-6542-6630

References

Arestis, P., and M. Sawyer. 2005. 'Aggregate Demand, Conflict and Capacity in the Inflationary Process.' *Cambridge Journal of Economics* 29 (6): 959–974.

Bastian, E. F., and M. Setterfield. 2020. 'Nominal Exchange Rate Shocks and Inflation in an Open Economy: Towards a Structuralist Inflation Targeting Agenda.' *Cambridge Journal of Economics* 44 (6): 1271–1299.

Bernanke, B. S., and O. J. Blanchard. 2023. 'What Caused the US Pandemic era Inflation.' NBER Working Paper 31417.

Blanchard, O.J. 2017. *Macroeconomics*. 7th edition. Boston: Pearson.

Blecker, R. A. 2011. 'Open Economy Models of Distribution and Growth.' In *A Modern Guide to Keynesian Macroeconomics and Economic Policies*, edited by E. Hein, and E. Stockhammer, 215–239. Cheltenham: Edward Elgar.

Blecker, R. A., and M. Setterfield. 2019. *Heterodox Macroeconomics: Models of Demand, Distribution and Growth*. Cheltenham: Edward Elgar Publishing.

Carlin, W., and D. Soskice. 2009. 'Teaching Intermediate Macroeconomics Using the 3-Equation Model.' In *Macroeconomic Theory and Macroeconomic Pedagogy*, edited by G. Fontana, and M. Setterfield, 13–35. Basingstoke: Palgrave Macmillan.

Carlin, W., and D. Soskice. 2015. *Macroeconomics: Institutions, Instability, and the Financial System*. Oxford: Oxford University Press.

Cassetti, M. 2002. 'Conflict, Inflation, Distribution and Terms of Trade in a Kaleckian Model.' In *The Economics of Demand-Led Growth*, edited by M. Setterfield, 189–214. Cheltenham: Edward Elgar.

Cassetti, M. 2003. 'Bargaining Power, Effective Demand and Technical Progress: A Kaleckian Model of Growth.' *Cambridge Journal of Economics* 27: 449–464.

Dutt, A. K. 1987. 'Alternative Closures Again: A Comment on 'Growth, Distribution and Inflation'.' *Cambridge Journal of Economics* 11 (1): 75–82.

Dutt, A. K. 1992. 'Conflict Inflation, Distribution, Cyclical Accumulation and Crises.' *European Journal of Political Economy* 8 (4): 579–597.

Hartwig, J. 2014. 'Testing the Bhaduri–Marglin Model with OECD Panel Data.' *International Review of Applied Economics* 28 (4): 419–435.

Hein, E. 2006. 'Wage Bargaining and Monetary Policy in a Kaleckian Monetary Distribution and Growth Model: Trying to Make Sense of the NAIRU.' *European Journal of Economics and Economic Policies: Intervention* 3 (2): 305–329.

Hein, E. 2014. *Distribution and Growth After Keynes: A Post-Keynesian Guide*. Cheltenham: Edward Elgar Publishing.

Hein, E. 2023a. *Macroeconomics After Kalecki and Keynes: Post-Keynesian Foundations*. Cheltenham: Edward Elgar.

Hein, E. 2023b. 'Varieties of Demand and Growth Regimes – Post-Keynesian Foundations.' *European Journal of Economics and Economics Policies: Intervention* 20 (3): 410–443.

Hein, E. 2024. 'Inflation is Always and Everywhere ... a Conflict Phenomenon: Post-Keynesian Inflation Theory and Energy Price Driven Conflict Inflation, Distribution, Demand and Employment.' *European Journal of Economics and Economic Policies: Intervention* 21 (2), forthcoming.

Hein, E., and E. Stockhammer. 2009. 'A Post-Keynesian Alternative to the New Consensus Model.' In *Macreoeconomic Theory and Macroeconomic Pedagogy*, edited by G. in Fontana, and M. Setterfield, 273–294. Basingstoke: Palgrave Macmillan.

Hein, E., and E. Stockhammer. 2010. 'Macroeconomic Policy Mix, Employment and Inflation in a Post-Keynesian Alternative to the New Consensus Model.' *Review of Political Economy* 22 (3): 317–354.

Hein, E., and E. Stockhammer. 2011. 'A Post-Keynesian Macroeconomic Model of Inflation, Distribution and Employment.' In *A Modern Guide to Keynesian Macroeconomics and Economic Policies*, edited by E. Hein, and E. Stockhammer, 112–136. Cheltenham: Edward Elgar Publishing.

Kaldor, N. 1955/56. 'Alternative Theories of Distribution.' *The Review of Economic Studies* 23 (2): 83–100.

Kaldor, N. 1957. 'A Model of Economic Growth.' *The Economic Journal* 67 (268): 591–624.

Kaldor, N. 1959. 'Economic Growth and the Problem of Inflation.' *Economica* 26 (104): 287–298.

Kalecki, M. 1954. *Theory of Economic Dynamics: An Essay on Cyclical and Long-Run Changes in Capitalist Economy*. London: Allen and Unwin.

Kalecki, M. 1971. *Selected Essays on the Dynamics of the Capitalist Economy, 1933–1970*. Cambridge: Cambridge University Press.

Keynes, J. M. 1930 [1973]. *A Treatise on Money, Vol. 1, Reprinted in: The Collected Writings of J.M. Keynes, Vol. V*. London: Macmillan.

Keynes, J. M. 1936 [1973]. *The General Theory of Employment, Interest, and Money, Reprinted in The Collected Writings of J.M. Keynes, Vol. VII*. London: Macmillan.

Kim, H. 2023. 'Inflation in OECD Countries: An Empirical Assessment of a Structuralist Theory of Inflation.' *Review of Political Economy*.

Lavoie, M. 1992. *Foundations of Post Keynesian Economic Analysis*. Aldershot: Edward Elgar Publishing Publishing.

Lavoie, M. 1995. 'Interest Rates in Post-Keynesian Models of Growth and Distribution.' *Metroeconomica* 46 (2): 146–177.

Lavoie, M. 2006. 'A Post-Keynesian Amendment to the New Consensus on Monetary Policy.' *Metroeconomica* 57 (2): 165–192.

Lavoie, M. 2022. *Post-Keynesian Economics: New Foundations*. Cheltenham: Edward Elgar.

Lavoie, M. 2024a. 'Conflictual Inflation and the Phillips Curve.' *Review of Political Economy*.

Lavoie, M. 2024b. 'Questioning Profit Inflation as an Explanation of the Post-Pandemic Inflation.' *European Journal of Economics and Economic Policies: Intervention* 21 (2): forthcoming.

Lorenzoni, G., and I. Werning. 2023. 'Inflation is Conflict.' NBER Working Paper w31099.

Marglin, S. A. 1984. 'Growth, Distribution and Inflation: A Centennial Synthesis.' *Cambridge Journal of Economics* 8 (2): 115–144.

Matamoros, G. 2023. 'Are Firm Markups Boosting Inflation? A Post-Keynesian Institutionalist Approach to Markup Inflation in Selected Industrialized Countries.' *Review of Political Economy*.

Morlin, G. S. 2023. 'Inflation and Conflicting Claims in the Open Economy.' *Review of Political Economy* 35(3): 762–790.

Onaran, Ö, and G. Galanis. 2014. 'Income Distribution and Growth: A Global Model.' *Environment and Planning A: Economy and Space* 46 (10): 2489–2513.

Onaran, Ö, and T. Obst. 2016. 'Wage-Led Growth in the EU15 Member-States: The Effects of Income Distribution on Growth, Investment, Trade Balance and Inflation.' *Cambridge Journal of Economics* 40 (6): 1517–1551.

Palley, T. I. 2007. 'Macroeconomics and Monetary Policy: Competing Theoretical Frameworks.' *Journal of Post Keynesian Economics* 30 (1): 61–78.

Palley, T. I. 2012. 'The Economics of the Phillips Curve: Formation of Inflation Expectations Versus Incorporation of Inflation Expectations.' *Structural Change and Economic Dynamics* 23: 221–230.

Robinson, J. 1956. *The Accumulation of Capital.* London: Macmillan.

Robinson, J. 1962. *Essays in the Theory of Economic Growth.* London: Macmillan.

Rochon, L.-P., and M. Setterfield. 2007. 'Interest Rates, Income Distribution, and Monetary Policy Dominance: Post Keynesians and the "Fair Rate" of Interest.' *Journal of Post Keynesian Economics* 30 (1): 13–42.

Rowthorn, R. E. 1977. 'Conflict, Inflation and Money.' *Cambridge Journal of Economics* 1 (3): 215–239.

Rowthorn, R. E. 2024. 'The Conflict Theory of Inflation Revisited.' *Review of Political Economy.*

Sasaki, H., R. Sonoda, and S. Fujita. 2013. 'International Competition and Distributive Class Conflict in an Open Economy KAleckian Model.' *Metroeconomica* 64 (4): 683–715.

Sawyer, M. 2002. 'The NAIRU, Aggregate Demand and Investment.' *Metroeconomica* 53 (1): 66–94.

Serrano, F., R. Summa, and G. Morlin. 2024. 'Conflict, Inertia, and Phillips Curve from a Sraffian Standpoint.' *Review of Political Economy.*

Setterfield, M. 2008. 'Macroeconomics Without the LM Curve: An Alternative View.' *Cambridge Journal of Economics* 33 (2): 273–293.

Setterfield, M. 2023. 'Inflation and Distribution During the Post-COVID Recovery: A Kaleckian Approach.' *Journal of Post Keynesian Economics* 46 (4): 587–611.

Stockhammer, E. 2008. 'Is the Nairu Theory a Monetarist, New Keynesian, Post Keynesian or a Marxist Theory?' *Metroeconomica* 59 (4): 479–510.

Storm, S., and C. W. M. Naastepad. 2013. 'Wage-Led or Profit-Led Supply: Wages, Productivity and Investment.' In *Wage-Led Growth: An Equitable Strategy for Economic Recovery*, edited by M. Lavoie, and E. Stockhammer, 100–124. Basingstoke: Palgrave Macmillan.

Summa, R., and J. Braga. 2020. 'Two Routes Back to the Old Phillips Curve: The Amended Mainstream Model and the Conflict-Augmented Alternative.' *Bulletin of Political Economy* 14 (1): 81–115.

Sylos-Labini, P. 1979. 'Prices and Income Distribution in Manufacturing Industry.' *Journal of Post Keynesian Economics* 2 (1): 3–25.

Tarling, R., and F. Wilkinson. 1985. 'Mark-Up Pricing, Inflation and Distributional Shares: A Note.' *Cambridge Journal of Economics* 9 (2): 179–185.

Vera, L. 2014. 'The Simple Post-Keynesian Monetary Policy Model: An Open Economy Approach.' *Review of Political Economy* 26 (4): 526–548.

Weber, I. M., and E. Wasner. 2023. 'Sellers' Inflation, Profits and Conflict: Why Can Large Firms Hike Prices in an Emergency?' *Review of Keynesian Economics* 11 (2): 1–21.

OPEN ACCESS

'Sellers' Inflation' and Monetary Policy Interventions: A Critical Analysis

Giuseppe Mastromatteo and Sergio Rossi

ABSTRACT
This paper analyses the phenomenon of 'sellers' inflation', that is to say, the increases in consumer prices as a result of firms' decision to increase their selling prices as much as possible in the aftermath of the war in Ukraine. This analysis focuses also on central banks' responses to such inflationary pressures, which monetary authorities have been trying to limit with several increases in their policy rates of interest. The paper explains the major shortcomings of this monetary policy strategy and its negative consequences for a number of economic agents. The last section puts forward an alternative economic policy stance, proposing in particular a series of 'green' monetary policy interventions to address these inflationary pressures in the general interest for the common good.

1. Introduction

The war in Ukraine has induced the phenomenon of 'sellers' inflation' (an expression used by Weber and Wasner 2023), that is, a series of increases in consumer prices as a result of firms' decision to increase their profits as much as possible, exploiting thereby the shortage of some raw materials both in the food and energy sectors (see Matamoros 2023a, 2023b). To restrain these inflationary pressures, central banks have been putting into practice a restrictive monetary policy, increasing their interest rates rapidly and in different steps that have contributed to slow down economic activities across the world and notably in many so-called 'advanced' countries — as if these inflationary pressures were the result of excessive demand on the market for produced goods and services, where the mainstream of the economics profession considers that 'too much money chases too few goods', as argued by Friedman (1960) and claimed by Bernanke and Blanchard (2023) recently (see Rossi 2022 for a critical appraisal of this orthodox view).

The next section presents the orthodox conception of actual inflationary pressures, with a critical approach that points out the mainstream's failures on macroeconomic grounds. The third section focuses on post-pandemic monetary policy interventions, which in fact aggravated these inflationary pressures instead of avoiding them with an appropriate co-ordinated intervention with the relevant fiscal authorities. The fourth section expands on this, suggesting an alternative economic policy stance, co-ordinating fiscal policy with a green monetary policy in order to address several economic issues in the general interest for the common good. The last section concludes, summarizing the major points of our analysis from a political economy perspective.

2. The Orthodox Analysis of Inflation and its Major Flaws

The mainstream's view on actual inflationary pressures considers them as if they were largely the result of excessive demand on the market for produced goods and services, induced by expansionary fiscal policies that have been adopted to address the COVID-19 crisis, and also as a result of 'quantitative easing' monetary policies in the aftermath of the global financial crisis. This is indeed the view of Bernanke and Blanchard (2023, p. 38), who consider that, in the US economy, 'the inflation reflected strong aggregate demand, the product of easy fiscal and monetary policies, excess savings accumulated during the pandemic, and the reopening of locked-down economies'. This explanation has been provided also in regard of other Western countries, particularly the European economy: 'the dynamics of demand and supply in the euro area have been similar to those in the United States. Specifically in the post-pandemic inflation surge, also both strong demand and weak supply factors appear to have been at work' (Eickmeier and Hofmann 2022, p. 4). These conclusions are also reached by many other mainstream economists (see Guerrieri et al. 2022; Shapiro 2022; Cline 2023; di Giovanni et al. 2023). As a matter of fact, in both the US and European economy 'there was little evidence of a wage—price spiral, in that workers did not achieve nominal wage gains sufficient to compensate them for unexpected price increases' (Bernanke and Blanchard 2023, p. 38). This is what a number of heterodox economists have pointed out in the post-pandemic period: 'the fall in the wage share has been accompanied by a fall in real wages, as nominal wages have not (yet) managed to catch up with prices' (Lavoie 2023a, Internet). To be sure, since the end of the COVID-19 pandemic, notably after the various lockdowns of a series of economic activities, an increasing number of individuals have been consuming much more goods and services. This induced a rapid increase in aggregate demand, so that the gap with actual supply could be reduced if not closed, with a positive impact on firms' sales figures, hence on their profits. Further, the economic consequences of the war that began in Ukraine on February 24, 2022 affected the consumer price level, which showed a rapid and mushroom growth across the world, particularly in different Western economies, notably in Europe and in the United States. Critics of so-called 'unconventional' monetary policy interventions in the aftermath of the global financial crisis that burst in 2008 have been pointing out these interventions as the main factor of those inflationary pressures that have been observed since 2022 in 'advanced' economies — as if '*inflation is always and everywhere a monetary [policy] phenomenon*' in the Friedman (1987, p. 17, italics in the original) sense, that is to say, originating in central banks' expansionary policies.

Now, instead of analysing the macroeconomic effects of restrictive monetary policies in the current inflationary environment, the orthodox view focuses on estimating the costs of reducing the measured rate of inflation, taking it for granted that there is no seriously viable and practicable alternative to pursuing a restrictive policy that causes recession or a reduction in national income (see notably Bernanke and Blanchard 2023).

The results of this view are summarized in a statistical indicator, the so-called 'sacrifice ratio', which measures how many percentage points of produced output the government is willing to give up each year in order to reduce the inflation rate by one percentage point (see Rossi 2004). To date, there is no longer any debate about the size of this sacrifice or how to distribute it in a balanced manner across the economic system, particularly as regards the labor market. To be sure, for each loss of produced output, there is also a sacrifice in terms of employment — hence an increase in unemployment, even though this phenomenon is not captured entirely by any official statistics. Further, empirical evidence across a variety of countries shows that inflation-targeting central banks have not been in a position to reduce the 'sacrifice ratio' or, in other words, to observe lower output and employment losses, as compared to those losses recorded in those countries whose central banks do not have an inflation-targeting strategy (see Rochon and Rossi 2006 for a critical appraisal of such a strategy).

The current macroeconomic situation and its short-run perspectives are problematic and therefore raise the need to consider the effects of these inflationary pressures on income and wealth distribution, within as well as between the relevant countries. The questions that are relevant in this regard and that must be urgently addressed by policy makers are manyfold: what is going to happen if the distributive conflict between firms and wage earners is left to the so-called 'market forces' of supply and demand in a situation of 'sellers' inflation'? Does the combination of rising wages for the necessary economic recovery and increasing policy rates of interest provide the best solution to dispose of these inflationary pressures? Are there any real possibilities to constrain the power of financial institutions and profit-oriented corporations in a framework of economic stagnation? To what extent is it possible to make real wages fall below subsistence levels and increase households' debt volumes, which to be sure are already problematic in different 'advanced' economies, particularly in a period where interest rates have shown an increasing trend, notably in the United States? Indeed, both in the United States and across the European Union, income inequalities — resulting from both the stagnation of real wages and job insecurity as a result of involuntary unemployment — have given rise to a mushroom growth of households' indebtedness since the early 1990s (see for instance Foster and Magdoff 2009 and Kotz 2009).

As Tori, Caverzasi, and Gallegati (2023) explain, the financialization process (see Epstein 2021) fostered by financial deregulation, liberalization and innovation, has been and still is the pivot around which the endogenous dynamics leading to the Great Recession unfolded and that still limits the effectiveness of monetary policies aimed at combating inflationary pressures. Indeed, the innovation process of banks and non-bank financial institutions, particularly in the United States, transformed them into 'financial commodity creators' and 'financial asset producers'. The somewhat 'forced' indebtedness of wage earners and consumers, as a result of increasing inequalities in wealth and income distribution, has been the lever to find 'new ways of financing assets' (Minsky 1986, p. 220), thus increasing the supply of credit with innovative approaches that allowed banks to expand their traditional role as credit providers and thereby become also 'producers of financial commodities' by not directly bearing their risks through different transfer mechanisms (the so-called 'originate-to-distribute' model). This expansion of the financial system has led to a surge in its level of indebtedness, thereby reducing the power of monetary and fiscal authorities to counter inflationary pressures with the same instruments they used to address those analogous pressures that emerged during the 1970s in Western economies.

Now, the emergence of inflationary pressures in the United States and across European countries has different supply-side causes, namely, the large impact of the COVID-19 pandemic on the labor market and the economic consequences of the war in Ukraine, which have induced a relevant increase in energy prices, import prices, as well as profit margins of a number of firms (see Ferguson and Storm 2023). Indeed, the lockdowns during the COVID-19 pandemic and the subsequent rebound of economic growth, as a result of expansionary fiscal and monetary policies across Western countries, induced an unexpected retreat from globalization, with a reshoring of many activities that made some goods more expensive to produce — a trend that was already observed during the Trump administration, and that the Biden administration did not interrupt as regards the United States. The war in Ukraine reinforced this trend across the Western economies, which more recently has been exacerbated by firms' increased mark-up rates. Indeed, particularly in Europe, rising profit margins have been responsible for almost half of the inflationary pressures observed since early 2022, as many firms have raised their selling prices more than their soaring costs for both energy and raw materials (Hansen, Toscani, and Zhou 2023). Figure 1 shows it clearly, as regards the evolution of profits and wages since the outbreak of the COVID-19 pandemic across the European Union.

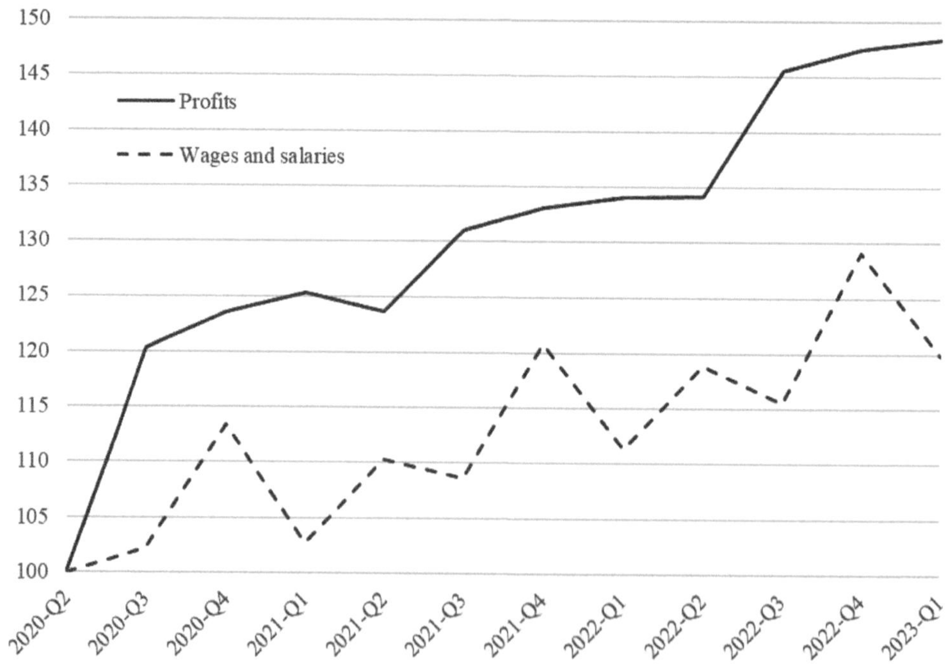

Figure 1. Evolution of profits and wages in the European Union (2020-Q2 = 100). Source: authors' elaboration on Eurostat data, available at https://ec.europa.eu/eurostat/databrowser/view/NAMQ_10_A10__custom_7139707/default/table and https://ec.europa.eu/eurostat/databrowser/view/TEINA520__custom_7139662/default/table (last accessed on 29 December 2023).

In Europe (more than in the United States), no price—wage spiral has been observed as a result of the inflationary pressures mentioned above. As a matter of fact, the growth rate of real GDP has been low since the beginning of the war in Ukraine. If so, then how can one explain that profit margins have been increased, pushing up the price level despite a stagnating demand on the market for produced goods and services? To be sure, there are no increases in real wages across Europe that could justify an increase in prices as large as it has been observed since early 2022. Indeed, these inflationary pressures have been the result of firms' increases of their mark-up, particularly for those firms whose market power allowed them to exploit this situation in order to record a rapid increase in profits so much so that the profit share of non-financial corporations increased, too (see Bivens 2022a; 2022b). Figure 2 illustrates this phenomenon across the European Union, which was initiated by the COVID-19 pandemic and further expanded by the war in Ukraine.

The increase in profits and in the profit share, and the stagnation of real wages, can be observed in the whole European Union since early 2020. For instance, Ragnitz (2022) shows that in Germany companies in some sectors took advantage of price increases to increase profits. As Boitani and Tamborini (2023) point out, this phenomenon has been present for some time in most 'advanced' countries and manufacturing sectors since the second half of 2021, although it appears more pronounced in some countries (the United States and the United Kingdom) and in some sectors (notably, agriculture, energy, food, construction, catering, and tourism) once the war in Ukraine burst in February 2022 (see also Saraceno 2023c).

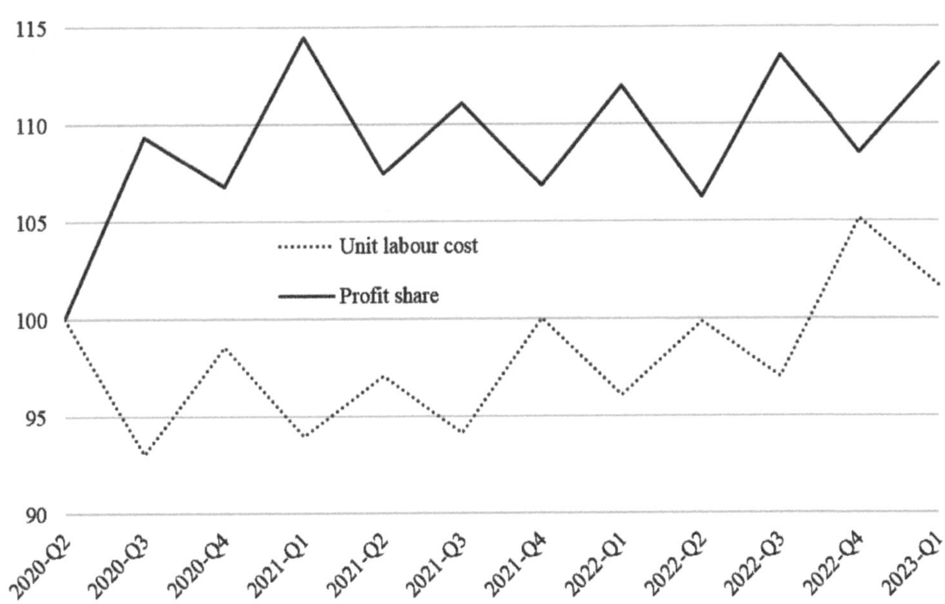

Figure 2. Evolution of unit labor cost and profit share in the European Union (2020-Q2 = 100). Source: authors' elaboration on Eurostat data, available at https://ec.europa.eu/eurostat/databrowser/view/TEINA520__custom_7139662/default/table and https://ec.europa.eu/eurostat/databrowser/view/NAMQ_10_LP_ULC__custom_7121733/default/table (last accessed on 29 December 2023).

To be sure, this 'sellers' inflation' is not only a European phenomenon, as it has also been observed in the United States since the outbreak of the COVID-19 pandemic in early 2020 (Figure 3).

For instance, Konczal and Lusiani (2022) show that, in 2021, mark-up rates and profits skyrocketed to their highest recorded level since the 1950s across the US economy, as firms 'increased their markups and profits [...] at the fastest annual pace since 1955' (Konczal and Lusiani 2022, p. 1): in this country profits account for 9.4 per cent of the 14.1 per cent increase in the GDP deflator from the third quarter of 2020 to the second quarter of 2022, while wages account for only 4.7 per cent of this increase across the US economy. Storm (2022, p. 38) confirms this observation, as he points out that '[m]ore than 38 per cent of the rise in the US inflation rate during 2020Q2 – 2022Q1 has been due to fatter profit margins, with higher unit labor costs contributing around 19 per cent of this increase.' Weber and Wasner (2023) agree, arguing that also in the US economy the post-pandemic inflationary pressures are predominantly 'seller-induced' and stem from the ability of firms with market power to raise prices. Such firms are price makers, but they actually decide to raise prices only if they expect their competitors to do the same. 'This requires an implicit agreement which can be coordinated by sector-wide cost shocks and supply bottlenecks' (Weber and Wasner 2023, p. 183). The most important sectors that have been adopting such a pricing strategy are chemicals, iron and steel, healthcare, and fossil fuels. Actually, the example of oil companies is really emblematic of this strategy: Breman and Storm (2023, p. 35) point out that speculative activity in the oil market 'has been responsible for 24 per cent–48 per cent of the increase' in crude oil prices during the period from October 2020 to

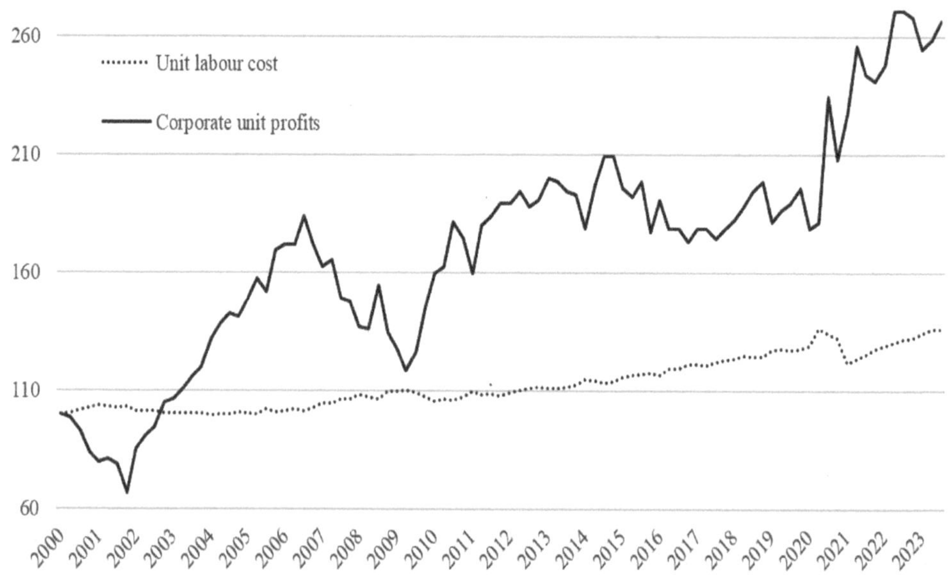

Figure 3. Evolution of unit labor cost and corporate unit profits in the United States (2000-Q1 = 100). Source: authors' elaboration on Bureau of Economic Analysis data, available at https://apps.bea.gov/iTable/?reqid = 19&step = 3&isuri = 1&nipa_table_list = 56&categories = survey (last accessed on 29 December 2023).

June 2022. According to their own calculations, 'these estimates translate into an oil price increase of around $18–$36 per barrel' and into an increase in the measured rate of inflation for consumption expenditures in the United States of about 0.75–1.5 percentage points from October 2020 to June 2022 (Breman and Storm 2023, pp. 35–36). The authors further notice (p. 36) that rising oil prices drove up the price of fertilizers, thereby much increasing the prices of basic food commodities (corn and soybeans). Oil speculators were therefore indirectly responsible for the increase in several food prices. Hence, Breman and Storm (2023, p. 36) conclude that higher oil prices have reduced consumers' purchasing power and disproportionately affected lower and middle-income households (who spend a larger share of their income on energy and food than richer households).

This framework of profit-driven inflation has been explained by Dögüs (2022), while the analysis of Weber and Wasner (2023) focuses on market concentration and firms' power allowing them to increase their mark-up, originating thereby many inflationary pressures as observed since March 2022. Both in Europe and in the United States, an increasing number of firms are profiting from inflationary pressures since early 2022, because wages have been increased much less than consumer prices. According to the European Central Bank calculations, in 2022 the standard of living for a representative employee in the euro area was 5 per cent lower than in 2021 (Bodnár et al. 2022). This situation is confirmed by Janssen (2023, Internet), who notices that across the European Union '[o]verall nominal wages still increased by 4.8 per cent on average in 2022 and seemed to continue their recovery after the pandemic. But with consumer prices peaking at 11.5 per cent in the EU-27 in October 2022, nothing was left of any recovery gains. On the contrary. Due to the inflation shock, workers lost an astonishing amount of purchasing power last year: real wages plunged by 4.0 per cent on average in the EU — an unprecedented loss.'

This wage squeeze, in fact, is the opposite of the wage-driven inflationary pressures observed in a number of Western countries during the 1970s — a period that still inspires the monetary policy decisions of a number of central banks confronted since 2022 with a series of problematic increases in the price level on the market for produced goods and services, both in Europe and in the United States. As a matter of fact, the US economy well illustrates these discrepancies between the wage-driven inflationary pressures during the two oil shocks of the 1970s and the 'sellers' inflation' observed at the time of writing (Figures 4 and 5).

As Figure 4 illustrates, during the first oil-price shock (1973–75) unit labor costs in the United States increased more than 20 per cent — from the first quarter of 1973 to the first quarter of 1975 — while corporate unit profits showed a reduction slightly higher than 10 per cent. A similar dynamics was observed in the second oil-price shock (1979–81) — as Figure 5 shows with regard to the US economy, where unit labor costs increased about 20 per cent while corporate unit profits were reduced by 20 per cent before coming back to their initial level in the first quarter of 1981. This historical evidence contrasts with the most recent statistics of the post-COVID-19 pandemic period in the United States, where the measured rate of inflation 'rose to 4.8 per cent in the second quarter of 2021, [while] profit margins of non-financial US corporations (after tax) broke a new record and climbed to 13.5 per cent, surpassing the previous series high during the post-war inflation in 1947' (Weber and Wasner 2023, p. 183).

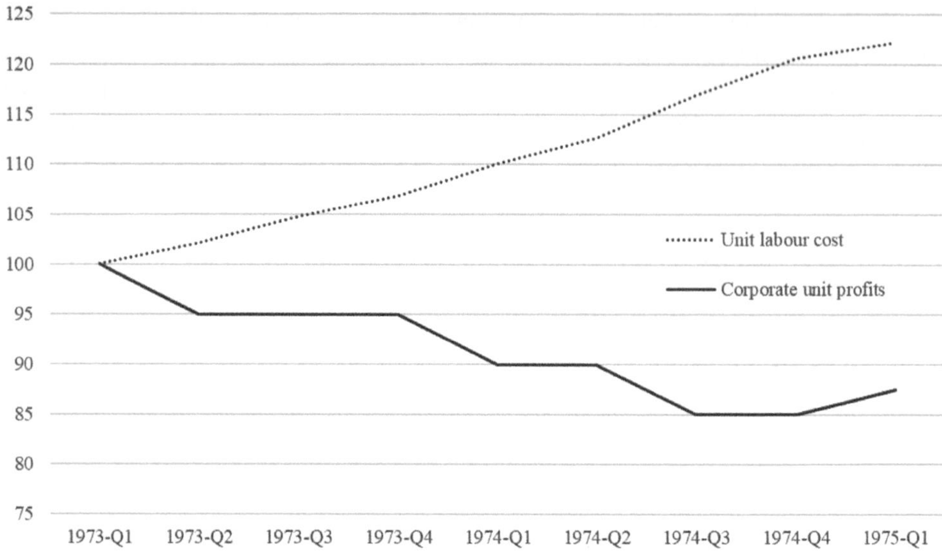

Figure 4. Evolution of unit labor cost and corporate unit profits in the 1970s first oil-shock in the United States (1973-Q1 = 100). Source: authors' elaboration on Bureau of Economic Analysis data, available at https://apps.bea.gov/iTable/?reqid = 19&step = 3&isuri = 1&nipa_table_list = 56&categories = survey (last accessed on 29 December 2023).

This relationship between an increase in firms' profits and in the general price level is a clear signal that those inflationary pressures observed since 2022 in the global economy are not the result of excessive demand on the market for produced goods and services. It

Figure 5. Evolution of unit labor cost and corporate unit profits in the 1970s second oil-shock in the United States (1979-Q1 = 100). Source: authors' elaboration on Bureau of Economic Analysis data, available at https://apps.bea.gov/iTable/?reqid = 19&step = 3&isuri = 1&nipa_table_list = 56&categories = survey (last accessed on 29 December 2023).

also indicates clearly that these pressures do not result from central banks' expansionary policies, contrary to the monetarists' claim, and cannot be explained with the so-called New-Keynesian consensus that considers aggregate demand to be higher than potential output (see Weber et al. 2022 for analytical elaboration). In both these views, inflation cannot result from an increase in firms' mark-up or their power to set prices. However, the relationship between the strong increase in profits and the general increase in prices observed since 2022 cannot be ignored, while there are no good indicators of excessive demand or a wage–price spiral (see Bivens 2022a, 2022b; Glover, Mustre-del-Rio, and von Ende-Becker 2023; Stiglitz and Regmi 2023). Leading central bankers in the United States and Europe have indeed clearly recognized the contribution of profits to inflation (see Brainard 2022; Schnabel 2022). This is so much so that inflationary pressures derived from firms' higher mark-up rates and market power are further increased by firms' compliance with the demand of institutional investors to demonstrate their ability to protect (and to increase) their respective market shares. 'If firms deviate from this price hike strategy, the threat of share sell-offs by financial investors can enforce compliance with such implicit agreements' (Weber and Wasner 2023, p. 186). As all firms want to protect their profit margins and know that other firms pursue the same goal, they may raise prices, trusting that other firms will follow suit. Indeed, if a firm deviates from this strategy of raising prices, the threat that a relevant number of financial investors will sell its shares may force it to comply with this strategy. This characteristic of the contemporary 'money manager capitalism' (Minsky 1993) is interesting, as it captures an element of the profit greed typical of our finance-led economic systems, so much so that it represents an additional opportunity for firms that was not present in the post-Great Recession stagnation period of 2007–2008.

A somewhat different perspective on current inflationary pressures has been provided by Lavoie (2023a, Internet), who denies the generalized existence of profit inflation. His argument is that '[w]hile one can certainly acknowledge that some industries such as the oil industry have benefitted from higher profit margins, [...], in general, the rise in profits and the profit share can be explained without resorting to an explanation based on firms taking advantage of the situation and raising markup rates' (Lavoie 2023a). Lavoie is indeed right in pointing out that, at the microeconomic level, '[f]irst, as firms produce and sell more units, their unit cost drops, and hence their realized profit per unit gets bigger, and secondly since they sell more units, they will make more profits.' Further, '[a]t the macroeconomic level, as the economy recovers, the presence of overhead labour costs explains that the profit share in value added will normally rise, despite constant markup rates' (Lavoie 2023a, Internet). This is what Nikiforos and Grothe (2023, Internet) have pointed out, explaining that profit-led inflation does not require an increase in markup rates. As Lavoie (2023a, Internet) observes — referring to Castro-Vincenzi and Kleinman (2023) — this occurs particularly in materials-intensive sectors. Further, 'in countries where there is a rise in the prices of materials and primary inputs, including energy, there is a rise in the share of profits in value added' (Lavoie 2023a, Internet; see also Lavoie 2023b, 2023c). In this regard, as Bellofiore and Coveri (2023, p. 26) point out, Lavoie's (2023a, 2023b, 2023c) writings have the merit to clarify four different magnitudes whose evolution can explain current inflationary pressures across the Western economies, namely: the total amount of profits, the share of profits in value added, the profit margin (that is, profit as a percentage of the total value of sales), and the mark-up rate (to wit, the mark-up set by firms on their normal unit production costs that enter into the determination of selling prices). In this regard, at the time of writing, '[t]he *rate of change* of prices is going down, but their *level* is permanently higher. In the process, wage earners have lost purchasing power, while profit earners have been able to defend and sometimes increase their profit margins' (Gallo 2024, Internet).

Therefore, since there is actually no real danger of starting a price–wage spiral, why did all central banks in Western countries put into practice a radically restrictive monetary policy to counteract those inflationary pressures that essentially depend neither on wage earners' power nor on aggregate demand? Let us address this issue in the next section to point out the major flaws of this monetary policy stance.

3. Post-Pandemic Monetary Policy Tightening: A Fundamental Critique

Rochon (2022a, p. 21) emphasizes that the New Consensus model — according to which 'changes in the rate of interest lead to expected changes in output' — is flawed and not grounded in empirical support (see also Rochon 2022b). Indeed, at a theoretical level, the transmission mechanism of monetary policy to real variables within the economic system is conditioned by multiple breaks in the chain of causal relations (see Rochon and Vallet 2022; Rochon and Seccareccia 2023). At the empirical level, there are many analyses with mixed findings, at best, of relevant effects of interest rates on investment and consumption (see, for instance, Cynamon, Fazzari, and Setterfield 2013; Sharpe and Suarez 2015). Raising interest rates to tame inflation requires repeated interventions by central banks, until their cumulative effect risks leading to a collapse of the whole economic system (Rochon 2022a). This is so much so that monetary policy lags are long and relevant, as the empirical evidence shows in a number of countries. As a matter of fact, the meta-analysis of Havranek and Rusnak (2013) pointed out that, on average, it takes from 12 to 18 months to see the effects of a change in the policy rate of interest on the so-called 'real' economy, and the transmission mechanism takes about two and a half years to be complete. These lags are particularly long for those countries having a highly developed financial system, because in these countries the central bank has much less influence on banks' decisions to open new credit lines. As Saraceno (2023b) notices, this means that the impact of the monetary policy tightening started around mid-2022 cannot be really observed before the end of 2023, when the economic system of Western countries may be suffering from a recession, particularly in the European Union and notably in some peripheral countries of the euro area. These observations help explaining why the timing of inflation containment, especially when addressed without resolving the problems of income and wealth distribution induced by actual inflationary dynamics, is misaligned with the recessionary consequences of inappropriate monetary policies.

Recessionary forces, generated by a series of monetary policy tightening, could indeed result in a balance sheet recession, that is, an economic recession that occurs when high levels of both private and public sector indebtedness make individuals, firms and States to save in order to repay their maturing debts rather than spending for consumption or investment purposes, causing first a slowdown and then a decline in output and income (see Koo 2011). This scenario can also give rise to a self-reinforcing spiral, as falling incomes make the amount of maturing debts even less sustainable, leading to larger reductions in both private and public spending. As a matter of fact, several collateral damages of monetary policy tightening were experienced in the early 1980s, when the drastic interventions to reduce the measured rate of inflation in the United States gave rise to a debt crisis in developing countries, which entered thereby in a lost decade for different Latin American and African economies. Now, as Storm (2022) notes, there is still a risk that the global recession triggered by a rapid and sharp rise of interest rates in the United States could permanently affect the growth and development processes in emerging economies, damaging the potential increases in domestic demand and capital accumulation in these countries, with a consequent drop in their ability to repay private and public debts. This is so much so that a number of other Western countries, beyond the United States, have been increasing repeatedly their rates of interest in 2022 as well as in 2023. These restrictive monetary policies, by the way, further increase the price level on the market for produced goods and services, since firms that need a new bank loan will have to pay higher rates of interest, thereby transferring to their selling prices these higher borrowing costs. This is the so-called 'Gibson paradox' (see, for instance, Levrero 2023). Hence, central banks will further push up their policy rates of interest, giving rise to a vicious circle that affects the whole economic system negatively as time goes by.

If an uncoordinated hike in the policy rates of interest, dictated by the desire of the US Federal Reserve to control inflationary pressures, were to lead to a global recession, it would raise serious questions about the workings of a system driven predominantly by the concerns of monetary authorities. It is true that a continuous increase in the price level on the market for produced goods and services induces the risk that inflation will become entrenched over time with expectations of an upward spiral, so much so that central banks will be forced to raise interest rates even more sharply. It is equally true that an over-intensity in the use of restrictive monetary policies would lead to a global recession without the certainty of averting this inflationary spiral. An entire generation of young people, whose education has already been damaged by COVID-19 lockdowns, will face therefore an increasingly problematic labor market. This situation is already a reality in the world's largest labor market, namely, China, where youth unemployment is around 20 per cent at the time of writing — similarly to the relevant figures for the so-called 'PIGS' countries in the euro area, namely, Portugal, Italy, Greece and Spain.

As Romaniello (2022) points out, the persistence of both high unemployment rates and inflationary dynamics is grafted onto an institutional context characterized by decades of weakening workers' power, thereby reducing the actual role of trade unions, and the precariousness of labor relations resulting from several 'structural' reforms. All these reforms, in fact, have not induced a reduction in unemployment rates, but have instead fully succeeded in weakening workers' wage claims. The unemployment rate aimed at by economic policies becomes only that which is compatible with a stable inflation rate, because it is the rate of unemployment necessary to weaken workers' bargaining power sufficiently to make them accept the wage rate reconcilable with the income distribution desired by corporations and global financial institutions (Romaniello 2022, p. 279). In this scenario, the anti-inflation recipe that finds majority consensus is precisely that of a strongly incisive and rapid monetary policy intervention to eradicate any expectations of further increases of the price level on the market for produced goods and services.

Now, as Weber and Wasner (2023) point out, conflict inflation driven by wage recovery could be the next stage in the current inflationary dynamics, and this could be exactly what central bankers want to avoid by continuing raising their policy rates of interest. However, such a monetary policy tightening affects both debtors and creditors with a series of negative effects: debtors are affected negatively as far as their income may be reduced across the labor market, while creditors could suffer from a reduction in the prices of their (real-estate and financial) assets. To be sure, borrowers have noticed a sharp increase in the variable rates of interest on their mortgage loans, which (together with a mushroom growth of consumer prices) have induced a reduction of disposable income to be spent on the market for produced goods and services, to support their living standard. These effects also impact on firms' investment negatively, since the level of aggregate demand on the product market is reduced thereby. Further, central banks' decisions to raise the policy rates of interest induce a redistribution of income from debtors to creditors, whose effect on total expenditure cannot be determined but probably is negative on macroeconomic grounds, considering that, generally speaking, the propensity to consume is higher for debtors than for creditors.

Now, these issues only concern income distribution. In highly financialized economies, where the prices of real-estate and financial assets have grown much more than income growth since the late 1980s, the monetary policy tightening that all major central banks have been putting into practice to curb inflationary pressures in the aftermath of the war in Ukraine could put financial stability at stake, with a series of dramatic effects across the 'real' economy, as a result of a sharp drop in the prices of real and financial assets. In this regard, Seccareccia (2017) points out that those quantitative easing interventions implemented by several central banks since the outbreak in 2008 of the global financial crisis deliberately sacrificed interest yields (driving interest rates to virtually zero) in order to preserve the market valuation of financial assets. As Wray and Kelton (2023, Internet) notice, '[g]radually, markets adapted to persistently low interest rates. In this new environment, leverage made sense. Holding long term assets made sense again. Financial markets bubbled.'

As Spanò (2023) explains cogently, in the conflict between creditors and debtors, rising the policy rates of interest implies that debtors lose real income, while creditors, even if they gain something in terms of income, suffer a price reduction of their financial assets. Generally speaking, economists focus on the former (income) effect, particularly since a large number of wage earners are affected by it. The latter (wealth) effect, however, is much more relevant for financial institutions, because a rise in interest rates induces a variety of them to sell their positions across financial markets, which can be affected by an increasing volatility, creating a framework of financial instability that could lead to a financial crisis eventually. This shows the need to rethink monetary policy interventions anew, integrating them into an appropriate policy mix that considers the general interest for the common good. Let us expand on this issue in the next section.

4. The Need of Rethinking Monetary Policy Interventions in an Appropriate Policy Mix

The COVID-19 pandemic has shown that fiscal and monetary policies must go together, to wit, should be co-ordinated to support economic activities, hence employment as well as financial stability of the economic system as a whole. In spite of this, the inflationary pressures induced by the war in Ukraine have been considered by policy makers simply as a result of excessive demand on the market for produced goods and services, thereby inducing central banks to raise their policy rates of interest markedly and repeatedly. In fact, as Saraceno (2023a) lucidly notes, instead of increasing the policy rates of interest, which impacts all sectors similarly, fiscal policy should have been preferred, as it could operate in a more targeted manner. For instance, fiscal authorities may implement some temporary price controls in the less competitive sectors of the economic system and in those where there are rents, providing incentives in those sectors where bottlenecks are the result of insufficient production capacity, adopting an active labor policy when the problem is labor supply, and supporting disposable income of those consumers that are most affected by inflationary pressures on the market for produced goods and services (see also Bofinger 2024).

In this regard, Saraceno (2023a) points out that the only way to avoid that a minority of powerful economic agents are in a position to take advantage of the current situation to the detriment of all other stakeholders (thereby progressively undermining the Welfare state created after the Second World War, which originated around thirty years of both economic growth and prosperity; the so-called 'Glorious Thirties') is for public policies to prioritizing collective interests. The instruments for this to occur exist and range from contingent measures such as price controls or the extraordinary and temporary taxation of extra profits — as advocated recently by economists from the International Monetary Fund (see Baunsgaard and Vernon 2022) — to those that eradicate the very foundations of income and wealth inequality in a more structural manner. For example, in the latter area, there might be a return to more progressive tax systems and greater international co-ordination to put an end to tax avoidance by transnational corporations and to avert a recessionary fiscal competition between countries. The recent decision by the member countries of the Organization for Economic Co-operation and Development to establish a minimum corporate tax rate and the obligation for transnational companies to declare their profits in the countries where the latter did originate (and not according to their tax domicile) represent an important step in this regard.

Indeed, the instruments of a policy mix different from the New Consensus are manifold, and monetary policy should provide incentives to both households and businesses for an appropriate ecological transition that guarantees price as well as financial stability in the economic system as a whole. Let us focus on these issues to illustrate the importance of monetary policy for the common good, moving away from the assumption of monetary policy neutrality, which has been influencing many central banks' interventions in order for them to avoid distortions in financial markets (Dikau and Volz 2021; van't Klooster and de Boer 2022). To be sure, as Rossi (2024) explains, no monetary policy decision is neutral, since it affects a number of variables across the whole economic system and alters both income distribution and capital allocation (see Rochon and Vallet 2022 for analytical elaboration on this). As a matter of fact, when a central bank carries out some asset purchase programs, it is not neutral as it supports the current capital allocation, thereby replicating existing market failures in a carbon-biased manner (Schnabel 2021; Kedward, Gabor, and Ryan-Collins 2022; Rochon 2022c). In particular, Matikainen, Campiglio, and Zenghelis (2017), Jourdan and Kalinowski (2019) as well as

Dafermos et al. (2020) have shown that the European Central Bank's interventions with quantitative easing instruments are biased in support of some sectors that are damaging the environment. Further, as D'Orazio (2021) points out, the macroprudential framework implemented by central banks at the time of writing does not really integrate ecological concerns, thereby further enhancing this carbon bias of any monetary policy decisions, which provide better funding conditions for pollutant activities in both the so-called 'real' economy and across financial markets (Couppey-Soubeyran 2020).

Let us propose, therefore, three 'green' monetary policy interventions to influence the banks' decisions to provide credit to firms, in order also to reduce current inflationary pressures due to 'profit inflation' in carbon-intensive activities such as the fossil-fuel sector (Solari, Le Bloc'h, and Rossi 2024).

First, central banks should differentiate the policy rate of interest applied in their own refinancing operations in regard of the volume of 'green' loans that banks provide in their domestic economy. This echoes the proposal by van't Klooster and van Tilburg (2020) about 'green' Targeted Long-Term Refinancing Operations (TLTROs) that the European Central Bank may put into practice to induce banks greening their portfolios. To date, these TLTROs aim at increasing banks' lending to support the 'real' economy, but without any consideration of the environmental consequences of these loans. These consequences could be mitigated by reducing the policy rates of interest for all lending operations that comply with some ecological objectives to be defined appropriately. In the current period of higher interest rates to curb inflationary pressures, this instrument could be used to protect non-harmful economic activities (see Monnet and van't Klooster 2023), supporting them in order to satisfy agents' demand so that no supply shortages or profit greed can exert an upward pressure on the price level in the market for produced goods and services. Similarly, any kind of refinancing operations carried out by central banks should have a policy rate of interest that integrates a 'climate premium' in light of the 'greenness degree' of the banks that are supported thereby, as Kempf (2020) has put to the fore to support a finance-led ecological transition. This premium has to be in line with the average degree of climate-related risk associated with the loans granted by a given bank. Such a penalty rate of interest would induce banks to look more carefully at the kinds of economic activities to which they provide credits, even though this must go along with the definition and implementation of an appropriate green taxonomy and rigorous verification of its compliance by all stakeholders (see D'Orazio and Popoyan 2022; Sawyer 2022).

Secondly, the list of eligible assets that central banks accept when they carry out any of their lending operations (rather than just for their repurchase agreements) should have a climate-related disclosure requirement and make sure that these assets are aligned with ecological targets (see Couppey-Soubeyran 2020). To date, as a matter of fact, central banks' lending has a carbon bias (Rochon 2022c), because their list of eligible assets is largely composed of bonds and equities issued by polluting firms (Pelizzon et al. 2020; Dafermos 2021). This allows these firms to maximize their profits, exerting thereby an upward pressure on the general price level when the factors summarized in the previous sections permit them to do so. In order to reduce these inflationary pressures at the time of writing, therefore, central banks or financial supervisory authorities should introduce a minimum share of 'green' assets that banks and non-bank financial institutions must respect when they need to borrow from the central bank (Oustry et al. 2020; Boneva,

Ferrucci, and Mongelli 2022). Greening the collateral framework of monetary policy interventions can thus contribute to price stability without damaging financial stability, provided that banks as well as non-bank financial institutions are sanctioned appropriately if they do not abide by the rules concerning the greenness of their portfolio. To support this framework, the relevant central banks could apply an (additional) haircut to all carbon-intensive assets, preventing 'greenwashing' strategies based on so-called 'green repos' (see Kedward, Gabor, and Ryan-Collins 2022).

Thirdly, central banks can intervene with a so-called 'green' quantitative easing, that is, purchasing huge volumes of government or corporate bonds issued to finance any kinds of climate-protecting economic activities. If so, then the carbon bias that, to date, affects monetary policy interventions would be much reduced (to disappear eventually), so that a number of carbon-intensive activities will be excluded from central banks' portfolio — particularly those financial assets currently issued by fossil fuel companies that at the time of writing are a major factor of profit inflation as explained in previous sections. Further, central banks might also implement quantitative easing interventions aimed at holding only financial assets that are consistent with social and ecological priorities, as proposed by van't Klooster and Fontan (2020). This monetary policy stance should also apply in the current period of quantitative tightening: 'brown' financial assets should be the first to be sold by central banks, to partially reinvest the relevant amounts in various low-carbon economic activities (Claeys 2023). This echoes Monnet and van't Klooster (2023), who point out that in case of maturing securities, central banks could also invest the corresponding amount in purchasing green bonds, thereby reducing the inflation rate across the market for produced goods and services in so far as carbon-intensive firms do not receive any incentive from the loan market that allows them to maximize their own profits through an increase in their selling prices.

To achieve these objectives, policy makers must coordinate their interventions in order to stabilize interest rates without leading to recessions, through a variety of instruments such as price controls that most affect the consumption of the less well-off (like energy, foodstuffs and services of collective public interest, such as health and education), fiscal policy, and the various forms of concertation and incomes policies that make it possible to determine wages, profit margins and public tariffs in a co-ordinated and co-operative manner with the aim of keeping inflation under control. The post-pandemic inflation is actually pointing out the importance of returning to a policy mix, co-ordinating the use of multiple instruments to achieve objectives that are sometimes even contradictory to each other (Saraceno 2023a).

Now, unlike past experiences, reinforced State intervention in the economic system and new opportunities for public and/or private borrowing are no longer enough. We should also rethink the organization of societies, that is, what, how and for whom to produce in the general interest for the common good (see Robinson 1972). This, however, implies several distributional conflicts that should be solved through the mutual convenience of all stakeholders to work together, in order to distribute in a well-balanced way all those increases in prosperity that result from investments, technological progress and the fight against inflation, once its actual origins are properly identified on economic grounds.

5. Conclusion

The analysis presented in this paper has pointed out the origins of current inflationary pressures, which can be identified in the increases of firms' profits in many economic activities that have been largely affected by the COVID-19 pandemic and the war that burst in Ukraine on February 24, 2022. In this regard, the current policy choices do not provide an appropriate solution to counter this economic situation: increasing the policy rates of interest does not reduce actual inflationary pressures, since the latter come from the supply side and not from the demand side, as the orthodox view pretends it. Further, monetary policy tightening increases the measured rate of inflation, as firms must pay a higher rate of interest when they need to refinance their bank loans, thereby transferring to consumer prices these higher borrowing costs. Such a restrictive monetary policy, by the way, could push the whole economic system into a sharp recession — which is then likely to increase financial instability across the global economy, as banks and non-bank financial institutions have to manage higher credit risks in a recessionary framework. As a matter of fact, consumption and investment seem to be quite insensitive to incremental increases in the rates of interest (so much so when the magnitude of these increases lies between 25 and 50 basis points), but are indeed sensitive to their cumulative increases — even though at the time of writing we are not at this point yet. However, as regards the labor market and wage levels, increasing the policy rates of interest in this framework reduces both the employment and the wage levels of an increasing number of workers, creating thereby the preconditions for growing instability and social unrest. Indeed, as Michał Kalecki would say, pushing real wages below the subsistence level through a sharp recession as well as higher unemployment is against the interests of firms, as it would drag the global economy into another great recession with extreme, disruptive and unresolved conflicts across the world.

As the current inflationary pressures have been induced by the effects of the COVID-19 pandemic and the war in Ukraine, in a context of already high financialization, there is a need to search for alternative instruments that are able to affect, also through fiscal and industrial policies, the redistributive conflicts of inflation by protecting the most fragile categories of economic agents. This paper suggests therefore an alternative scenario to the mainstream's view — where monetary policy interventions make it possible to curb actual inflationary pressures and support economic activities with a view to ecological transition considering the general interest for the common good, so that there will be no further polarization of social classes and, most importantly, without imposing another reduction of well-being to the poor and middle class (Bibi 2023 expands on this). Only in this situation will 'sellers' inflation' represent an opportunity for a radical change in economic policies as well as activities in so-called 'advanced' economies disposing of income as well as wealth distributional conflicts when carrying out a properly defined ecological transition with the support of central banks. Let us hope that policy makers will have enough time to consider and implement this proposal, before the next global crisis occurs, because otherwise the future will be highly dramatic for an increasing number of economic agents across the world — which at the time of writing is already largely affected by the on-going polycrisis that creates so many fears and troubles for many stakeholders.

Acknowledgements

The authors are grateful to Louis-Philippe Rochon for his much constructive comments on a first draft of this paper. They also thank two anonymous referees for their critiques, which have been considered in this revised version extensively. Research assistance by Maurizio Solari is gratefully acknowledged. The usual disclaimer applies.

Disclosure Statement

No potential conflict of interest was reported by the author(s).

ORCID

Giuseppe Mastromatteo http://orcid.org/0000-0002-7809-8832
Sergio Rossi http://orcid.org/0009-0002-5926-5356

References

Baunsgaard, T., and N. Vernon. 2022. *Taxing Windfall Profits in the Energy Sector.* Washington, DC, USA: International Monetary Fund Note. No. 2022/002.

Bellofiore, R., and A. Coveri. 2023. '*Zwischen den Zeiten*: problemi e contraddizioni del capitalismo negli anni del ritorno dell'inflazione', *Officina Primo Maggio*, December, pp. 1–46, Available at http://sinistrainrete.info/pdf/InflazioneBellofioreCoveriOPM.pdf (last accessed on 11 March 2024).

Bernanke, B., and O. Blanchard. 2023. 'What Caused the U.S. Pandemic-Era Inflation?', Conference Draft, Hutchins Center on Fiscal & Monetary Policy at Brookings, 23 May, https://www.brookings.edu/research/what-caused-the-u-s-pandemic-era-inflation/.

Bibi, S. 2023. 'The Distributive Monetary Analysis of a (un)Sustainable Economy.' *Review of Political Economy*, doi:10.1080/09538259.2023.2189516.

Bivens, J. 2022a. 'Corporate Profits Have Contributed Disproportionately to Inflation. How Should Policymakers Respond?' *Economic Policy Institute*, Available at www.epi.org/blog/corporate-profits-have-contributed-disproportionately-to-inflation-how-should-policymakers-respond/ (last accessed on 11 March 2024).

Bivens, J. 2022b. 'Wage Growth has Been Dampening Inflation all Along – and has Slowed Even More Recently.' *Economic Policy Institute*, Available at www.epi.org/blog/wage-growth-has-been-dampening-inflation-all-along-and-has-slowed-even-more-recently/ (last accessed on 11 March 2024).

Bodnár, K., E. Gonçalves, L. Górnicka, and G. Koester. 2022. 'Wage Developments and Their Determinants Since the Start of the Pandemic.' *European Central Bank Economic Bulletin* 8: 117–137.

Bofinger, P. 2024. *Fighting Inflation with Conventional and Unconventional Fiscal Policy.* Düsseldorf (Germany): Institut für Makroökonomie und Konjunkturforschung Study, no. 92, Available at https://www.imk-boeckler.de/de/faust-detail.htm?sync_id=HBS-008797 (last accessed on 11 March 2024).

Boitani, A., and R. Tamborini. 2023. 'Inflazione da profitti o profitti da inflazione?', *Menabò*, (192), Available at https://eticaeconomia.it/inflazione-da-profitti-o-profitti-da-inflazione/?fbclid=IwAR2YXil6flB0dFh3Vwj5uBVd70gn936iLklrjDt_uzE5aWNATRn5LxtyuWM (last accessed on 11 March 2024).

Boneva, L., G. Ferrucci, and F. P. Mongelli. 2022. 'Climate Change and Central Banks: What Role for Monetary Policy?' *Climate Policy* 22 (6): 770–787.

Brainard, L. 2022. '*Bringing inflation down*.' Paper presented at the Clearing House and Bank Policy Institute 2022 Annual Conference, Available at www.federalreserve.gov/newsevents/speech/brainard20220907a.htm (last accessed on 11 March 2024).

Breman, C., and S. Storm. 2023. 'Betting on Black Gold: Oil Speculation and U.S. Inflation (2020–2022)', *Institute for New Economic Thinking Working Paper*, no. 208, Available at www.

ineteconomics.org/uploads/papers/WP_208-Storm-and-Breman-Oil-price-speculation-and-inflation.pdf (last accessed on 11 March 2024).

Castro-Vincenzi, J., and B. Kleinman. 2023. 'Intermediate Input Prices and the Labor Share', *Econometrica*, Available at https://www.castrovincenzi.com/s/LaborShare2.pdf (last accessed on 11 March 2024).

Claeys, G. 2023. 'Finding the Right Balance (Sheet): Quantitative Tightening in the Euro Area', *Monetary Dialogue Papers*, Available at https://www.bruegel.org/sites/default/files/2023-03/Claeys%20QT%202023%20Final.pdf (last accessed on 11 March 2024).

Cline, W. R. 2023. 'Fighting the Pandemic Inflation Surge of 2021-2022', *Economics International Inc. Working Paper*, no. 23-1.

Couppey-Soubeyran, J. 2020. 'The Role of Monetary Policy in the Ecological Transition: An Overview of Various Greening Options', Veblen Institute for Economic Reforms, Available at https://www.veblen-institute.org/IMG/pdf/the_role_of_monetary_policy_in_the_ecological_transition_an_overview_of_various_greening_options.pdf (last accessed on 11 March 2024).

Cynamon, B. Z., S. Fazzari, and M. Setterfield, eds. 2013. *After the Great Recession: The Struggle for Economic Recovery and Growth*. Cambridge, UK: Cambridge University Press.

Dafermos, Y. 2021. 'Climate Change, Central Banking and Financial Supervision: Beyond the Risk Exposure Approach.' *SOAS Department of Economics Working Paper*, no. 243.

Dafermos, Y., D. Gabor, M. Nikolaidi, A. Pawloff, and F. van Lerven. 2020. 'Decarbonising is Easy: Beyond Market Neutrality in the ECB's Corporate QE', New Economics Foundation, Available at https://neweconomics.org/uploads/files/Decarbonising-is-easy.pdf (last accessed on 11 March 2024).

di Giovanni, J., Ş Kalemli-Özcan, A. Silva, and M. A. Yildirim. 2023. 'Quantifying the Inflationary Impact of Fiscal Stimulus Under Supply Constraints.' *AEA Papers and Proceedings* 113: 76–80.

Dikau, S., and U. Volz. 2021. 'Central Bank Mandates, Sustainability Objectives and the Promotion of Green Finance.' *Ecological Economics* 184, doi:10.1016/j.ecolecon.2021.107022.

D'Orazio, P. 2021. 'Towards a Post-Pandemic Policy Framework to Manage Climate-Related Financial Risks and Resilience.' *Climate Policy* 21 (10): 1368–1382.

D'Orazio, P., and L. Popoyan. 2022. 'Realising Central Banks' Climate Ambitions Through Financial Stability Mandates.' *Intereconomics* 57 (2): 103–111.

Dögüs, I. 2022. 'Market Power and Inflation', *Monetary Policy Institute Blog*, Available at https://medium.com/@monetarypolicyinstitute/market-power-and-inflation-ea917ac86f67 (last accessed on 11 March 2024).

Eickmeier, S., and B. Hofmann. 2022. 'What Drives Inflation? Disentangling Demand and Supply Factors' *Deutsche Bundesbank Discussion Paper*, no. 46/2022.

Epstein, G. A. 2021. 'Financialization.' In *An Introduction to Macroeconomics: A Heterodox Approach to Economic Analysis*, Second Edition, edited by L.-P. Rochon, and S. Rossi. Cheltenham, UK: Edward Elgar.

Ferguson, T., and S. Storm. 2023. 'Myth and Reality in the Great Inflation Debate: Supply Shocks and Wealth Effects in a Multipolar World Economy.' *International Journal of Political Economy* 52 (1): 1–44.

Foster, J. B., and F. Magdoff. 2009. *The Great Financial Crisis: Causes and Consequences*. New York: NYU Press.

Friedman, M. 1960. *A Program for Monetary Stability*. New York: Fordham University Press.

Friedman, M. 1987. 'Quantity Theory of Money.' In *The New Palgrave: A Dictionary of Economics*, edited by J. Eatwell, M. Milgate, and P. Newman. London: Macmillan.

Gallo, E. 2024. 'Unpacking Decreasing Inflation: Profit Inflation vs. the Heroic Central Bank', *Monetary Policy Institute Blog* #122, 27 February, Available at https://medium.com/@monetarypolicyinstitute/unpacking-decreasing-inflation-profit-inflation-vs-the-heroic-central-bank-76aae6327051 (last accessed on 11 March 2024).

Glover, A., J. Mustre-del-Rio, and A. von Ende-Becker. 2023. 'How Much Have Record Corporate Profits Contributed to Recent Inflation?' *Federal Reserve Bank of Kansas City Economic Review* 1: 1–13.

Guerrieri, V., G. Lorenzoni, L. Straub, and I. Werning. 2022. 'Macroeconomic Implications of Covid-19: Can Negative Supply Shocks Cause Demand Shortages?' *American Economic Review* 112 (5): 1437–1474.

Hansen, N.-J., F. Toscani, and J. Zhou. 2023. 'Europe's Inflation Outlook Depends on how Corporate Profits Absorb Wage Gains', *The Business Standard*, 26 June, Available at www.tbsnews.net/world/global-economy/europes-inflation-outlook-depends-how-corporate-profits-absorb-wage-gains (last accessed on 11 March 2024).

Havranek, T., and M. Rusnak. 2013. 'Transmission Lags of Monetary Policy: A Meta-Analysis', *International Journal of Central Banking* 9 (4): 39–75.

Janssen, T. 2023. 'From Inflation Shock to a Sharp Distributional Conflict', *Social Europe*, 27 July, Available at www.socialeurope.eu/from-inflation-shock-to-a-sharp-distributional-conflict (last accessed on 11 March 2024).

Jourdan, S., and W. Kalinowski. 2019. 'Aligning Monetary Policy with the EU's Climate Targets', *Veblen Institute for Economic Reforms and Positive Money Working Paper*, Available at https://www.veblen-institute.org/IMG/pdf/aligning_monetary_policy_with_eu_s_climate_targets.pdf (last accessed on 11 March 2024).

Kedward, K., D. Gabor, and J. Ryan-Collins. 2022. 'Aligning Finance with the Green Transition: From a Risk-Based to Allocative Green Credit Policy Regime.' *UCL Institute for Innovation and Public Purpose Working Paper*, no. 2022-11. last accessed on 11 March 2024.

Kempf, H. 2020. 'Verdir la politique monétaire.' *Revue d'économie politique* 130 (3): 311–343.

Konczal, M., and N. Lusiani. 2022. 'Prices, Profits, and Power: An Analysis of 2021 Firm-Level Markups', Mimeo, Available at https://rooseveltinstitute.org/wp-content/uploads/2022/06/RI_PricesProfitsPower_202206.pdf (last accessed on 11 March 2024).

Koo, R. C. 2011. 'The World in Balance Sheet Recession: Causes, Cure, and Politics.' *Real World Economics Review* 58: 19–37.

Kotz, D. M. 2009. 'The Financial and Economic Crisis of 2008: A Systemic Crisis of Neoliberal Capitalism.' *Review of Radical Political Economics* 41 (3): 305–317.

Lavoie, M. 2023a. 'Some Controversies in the Causes of Postpandemic Inflation', *Monetary Policy Institute Blog* #77, 14 May, Available at https://medium.com/@monetarypolicyinstitute/some-controversies-in-the-causes-of-the-post-pandemic-inflation-1480a7a08eb7 (last accessed on 11 March 2024).

Lavoie, M. 2023b. 'Profit-Led Inflation Redefined: Response to Nikiforos and Grothe', Institute of New Economic Thinking, 6 June, Available at https://www.ineteconomics.org/perspectives/blog/profit-led-inflation-redefined-response-to-nikiforos-and-grothe (last accessed on 11 March 2024).

Lavoie, M. 2023c. 'Profit Inflation and Markups Once Again', Institute of New Economic Thinking, 15 June, Available at https://www.ineteconomics.org/perspectives/blog/profit-inflation-and-markups-once-again (last accessed on 11 March 2024).

Levrero, S. E. 2023. 'Gibson Paradox.' In *Elgar Encyclopedia of Post-Keynesian Economics*, edited by L.-P. Rochon, and S. Rossi. Cheltenham, UK: Edward Elgar.

Matamoros, G. 2023a. 'Are Firm Markups Boosting Inflation? A Post-Keynesian Institutionalist Approach to Markup Inflation in Select Industrialized Countries.' *Review of Political Economy*, doi:10.1080/09538259.2023.2244440.

Matamoros, G. 2023b. 'Once Again on Profit Inflation: A Follow-up on Marc Lavoie's Blog', *Monetary Policy Institute Blog* #82, 5 June, Available at https://medium.com/@monetarypolicyinstitute/once-again-on-profit-inflation-a-follow-up-on-marc-lavoies-blog-78f2986e3a39 (last accessed on 11 March 2024).

Matikainen, S., E. Campiglio, and D. Zenghelis. 2017. 'The Climate Impact of Quantitative Easing', *Grantham Research Institute on Climate Change and the Environment Policy Paper*, Available at https://www.lse.ac.uk/granthaminstitute/wp-content/uploads/2017/05/ClimateImpactQuantEasing_Matikainen-et-al.pdf (last accessed on 11 March 2024).

Minsky, H. P. 1986. *Stabilizing an Unstable Economy*. London, UK: Yale University Press.

Minsky, H. P. 1993. 'Schumpeter and Finance.' In *Market and Institutions in Economic Development: Essays in Honour of Paolo Sylos Labini*, edited by S. Biasco, A. Roncaglia, and M. Salvati. New York: St. Martin's Press.

Monnet, E., and J. van't Klooster. 2023. 'Using Green Credit Policy to Bring Down Inflation: What Central Bankers Can Learn from History', *The Inspire Sustainable Central Banking Toolbox Policy Briefing Paper*, no. 13, Available at https://www.inspiregreenfinance.org/publications/using-green-credit-policy-to-bring-down-inflation-what-central-bankers-can-learn-from-history/ (last accessed on 11 March 2024).

Nikiforos, M., and S. Grothe. 2023. 'Markups, Profit Shares, and Cost-Push-Profit-Led Inflation', Institute for New Economic Thinking, 6 June, Available at https://www.ineteconomics.org/perspectives/blog/markups-profit-shares-and-costpush-profit-led-inflation (last accessed on 11 March 2024).

Oustry, A., B. Erkan, R. Svartzman, and P.-F. Weber. 2020. 'Climate-Related Risks and Central Banks' Collateral Policy: A Methodological Experiment.' *Revue économique* Vol. 73 (2): 173–218.

Pelizzon, L., M. Riedel, Z. Simon, and M. G. Subrahmanyam. 2020. 'Collateral Eligibility of Corporate Debt in the Eurosystem.' *SAFE Working Paper*, no. 275. last accessed on 11 March 2024.

Ragnitz, J. 2022. 'Gewinninflation und Inflationsgewinner.' *ifo Dresden berichtet* 29 (5): 24–28.

Robinson, J. 1972. 'The Second Crisis of Economic Theory.' *American Economic Review* 62 (1–2): 1–10.

Rochon, L.-P. 2022a. 'The General Ineffectiveness of Monetary Policy or the Weaponization of Inflation.' In *The Future of Central Banking*, edited by S. Kappes, L.-P. Rochon, and G. Vallet. Cheltenham, UK: Edward Elgar.

Rochon, L.-P. 2022b. 'The Impotence of Monetary Policy', *Monetary Policy Institute Blog*, Available at https://medium.com/@monetarypolicyinstitute/the-impotence-of-monetary-policy-180fb24d0f28 (last accessed on 11 March 2024).

Rochon, L.-P. 2022c. 'Sesgos inherentes de la política monetaria.' In *Política fiscal y monetaria. Confinamiento, pandemia y recuperación inestable*, edited by A. Girón. Mexico: Instituto de Investigaciones Económicas, Universidad Nacional Autónoma de México.

Rochon, L.-P., and S. Rossi. 2006. 'Inflation Targeting, Economic Performance, and Income Distribution: A Monetary Macroeconomics Analysis.' *Journal of Post Keynesian Economics* 28 (4): 615–638.

Rochon, L.-P., and M. Seccareccia. 2023. 'A Primer on Monetary Policy and its Effect on Income Distribution: A Heterodox Perspective.' In *Central Banking, Monetary Policy and Income Distribution*, edited by S. Kappes, L.-P. Rochon, and G. Vallet. Cheltenham, UK: Edward Elgar.

Rochon, L.-P., and G. Vallet. 2022. 'The Institutions of the People, by the People and for the People? Addressing Central Banks' Power and Social Responsibility in a Democracy.' *PSL Quarterly Review* 75 (301): 83–102.

Romaniello, D. 2022. '*Unemployment gap*, isteresi e disoccupazione di lunga durata: quale ruolo nella comprensione dell'inflazione?' *Moneta e Credito* 75 (299): 267–283.

Rossi, S. 2004. 'Inflation Targeting and Sacrifice Ratios: The Case of the European Central Bank.' *International Journal of Political Economy* 34 (2): 69–85.

Rossi, S. 2022. 'Milton Friedman and the Monetarist School.' In *A Brief History of Economic Thought: From the Mercantilists to the Post-Keynesians*, edited by H. Bougrine, and L.-P. Rochon. Cheltenham, UK: Edward Elgar.

Rossi, S. 2024. 'The Political Benefits of 'Unconventional' Monetary Policies in Times of Crisis.' *Review of Political Economy* 36 (2): 533–545.

Saraceno, F. 2023a. 'Inflazione: strategie di policy mix globale', Istituto per gli Studi di Politica Internazionale, 15 June, Available at https://www.ispionline.it/it/pubblicazione/inflazione-strategie-di-policy-mix-globale-132334 (last accessed on 11 March 2024).

Saraceno, F. 2023b. 'The Damage of Monetary Tightening Is About to Begin', *Sparse Thoughts of a Gloomy European Economist Blog*, 4 August, Available at https://fsaraceno.wordpress.com/2023/08/04/the-damage-of-monetary-tightening-is-about-to-begin/ (last accessed on 11 March 2024).

Saraceno, F. 2023c. *Oltre le banche centrali: inflazione, disuguaglianza e politiche economiche.* Rome: LUISS University Press.

Sawyer, M. 2022. 'Monetary Policy, Environmental Sustainability and the Climate Emergency.' In *Central Banking, Monetary Policy and the Environment*, edited by L.-P. Rochon, S. Kappes, and G. Vallet. Cheltenham, UK: Edward Elgar.

Schnabel, I. 2021. 'From Green Neglect to Green Dominance?', Speech Given at the Conference on Greening Monetary Policy: Central Banking and Climate Change, Cleveland, 3 March, Available at https://www.ecb.europa.eu/press/key/date/2021/html/ecb.sp210303_1_annex~3c03f9a09c.en.pdf (last accessed on 11 March 2024).

Schnabel, I. 2022. 'The Globalisation of Inflation', Bank for International Settlements, Available at www.bis.org/review/r220513b.htm (last accessed on 11 March 2024).

Seccareccia, M. 2017. 'Which Vested Interests do Central Banks Really Serve? Understanding Central Bank Policy Since the Global Financial Crisis.' *Journal of Economic Issues* 51 (2): 341–350.

Shapiro, A. H. 2022. 'How Much do Supply and Demand Drive Inflation?' *Federal Reserve Bank of San Francisco Economic Letter* 2022-15: 1–6.

Sharpe, S. A., and G. A. Suarez. 2015. 'Why Isn't Investment More Sensitive to Interest Rates: Evidence from Surveys.' In *Finance and Economics Discussion Series*, no. 2014-002. Washington DC, USA: Finance and Economics Discussions Series.

Solari, M., A. Le Bloc'h, and S. Rossi. 2024. 'Ecological Transition in a Monetary Economy of Production: A Heterodox Approach.' *Eurasian Economic Review* 14 (1): 13–37.

Spanò, M. 2023. 'La politica economica tra inflazione e stabilità finanziaria', *La Fionda*, 24 March, Available at https://www.lafionda.org/2023/03/24/la-politica-economica-tra-inflazione-e-stabilita-finanziaria/ (last accessed on 11 March 2024).

Stiglitz, J. E., and I. Regmi. 2023. 'The Causes of and Responses to Today's Inflation.' *Industrial and Corporate Change* 32 (2): 336–385.

Storm, S. 2022. 'Inflation in the Time of Corona and war.' *Institute for New Economic Thinking Working Paper* 185.

Tori, D., E. Caverzasi, and M. Gallegati. 2023. 'Financial Production and the Subprime Mortgage Crisis.' *Journal of Evolutionary Economics* 33: 573–603.

van't Klooster, J., and N. de Boer. 2022. 'What to do with the ECB's Secondary Mandate.' *JCMS: Journal of Common Market Studies* 61 (3): 730–746.

van't Klooster, J., and C. Fontan. 2020. 'The Myth of Market Neutrality: A Comparative Study of the European Central Bank's and the Swiss National Bank's Corporate Security Purchases.' *New Political Economy* 25 (6): 865–879.

van't Klooster, J., and R. van Tilburg. 2020. 'Targeting a Sustainable Recovery with Green TLTROs', Positive Money Europe & Sustainable Finance Lab, Available at http://www.positivemoney.eu/wp-content/uploads/2020/09/Green-TLTROs.pdf (last accessed on 11 March 2024).

Weber, I. M., J. L. Jauregui, L. Teixeira, and L. N. Pires. 2022. 'Inflation in Times of Overlapping Emergencies: Systemically Significant Prices from an Input-Output Perspective.' *University of Massachusetts Amherst Economics Department Working Paper*, no. 340.

Weber, I. M., and E. Wasner. 2023. 'Sellers' Inflation, Profits and Conflict: Why Can Large Firms Hike Prices in an Emergency?' *Review of Keynesian Economics* 11 (2): 183–213.

Wray, L. R., and S. Kelton. 2023. 'Magical Monetary Thinking at the Fed Killed SVB', 18 March, Available at https://open.substack.com/pub/stephaniekelton/p/magical-thinking-monetary-thinking?utm_source = direct&utm_campaign = post&utm_medium = web (last accessed on 11 March 2024).

Conflict Inflation and the Role of Monetary Policy

Pedro Clavijo-Cortes

ABSTRACT

The aim of this study is twofold: on the one hand, to provide evidence of the positive association between the inflation rate and the labor share in the US; on the other, to show that monetary policy slows inflation by depressing the labor share. With the help of Bayesian econometrics, the paper shows evidence of a conflict Phillips curve. Furthermore, a structural vector autoregressive model reveals the detrimental effects of interest rate hikes on the labor share. Together, these results mean the monetary policy of administered interest rates resolves the class conflict in favor of capital to control inflation. Scrutiny of the US monetary policy development and a model of a controlled predator-prey system prepare the way for the empirical sections. Finally, the paper concludes that controlling the distributive conflict matters for impinging on inflation and that the Fed might follow alternative monetary rules to cease being the third party participating in the distributive conflict.

1. Introduction

This paper contributes to the scant empirical literature on the connection between inflation, functional distribution of income, and monetary policy in the US context. The theoretical literature on conflict inflation is vast and varied, a testament to the constant interest in the topic in heterodox economics (see, e.g., Goodwin (1967); Rowthorn (1977); Marglin (1984); Dutt (1992); Rochon and Setterfield (2007); Vera (2010); Lavoie (2022); among many others). Empirical investigation, however, is meager (see, e.g., Barbosa-Filho (2014); Perrotini Hernández and Vázquez Muñoz (2017); Taylor and Barbosa-Filho (2021)). Apart from that, the sharp rise in inflation that began after the COVID-19 pandemic and the subsequent policy response by central banks have spawned a renewed interest in this central relationship.

The null hypothesis I defend in this paper, firmly rooted in the heterodox tradition in economics, considers that the issues of inflation, income distribution, and monetary policy are tied not instrumentally but, if you will, constitutively. The theoretical scheme underpinning conflict inflation maintains that inflation is determined by class conflict over the distribution of national income, and the monetary authority, with its policy of administered interest rates, bends income distribution toward the profit share to restore price stability. Underlying this theory is the simple argument that inflation captures the balance of power between capitalists wishing to raise profitability and workers procuring wage increases whenever they feel strong enough to do so. This understanding of conflict inflation is the basic logic supporting this study.

Conflict inflation theory is rationalized as a coordination problem among classes regarding how national income is distributed. In this respect, Tobin (1981) considers inflation to be a temporary reconciliation of the conflicting and excessive claims both classes make on the resources available for distribution. Excess claims over the available real income are conceptualized in the form of an aspiration gap (Rowthorn 1977). The gap is simply the difference between the actual and the target labor share capitalists aspire to achieve that is consistent with a specific target share of profits. If both labor shares are similar, there is no rivalry among classes regarding how income is distributed, and therefore, prices remain unchanged. However, if they diverge and the actual exceeds the target labor share significantly, conflict triggers, and capitalists respond by increasing prices to reduce the real purchasing power of wages and achieve their desired profit share; see, e.g., Rochon and Setterfield (2007).

The idea of conflict inflation has also been explored within new-Keynesian macroeconomics. Lorenzoni and Werning (2023) render it into mainstream economics, arguing that inflation is due to disagreement on relative prices that leads to conflict. Woodford (2001) argues that the empirical failures of the new-Keynesian Phillips curve result from using detrended GDP to measure the output gap. He notes that the sticky-price models underpinning the new-Keynesian Phillips curve imply that labor share is the correct driving variable in this equation. Woodford presents evidence that using a direct measure of real marginal cost results in a better-fitting inflation equation and concedes that the labor share 'is a much better measure of the true output gap, at least for purposes of explaining inflation variation.' Sbordone (2002), and Galí and Gertler (1999) also suggest using labor's share of income as a proxy for nominal marginal cost in the new-Keynesian Phillips curve estimations. More recently, Ratner and Sim (2022) find that a reduction in inflation volatility is possible just by bending the power balance toward capital; the decline of trade union power helps explain the secular decline of the labor share and the rise of the profit share.

Although the new-Keynesian approaches are compelling, they find it problematic to analytically accommodate conflict inflation theory at the core of its 3-equation model. This is because it, in turn, implies that the monetary authority should raise interest rates in response to increases in the labor share. However, conducting monetary policy this way suggests following a discriminatory rule against workers, which meets resistance since it is at odds with the general principle of independence of a technical monetary authority that is free of political values. For example, Ratner and Sim (2022) maintain that the impact of Volcker's monetary policy has been exaggerated and that the inflation of the 1970s was solved through structural changes in the labor market that reduced workers' bargaining power rather than monetary policy. Their evaluation of the Volcker shock renders monetary policy irrelevant in income distribution assessments and invites the conclusion that those aggressive increases in real interest rates played no role in resolving the inflationary conflict.

Post-Keynesian macroeconomics, on the contrary, accepts that monetary policy has severe distributional effects. For Niggle, 'monetary policy, through its effects on interest rates, debt to income ratios, and interest income, has contributed substantially to the observed increasing inequality in the personal distribution of income in the United States since the 1960s' (Niggle 1989, 820). Specifically, he argues that monetary policy is transmitted to the functional distribution of income through the mechanism of the level of interest rates. Seccareccia and Lavoie (2016), following a Keynes-Pasinetti perspective, find that higher interest rates redistribute income favoring the affluent (rentiers and capitalists). This aligns with Rochon and Setterfield (2007), who show that the *raison d'etre* of monetary policy is to guarantee the conditions of profitability through interest rate changes to the detriment of wage participation in national income.

The post-Keynesian interpretation of the monetary policy instrument as a distributive variable stems from the theory of endogenous money that makes the interest rate exogenous to the economic system and, therefore, an administered variable. An implication of endogenous money and conflict inflation theories for making monetary policy is that the central bank must accommodate excess claims on the national income into its reaction function and set the interest rate accordingly to close the inflation loop. Hence, when the central bank acts to mediate the distributive conflict by setting the interest rate, it follows a discriminatory policy against one of the classes. In other words, it becomes a third party participating in the distributive conflict.

The mechanism through which interest rate changes stabilize inflation is the redistribution of income between classes, particularly by lowering labor share. Heterodox economic theory posits different ways that monetary policy can affect labor share. For instance, Pivetti (2010) shows that raising the policy rate instrument by the central bank induces capital to adjust their markups, which reduces real wages and inflation. Besides that, one might argue that the rise in interest rates weakens aggregate demand and employment. This reduces workers' bargaining power due to higher unemployment, leading to wages growing below productivity, thus reducing labor's income share and, ultimately, inflation. In either case, the burden of inflation lies with workers who must tolerate a devaluation of their income and reformulate their expectations for subsequent wage demands since they recognize that the monetary authority is determined to curb excessive demands by imposing wage moderation through recessions and unemployment.

This study contributes to the existing empirical literature on conflict inflation and monetary policy in two ways. First, in Section Three, using a Bayesian bivariate time-varying model for inflation, in which the aspiration gap is identified as the variable that governs inflation dynamics, I provide strong evidence of a positive and well-defined association in the data between inflation and income distribution. Second, in Section Four, I add the interest rate and show, with the help of a structural vector autoregressive (SVAR) model, that monetary shocks depress the labor share and thus reduce inflation. The structural approach adopted in this work benefits from recent contributions to SVAR literature. In specific, I trace the system's stochastic variations back to unique, informative covariance changes. But first, Section Two elaborates on a historical narrative of the pattern of the postwar development of the US monetary policy based on a bare-bones model of a controlled predator-prey system. The model and narrative introduced next provide informational content to the empirical sections for a dynamic analysis of how inflation and income distribution have interacted with US monetary policy.

2. The US Monetary Policy and its Control Strategy: An Overview

In this section, I provide evidence supporting conflict inflation theory as a good description of the US inflation, labor share, and interest rate behaviors. Figure 1 portrays the three variables of interest for this study and highlights prominent episodes and events that I refer to along the way. The data used are described in detail in Appendix.

Considering that inflation is, at its core, an expression and the outcome of class conflict, the inflation rate used in this study excludes food and energy. In this regard, Taylor and Barbosa-Filho (2021) find that apart from the labor share, import prices and material costs have also been key in explaining an inflation index that includes food and energy. The labor share is measured by the percentage of labor compensation in the Net Domestic Income. Finally, the interest rate is the zero-lower-bound-adjusted Federal Funds rate (Wu and Xia 2016). The interest rate is adjusted to capture the hypothetical monetary policy rates below the zero lower bound and thus to examine the macroeconomic effects of low interest rates. Also, to preempt issues regarding identifying monetary shocks at the zero lower bound.

From Figure 1, four observations, in particular, stand out. First, there is a sequence of movements among the variables: the three series peak during the 1980s and, following the Great Inflation period, start declining. Second, the inflation rate and the labor share, on one side, and the interest rate and the labor share, on the other, show comovements throughout the sample. Third, the labor share shows a hump shape, which confirms its deterioration after the 1980s. Fourth, etched in US economic history, the Volcker shock is present in the three variables and stands as a turning point after the 1980s.

The comovements between the inflation rate and the labor share suggest a positive relationship that, in line with conflict inflation theory, indicates that increases in labor share accelerate the impetus of the price level. The positive association between these

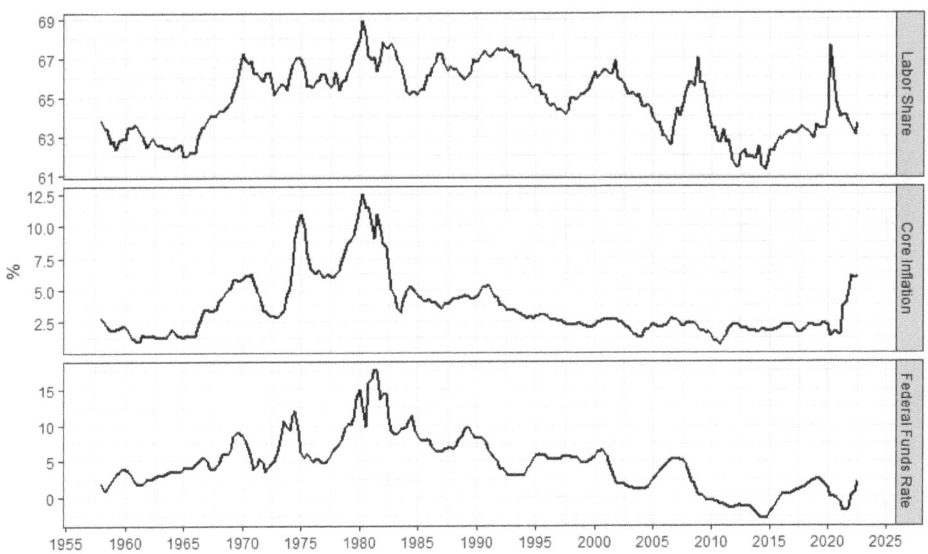

Figure 1. Labor Share, Inflation, and Interest Rate in the US: 1958:Q1 to 2022:Q3.

two can be appreciated more readily in Figure 2, which shows the inflation rate vis-à-vis the labor share and the fitted regression line.

Figure 2 spotlights some tipping points in the labor share and inflation relationship that begin to tell the story. Beginning at the red dot in the Figure, since the early 1960s, both variables exhibit a protracted increase until the 1980s, when this trajectory reverses. Then, in the late 1990s, both labor share and inflation decline precipitously and reach a new low in the mid-2010s. Since then, both variables have picked up, but inflation has outpaced wage share since the COVID-19 pandemic. However, what impact the pandemic itself might have on the labor share and inflation relationship once its effects unwind remains uncertain.

Thus, the central aspect that stands out from Figure 2 is the counter-clockwise pattern in inflation rate and labor share. This is an empirically relevant pattern since it indicates that, in general, these two exhibit a 'predator-prey' dynamic in which fluctuations in the labor share (predator) 'chase' fluctuations in the inflation rate (prey). The predator-prey dynamic between labor share and inflation is consistent with Goodwin's (1967) model, in which the labor share acts like the predator and employment as the prey, assuming inflation and employment move in tandem. What is, therefore, the role of the interest rate in this Goodwin system? As shown below, the interest rate constitutes predator control; the interest rate helps prey to be resilient to predation. In this regard, a recurrent pattern is evident in Figure 1. The Fed moved the federal funds rate sharply higher during those periods when the labor share trended up. In fact, the interest rate shows a variability pattern closer to that of the labor share and appears to track the latter more closely than it tracks inflation.

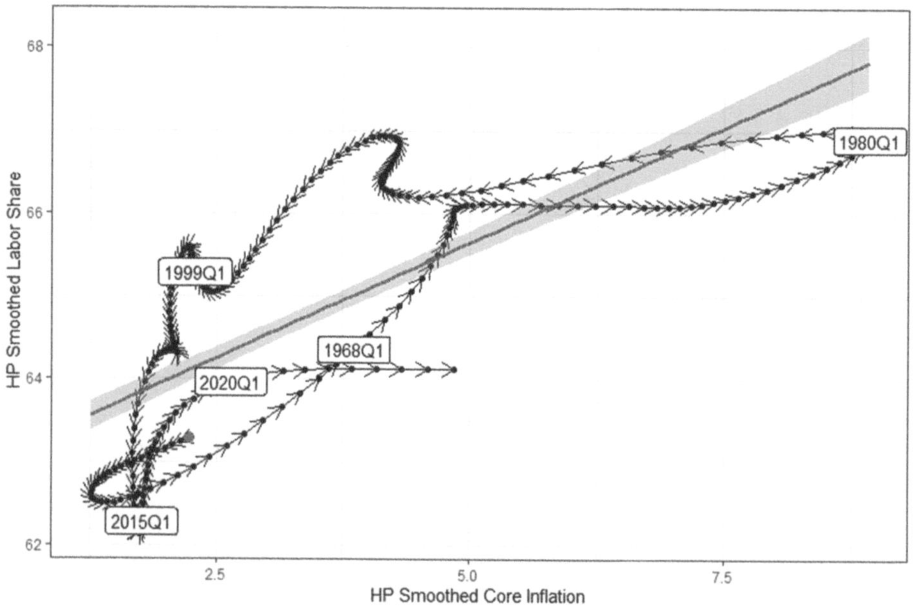

Figure 2. Inflation and Labor Share.

Note: Inflation and labor share are smoothed using the Hodrick–Prescott (HP) filter ($\lambda = 1600$) to neatly illustrate the trajectory. The red dot indicates the starting point. The upward-sloping line is the fitted regression line.

It is well known that Goodwin's (1967) model predicts perpetual distributional cycles around a steady state without ever reaching it. Tobin advances that under conflict inflation, there is no equilibrium path between inflation and income distribution, and inflation 'will continue and indeed accelerate so long as the basic conflicts of real claims and real power continue' (Tobin 1981, 28). Rapping also concedes that 'Inflation proceeds so long as there is no political and economic structural resolution to the problem of distribution and growth' (Rapping 1979, 34–35). But then, how does the economy reach equilibrium? In Olivier Blanchard's opinion, equilibrium is reached only when the various players are forced to accept the distributional outcome. Naturally, this begs the question of forced by whom. That is the crucial issue: they are forced by the monetary authority that enforces a distributional outcome compatible with low and stable inflation through interest rate adjustments. As shown later, the US experience suggests the Goodwin system has been under a control strategy by the central bank.

To illustrate, consider the following controlled prey-predator system for the inflation rate π_t and the labor share ψ:

$$\dot{\pi} = (\tau_1 - \delta_1 \psi)\pi \tag{1}$$

$$\dot{\psi} = (\delta_2 \pi - \tau_2)\psi - \kappa i \psi \tag{2}$$

where τ_1, τ_2, δ_1, δ_2 and κ are positive constants, $\dot{z} = \frac{dz}{dt}$, and i is the interest rate that stands for the control variable, which satisfies $0 \leq i \leq i_{max}$. The condition that the interest rate must be positive is imposed and i_{max} is a constant representing the maximum interest beyond which macroeconomic stability is compromised. This model captures the idea that the way to control inflation (prey) is by employing an interest rate (predator control) policy that reduces the labor share (predator) (Goh, Leitmann, and Vincent 1974). The system features a non-trivial equilibrium point E with the desirable property of constant inflation. Thus, we can assume that E is a desirable target for the central bank.

The performance of the central bank in the fight against inflation is measured via a loss function given by.

$$L = \int_{t_0}^{t_f} [c_\pi \pi + c_i i]\, dt, \ (c_\pi, c_i > 0), \tag{3}$$

with t_f denoting the time it takes the central bank to bring inflation under control. The central bank's problem is to find a value for the control variable, $i^\star$, which will drive the system from an arbitrary initial state to the equilibrium E such that the loss function L is minimized subject to (1)–(2). The control strategy is displayed in Figure 3.

The economic intuition of the dynamics underlying the system is as follows. Assume the economy starts at K, where it can move under null control until it reaches M. During the transition toward M, the class conflict escalates, and inflation and labor share increase. At M, both state variables are above their equilibrium values and the central bank raises the interest rate at its maximum value, driving the economy toward its equilibrium point, E. Once the economy is at equilibrium, the interest rate is 'switched off,' and both state variables remain constant. At this point, $i^\star$ is the rate associated with stability between price and labor share and represents the income distribution variable in the model.

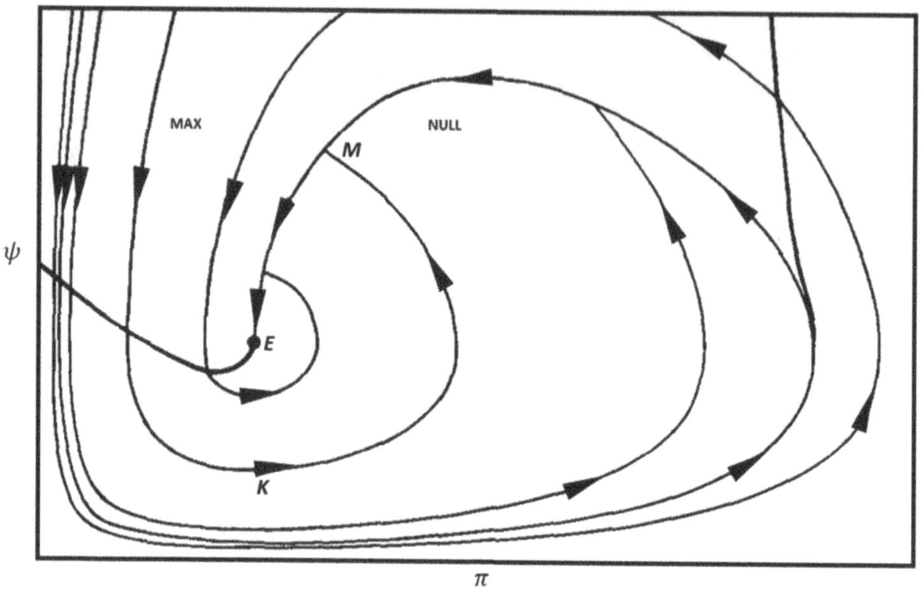

Figure 3. Control of inflation by reducing the labor share

This simple model illustrates how the central bank acts as a third actor in the class struggle, resolving the conflict in favor of the profit share to stabilize inflation. In the US, the Fed strengthened its third position in the 1970s when the Federal Open Market Committee (FOMC) reinforced its commitment to low and stable inflation to gain credibility. The transcripts of the FOMC indicate that Volcker and his Federal Reserve colleagues thought that acquiring credibility for low inflation was central to the success of their campaign against inflation, and they regarded long-term interest rates as indicators of inflation expectations and of the credibility of their disinflationary policy (Goodfriend and King 2005). But, of course, it is not just the credibility but the nature of the threat that matters. In the nature of the case, the threat of breaking the back of the labor share to restore price stability.

2.1. Monetary Policy and Distributive Regimes in the US

Different monetary regimes in the economy provide a means for assessing the control strategy and role of the Fed in the US conflict inflation process. Motivated by Seccareccia (2019), I divide the sample period into three stages. These are the Keynesian era until the 1970s, the monetarist age until the 1990s, and the inflation-targeting regime onward.[1]

2.1.1. The Keynesian Era

The Keynesian era is commonly understood as a period of growth but with significant volatility. During this period, and in line with the Polanyi perspective (Pollin 2000),

[1]Seccareccia (2019) further distinguishes a flexible inflation targeting sub-regime that starts after the Great Financial Crisis. However, for this paper, the distinction of this sub-regime would not change how monetary policy is generally conducted under the new consensus.

economic policy concentrated on redistributing income to overcome inequalities, particularly in labor and financial markets. The economy hovered around a reasonable approximation of full employment underpinned by financial efficiency and stability. Inflation was not a preoccupation of the economic policy until the first oil price shock of the 1970s. Toward the end of the 1960s, inflation ran at about a 3 per cent annual rate, and the real interest rate gravitated around approximately zero percent. The interest rate was characterized by significantly high variance around the mean, signifying decisive discretionary policy actions of the central bank, which was not wedded to any simple type of interest rate policy rule (Seccareccia 2019).

In the course of the Keynesian era, the welfare state strengthened trade unions' power, and the long period of price stability reflected an implicit political agreement (Vernengo 2022). This political agreement meant a gradual redistribution of income and power to workers promoted by democratic reforms. Those reforms implied wages would only increase at the same pace as productivity gains, keeping inflation under control. The reductions in costs associated with increasing productivity were not reflected in lower prices or higher profits for capital but passed on as wages. Thus, it comes as no surprise that the inflation rate epitomized economic policy and political agreements at the time (Glyn et al. 1990). Toward the end of the era, the exhaustion of Keynesian-style policies led to the erosion of the golden age of US capitalism and weaker economic performance. As lower output meant fewer resources available for distribution between workers with influence over the labor share and capitalists with the power to mark up costs, inflation was the outcome. This would mark the transition from *K* to *M* in Figure 3.

2.1.2. The Monetarist Age

With the fall of the Keynesian establishment and economic sluggishness, capital claimed back the income and power concessions made to labor. The rise of monetarism rooted out Keynesian activism and replaced it with policies aimed at reversing the previous era's income redistribution pattern that had led to greater bargaining power for workers in labor markets. The triumph of monetarism placed monetary policy as the only macroeconomic instrument and constrained it in the pursuit of the single objective of eliminating inflationary pressures. Monetary policy was tasked with lowering the inflation rate to a foreseeable level to protect wealth-holders from unexpected inflation and the erosion of rentier income and wealth (Seccareccia 2019). In fact, during the Keynesian era, deflationary periods vanished from the data (Vernengo 2022), causing the real interest rate to decline compared to productivity growth, favoring wage earners.

The monetary policy under Volcker's chairmanship, it is said, targeted monetary variables such as bank reserves and allowed wider interest rate fluctuations, as monetarism prescribed. However, FOMC transcripts suggest that the Fed switched to the more conventional managing of the federal funds rate more closely toward the end of the 1970s. Indeed, Volcker accepted that 'the only reasonable conclusion is not to put much weight on the aggregates' (FOMC transcript, April 1979, 15). Monetarism was a facade, as Governor Nancy H. Teeters admitted: 'I do think that the monetary aggregates provided a very good political shelter for us to do the things we probably couldn't have done otherwise' (FOMC transcript, February 1983, 26). Monetarism served to obfuscate the fact that the Fed was managing the interest rate while the FOMC ascribed those interest rate hikes to market forces (FOMC transcript, March 1988, 12). As it is now well acknowledged, inflation stabilization was not the result of lower monetary emissions so much as the fact of significantly higher interest rates (Goodfriend and King 2005).

Moreover, and still more telling, the Volcker Fed delivered the clear message that wage demands would have a harsh response by the monetary authority that, if necessary, would induce a recession and unemployment to impose wage moderation. The Volcker shock, combined with other policy measures, instituted a distribution pattern bound to act in the interests of capital. Also, the shock left a mass of 'traumatized workers' reluctant to demand significant wage increases and whose passiveness allowed capitalists to raise their margins safely without creating inflationary pressures in what has come to be known as the Great Moderation. Volcker's aggressive tightening represents the Fed's control strategy that led the economy toward equilibrium in the aftermath of the Great Inflation period.

2.1.3. The Inflation-targeting Regime

By the end of the 1990s, the 'years of monetarism experimentation' conclude, and a new consensus in macroeconomics emerges with the economy in a state of control at *E*. The new consensus vindicates the monetarist objective of fighting inflation over fighting unemployment, albeit now the monetary policy is conceived as the 'science' of administering the interest rate (Clarida, Galí, and Gertler 1999). The goal of low and stable inflation with interest rate management is materialized in a monetary policy prescription called inflation targeting. Inflation targeting rests on institutional arrangements such as the independence of the central bank to choose its policy instrument and public commitment to price stability as the primary long-run goal of monetary policy. As importantly, it is inextricably connected with Taylor-type reaction functions (Taylor 1993). In this regard, Benati and Goodhart (2010) argue that following a policy rule is observationally equivalent to following an inflation target and vice versa.

Taylor starts up a small empirical industry to estimate reaction functions. Remarkably, several of those studies find that Taylor rules have been ruling monetary policy since Volcker's chairmanship; see, Clarida, Galí, and Gertler (2000); Orphanides (2004); Rudebusch (2006); Kim and Nelson (2006); among others. In this regard, Perrotini Hernández and Vázquez Muñoz (2017) estimate a reaction function and show that the Fed has been adjusting the interest rate to the wage rate, suggesting that the latter is the actual nominal anchor of inflation targeting instead of the inflation rate, as typically argued. If we connect the dots, we shall find that the Fed has been using the wage rate as its nominal anchor and setting the interest rate accordingly to impinge on inflation since the 1980s.[2] Apparently, at least behind closed doors, the Fed has acknowledged since Volcker's chairmanship that money is endogenous and inflation a distributive outcome. Ideas partially contained in the new consensus.

As mentioned earlier, the post-pandemic recovery has been distinguished by a burst of inflation that has interrupted the long period of inflation stability. A feature of the recovery has been a tight labor market related to the COVID-19 effects that has circumstantially improved workers' leverage,[3] leading to an upward adjustment of wages. In fact,

[2] Although monetary policy may focus on avoiding deflation and secular stagnation in periods when the labor market is weak, such as in the aftermath of the Great Financial Crisis (Seccareccia and Matamoros 2023).

[3] Here, worker leverage should not be confused with collective bargaining power, which is comprised of strong trade unions and the political integration of labor. Workers have enjoyed higher leverage and wages after the pandemic

nominal wages grew at an annual rate of 3 per cent on average between 2018 and 2019, in contrast to 5 per cent during 2021 and 2022, the highest rate in more than two decades.[4] Higher wages imply, *ceteris paribus*, lower markups to which capitalists respond by raising prices to protect their profit share. If the inflation rate exceeds any increase in the wage rate, profits rise, as has happened after the pandemic.

Given that the wage rate is the nominal anchor of monetary policy, the Fed's reaction function demands rate hikes to subdue wages and bring the economy back to controlled inflation. For instance, Powell has recently argued that it is imperative 'to get wages down and then get inflation down.' Nonetheless, the significance of this modest nominal wage increase in driving inflation is a matter of debate. Particularly considering the intricate tangle of other critical factors of post-pandemic inflation dynamics, such as supply blockages, the war in Ukraine, and rising profits; see Vernengo and Caldentey (2023); and Weber and Wasner (2023). Notwithstanding, Powell considers labor market tightness crucial as it has caused a 'real imbalance in wage negotiating.' Hence, the interest rate hikes shall continue until unemployment provides sufficient slack in the labor market to reverse the uptick in wage inflation, regardless of whether this is the primary source of inflationary pressures. The Fed's policy response to the post-pandemic inflation can be seen as a confirmation of its commitment to maintaining a 'benign wage environment' and an effort to preempt attempts to catch up by workers with compensatory wage settlements that could impart greater persistence to what would otherwise be a transitory increase in inflation.

The sections below provide statistical elements to assess conflict and the role of the monetary authority in controlling inflation.

3. The Inflation-Income Distribution Connection: The Conflict Phillips Curve

To study the positive comovements of the labor share and inflation advanced in Figure 2, I estimate a dyadic model for inflation, π_t, and labor share, ψ_t of the form:

$$\pi_t = \beta_1 \pi_{t-1} + \beta_t^{\psi}(\psi_t - \psi_t^{\star}) + \varepsilon_t^{\pi}; \tag{4}$$

$$(\psi_t - \psi_t^{\star}) = \alpha(\psi_{t-1} - \psi_{t-1}^{\star}) + \varepsilon_t^{\psi}. \tag{5}$$

This model incorporates the property that the conflict Phillips curve is driven by deviations of the labor share from its trend, $\psi_t^{\star}$ so that $\psi_t - \psi_t^{\star}$ represents the aspiration gap. Trend labor share is an unobserved latent state modeled as a smooth stochastic process. Thus,

$$\psi_t^{\star} = \psi_{t-1}^{\star} + \varepsilon_t^{\star}, \quad \varepsilon_t^{\star} \overset{i.i.d.}{\sim} N(0, \sigma_{\varepsilon,\star}^2). \tag{6}$$

because the circumstantial tightening of the labor market has resulted in labor scarcity in some sectors. In this regard, Joan Robinson (1947, 9) stated that "when there is a scarcity of labour, employers themselves have an incentive to raise wages. On the assumption of perfect mobility, full employment will be reached in all trades at the same time, and when there is a scarcity of labour each employer will be in a situation in which he could increase his profits if he were able to secure more workers, even at a somewhat higher wage. But more workers are only to be had by tempting them away from other employers."

[4]Numbers come from the employment cost index (ECI) published by the Bureau of Labor Statistics.

Trend labor share can be interpreted as the target labor share to which capitalists aspire, and therefore its evolution measures, among other things, the bargaining power of labor vis-à-vis capital. The value of this desired share and the speed at which the labor share converges to it are influenced by variables such as the unemployment rate, the degree of unionization, market structure, labor productivity growth, and the rate of spare capacity; or more generally, variables that capture the relative bargaining positions of workers and firms and the broader state of the economy; see Rowthorn (1977) and Dutt (1992).

Likewise, the time-varying coefficient in the conflict Phillips curve equation, β_t^{ψ}, evolves according to a random walk.

$$\beta_t^{\psi} = \beta_{t-1}^{\psi} + \varepsilon_t^{\beta}, \quad \varepsilon_t^{\beta} \overset{i.i.d.}{\sim} N(0, \sigma_{\varepsilon,\beta}^2). \tag{7}$$

The time variation in β_t^{ψ} is an extension of the conventional Phillips curve that helps assess the strength of the labor share-inflation relation over time. β_1, for its part, is modeled as a constant parameter.

Note the labor share equation (5) implies an AR(1) behavior for the labor share. The AR(1) assumption might be empirically sensible, but it was selected using the Schwarz information criteria and the diagnostic checking tests proposed by Harvey (1985). Note also that a constant coefficient in the labor share equation is assumed.

The errors in (4) and (5) are assumed to be independent of one another at all leads and lags and exhibit stochastic volatility. Thus,

$$\varepsilon_t^q \overset{i.i.d.}{\sim} N(0, \exp\{h_t^q\}), \tag{8}$$

$$h_t^q = h_{t-1}^q + e_t^{h^q}, \tag{9}$$

$$e_t^{h^q} \overset{i.i.d.}{\sim} N(0, \sigma_{e,h^q}^2), \tag{10}$$

for $q = \pi, \psi$.

3.1. Bayesian Estimation

Equations (4)–(10) constitute a State Space model, so the Kalman filter might be used to filter the unobserved states from the data and construct the likelihood function to estimate the unknown parameters using Maximum Likelihood (ML). However, the stochastic volatility components imply a nonlinear and non-Gaussian estimation problem for which the standard approach via the Kalman filter and ML is not directly applicable. Because the model forms a nonlinear state space model with stochastic volatility, the ML estimation requires a heavy computational burden to repeat the filtering many times to evaluate the likelihood function for each set of parameters until the maximum is reached. Hence, I alternatively employ Bayesian machinery for precisely and efficiently estimating the parameters and extracting the unobserved states.

Bayesian estimation has advantages over standard ML estimation and filtering techniques, such as the HP filter and alike. For instance, it directly provides an entire distribution of all parameters and states, allowing us to analyze the uncertainty around state estimates. The treatment of state variables and parameters as jointly distributed random variables means that estimates of each appropriately reflect uncertainty about the other. Thus, with the Bayesian approach, credible bands around the states combine states and parameters uncertainty (Kim and Nelson 1999). Additionally, it uses prior distributions on reasonable regions of the parameter space to down weight the likelihood function in regions of the parameter space that are inconsistent with out-of-sample information or in which the model is not interpretable (see Berger, Everaert, and Vierke 2016 and Clavijo-Cortes 2023). The specific sampler used is described in detail in Appendix.

3.2. Estimation Results

Figures 4–6 and Table 1 show the estimates of unobserved states and model parameters. The sampler is run for 50,000 iterations omitting the first 20,000 random draws due to burn-in.

Figure 4 panel A portrays the labor share and its trend. The main characteristic is how the aspiration gap (the difference between the two) widens during the 1970s and 1980s, reflecting workers' strong bargaining power. While target labor share declines during those years, actual labor share exceeds it substantially, widening the gap and propelling inflationary pressures. The gap expansion is perceived as threatening the profit share, generating an intense response from capitalists, and leading to high inflation. On this view, it is good practice to keep in mind that a higher labor share by itself does not cause higher prices; it only causes a lower profit share, for these two are inversely related. While the conflict inflation theory is usually stated with regard to workers' wage demands, conflict inflation binds both classes, emphasizing that inflation is always and everywhere the result of capitalists hiking prices to sustain or even increase profitability. Now, following the Volcker shock, the gap starts closing toward the end of the 1990s. Since the 2000s, the labor share gap narrows, and the labor share remains close to its trend.

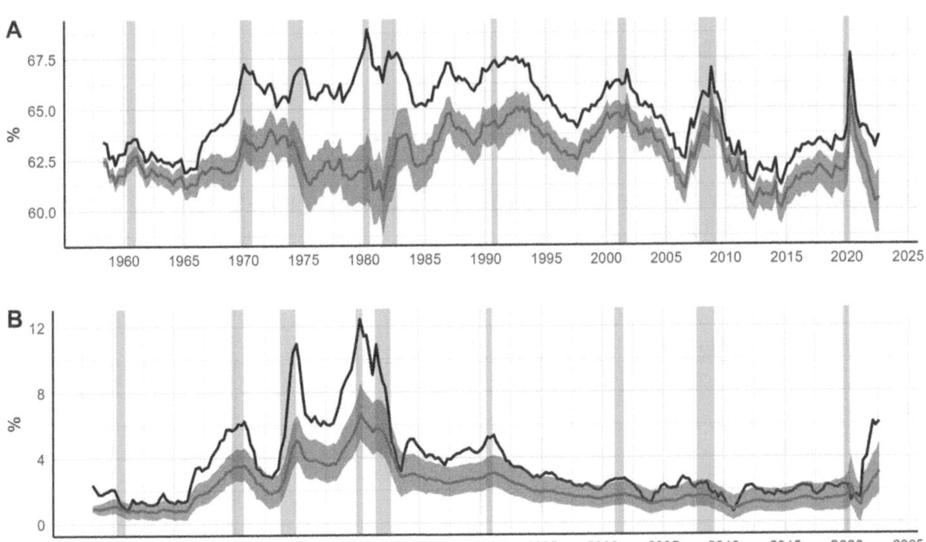

Figure 4. A. Labor Share(Black) and its trend(Red) **B.** Inflation(Black) and aspiration gap(Red). Bands represent the 90% credible interval. Grey bars indicate NBER recession dates.

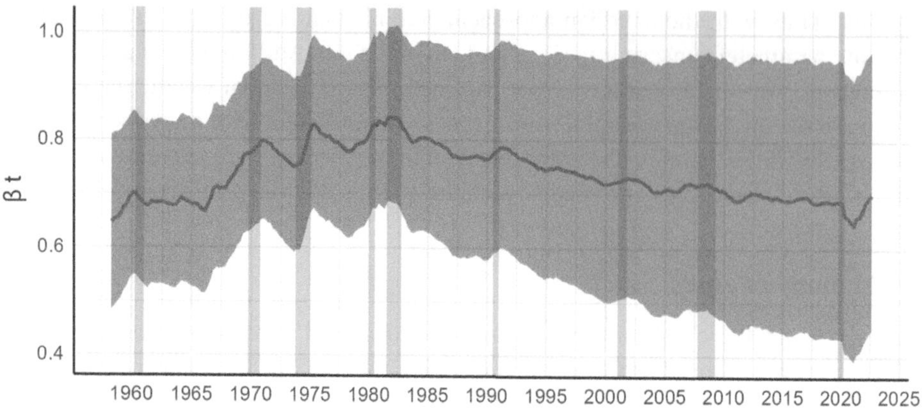

Figure 5. Time-varying conflict Phillips curve slope. Bands represent the 90% credible interval. Grey bars indicate NBER recession dates.

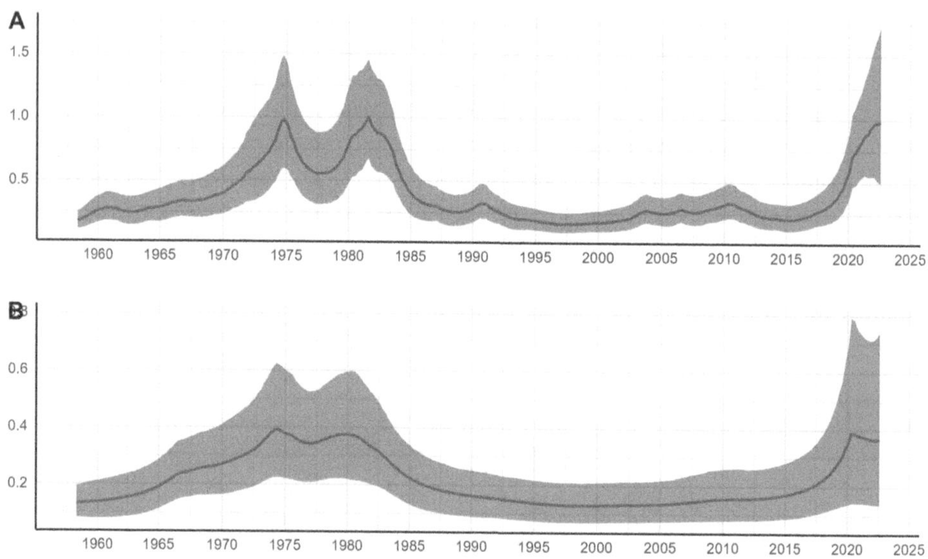

Figure 6. A. Stochastic volatility inflation equation. **B.** Stochastic volatility labor share equation. Bands represent the 90% credible interval.

Table 1. Parameters estimates.

			Posterior	
Coefficients		Mean	2.5%	97.5%
1st AR lag of inflation	β_1	0.52	0.46	0.55
1st AR lag of labor share gap	α	0.98	0.97	0.99
var. of time-varying Phillips curve slope	$\sigma^2_{\varepsilon,\beta}$	0.09	0.08	0.10
var. of labor share trend	$\sigma^2_{\varepsilon,\star}$	0.56	0.49	0.62
var. of SV: inflation equation	σ^2_{η,h^π}	0.14	0.09	0.21
var. of SV: labor share equation	σ^2_{η,h^ψ}	0.08	0.01	0.17

The variability of trend labor share is determined by a conjunction of variables, including those that capture classes' bargaining power, as well as the secular trend of the economy. For instance, since the mid-1980s, trend labor share moves up even when workers' bargaining power and conflict begin to wane. This observed increase in trend labor share might be attributed in part to firms having incomplete bargaining power. Under such conditions, firms cannot fully materialize their aspirations due, for example, to technically induced productivity changes that generate output surpluses that must be distributed among profits and wages such that the gap closes.

Figure 4 panel B shows the inflation rate and aspiration gap. Overall, the aspiration gap tracks the behavior of actual inflation very well. It is particularly interesting to observe that it does a good job of explaining the behavior of inflation over the sample period. For instance, the inflation peaks during the 1970s and early 1980s also correspond to extremes in the gap. Those peaks in the gap imply conflicting claims on income coming from workers during that period and correspond to the most significant deviations of the labor share from its trend reported in Figure 4 panel A. After the mid-1980s, the inflation and labor share gap stabilize around low levels. Since the late 1980s, the labor share deviation from its trend has shrunk, helping maintain a low and stable inflation rate. Note how the inflation rate rises more rapidly than the labor share in those periods of high income claims by workers, forcing down the labor share and raising the profit share.

A final cautionary note regarding the interpretation of the gap widening in the aftermath of the pandemic is in order. The labor share gains that came with the pandemic include the stimulus money for pandemic response and recovery, which was not an increase in labor's bargaining power. The COVID-19 pandemic recovery has incidentally improved workers' leverage due to a resurgence in demand for labor, a sluggish labor supply, and higher turnover rates, but the tight labor market and rapid relative wage growth have primarily benefited workers in low-wage sectors (Autor, Dube, and McGrew 2023). Sectors that have less labor organization. Hence, we should be cautious when interpreting those labor share deviations from its trend and not assume the gains are tantamount to increased labor's bargaining power. Instead, we should acknowledge that the overall labor organization is still weak and that the gap will close again once the COVID-19 pandemic effects fade away.

I now turn to examine how strong the inflation-labor share connection is. Figure 5 reports the posterior mean of the coefficient controlling the slope of the Phillips curve β_t^{ψ}, which is, as expected, a positive number. The parameter has moved during the sample, reaching its highest value during the 1980s and showing a mild decline since then. β_t^{ψ} has fluctuated around a value of 0.7 throughout the sample, which we might interpret as a substantial value especially compared to the vanishing slope of the conventional Phillips curve. Its peak during the 1980s reaffirms the intense class conflict and strained labor relations at that period. In comparison, although the post-pandemic uptick indicates a revitalized workers' leverage, it is far from an economy-wide rise in labor organization as in the 1980s, since the union side represents a small part of the economy. Besides, following the pandemic, the value of β_t^{ψ} merely reaches pre-pandemic levels.

Notwithstanding weak labor organization, the substantial value of β_t^{ψ} suggests that conflict inflation has been latent even in periods of low and stable inflation. It should be pointed out that all levels of inflation, high and low, are a sign of conflict, as inflation is simply 'a particular aspect of the much more general phenomenon of class struggle' (Noyola, 1956 [2011], 162). For instance, the national accounts arithmetic shows that for capital to have safely raised the markups to boost profit shares without causing inflation during the Great Moderation, the labor share necessarily had to decline, which was possible thanks to the well-documented annihilation of the working-class threat.

Figure 6 reports the stochastic volatility estimates for the inflation rate and labor share equations. The two series of volatility estimates are time-varying and show similar patterns. Both volatilities rise significantly in the 1970s and early 1980s and fall astoundingly after about 1981, reaching their minimum recently. The Great Financial Recession increases inflation volatility slightly. The rise, however, is short-lived, and volatility recovers its declining pattern following the worst of the Recession. Labor share volatility remains low and stable during the Great Moderation. This phenomenon can be taken as proof of the amply documented wage suppression. Finally, we observe both series increase significantly with the pandemic reaching levels not seen since the Great Inflation period. However, while labor share volatility shows signs of declining, inflation volatility remains high, suggesting other forces are also at work.

In summary, although the inflation process during the Great Inflation period seems explained by the manifestation of class conflict,[5] the combination of a low conflict Phillips curve slope, the decline in labor share volatility, and high inflation volatility suggests that post-pandemic inflation might be driven by other factors such as the COVID-19-induced supply chain bottlenecks and demand shifts.

Finally, Table 1 shows the posterior mean for all model parameters and the 5th and 95th percentiles of the posterior distributions. The value of α implies the labor share equation is very persistent, as the posterior mean for α is close to one. For its part, the AR lag of the inflation equation is lower, suggesting a less persistent inflation process.

4. The Role of Monetary Policy: A Nonlinear SVAR

In contemplating the positive connection between inflation and income distribution, one cannot avoid addressing the question of monetary policy's role in mediating class conflict. To assess monetary policy's position, I use a SVAR model that exploits the basic axiomatic foundations of predator-prey models (see Barbosa-Filho and Taylor 2006) to determine the system's reaction to a monetary shock. Consider the following SVAR model of order p,

$$y_t = A_0 + A_1 y_{t-1} + \cdots + A_p y_{t-p} + \mathrm{B}\varepsilon_t, \tag{11}$$

where $y_t = [\psi_t^g, \pi_t, i_t]'$ is the vector that contains the endogenous variables aspiration gap as defined above, inflation, and federal funds rate; $A_j, j = 0, \ldots, p$, represent parameter matrices; the nonsingular matrix B captures instantaneous effects of the structural shocks on the variables in the system; and ε_t denotes the vector of structural shocks which are typically presumed uncorrelated across equations and over time with mean zero and unit covariance matrix.

[5]Some literature strands would disagree that conflict even seems relevant to the Great Inflation, arguing that conflict was not as relevant as usually regarded during this period; see Alvarez et al. (2022).

As known, the impacts of the structural shocks ε_t on the variables in the system y_t cannot be identified without further external assumptions. Identifying external information might stem from two sources: (i) theoretical considerations that impose economic restrictions such as short-run restrictions (Sims 1980), long-run restrictions (Blanchard and Quah 1989), and specific sign restrictions (Uhlig 2005); or (ii) from statistical methods that exploit stylized features, such as heteroscedasticity of structural shocks (Lanne and Lütkepohl 2008; Rigobon 2003). Here, I follow the modern approach developed recently by Herwartz and Plödt (2016) that conflates both identification strategies. In particular, I identify monetary policy shocks via sign restrictions and changes in volatility.

The hybrid identification strategy proposed by Herwartz and Plödt (2016) presumes that blending alternative identification schemes aims at a most accurate description of a system's responses to structural shocks on impact and over time. Overall, relying exclusively on theory restrictions might be unsatisfactory given those volatility changes in the data reported before (see Figure 6). It appears worthwhile to exploit information on observable heteroskedasticity, especially when it has been shown that distinct covariance estimates may allow obtaining structural shocks from the estimated reduced form residuals. Thus, the hybrid approach exploits covariance shifts whenever diagnosed by pretests; otherwise, it relies on the complete set of sign restrictions.

To identify the signs of the elements in matrix B, I employ a minimal identification structure that captures the narrative and intuition presented so far. Consider a parsimonious 3-equation model similar to that proposed by Estrella (2015) such that.

$$\psi_t^g = a_1\psi_{t-1}^g + a_2(i_t - \pi_t) + \eta_t \tag{12}$$

$$\pi_t = b_1\pi_{t-1} + b_2\psi_t^g + \epsilon_t \tag{13}$$

$$i_t = c_1 i_{t-1} + c_2\pi_t + c_3\psi_t^g + \nu_t \tag{14}$$

where $a_1 > 0$, $a_2 < 0$; $b_1 > 0$, $b_2 > 0$; and $c_k > 0$, for $k = 1,\ 2,\ 3$.

Although outwardly equations (12)-(14) resemble the new-Keynesian 3-equation model, it essentially incorporates several heterodox insights. For instance, (12) captures the aforementioned idea that the monetary authority applies interest rate-management policies to close the labor share gap, as introduced in Section Three. (13) is the conflict Phillips curve of Section Three stating that deviations in the labor share from its trend trigger inflation. Finally, (14) incorporates the notion that the central bank accommodates conflicting claims on income via the inflation rate and aspiration gap into its reaction function to set the policy rate. The set of equations (12)-(14) carries severe implications for monetary policy. Importantly, it suggests that the interest rate is the policy instrument used to settle the class conflict, and monetary policy impinges on inflation essentially through income distribution. This identification strategy provides structure to the estimation while emphasizing with its 3 equations that conflict inflation involves three parties: wage, profit, and the central bank with its discriminatory rule.

The pattern of signs of matrix B, which contains the elements that represent the instantaneous effects of the shocks on the variables, is summarized in Table 2 (I give the full expression for the impulse response matrix B in Appendix).

Table 2. Imposed sign restrictions in the SVAR estimation.

Variable	Shock		
	$\varepsilon_{\psi^\beta} \rightarrow$	$\varepsilon_{\pi} \rightarrow$	$\varepsilon_{i} \rightarrow$
ψ^β	+	−	−
π	+	+	−
i	+	+	+

The matrix implies a unique pattern of sign restrictions corresponding to each structural shock that one can exploit in the SVAR if there is no statical evidence of covariance shifts. Those signs are consistent with the economic intuition behind the idea of conflict inflation exploited in this study, in which a labor share shock leads to a positive response of all three variables. An inflation shock invokes a positive response of inflation and the interest rate and a negative response of the labor share gap. Moreover, the monetary policy shock is identified by forcing labor share and inflation to fall and the interest rate to rise.

For its part, the implementation of changes in volatility is justified by Figure 6. However, applying identification by means of changes in volatility requires determining the time location of the change in volatility. One might rely on historical information or resort to empirical literature. Here, I rely on the results presented in Section Three and set a break in 1981Q3 that captures the Volcker shock. This implies a model with two volatility regimes (one before and one after the break), where the corresponding covariance matrices obey the decompositions $\Sigma_1 = BB^{'}$ and $\Sigma_2 = B\Lambda B'$, where Λ is a diagonal matrix with diagonal elements $\lambda_{kk} > 0, k = 1, \ldots, K$. Nonetheless, a unique identification by means of heteroskedasticity requires that the parameters in Λ must be different.

Finally, I choose a lag length of $p = 6$ based on the LM test for the absence of serial correlation. Even though standard information criteria suggest a lag length of 4, it is necessary to include more lags to avoid serial correlation.

4.1. Monetary Policy Shocks

I start by showing the estimated matrices B and Λ with standard errors in parentheses:

$$\hat{B} = \begin{bmatrix} \underset{(0.018)}{0.110} & \underset{(0.004)}{-0.024} & \underset{(0.012)}{-0.099} \\ \underset{(0.053)}{0.340} & \underset{(0.015)}{0.110} & \underset{(0.037)}{-0.270} \\ \underset{(0.117)}{0.978} & \underset{(0.028)}{0.072} & \underset{(0.088)}{0.540} \end{bmatrix}; \hat{\Lambda} = \begin{bmatrix} \underset{(0.074)}{0.124} & 0 & 0 \\ 0 & \underset{(0.496)}{2.651} & 0 \\ 0 & 0 & \underset{(0.023)}{0.397} \end{bmatrix}. \tag{15}$$

Wald statistics for testing the equality of the diagonal elements of $\hat{\Lambda}$ are documented in Table 3. All three tests reject equality at the 5 per cent level, proving that the statistical identification is an informative means to identify the shocks in this model.

Table 3. Test for equality of diagonal elements of $\hat{\Lambda}$.

H_0	Wald test	*P*-value
$\lambda_{11} = \lambda_{22}$	16.4385	0.0002
$\lambda_{11} = \lambda_{33}$	45.6974	0.0000
$\lambda_{22} = \lambda_{33}$	6.6275	0.0363

Furthermore, by contrasting the sign pattern of the columns of B in equation (15) with the sign restrictions specified in Table 2, we can notice it supports the theory-based assumptions regarding labor share, inflation, and monetary policy shocks. The signs of the estimated matrix B match the assumptions relating to the qualitative effects of an unexpected monetary policy tightening. In line with a labor share shock, the impact effects of the first shock (first column of B) are all positive. The second shock leads to a positive contemporaneous response of inflation and the interest rate and to a negative contemporaneous response of the labor share gap (second column of B). The third shock increases the interest rate and decreases inflation and labor share (third column of B). As the theory-based sign pattern does not conflict with the data in the SVAR, it offers a reasonable device for subsequent economic interpretation of the statistically identified shocks via impulse-response analysis.

To illustrate model implied dynamics, Figure 7 reports the overall effects of a positive monetary policy shock together with 68 per cent bootstrap confidence bands.

The results in Figure 7 indicate that rises in the interest rate are detrimental to both the share of national income going to labor and the inflation rate. This result exposes the distributional channel of monetary policy: the monetary authority impinges on inflation by depressing the labor share via interest rate hikes. Additionally, the impulse response functions show that positive impulses in the labor share lead to a rise in inflation. This outcome is consistent with the idea that following a labor share increase, capitalists respond by increasing prices to reduce the real purchasing power of wages and achieve their desired profit share. For its part, a surge in inflation leads first to a decrease in the labor share and then to an increase in it. Overall, these empirical results are congruent with the conflict inflation theory and the role of monetary policy in settling it.

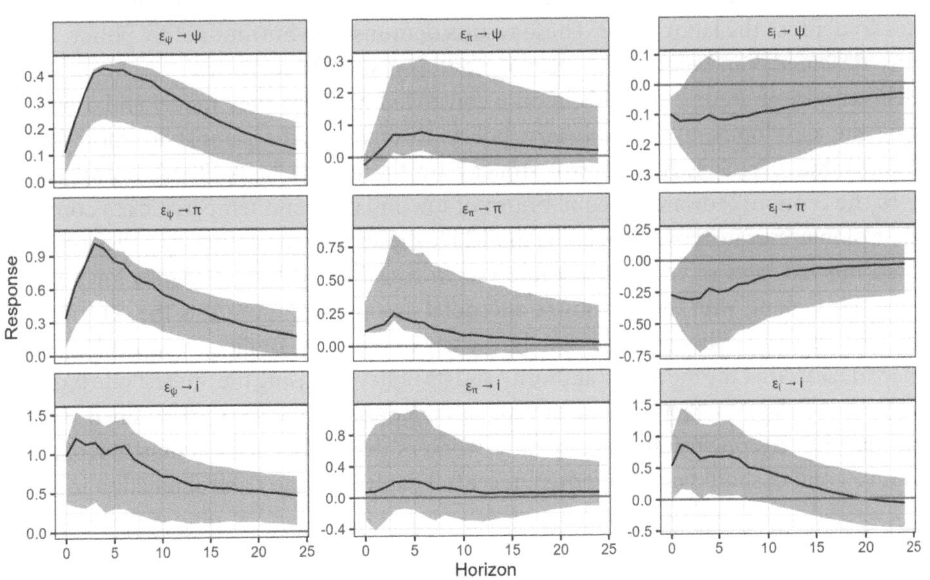

Figure 7. Impulse-response functions with 68% confidence bands based on 1000 bootstrap replications. Structural shocks identified through an unconditional shift in the covariance structure.

This econometric setup and its results imply that interest rate can be used as a distributional policy to deliver stability to the economy. This is partly why post-Keynesians reject an activist approach to monetary policy and favor some parking-it rules, such as what Lavoie calls the income distributive rule. In Lavoie's (1996, 537) words: 'monetary policy should not so much be designed to control the level of activity, but rather to find the level of interest rates that will be proper for the economy from a distribution point of view. The aim of such a policy should be to minimize conflict over income shares, in the hope of simultaneously keeping inflation low and activity high.' In general, post-Keynesian macroeconomics is rich in alternative policy rules that the monetary authority might follow to cease to be the third party in the class struggle (see Rochon and Setterfield 2007).

5. Final Remarks

This study supports the well-established and positive association between inflation and labor share advanced by the heterodox tradition in economics. The estimation results show that the connection between inflation and income distribution remained robust throughout the sample periods, particularly during the Great Inflation. The estimated aspiration gap traces the movements of inflation and estimates a steep slope for the conflict Phillips curve. However, the post-pandemic upsurge in inflation seems to reflect other multiple drivers, including supply chain bottlenecks, rising transport costs, and COVID-19-related base effects.

The paper takes advantage of recent contributions to the literature on identification in SVAR models to provide insights into the dynamic and contemporaneous interplay between three key variables: inflation, income distribution, and monetary policy. Using a 3-equation macroeconomic model, it is shown that there is a distributional channel through which the monetary policy of administered interest rates affects inflation. Put differently, the monetary authority slows inflation by using interest rate hikes to depress the labor share. These results demonstrate how monetary policy, as currently designed, can be not only recessive but also socially regressive.

The empirical argument builds upon a controlled predator-prey model and a narrative about the developments in monetary policy throughout the sample to show the US economy has been under a control strategy by the central bank. This control strategy drives the economy toward an equilibrium of low inflation and tempered class conflict by means of interest rate movements. The model illustrates how the monetary policy of administered interest rates serves capitalist interests in resisting workers' demands for improved wages. This, along with the narrative's anecdotal account, captures how the central bank's tuned interest rate policy places it as a third party in the class conflict. In particular, the evidence suggests that the monetary authority and its policy of raising the interest rate have been resolving the class conflict in favor of capital by depressing the labor share since Volcker's chairmanship. In conclusion, the restraint of workers' demands and the attenuation of the distributive conflict should not be ignored in central bank efforts to control inflation in the US.

Acknowledgements

With the usual disclaimer, I want to thank Holly Sue Hatfield and two anonymous referees for their valuable comments that helped to improve the paper. The views expressed in this paper are my own and should not necessarily be attributed to others at the New Mexico Taxation and Revenue Department.

Disclosure Statement

No potential conflict of interest was reported by the author(s).

ORCID

Pedro Clavijo-Cortes http://orcid.org/0000-0002-1021-6206

References

Alvarez, J., J. Bluedorn, N.-J. Hansen, Y. Huang, E. Pugacheva, and A. Sollaci. 2022. 'Wage-Price Spirals: What is the Historical Evidence?' International Monetary Fund, IMF Working Paper 22/221.

Autor, D., A. Dube, and A. McGrew. 2023. 'The Unexpected Compression: Competition at Work in the Low Wage Labor Market.' NBER Working Paper No. 31010.

Barbosa-Filho, N. H. 2014. 'A Structuralist Inflation Curve Structuralist Inflation Curve.' *Metroeconomica* 65: 349–376.

Barbosa-Filho, N. H., and L. Taylor. 2006. 'Distributive and Demand Cycles in the US Economy — A Structuralist Goodwin Model.' *Metroeconomica* 57: 389–411.

Benati, L., and C. Goodhart. 2010. 'Monetary Policy Regimes and Economic Performance: The Historical Record, 1979-2008.' In *Handbook of Monetary Economics*, edited by B. M. Friedman, and M. Woodford, Vol. 3, 1st ed., Chapter 21. North Holland: Elsevier.

Berger, T., G. Everaert, and H. Vierke. 2016. 'Testing for Time Variation in an Unobserved Components Model for the U.S. economy.' *Journal of Economic Dynamics and Control* 69: 179–208.

Blanchard, O. J., and D. Quah. 1989. 'The Dynamic Effects of Aggregate Demand and Supply Disturbances.' *American Economic Review* 79: 655–673.

Carter, C. K., and R. Kohn. 1994. 'On Gibbs Sampling for State Space Models.' *Biometrika* 81: 541–553.

Clarida, R., J. Galí, and M. Gertler. 2000. 'Monetary Policy Rules and Macroeconomic Stability: Evidence and Some Theory*.' *Quarterly Journal of Economics* 115: 147–180.

Clarida, R., J. Galí, and M. Gertler. 1999. 'The Science of Monetary Policy: A New Keynesian Perspective.' *Journal of Economic Literature* 37: 1661–1707.

Clavijo-Cortes, P. 2022. 'Output Hysteresis in the US: New Evidence from a Time-Varying Verdoorn's law.' *Journal of Economic Studies* 49 (1): 185–197.

Clavijo-Cortes, P. 2023. 'Is Unemployment Hysteretic or Structural? A Bayesian Model Selection Approach.' *Empirical Economics* 65: 2837–2866.

De Jong, P., and N. Shephard. 1995. 'The Simulation Smoother for Time Series Models.' *Biometrika* 82: 339–350.

Dutt, A. K. 1992. 'Conflict Inflation, Distribution, Cyclical Accumulation and Crises.' *European Journal of Political Economy* 8: 579–597.

Estrella, A. 2015. 'The Price Puzzle and VAR Identification.' *Macroeconomic Dynamics* 19: 1880–1887.

Galí, J., and M. Gertler. 1999. 'Inflation Dynamics: A Structural Econometric Analysis.' *Journal of Monetary Economics* 44: 195–222.

Glyn, A., A. Hughes, A. Lipietz, and A. Singh. 1990. 'The Rise and Fall of the Golden age.' In *The Golden Age of Capitalism: Reinterpreting the Postwar Experience*, edited by S. A. Marglin and J. B. Schor, 39–125. Oxford: Oxford University Press.

Goh, B. S., G. Leitmann, and T. L. Vincent. 1974. 'Optimal Control of a Prey-Predator System.' *Mathematical Biosciences* 19: 263–286.

Goodfriend, M., and R. G. King. 2005. 'The Incredible Volcker Disinflation.' *Journal of Monetary Economics* 52: 981–1015.

Goodwin, R. M. 1967. 'A Growth Cycle.' In *Socialism, Capitalism and Economic Growth*, edited by C. Feinstein. Cambridge, UK: Cambridge University Press.

Harvey, A. C. 1985. 'Trends and Cycles in Macroeconomic Time Series.' *Journal of Business and Economic Statistics* 3: 216–227.

Harvey, A. C. 1993. *Time Series Models*. 2nd ed. Cambridge: The MIT Press.

Herwartz, H., and M. Plödt. 2016. 'Simulation Evidence on Theory-Based and Statistical Identification Under Volatility Breaks.' *Oxford Bulletin of Economics and Statistics* 78: 94–112.

Kim, C.-J., and C. R. Nelson. 1999. *State-Space Models with Regime Switching: Classical and Gibbs-Sampling Approaches with Applications*. Cambridge: MIT Press.

Kim, C.-J., and C. R. Nelson. 2006. 'Estimation of a Forward-Looking Monetary Policy Rule: A Time-Varying Parameter Model Using ex Post Data.' *Journal of Monetary Economics* 53: 1949–1966.

Kim, S., N. Shephard, and S. Chib. 1998. 'Stochastic Volatility: Likelihood Inference and Comparison with Arch Models.' *Review of Economic Studies* 65: 361–393.

Lanne, M., and H. Lütkepohl. 2008. 'Identifying Monetary Policy Shocks via Changes in Volatility.' *Journal of Money, Credit and Banking* 40: 1131–1149.

Lavoie, M. 1996. 'Monetary Policy in an Economy with Endogenous Credit Money.' In *Money in Motion: The Post Keynesian and Circulation Approaches*, edited by G. Deleplace, and E. J. Nell, 532–545. London: Palgrave Macmillan UK.

Lavoie, M. 2022. *Post-Keynesian Economics. New Foundations*. Cheltenham, UK: Edward Elgar Publishing.

Lorenzoni, Guido, and Werning, Iván. 2023. 'Inflation is Conflict.' National Bureau of Economic Research, Inc, NBER Working Papers 31099.

Marglin, S. A. 1984. 'Growth, Distribution, and Inflation: A Centennial Synthesis.' *Cambridge Journal of Economics* 8: 115–144.

Niggle, C. J. 1989. 'Monetary Policy and Changes in Income Distribution.' *Journal of Economic Issues* 23: 809–822.

Noyola Vázquez, J. 1956 [2011]. 'El Desarrollo Económico y la Inflación en México y Otros Países Latinoamericanos.' *Ola Financiera* 2 (3): 161–177.

Omori, Y., S. Chib, N. Shephard, and J. Nakajima. 2007. 'Stochastic Volatility with Leverage: Fast and Efficient Likelihood Inference.' *Journal of Econometrics* 140: 425–449.

Orphanides, A. 2004. 'Monetary Policy Rules, Macroeconomic Stability, and Inflation: A View from the Trenches.' *Journal of Money, Credit, and Banking* 36: 151–175.

Perrotini Hernández, I., and J. A. V. Muñoz. 2017. 'Is the Wage Rate the Real Anchor of the Inflation Targeting Monetary Policy Framework?' *Investigación Económica* 76: 9–54.

Pivetti, M. 2010. 'Interest and the General Price Level: Some Critical Notes on 'The New Consensus Monetary Policy Model'.' In *Production, Distribution and Trade: Alternative Perspectives*, edited by H. D. Kurz, B. Schefold, A. Birolo, D. Foley, and I. Steedman. 1st ed., Chapter 13. New York: Routledge.

Pollin, R. 2000. 'Globalization, Inequality and Financial Instability: Confronting the Marx, Keynes and Polanyi Problems in the Advanced Capitalist Economies.' Political Economy Research Institute, University of Massachusetts at Amherst, Working Papers.

Rapping, L. A. 1979. 'The Domestic and International Aspects of Structural Inflation.' In *Essays in Post-Keynesian Inflation*, edited by J. Gapinski, and C. E. Rockwood, 31–53. Cambridge, MA: Ballinger Publishing Company Cambridge.

Ratner, D., and J. W. Sim. 2022. *Who Killed the Phillips Curve? A Murder Mystery Finance and Economics Discussion Series 2022-028*. Washington, DC: Board of Governors of the Federal Reserve System (U.S.).

Rigobon, R. 2003. 'Identification Through Heteroskedasticity.' *Review of Economics and Statistics* 85: 777–792.

Robinson, J. 1947. *Essays in the Theory of Employment*. 2nd ed. Oxford: Basil Blackwell.

Rochon, L.-P., and M. Setterfield. 2007. 'Interest Rates, Income Distribution, and Monetary Policy Dominance: Post Keynesians and the "Fair Rate" of interest' *Journal of Post Keynesian Economics* 30: 13–42.

Rowthorn, R. E. 1977. 'Conflict, Inflation and Money.' *Cambridge Journal of Economics* 1: 215–239.

Rudebusch, G. D. 2006. 'Monetary Policy Inertia: Fact or Fiction?' *International Journal of Central Banking* 2: 85–135.

Sbordone, A. M. 2002. 'Prices and Unit Labor Costs: A New Test of Price Stickiness.' *Journal of Monetary Economics* 49: 265–292.

Seccareccia, M. 2019. 'From the age of Rentier Tranquility to the new age of Deep Uncertainty: The Metamorphosis of Central Bank Policy in Modern Financialized Economies.' *Journal of Economic Issues* 53: 478–487.

Seccareccia, M., and M. Lavoie. 2016. 'Income Distribution, Rentiers, and Their Role in a Capitalist Economy.' *International Journal of Political Economy* 45: 200–223.

Seccareccia, M., and G. Matamoros. 2023. 'Is "Inflation First" Really "Rentiers First"? The Taylor Rule and Rentier Income in Industrialized Countries.' Institute for New Economic Thinking, Working Paper 209.

Sims, C. A. 1980. 'Macroeconomics and Reality.' *Econometrica* 48: 1–48.

Taylor, J. B. 1993. 'Discretion Versus Policy Rules in Practice.' *Carnegie-Rochester Conference Series on Public Policy* 39: 195–214.

Taylor, L., and N. H. Barbosa-Filho. 2021. 'Inflation? It's Import Prices and the Labor Share!.' *International Journal of Political Economy* 50: 116–142.

Tobin, J. 1981. 'Diagnosing Inflation: A Taxonomy.' In *Development in an Inflationary World*, edited by M. Flanders, and A. Razin. New York: Academic Press.

Uhlig, H. 2005. 'What are the Effects of Monetary Policy on Output? Results from an Agnostic Identification Procedure.' *Journal of Monetary Economics* 52: 381–419.

Vera, L. 2010. 'Conflict Inflation: An Open Economy Approach.' *Journal of Economic Studies* 37: 597–615.

Vernengo, M. 2022. 'The Inflationary Puzzle.' *Catalyst* 5: 90–113.

Vernengo, M., and E. P. Caldentey. 2023. 'Price and Prejudice: Reflections on the Return of Inflation and Ideology.' *Review of Keynesian Economics* 11 (2): 129–146.

Weber, I. M., and E. Wasner. 2023. 'Sellers' Inflation, Profits and Conflict: Why Can Large Firms Hike Prices in an Emergency?' *Review of Keynesian Economics* 11 (2): 183–213.

Woodford, M. 2001. 'The Taylor Rule and Optimal Monetary Policy.' *American Economic Review* 91: 232–237.

Wu, J. C., and F. D. Xia. 2016. 'Measuring the Macroeconomic Impact of Monetary Policy at the Zero Lower Bound.' *Journal of Money, Credit and Banking* 48: 253–291.

Appendix

Data

I use quarterly data for the US economy from 1958:Q1 to 2022:Q3. The variables are:

- The Consumer Price Index (CPI) for All Urban Consumers: All Items Less Food and Energy. I computed the inflation rate π_t as the year-over-year log percentage change of the CPI index, i.e., $\pi_t = 100 \times \ln\,(CPI_t/CPI_{t-4})$.
- The labor share is 100× the quotient of National Income: Compensation of Employees, Paid over Net Domestic Income.
- The interest rate is the Federal Funds Effective Rate. To adjust the interest rate, I used the Wu-Xia Shadow Federal Funds Rate for the periods when the rate reached the zero lower bound. These periods are 2009Q3–2015Q4, and 2020Q4–2021Q4.

All variables are freely available in the Federal Reserve Bank of St. Louis Economic Database (FRED) and the Federal Reserve Bank of Atlanta.

Priors and MCMC Algorithm used in the Bivariate Model

For the Bayesian estimation, the following independent prior distributions and proper but relatively informative hyperparameters are chosen for the model parameters: $\beta_1 \sim \mathcal{N}(0.5, 0.25^2)$; $\alpha \sim \mathcal{N}(0.5, 0.25^2)$; $\sigma^2_{\varepsilon,\star} \sim \mathcal{IG}(10, 0.18)$; $\sigma^2_{\varepsilon,\beta} \sim \mathcal{IG}(10, 0.1)$; and $\sigma_{\varepsilon,h^e} \sim \mathcal{IG}(10, 0.9)$ for $e = \pi, \psi$; where $\mathcal{IG}(\cdot,\cdot)$ and $\mathcal{N}(\cdot,\cdot)$ denote the inverse gamma and normal distributions. The informative prior used for β_1 and α implies that the 95 per cent interval of the prior belief ranges roughly from 0 to 1. This prior choice reflects the wide range of estimates found in the literature, particularly for β_1, and ensures that both parameters lie in the stationary region. Thus, I preempt explosive behaviors that would be hard to explain in the context of the US inflation and labor share dynamics. The rest of the priors have been set similar to those in the literature (see Berger, Everaert, and Vierke 2016 and Clavijo-Cortes 2022).

The system of equations presented in Section Three can be cast in a state space form given by

$$y_t = Zx_t + \epsilon_t, \quad \epsilon_t \overset{i.i.d.}{\sim} N(0, H) \tag{A1}$$

$$x_t = Tx_{t-1} + R\eta_t, \quad \eta_t \overset{i.i.d.}{\sim} N(0, Q). \tag{A2}$$

Notation matches that of Harvey (1993). Here,

$$y_t = [\pi_t - \beta_1 \pi_{t-1}, \psi_t]'; \; x_t = [\psi_t^\star, \psi_t^g]' \tag{A3}$$

$$Z = \begin{bmatrix} 0 & \beta_t^\psi \\ 1 & 1 \end{bmatrix}; \; T = \begin{bmatrix} 1 & 0 \\ 0 & \alpha \end{bmatrix}; \; R = \begin{bmatrix} 1 & 0 \\ 0 & 1 \end{bmatrix} \tag{A4}$$

$$H = \begin{bmatrix} \exp\{h_t^\pi\} & 0 \\ 0 & 0 \end{bmatrix}; \; Q = \begin{bmatrix} \sigma^2_{\varepsilon,\star} & 0 \\ 0 & \exp\{h_t^\psi\} \end{bmatrix} \tag{A5}$$

Similarly, the state space representation of the time-varying parameter β_t^ψ is:

$$y_t = [\pi_t - \beta_1 \pi_{t-1}]'; \; x_t = \beta_t^\psi \tag{A6}$$

$$Z = [\psi_t^g]; \; T = [1]; \; R = [1] \tag{A7}$$

$$H = [\exp\{h_t^\pi\}]; \; Q = [\sigma^2_{\varepsilon,\beta}] \tag{A8}$$

Step 1:
The Gibbs MCMC sampler exploits this state-space representation to create posterior draws of x_t using Kalman filtering and Kalman smoothing built on the insights of De Jong and Shephard (1995) and Carter and Kohn (1994) for Gibbs sampling. For given parameter matrices Z, T, R, H, and Q, and an initial guess for the hyperparameters, I start by filtering and sampling the unobserved components.

Step 2:
Conditioning on the unobserved components sampled in Step 1, the hyperparameters β_1 and α can be expressed as unknown parameters in the standard static linear regression model,

$$y = Xb + u; \; u \overset{i.i.d.}{\sim} N(0, \Sigma), \tag{A9}$$

where $\Sigma = \text{diag}(\exp\{h_1^e\}, \ldots, \exp\{h_T^e\})$ and $b \sim \mathcal{N}(a_0, A_0)$ with

$$a_T = A_T(X'\Sigma^{-1}y + A_0^{-1}a_0), \tag{A10}$$

and

$$A_T = (X'\Sigma^{-1}X + A_0^{-1})^{-1}. \tag{A11}$$

I sample the variances from their respective full conditional distributions. Thus,

$$\sigma^2_{\varepsilon,\beta} \sim IG\left(\frac{T-1}{2} + \nu_\beta, S_\beta + \frac{\sum_{t=2}^{T}\left(\beta_t^{\psi} - \beta_{t-1}^{\psi}\right)^2}{2}\right), \tag{A12}$$

$$\sigma^2_{\varepsilon,\star} \sim IG\left(\frac{T-1}{2} + \nu_\star, S_\star + \frac{\sum_{t=2}^{T}\left(\psi_t^{\star} - \psi_{t-1}^{\star}\right)^2}{2}\right), \tag{A13}$$

and

$$\sigma^2_{\varepsilon,h^e} \sim IG\left(\frac{T-1}{2} + \nu_h, S_h + \frac{\sum_{t=2}^{T}\left(h_t^{e} - h_{t-1}^{e}\right)^2}{2}\right), \tag{A14}$$

where $\nu_{h^e} = \nu_{\beta^\psi} = \nu_\star = 10$, and $S_{h^e} = 0.9$, $S_\star = 0.18$ and $S_\beta = 0.09$.

Step 3:
Sample the stochastic volatilities. The stochastic volatility component $\exp\{h_t\}$ is non-linear but can be linearized by taking the logarithm of its square

$$\ln\left(\exp\{h_t\}\eta_t^{g^c}\right)^2 = 2h_t + \ln\left(\eta_t^{g^c}\right)^2, \tag{A15}$$

where $\ln(\eta_t^{g^c})^2$ is log-chi-square distributed with expected value -1.2704 and variance $3.1416^2/2$. Following Kim, Shephard, and Chib (1998), I approximate the linear model by an offset mixture time series model as

$$g_t = 2h_t + \epsilon_t, \tag{A16}$$

where $g_t = \ln\left(\left(\exp\{h_t\}\eta_t^{g^c}\right)^2 + c\right)$ with $c = 0.001$ being an offset constant to ensure the term inside the ln is bounded away from zero, and the distribution of ϵ_t being the following mixture of normal

$$f(\epsilon_t) = \sum_{i=1}^{M} q_i f_N(\epsilon_t | m_i - 1.2704, v_i^2), \tag{A17}$$

with component probabilities q_i, means $m_i - 1.2704$, and variances v_i^2. Following Omori et al. (2007), I use a mixture of $M = 10$ normal distributions to approximate the log-chi-square distribution. Values for $\{q_i, m_i, v_i^2\}$ are provided by Omori et al. (2007) in Table 1.

SVAR Identification

The B matrix that contains the elements representing the instantaneous effects of the shocks on the variables is given by

$$B = \begin{pmatrix} 1 - \frac{a_2 b_2}{1 + a_2 b_2} + \frac{a_2(b_2 c_2 + c_3)}{(1 + a_2 b_2)(-a_2 c_3 - a_2 b_2 c_2 + 1 + a_2 b_2)} & \frac{-a_2^2 b_2 + a_2^2 b_2 c_2 + a_2 c_2 - a_2}{(a_2 b_2 + 1)(a_2 b_2 - a_2 c_3 - a_2 b_2 c_2 + 1)} & \frac{a_2}{a_2 b_2 - a_2 c_3 - a_2 b_2 c_2 + 1} \\ \frac{b_2}{a_2 b_2 - a_2 c_3 - a_2 b_2 c_2 + 1} & \frac{1 - a_2 c_3}{a_2 b_2 - a_2 c_3 - a_2 b_2 c_2 + 1} & \frac{a_2 b_2}{a_2 b_2 - a_2 c_3 - a_2 b_2 c_2 + 1} \\ \frac{b_2 c_2 + c_3}{-a_2 c_3 - a_2 b_2 c_2 + 1 + a_2 b_2} & -\frac{a_2 c_3 - c_2}{-a_2 c_3 - a_2 b_2 c_2 + 1 + a_2 b_2} & \frac{1 + a_2 b_2}{-a_2 c_3 - a_2 b_2 c_2 + 1 + a_2 b_2} \end{pmatrix}$$

Conflict, Inertia, and Phillips Curve from a Sraffian Standpoint

Franklin Serrano, Ricardo Summa and Guilherme Spinato Morlin

ABSTRACT

The recent post-Keynesian debate on conflict inflation revolves around plausible magnitudes of the parameters of the standard model. We assess this debate by examining the economic meaning of the 'bargaining' and 'indexation' parameters, and proposing a reinterpretation in which the bargaining power is reflected in the relative frequency of wage and price increases in a period. Inflation then depends on the size of the inconsistent distributive claims and the absolute frequency of wage and price increases. Distribution depends on the relative frequency of such increases. From the latter we derive the real wage and profit resistance parameters, which determine the structural degree of inflation inertia. By adding the employment rate as a determinant of the desired real wage, we get a conflict-augmented Phillips curve. We show how different assumptions on the real resistance parameters affect the shape of the Phillips curve and the distributive outcomes in different conflict inflation models. A NAIRU occurs only when there is both full real wage and real profit resistance. Conflict generates inflation (not acceleration) with less extreme assumptions. The old-type conflict-augmented Phillips curve, with income distribution depending on the relative frequency of wage and price adjustments, is the most plausible case.

1. Introduction

There is an ongoing controversy between influential textbooks in post-Keynesian economics about how to model conflict inflation adequately. The standard post-Keynesian view follows the conflict inflation model proposed by Dutt (1987), where inflation makes the conflicting claims compatible, and usually generates a stable level of inflation (and not accelerating inflation). This view is now consolidated in the textbooks by Blecker and Setterfield (2019, pp. 209–222) and Lavoie (2022, pp. 592–629), but has recently been the object of criticism by Hein (2023, pp. 136–151) in his textbook. Building on previous work (Stockhammer 2008; Hein and Stockhammer 2009, 2010), he criticizes the assumptions of the standard model. Hein argues that the assumptions of partial indexation of wages and/or prices in the models proposed by Blecker and Setterfield (2019) and Lavoie (2022) are inconsistent with workers and firms bargaining for desired real wages and profits. If workers and firms bargain for targeted real wages and profits, it would not be rational to negotiate less than full pass-through of past price and wage inflation when setting nominal wage contracts and prices. Hence, Hein (2023) proposes an alternative framework in which conflicting claims lead directly to inflation acceleration.

We assess this debate by examining the theoretical foundations of the standard conflict model, taking a closer look into the economic meaning and possible determinants of the 'bargaining' and 'indexation' parameters. After presenting the model (Section Two) and the recent controversy (Section Three), we propose a Sraffian reinterpretation of the model coefficients (in Section Four), in which the relative bargaining power of firms and workers is objectively reflected in the relative frequency of wage and price increases within a given period (see also Serrano, Aidar, and Bhering 2024). Based on our reinterpretation, conflict inflation depends on the size of the inconsistency between the distributive claims of firms and workers and the absolute frequency of wage and price increases, while the distributive outcome depends on the relative frequency of such increases. From these relative frequencies of nominal wage and price increases within a given period, we then derive the real wage and profit resistance parameters of the model. These parameters determine the structural degree of inflation inertia within the system.

By further adding the employment rate as one of the determinants of the desired real wage, in Section Five, we obtain a conflict-augmented Phillips curve in line with Serrano (2019), Summa and Braga (2020), Braga and Serrano (2023) and Morlin and Pariboni (2023). We show how different assumptions on the real resistance parameters affect the shape of the Phillips curve and the distributive outcomes in different heterodox and mainstream models of conflict inflation. Our results reveal that a NAIRU can only occur when there is *both* full real wage and real profit resistance. Under less extreme conditions, as usually neither workers nor firms can increase their corresponding nominal wages and prices as often as they wish (and, especially, not continuously), distributive conflict generates a level of inflation instead of an acceleration of inflation. In our final remarks (Section Six) we conclude that, apart from very special circumstances, an old-type non-accelerationist conflict-augmented Phillips curve presents itself as the most satisfactory both theoretically and empirically (Stirati and Paternesi-Meloni 2018).

2. Inflation and Conflicting Claims

We start with a brief discussion of the two key points of what we call a Sraffian approach to conflict inflation (Serrano 1993). The first is the key distinction between demand-pull and cost-push inflation. Demand-pull inflation occurs when effective demand — i.e., the nominal aggregate demand divided by the supply or normal price — is higher than the potential output, causing a rise in market prices as a result of scarcity. Cost-push inflation comes from nominal increases in the normal or supply price of one unit of output, i.e., follows from the rise in at least one of the technical coefficients or nominal distributive variables that compose the normal price.[1] Cost-push inflation occurs when effective demand is lower than or

[1]In the case of an open economy, the rise in supply prices can be caused by the rise in the exchange rate and/or exogenous international prices of inputs or other tradable goods (see Morlin 2023).

equal to potential output and has nothing to do with scarcity.[2] Conflict inflation is thus cost-push inflation.

The second key point is that inflation is not neutral with respect to income distribution. In our view, the cost-push ultimately comes from conflicting claims over distribution. In this paper, we examine the conflict between workers and capitalists that determines the distribution between the real wage and the normal rate of profits. In a fiat money economy, workers can set money wages, but cannot directly determine real wages since they do not control the price level. On the other hand, and this is often overlooked, even if firms set their nominal profit rate on their historical costs, they do not directly determine the real rate of profits on their replacement costs, as they do not control the rate of increase of their nominal unit wage costs occurring between each price increase. It is the joint dynamics of these nominal variables that will determine both the rate of inflation and actual income distribution.

2.1. The Basic Conflict Inflation Model

In our discussion of conflict inflation, we shall make use of the simplest possible 'corn model'. We consider an economy that uses a single method to produce only one basic good ('corn'), which is also the single wage good and the circulating capital input. Production uses homogenous labor, besides corn itself. Real wages (assumed to be well above some minimum incompressible subsistence level) are paid at the end of the period. The price level equation, assuming a uniform real normal rate of profits on replacement costs (between different producers) for this economy, is given by:

$$P = aP(1 + r) + bPl \tag{1}$$

Where P corresponds to the price level of a unit of gross output, a is the technical coefficient of the circulating capital input required to produce one unit of output, r is the real rate of profit, b is the real wage, and l is the technical coefficient of labor required to produce one unit of output. The net output is given by $(1 - a)$. Therefore, we can define $B = (1 - a)/l$ as the net output per worker (the maximum real wage) and symmetrically $R = (1 - a)/a$ as the normal net output to capital ratio (the maximum rate of profit). Finally, we can derive a wage curve that shows the set of distributive possibilities:[3]

$$1 = \frac{b}{B} + \frac{r}{R} \tag{2}$$

[2]Note that in this approach capital and labor are not smoothly substitutable and potential output is determined by the size of the capital stock and its efficiency, as labor is realistically assumed to be usually available in quantities larger than those necessary to fully operate the available stock of fixed capital (Garegnani 1979; Serrano 2019; and Morlin and Pariboni 2023).

[3]We call our reinterpretation 'Sraffian' as the possibilities for income distribution are based on this wage curve. The latter describes the inverse relation between the level of real wages and the normal profit rate (Sraffa 1960). This allows us to represent the distributive conflict between workers and firms, serving as the foundation of our conflict inflation model. We derive the wage curve in a simple model with only one commodity being the circulating capital and consumption good, but the same results can be obtained in an economy with many commodities, fixed capital, and joint production, with all commodities being separately producible (Kurz and Salvadori 1997, pp. 236–240; Petri 2021, pp. 831–913).

Let us connect our simple Sraffian model with the standard conflict inflation model (Dutt 1987)[4] that is now consolidated in post-Keynesian textbooks (Blecker and Setterfield 2019, pp. 209–222; Lavoie 2022, pp. 592–629). From equation (2), we know that the sum of the share of profits and wages must be equal to 1. The basic assumption of a conflicting claims model is that workers desire a real wage, b^w, incompatible with the real rate of profit desired by the firms, r^k. Equation (3) defines the real wage desired by firms b^k, derived from their desired profit rate.

$$b^k = B\left(1 - \frac{r^k}{R}\right) \tag{3}$$

If the real wage aspired by workers is greater than the real wage that corresponds to firms' desired real rate of profits (that is, $b^w > b^k$), then there are conflicting claims over distribution.

The basic model relates this distributive conflict to cost-push inflation by taking the price and nominal wage inflation rates, $\hat{p}$ and $\hat{w}$, as a function of firms' and workers' aspiration gaps, i.e., the difference between their target and the actual real wage (throughout the paper a minus one subscript will mean a lagged variable)[5]:

$$\hat{w} = \beta^w(b^w - b_{-1}) \tag{4}$$

$$\hat{p} = \beta^k(b_{-1} - b^k) \tag{5}$$

This conflictual process of increases in nominal wages and prices will tend to make them converge to a common rate of wage and price inflation (equation 6) which will also correspond to a particular state of the distribution of income.

$$\hat{p} = \hat{w} \tag{6}$$

Therefore, the actual real wage b and the rate of inflation converge to their equilibrium levels b^* and $\widehat{p^*}$, as shown in equations (7) and (8).

$$b^* = \frac{\beta^w b^w + \beta^k b^k}{\beta^w + \beta^k} \tag{7}$$

$$\widehat{p^*} = \frac{\beta^w \beta^k (b^w - b^k)}{\beta^w + \beta^k} \tag{8}$$

In the equilibrium, the real wage lies between the levels desired by workers and by the firms, depending on the *relative* magnitude of the two bargaining power coefficients, $\beta^w$and β^k. Moreover, the rate of inflation depends on the magnitude of the distributive conflict $(b^w - b^k)$ and the *absolute* magnitude of the bargaining power coefficients, β^w and β^k.

[4]Rowthorn (1977) is often considered the seminal contribution to conflict inflation modeling. Hein (2023) associates his perspective — which we will discuss below — with Rowthorn's approach to modeling conflict inflation and distinguishes it from Dutt's (1987) approach. For the sake of our exposition, we consider Dutt's approach as the standard conflict inflation model, since it is closely related to the textbook versions of Blecker and Setterfield (2019) and Lavoie (2022).

[5]Throughout this paper, both for the sake of simplicity and ease of comparison with the post-Keynesian literature we shall use the conflict inflation models in their simplified linearized forms. This is not a real problem, as the formally more exact version of the equations gives the same qualitative results, as can be seen in Serrano, Aidar, and Bhering (2024).

We can have four possibilities for the closure of such a model depending on the bargaining power of workers and firms (β^w and β^k): (1) when workers have very strong bargaining position, and β^w tends to infinity, but firms have a finite β^k; (2) when firms have a very strong bargaining position and β^k tends to infinity, but workers have a finite β^w; (3) when both firms and workers have a very strong bargaining position and both β^w and β^k tend to infinity; (4) when neither firms nor workers have a very strong bargaining position and β^w and β^k are finite.

In case (1), when workers have a very strong bargaining position and β^w tends to infinity, the real wage converge to workers' target $\lim_{\beta^w \to \infty} b^* = b^w$. Any response from firms through price increases (i.e., any $\beta^k > 0$) only generates inflation without affecting the real wage level. The equilibrium inflation rate, in that case, is described by equation (9).

$$\lim_{\beta^w \to \infty} \widehat{p^*} = \beta^k (b^w - b^k) \tag{9}$$

Conversely, in case (2), if the firms have a very strong bargaining position, i.e., β^k tends to infinity, the real wage target for firms prevails, $\lim_{\beta^k \to \infty} b^* = b^k$. In this case, money wage increases only generate inflation and workers cannot affect the real wage.

$$\lim_{\beta^k \to \infty} \widehat{p^*} = \beta^w (b^w - b^k) \tag{10}$$

The third case occurs when both firms and workers have a very strong bargaining position, with both β^w and β^k tending to infinity. In this case, the incompatibility between desired real wages and real rate of profit causes the acceleration of inflation. Since workers and firms strongly react to increases in prices and wage costs, no finite inflation rate can reconcile the conflicting claims. Therefore, inflation can accelerate continuously for any degree of conflict over distribution (i.e., any positive difference between $b^w$and b^k).

Finally, in case (4), both parameters β^w and β^k are finite, and neither workers nor firms have completely strong bargaining power to fully achieve their distributive targets. Equation (7) shows that the equilibrium real wage lies between both sides' targets, leaning towards the side with the stronger bargaining parameter. Equation (8) shows that equilibrium inflation depends on the magnitude of the conflict ($b^w - b^k$) and the absolute magnitude of the bargaining power parameters. Therefore, there is a finite inflation rate capable of reconciling conflicting claims in this fourth case.

2.2. Extended Model with the 'Indexation' Parameters

The more complete version of the model usually adds what is known as price and wage 'indexation', which usually does not refer exclusively nor even predominantly to formal indexation of contracts, but more generally to the reaction of money wage and price increases to expected, past, or even current price and wage increases.

Some authors (Hein and Häusler 2024) interpret the 'indexation' parameters as reflecting expectations, and discuss the effect of different assumptions on expectation formation and their correctness on the level of inflation and income distribution. Following

Rowthorn (1977) and Palley (2018), in this subsection we will try to show that in the end what really matters in the long run is the degree by which these expectations, however formed, are actually incorporated in wage and price increases.

In order to do this, we start our discussion taking those parameters as representing the effects of expected wage ($\widehat{w^e}$) and price inflation ($\widehat{p^e}$) by firms and workers, respectively.[6] The parameters α^w and α^k link nominal wage changes to expected inflation and price increases to expected wage inflation, as in equations (11) and (12).[7]

$$\hat{w} = \beta^w(b^w - b_{-1}) + \alpha^w \widehat{p^e} \tag{11}$$

$$\hat{p} = \beta^k(b_{-1} - b^k) + \alpha^k \widehat{w^e} \tag{12}$$

Expectations now play a role in determining inflation and distribution. We will see, case by case, how different assumptions on the formation of expectations lead to different results in light of our conflict inflation model.

2.2.1. The Case of 'Anchored Expectations'

We start with a general case in which (price and wage) inflation expectations depend both on an exogenous expected term, $\overline{\hat{p}^e}$ and $\overline{\hat{w}^e}$, and on lagged (price and wage) inflation. The exogenous expected term reflects what is nowadays called 'anchored expectations' (Blanchard 2016). The parameters γ^w and γ^k reflect by how much expectations depend on past inflation. Let us call them expectations parameters. Then, we can write price and wage inflation expectations as the following weighted averages:

$$\widehat{p^e} = \gamma^w p_{-1} + (1 - \gamma^w)\, \overline{\hat{p}^e} \tag{13}$$

$$\widehat{w^e} = \gamma^k w_{-1} + (1 - \gamma^k)\overline{\hat{w}^e} \tag{14}$$

We can solve equations (11) to (14) for b^* and $\widehat{p^*}$ with the condition that $\hat{p} = \hat{w} = \hat{p}_{-1} = \hat{w}_{-1}$:

$$b^* = \frac{(1 - \alpha^k\gamma^k)\beta^w b^w + (1 - \alpha^w\gamma^w)\beta^k b^k}{(1 - \alpha^k\gamma^k)\beta^w + (1 - \alpha^w\gamma^w)\beta^k} + \frac{(1 - \alpha^k\gamma^k)\alpha^w\,(1 - \gamma^w)\overline{\hat{p}^e} - (1 - \alpha^w\gamma^w)\alpha^k(1 - \gamma^k)\overline{\hat{w}^e}}{(1 - \alpha^k\gamma^k)\beta^w + (1 - \alpha^w\gamma^w)\beta^k} \tag{15}$$

$$\widehat{p^*} = \frac{\beta^w\beta^k(b^w - b^k)}{(1 - \alpha^k\gamma^k)\beta^w + (1 - \alpha^w\gamma^w)\beta^k} + \frac{\beta^k\alpha^w(1 - \gamma^w)\overline{\hat{p}^e} + \beta^w\alpha^k\,(1 - \gamma^k)\overline{\hat{w}^e}}{(1 - \alpha^k\gamma^k)\beta^w + (1 - \alpha^w\gamma^w)\beta' k} \tag{16}$$

These results seem quite complex and dependent on many parameters, but we can observe some general patterns. Solution (15) shows that the equilibrium real wage

[6]A similar representation of this version is presented in Blecker and Setterfield (2019) and Lavoie (2022). and is used by Hein (2023) to represent both Blecker and Setterfield (2019) and Lavoie (2022) with the aim to criticize them.

[7]In fact, there is also a fundamental asymmetry in the formation of expectations, as firms probably know better how much the wages they pay are currently increasing, so it is unclear why one should use expected wage increases in firms' price equation. Lavoie (2022, pp. 601–602) addresses this asymmetry by assuming that workers consider expectations equal to past inflation while firms consider the current nominal wage change in their equations. We will skip this possible asymmetry and keep the general formulation in which both expectations for firms and workers are incorporated into prices and wages.

depends on two components: the first is an average between the desired real wage targets (weighted according to parameters of bargaining, indexation, and expectations), and the second is the difference between exogenous expectations (also weighted by the parameters of bargaining, indexation, and expectations). Given these parameters, if workers have a sufficiently higher inflation expectation than firms, ($\overline{\hat{p}^e} > \overline{\hat{w}^e}$, and this difference is sufficient to compensate for the difference in the expectation parameters when they are greater for firms than for workers) the equilibrium real wage will increase. Solution (16) shows that inflation depends on the conflicting claims (again weighted by the parameters of bargaining, indexation, and expectations) and on the average (weighted by the parameters of bargaining, indexation, and expectations) between price and wage expectations. Moreover, we can see that in this general case, where γ^k, $\gamma^w < 1$, inflation tends to be finite, even when there is full indexation ($\alpha^w = \alpha^k = 1$). The finite equilibrium inflation rate can be achieved independently of the convergence or divergence between the exogenous components of expectations of workers ($\overline{\hat{p}^e}$) and firms ($\overline{\hat{w}^e}$).

If inflation expectations are completely anchored, i.e., γ^k, $\gamma^w = 0$, the solution of the model becomes simpler, although the results are similar. Divergence between workers and firms about anchored expectations affects distribution. Inflation is finite even when the anchored expectations are fully passed on to prices and wages ($\alpha^w = \alpha^k = 1$):

$$b^* = \frac{\beta^w b^w + \beta^k b^k}{\beta^w + \beta^k} + \frac{\alpha^w \overline{\hat{p}^e} - \alpha^k \overline{\hat{w}^e}}{\beta^w + \beta^k} \tag{17}$$

$$\widehat{p^*} = \frac{\beta^w \beta^k (b^w - b^k)}{\beta^w + \beta^k} + \frac{\beta^k \alpha^w \overline{\hat{p}^e} + \beta^w \alpha^k \overline{\hat{w}^e}}{\beta^w + \beta^k} \tag{18}$$

Finally, we can consider the case in which both sides converge in their anchored expectations, with $\overline{\hat{p}^e} = \overline{\hat{w}^e}$. Equations (19) and (20) show the equilibrium real wage and inflation rate for this case. As in the previous cases, the equilibrium real wage still depends on a first term which consists of a weighted average of the income claims of workers and firms. The second term now depends on the values of α^w and α^k, which reflect the impact of expected inflation on price and nominal wage increases.

$$b^* = \frac{\beta^w b^w + \beta^k b^k}{\beta^w + \beta^k} + \frac{(\alpha^w - \alpha^k)\overline{\hat{p}^e}}{\beta^w + \beta^k} \tag{19}$$

$$\widehat{p^*} = \frac{\beta^w \beta^k (b^w - b^k)}{\beta^w + \beta^k} + \frac{(\beta^k \alpha^w + \beta^w \alpha^k)\ \overline{\hat{p}^e}}{\beta^w + \beta^k} \tag{20}$$

If workers have a greater ability (say, due to greater bargaining power) to include expected price inflation in wage increases than firms' ability to include the expected common wage inflation in price increases (i.e., if $\alpha^w > \alpha^k$), then the common exogenous expected inflation term positively affects the equilibrium real wage. Conversely, common exogenous expected inflation has a negative impact on the equilibrium real wage if firms are more capable of including expectations in their price increases than workers in their nominal wage gains (i.e., if $\alpha^w < \alpha^k$). Finally, in the particular case in which both sides include expectations in the same proportion (i.e., $\alpha^w = \alpha^k$, for any value of both, including when both are equal to one), the expectational component disappears from the determination of the equilibrium real wage. In this case in which both sides fully include expectations (i.e., $\alpha^w = \alpha^k = 1$), the equilibrium inflation rate only deviates from the expected inflation due to conflict. In the absence of conflict, equilibrium inflation is equal to the expected inflation. With positive aspiration gaps, however, the expectations about inflation will certainly prove to be wrong.

It seems quite unrealistic to conclude that income distribution, in equilibrium, can be a result of which social class — capitalists or workers — is more pessimistic about the future (in the sense that one wrongly expects permanently higher inflation than the other). Moreover, it seems difficult to accept that expectations, or at least part of them, are exogenous or anchored in the long run, despite what is happening with actual price and wage inflation. Empirical evidence shows that inflation expectations are not independent of past inflation (Fair 2022) and that workers, in practice, use the observed increases in their cost of living when negotiating labor contracts (see Braga and Serrano 2023, for references).

Finally, even the idea of exogenous anchored expectations, put out by Blanchard (2016), was recently amended with the assumption that the long-run exogenous anchored expectation is (slowly) corrected by past inflation (Blanchard and Bernanke 2023, p. 9). A simple way to do this is to replace the fixed expectation with an expectational term which evolves according to past inflation.

2.2.2. The Case of Adaptive Expectations

Let us consider the case in which the expectational term evolves according to past inflation. Consider that both workers and firms have adaptive expectations. These are initially exogenous and then will be gradually corrected by observed past inflation. We can get do this by introducing $\overline{\hat{p}^e} = \widehat{p^e_{-1}}$ and $\overline{\hat{w}^e} = \widehat{w^e_{-1}}$ in equations (13) and (14).

If expectations parameters are $0 < \gamma^w, \gamma^k < 1$, expectations of price and wage inflation converge to past observed values ($\widehat{p^e} = \widehat{p_{-1}}$ and $\widehat{w^e} = \widehat{w_{-1}}$). In this case, the result will be the same as the case of naive adaptive expectations for both workers and firms, that is, when $\gamma^w = \gamma^k = 1$. Exogenous initial expectations can affect distribution and inflation out of the equilibrium, but this effect fades away as inflation expectations converge to past inflation. The model with adaptive expectations thus becomes:

$$\hat{w} = \beta^w(b^w - b_{-1}) + \alpha^w \widehat{p_{-1}} \tag{21}$$

$$\hat{p} = \beta^k(b_{-1} - b^k) + \alpha^k \widehat{w_{-1}} \tag{22}$$

Equilibrium requires that $\hat{p} = \hat{w} = \hat{p}_{-1} = \hat{w}_{-1}$. Therefore, workers and firms correct persistent mistakes in their expectations, unlike in the previous anchored case. Equations (23) and (24) show the solutions for the real wage and inflation:

$$b^* = \frac{\left(\frac{\beta^w}{1-\alpha^w}\right)b^w + \left(\frac{\beta^k}{1-\alpha^k}\right)b^k}{\left(\frac{\beta^w}{1-\alpha^w}\right) + \left(\frac{\beta^k}{1-\alpha^k}\right)} \tag{23}$$

$$\widehat{p^*} = \frac{\beta^w \beta^k (b^w - b^k)}{\beta^w (1 - \alpha^k) + \beta^k (1 - \alpha^w)} \tag{24}$$

The solutions (23) and (24) of the model with adaptive expectations show that the parameters that measure the degree of wage and price indexation (α^w and α^k) together with the bargaining parameters (β^w and β^k) are important to the equilibrium real wage and inflation. The higher the degree of wage indexation to prices, the greater the equilibrium real wage and the inflation rate will be. The higher the degree of price indexation to wages, the greater the inflation rate and the lower the equilibrium real wage.

Moreover, from equations (21) and (22), even with finite bargaining power coefficients β^w and β^k, we can obtain the solutions in which one side's target completely determines distribution if the corresponding indexation parameter is equal to 1. In other words, if the degree of indexation of wages (α^w) is equal to one, the equilibrium real wage will be equal to workers' desired real wage. We then have one situation analogous to case 1 discussed in subsection 2.1. Conversely, a situation analogous to case 2, subsection 2.1, occurs if, despite finite bargaining power coefficients β^w and β^k, the degree of indexation of prices to wage costs (α^k) is equal to one. In this case, the real wage will be equal to the target real wage for the firms, b^k. The third case, analogous to case (3), subsection 2.1, occurs when both α^w and α^k are equal to one. We will then have hyperinflation as a result of any permanent degree of conflict (i.e., whenever $b^w > b^k$). Finally, a result analogous to case 4 of subsection 2.1 appears when both bargaining power coefficients β^w and β^k are finite and the degrees of indexation α^w and α^k are lower than 1.

Notice that the same result of conditions (23) and (24) can be obtained if we suppose that workers and firms understand very well the process of inflation and have rational and correct expectations of price and wage so that $\widehat{p^e} = \hat{p}$, as assumed, for example, by Palley (2018), and $\widehat{w^e} = \hat{w}$, as supposed, for example, by Lavoie (2022).

We conclude then, following Palley (2018) that whether expectations are forward or backward looking (unless they unrealistically remain incorrect and unrevised anchored forever) is not too important in the long run. What is really important to the result of distribution and inflation are the magnitudes of the parameters α^w and α^k.

3. Theoretical Controversies on Conflicting Claims Modeling

As explained in Section Two, conflict inflation models appear in two versions: one with only the 'bargaining' parameters, that is, relating aspiration gaps to price and nominal wage growth; and another more complete version, with 'bargaining' and 'indexation' parameters, the latter relating expected or past wage and price inflation to price and nominal wage growth.

Our first remark here asserts that the difference between these two versions of the conflict inflation model is not fully explained in the textbooks (Blecker and Setterfield 2019; Lavoie 2022; and Hein 2023). Blecker and Setterfield (2019) first present the model with only the 'bargaining parameters'. They relate these parameters to 'institutional aspects of the labour market and labour bargaining, such as the frequency of contract renegotiations or wage increases and the ability of workers (or their unions) to win the increases they seek' (p. 212) and 'the speed of adjustment of prices' (p. 213). Then, they present the second version of the model, with 'bargaining' and 'indexation' parameters. The authors justify the use of the second model in a 'high-inflation environment' (p. 219). However, they do not explain in detail the meaning of the 'bargaining' and 'indexation' parameters when they are taken together.[8]

Lavoie (2022) also presents conflict inflation models with these two specifications. The first with only 'bargaining' parameters would consist of 'a simplified version' which 'can very well represent conflicting-claims (...) without losing much substance' (Lavoie 2022, p. 602). The second, including 'bargaining' and 'indexation', would represent a more complete version that, according to him, does not change the main results. Therefore, Lavoie (2022) also does not discuss in detail the exact meaning of the 'bargaining' and 'indexation' parameters when combined in the same model.

Our second assessment is about the recent post-Keynesian debate itself. The debate seems to be centered on the plausibility of the values of the 'bargaining' and 'indexation' parameters of the standard model. However, we think that this debate reflects a more theoretical contention on the meaning of the 'bargaining' and the 'indexation' parameters.

On the one side of this controversy, we have Blecker and Setterfield (2019) and Lavoie (2022) who consider the 'bargaining' and 'indexation' parameters as smaller than one, and associate conflicting claims as generating inflation. On the other side, we have Hein (2023) who criticizes the idea that these parameters should be smaller than one and believes that conflicting claims should be associated with accelerating inflation.

The defense of the arguments from the authors that believe that the 'indexation' parameters are smaller than one (at least in the short run) are grounded on empirical regularities (Blecker and Setterfield 2019; Lavoie 2022; Setterfield and Blecker 2022). Lavoie (2022, p. 603) provides a list of references with evidence of incomplete incorporation of past inflation to wage increases. According to him, wage agreements seem to usually incorporate only partially past inflation and estimated wage indexation coefficients in the wage inflation equation seem to be lower than 1. As noticed by Palley (2018), this has nothing to do with how workers form expectations but with their limited power to incorporate all the expected or past inflation into their money wage increases. Also, there is empirical evidence that the pass-through of changes in labor costs to prices is partial and asymmetric (Sylos-Labini 1979, 1982).

Hein (2023, pp. 136–151), however, criticizes the plausibility of the assumption of the values of the 'indexation' parameters being smaller than one. He argues that this should be inconsistent with rational behavior of workers and firms. If workers bargain a desired real wage, it should be irrational for them to claim only part of past inflation in their wage negotiations. Therefore, α^w should be equal to one and should not depend on workers' relative bargaining power (Hein 2023). If workers have a reduced bargaining power, this should be reflected in a lower level of workers' desired real wage (b^w). In the same vein, assuming $\alpha^k < 1$ in the equation of price increases is inconsistent with the idea of a desired real wage by firms, as to achieve such a target, firms cannot pass on only part of their cost increases. Hence, firms should also completely pass through nominal wage increases to prices, with $\alpha^k = 1$.

[8] In inflation debates, past or expected inflation usually becomes relevant when it persists at moderate or high levels. For instance, Rowthorn (1977, p. 226) assumes that there is a threshold 'below which expected inflation is ignored completely, and above which it is fully taken into account by all concerned'. Similar arguments were put forward in earlier debates about wage inflation (see Forder 2014, pp. 81–89).

In fact, we can add a further criticism on what seems to be an inconsistent treatment of the two parameters of the model as being independent of each other. As we discussed in subsection 2.2, case 2, firms can fully protect their desired real profit rate either when they have an infinite bargaining power coefficient, β^k, or when the 'indexation' coefficient on wage increases in the price increase equation, α^k, is equal to one. However, how can the rate of profit remain at the desired level if at the same time in the same model it is assumed in the other parameter that higher costs are not being fully passed on to price increases? But what, then, is this 'bargaining power', whether 'infinite' or not, if not the capacity to fully pass on cost increases into prices? Why then do we have two independent 'bargaining' and 'indexation' coefficients? Similar objections could be made concerning the money wage increase equation.

So, it seems that the precise meaning behind these 'bargaining' and 'indexation' parameters, both separately and especially when taken together, are less than totally clear, and their theoretical foundations deserve a closer look.

4. A Reinterpretation Proposal

4.1. From 'Bargaining' to Frequency

To clarify the precise meaning behind the 'bargaining' and 'indexation' parameters, let us start with the standard model with only the 'bargaining' parameters. We already discussed the implications of the different values of the β coefficients. But let us take a step back and reflect on the meaning of such parameters.

In his seminal paper, Rowthorn (1977, p. 218) interprets the parameter β as the product of two elements: (1) the number of price (or wage) increases, T, within the period of analysis; and (2) the proportion of the aspiration gap that is filled in each increase, λ. Thus, for workers and firms, their respective bargaining parameters are $\beta^w = T^w\lambda^w$ and $\beta^k = T^k\lambda^k$.[9]

Let us begin by discussing the meaning and the probable values of these λ coefficients, related to the proportion of the aspiration gaps filled for workers and firms in each wage and price increase. Consider first the case of wage increases (equation 4). If workers really want to get a desired real wage b^w, the value of λ^w should not be below one. A λ^w lower than one would mean that the nominal wage would have increased less than the gap between the actual real wage b_{-1} and the desired real wage b^w. For the same reason, λ^w should not be greater than one, as in this case, workers would be trying to get a real wage higher than the target b^w at each wage bargain. The same could be said about firms. If they have a given target for the profit rate r^k that implies that their desired real wage is b^k and not more nor less than that, then λ^k should also be set to one.

Of course, we could introduce some kind of heterogeneity between workers, such as that not all workers get wage increases each time, or that they have heterogeneous or

[9]Note that Rowthorn used his explanation of the bargaining parameter mentioned above as depending on the number of 'bargains per year' price (or wage) increases (and the proportion of the respective aspiration gaps that is filled in each increase) and the inconsistent distributive claims not to explain total inflation, but only the part that he called 'anticipated inflation'. To the latter he would add (no doubt influenced by the monetarist debates of the time) what he called unanticipated inflation, i.e., 'the difference between price rises which actually occur and those anticipated in the wage bargain' (Rowthorn, p. 218). We have no use for this distinction between anticipated and unanticipated inflation and thus we are explaining total inflation.

biased expectations. In that case, λ^w would be lower than one. Formally, we could say the same for prices. The parameter λ^k could be lower than one if not all firms change prices each period.[10] But note that we can make matters simpler by merely noting that a partial adjustment $\lambda < 1$ is formally equivalent to less frequent adjustments T of the full aspiration gap. For instance, $\lambda = 0{,}5$ is clearly equivalent to having full adjustments twice less often. From this we can define $N = \lambda T$ as the equivalent frequency of full adjustments of the aspiration gap.

For the sake of simplicity, in our simple framework with homogenous labor and only one good being produced, we assume $\lambda^w = \lambda^k = 1$. Thus $N = T$ for both workers and firms, implying that both workers and firms get in each wage and price increase exactly what is necessary to fulfill their aspiration gaps. But the analysis could easily be adapted to deal with more complex cases in which there is partial adjustment with either λ^w or λ^k smaller than one, and similar conclusions would follow.

We shall thus assume from now on that the 'bargaining' parameters β^w and β^k will be determined by the frequency of wage and price increases in a given period, $\beta^w = N^w$ and $\beta^k = N^k$. So, we can rewrite equations (4) and (5) as:

$$\hat{w} = N^w(b^w - b_{-1}) \tag{25}$$

$$\hat{p} = N^k(b_{-1} - b^k) \tag{26}$$

Again, as in Section Two, we can find the equilibrium condition for the real wage and inflation when $\hat{p} = \hat{w}$:

$$b^* = \frac{N^w b^w + N^k b^k}{N^w + N^k} \tag{27}$$

$$\widehat{p^*} = \frac{N^w N^k (b^w - b^k)}{N^w + N^k} \tag{28}$$

The equilibrium real wage (b^*) is an average between the desired real wages of workers and firms, with the weight being more favorable for workers or firms depending on their relative frequency of wage and price increases. Equilibrium inflation ($\widehat{p^*}$) depends on the absolute number of increases in wages and prices. Inflation is higher the more frequent both price and wage increases are. Hence, the absolute number of increases in wages and prices matters for determining the equilibrium inflation rate. On the other hand, only the relative frequency of wage and price increases is relevant to the equilibrium real wage.

Our reinterpretation gives us a more objective way to deal with the bargaining power of workers and firms, given their desired real wage and profit rate. A stronger bargaining power of either workers or firms, apart from possibly increasing their respective aspiration gaps, manifests itself objectively, and thus can be also measured, as more frequent wage or price increases.

[10]The problem here is that if two firms sell the same goods, it is difficult to guarantee that due to competition, a situation when one firm changes price and the other not would occur systematically, as demand would shift completely to the firm that keeps the lowest price and this possibility would prevent the firm from changing its price. In new-Keynesian models, this kind of competition is ruled out, as firms adjust prices according to a given probability distribution — when they receive 'the visit of the Calvo Fairy' — and this kind of behavior is justified by market imperfections, such as that firms are monopolistic and produce goods that are imperfect substitutes for the goods produced by their competitors.

Notice that our interpretation is consistent with the pioneering work of Okishio (1959 [1977]), and his main results could be represented in terms of equations 25–28. Okishio first presented his model supposing that, in each wage and price increase, workers and firms get exactly what is necessary to fulfill their aspiration gaps and that workers and firms can set wages and prices only once within a given period, i.e., $N^w = N^k = 1$. He gets the result that the real wage b^* will be an average between the target real wages of firms and workers and the rate of inflation $\widehat{p^*}$ will be equal to the size of the distributive conflict. In the end of the paper, Okishio briefly discusses what would happen if wages were increased less often than prices. To do so, he compares a situation in which wages and prices increase twice within the period of analysis ($N^w = 2$ and $N^k = 2$), with a second situation in which firms set prices twice while workers only once ($N^w = 1$ and $N^k = 2$) over the same period. As a result, not only inflation decreases in the second case, but also the profit rate increases, and consequently, the real wage decreases. With this example, Okishio (1977[1977]) showed that inflation depends on the absolute number of wage and price increases and that changes in the relative frequency of wage and price adjustments will affect the distribution outcome. What we are proposing here is an attempt to generalize his results using the simpler analytical framework of Dutt (1987).

Our reinterpretation is also in line with the views held by the old Cambridge Economic Policy Group — CEPG (Coutts, Tarling, and Wilkinson 1976; Godley and Cripps 1983; Tarling and Wilkinson 1985) to whom (similarly to Okishio 1959[1977]) conflict inflation depends on the conflicting claims and the absolute number of wage and price increases, while the distributive outcome depended on the relative frequencies of such increases.

Coutts, Tarling, and Wilkinson (1976, p. 24) contrast the 'expectational' view of the monetarists to the CEPG's own 'compensational' view of wage bargaining and money wage increases. In the approach of Okishio and the CEPG, expected inflation does not play a direct role on determining inflation. Generalized broad expectations of inflation can play an important role indirectly, to the extent that this will be one of the factors (though not the only one) that determines the actual frequency of wage and price increases.

4.2. From 'Indexation' to Real Resistance and Structural Inertia

When we turn to discuss the other 'indexation' parameter we are faced with an apparent difficulty. By considering the actual frequency of wage and price increases within the period we have already taken care of the reaction of both money wages and prices to previous increases in prices and wages respectively. Thus, there is simply no room to add new assumptions about indexation without falling into the contradictions mentioned at the end of Section Three.

However, we can rewrite our model (that springs from equations 25 and 26) in a way that allows for a comparison with the literature.

To do so, let us redefine the 'indexation' parameters α^w and α^k as real wage and real profit rate resistance parameters, which show by how much money wages and prices react to price and wage inflation. Under this new definition, we can see that, in our model, α is equal to zero either for wages or prices or both when there is no resistance, as in the first Okishio example in which there is only a single wage and price increase (equal to the respective aspiration gaps) in each period (N = 1). On the other hand, these suitably redefined α coefficients would be equal to one when the real wage or price resistance reaction is so strong that it prevents price or wage inflation from eroding the real wage or rate of profits, accordingly (namely when the relevant N tends to infinity and there are continuous adjustments). Finally, in intermediate cases of many but not continuous wage or price increases within each period, the α parameters should remain between zero and one (as it is for firms in the second example of Okishio discussed above, where firms adjust prices two times per period).

Therefore, we can present our reformulated model (equations 25–26) in terms of the aspiration gaps and these real resistance coefficients as:

$$\hat{w} = (b^w - b_{-1}) + \alpha^w \widehat{p_{-1}} \tag{29}$$

$$\hat{p} = (b_{-1} - b^k) + \alpha^k \widehat{w_{-1}} \tag{30}$$

We can further relate our (now redefined) real resistance parameters, α^w and α^k, directly to the frequency of wage and price adjustments (see also Serrano, Aidar, and Bhering 2024). To see this correspondence, we add to equations (29) and (30), the equilibrium conditions $\hat{p} = \hat{w} = \hat{p}_{-1} = \hat{w}_{-1}$. This allows us to rewrite them as follows below:

$$\hat{w} = \frac{1}{1 - \alpha^w}(b^w - b_{-1}) \tag{31}$$

$$\hat{p} = \frac{1}{1 - \alpha^k}(b_{-1} - b^k) \tag{32}$$

By comparing equations (31) and (32) with the corresponding equations (25) and (26) of our reformulated basic model, the necessary relation between the real resistance coefficients and the frequency of wage and price increases becomes clear:

$$\alpha^w = 1 - \frac{1}{N^w} \tag{33}$$

$$\alpha^k = 1 - \frac{1}{N^k} \tag{34}$$

From (33) and (34), we can see that the coefficients of 'indexation' can only be equal to one if the number of price (or wage) increases tends to infinity. This means that prices (or wages) must increase *continuously* within the period of analysis to keep the desired level of the distributive variable by firms (or workers). Otherwise, for a finite number of adjustments within each period, the real resistance coefficients increase with a higher frequency of price and wage adjustments, but always stay below one.[11]

Solving the model for the equilibrium real wage and inflation, we get:

$$b^* = \frac{(1 - \alpha^k)b^w + (1 - \alpha^w)b^k}{(1 - \alpha^k) + (1 - \alpha^w)} \tag{35}$$

$$\widehat{p^*} = \frac{(b^w - b^k)}{(1 - \alpha^k) + (1 - \alpha^w)} \tag{36}$$

[11]Note that this equation does not work if $N = 0$. But in this case either the money wage or the price level or both are constant over time and thus there is no conflict inflation anyway.

Equation (35) shows that the relative size of the real resistance coefficients affects the result for income distribution. And equation (36) shows that inflation will be a positive function of the size of the conflicting claims $b^w - b^k$ and of both real resistance coefficients (and will be infinite for any positive distributive conflict only in the case in which both real resistance coefficients are equal to one).

The upshot of our critique and reformulation of the standard conflicting claims model is that while the model cannot have the two independent 'bargaining power' and 'indexation' parameters, it can and it should be used, either by making the frequency of wage and price increases determine directly the extent of the 'bargaining power' of each side of the conflict (as in equations 25 and 26) or instead by representing the relative bargaining power as the degree of real wage and real rate of profit resistance (as in equations 29 and 30). Since both representations concern exactly the same model, the choice between which form to use in a particular application depends on which aspect of the conflict inflation process one wants to examine.

In particular, the representation of the model in terms of real resistance coefficients allows us to overcome the criticism put forward by Hein (2023) concerning the inconsistency of assuming the 'indexation' parameters on wages and/or prices as being lower than one. The inconsistency is resolved when we realize that these parameters express the real resistance, not indexation, and therefore are unrelated to expectations. In fact, in our formulation workers and firms do ask exactly what they aspire each time they have a chance to increase their nominal wages or prices. But as long as neither workers nor firms have the power to increase wages and prices continuously, their respective real resistance parameters will be lower than one. According to this specification, workers may always ask for full compensation for past inflation. But they do not have the power to obtain nominal wage increases as often as they would like. In the same vein, there is no reason to assume that firms always have the power to increase prices as often as they would like, something that, due to the pressure of competition, would require some sort of perfect coordination and collusion among them.

Note that, in this representation of the model, the real resistance coefficients determine the structural degree of inflation inertia in the system, with no need for assumptions on expectations and their formation. Moreover, the fact that in most relevant cases the real resistance coefficients are likely to be lower than one confirms that in principle a given distributive conflict determines a particular level of inflation, and not its acceleration (Serrano 1986). This level will be a multiple of the sum of the real resistance coefficients that determine the degree of inflation inertia of the economy.

4.3. Real Resistance, Inertia and Inflation

We can now use our simple conflict inflation model to critically discuss the four possible cases mentioned in Section Two, as resulting from different assumptions about the real resistance of wages and profits, deriving from different assumption concerning the frequencies of wage and price increase (Serrano, Aidar, and Bhering 2024).

The first two cases are: (a) the one in which workers have complete real wage resistance, but firms do not have complete real profit resistance; and (b) the one in which firms have complete real profit resistance but workers do not have complete real wage resistance. From equation (31) it is easy to see that in case (a) as $\alpha^w = 1$ and $1 > \alpha^k > 0$, the equilibrium real wage is equal to the workers' target ($b^* = b^w$). In that case, a firm's target differing from workers' will only increase inflation without changing distribution. Also, the frequency of price increases, as measured by α^k, will only affect inflation but not distribution. If that was the case, perhaps we should ask: why do firms keep increasing their prices? The same question is valid for the opposite case when firms can fully protect their real rate of profits, but workers do not have any power to affect their real wages. If this is the case, why would workers keep asking for money wage increases, given that they cannot change distribution but only increase inflation? And why would firms make so much effort to deny increasing money wages as much as their workers want, if granting these increases would have no effect on their real rate of profits?[12] If one side has complete real resistance, it would be rational for the other side's real resistance to fall to zero.[13]

The third case occurs when both firms and workers have perfect real profit and real wage resistance ($\alpha^w = \alpha^k = 1$). In this case, any conflict accelerates inflation, as the level of wage and price inflation cannot change income distribution. As we discussed before, this case is quite extreme since it implies that both sides can *continuously* increase nominal wages and prices. Situations of accelerating inflation, very high inflation regimes, and even hyperinflation episodes can happen if fierce distributive conflict, with both sides having strong bargaining power, leads to an increase in the frequency of price increases and the shortening of the duration of wage contracts. However, even in such situations, the idea that distribution is completely determined independently of wage and price inflation, and thus inflation is neutral to distribution, seems a bit difficult to accept.[14]

Finally, we have the case where both firms and workers have incomplete real profit and wage resistance, as expressed in their inability to continuously adjust prices and wages. This seems to us the most plausible case empirically (apart from very special and extreme circumstances alluded to above), and is consistent with the views of Okishio, the CEPG and Sylos-Labini (1982).

5. Conflict Augmented Phillips Curve

We can now discuss what we call conflict-augmented Phillips curve (Serrano 2019; Summa and Braga 2020; Morlin and Pariboni 2023). In the last sections, we have defined the desired real wages by workers and firms (and so the desired real profit rate) as exogenous variables. To transform our system of conflict inflation into a Phillips curve, we add one new assumption. We assume that the real wage desired by workers is a

[12]Many post-Keynesian and Kaleckian authors and also the well-known theory of inertial inflation (Modigliani and Padoa-Schioppa 1978; Lopes 1986; Pereira and Nakano 1987; Ros 1989) assume that firms have perfect real rate of profit (real markup, in their case) resistance and have never satisfactorily explained these basic questions (Serrano 1986, 2010).

[13]Lorenzoni and Werning (2023, p. 15) consider the possibility of this case where workers (or firms) have full capacity to index their real variables and firms (workers) not, and conflict only produces inflation but not changes in real variables. That the losers in this process would keep increasing their nominal wages (or prices) with no real effect seem even more implausible in this context, given the usual assumptions of extreme rationality embedded in New Keynesian models.

[14]In historical experiences of very high and unstable rates of inflation, as in Brazil in the 1980s, for instance, this process of shortening the length of nominal wage contracts and increase in frequency of price increases was aggravated by the daily formal indexation of the nominal exchange rate and the basic nominal interest rate. The resulting rate of inflation was, of course, quite high but hardly neutral in distributive terms.

positive function of the level of the employment rate, $\frac{L}{N}$, where L stands for the level of employment, and N is the working age population.[15] Besides the labor market effect, workers' real wage target also depends on institutional factors, represented by the exogenous parameter b_0^w. The employment rate reflects the assumption that less slack in the labor market would strengthen the bargaining power of workers, who change their desired real wage accordingly. On the other hand, we keep firms' target exogenous. Thus, firms' real wage target does not respond to changes in employment or the utilization rate.[16] Therefore, equations 37 and 38 below show these assumptions:

$$b^w = b_0^w + \rho^w\left(\frac{L}{N}\right) \tag{37}$$

$$b^k = b_0^k \tag{38}$$

Inserting equations (37) and (38) into equation (36) gives us the following long run 'old' Phillips curve, in which a higher employment ratio leads to a higher level of inflation:

$$\widehat{p^*} = \frac{(b_0^w - b_0^k)}{(1-\alpha^k)+(1-\alpha^w)} + \frac{\rho^w}{(1-\alpha^k)+(1-\alpha^w)}\left(\frac{L}{N}\right) \tag{39}$$

It is important to notice that the old-type Phillips curve will occur if at least one of the real resistance coefficients of workers or firms is smaller than 1.[17] We will only have an 'accelerationist-type' Phillips curve when both real resistance coefficients are equal to one. In that case, there is a single employment rate that makes distributive claims compatible and inflation stable (a single NAIRU[18]). At any other level of the employment rate, inflation will be either accelerating or decelerating continuously. We can find this

---

[15]We use this definition of the employment rate as a general indicator for labor market slack. Of course, other measures of labor market slack are used in the empirical literature to relate labor market conditions to wage and/or price dynamics (Blanchflower and Bryson 2023). As the objective of our paper is purely theoretical and our general formulation of conflict inflation and Phillips curve is compatible with any indicator of labor market slack, we choose this variable as it is widely used in theoretical literature and so it is more comparable with other models.

[16]Alternatively, we could add the assumption that firms increase their desired real profit rate when the actual degree of capacity utilization is above its normal or planned degree. But if investment is induced and productive capacity adjusts to the trend of demand and there is tendency towards the normal degree of utilization through the operation of the Sraffian Supermultiplier, this effect of demand shocks on profit margins and prices would anyway be temporary, as shown in Serrano (2019) and Morlin and Pariboni (2023). But even this transient effect is unlikely to happen in practice, as it is not realistic to think that firms change profit margins and prices as a response to the degree of capacity utilization while it is below its maximum degree of utilization, in the sense that capacity is fully utilized, and it is not possible to expand production at all. Since cyclical fluctuations in capacity utilization tend to remain below this full capacity level, they tend not to exert any pressure on prices and the profit rate. In fact, as long as there is spare capacity, competition constrains the ability of firms to increase the desired real profit rate (Lavoie 2023). But even if the maximum degree of utilization were to be reached on some occasions, these episodes of proper demand inflation would be temporary, as during the ongoing Supermultiplier process, capacity utilization would not remain at the maximum degree of utilization for long time (even if the convergence to the normal degree of utilization is slow).

[17]See Serrano (2019, pp. 9–10) and Summa and Braga (2020, pp. 92–93).

[18]In fact, considering that we are working with the employment ratio, rather than the unemployment rate, we should refer to a SIRE (Stable Inflation Rate of Employment), as done by Hein (2023) among others. For the sake of exposition, however, we keep the concept of NAIRU in the text since it expresses the same idea, and this concept is more common in the literature.

type of NAIRU derived from conflict inflation models in the literature, as we will discuss further in subsection 5.1.

We can insert equations (37) and (38) into equation (35) to see the effect of the employment rate on equilibrium real wage:

$$b^* = \frac{(1-\alpha^k)b_0^w + (1-\alpha^w)b_0^k}{(1-\alpha^k)+(1-\alpha^w)} + \frac{\rho^w\left(\frac{L}{N}\right)}{(1-\alpha^k)+(1-\alpha^w)} \tag{40}$$

The real wage is positively related to the employment rate as long as $\alpha^k < 1$. If firms have real profit resistance, $\alpha^k = 1$, they can set real wage according to their target, $b^* = b_0^k$ and real wage will not depend on the employment rate.

In the next subsections, we show how different assumptions on the real resistance parameters affect the shape of the Phillips curve and the distributive outcomes in different conflict inflation models, as special cases of our reformulated model. We will relate our 'four cases' (discussed in sections 2.1 and 4.3), as expressed by the magnitude of the parameters, to the consequences to both the 'nominal' (equation 39) and the 'real' (equation 40) Phillips curves.

5.1. Conflict, Accelerationist Phillips Curves and NAIRU

The accelerationist Phillips curve based on conflicting claims appears in some contributions in the mainstream. One example is found in Carlin and Soskice (1990), who assume both α parameters as equal to one to get a NAIRU. These parameters reflect complete real wage and profit (mark-up) resistance from workers and firms. Their model also assumes that the real mark-up set by firms is exogenous. Any employment rate different than the NAIRU leads to continuously accelerating or decelerating inflation (see equation 39, for $\alpha^w = \alpha^k = 1$). This process, however, has no impact on distribution (see equation 40, for $\alpha^w = \alpha^k = 1$).

The same accelerationist Phillips curve can be found in a recent contribution by Blanchard and Bernanke (2023). They first suppose that both firms and workers have complete real wage and profit resistance regarding their expectations (i.e., $\alpha^k = \alpha^w = 1$). They assume that firms know the actual increase in nominal wages and fully incorporate it into prices. Workers' expectations, however, are anchored, as they depend strongly on exogenous expectations and few on past inflation. In terms of our model with equations (13), (14), (15) and (16), this would mean a γ^w positive but very close to zero for workers and $\gamma^k = 1$ for firms. In the short-run, this assumption produces an old-type Phillips curve with non-accelerationist results. However, note that this is only a nominal wage Phillips curve, as the real mark-up is exogenous. In the long run, anchored expectations follow an adaptive mechanism, despite the strong weight on the exogenous initial expectation. As we showed in sub-section 2.2, this adaptive mechanism will make anchored expectations to (slowly) converge to past inflation. Thus, wage inflation will be fully indexed to past inflation in the long run. The accelerationist Phillips curve from Blanchard and Bernanke (2023), thus, produces slow inflation acceleration in the short-run, due to this sluggish process of adjustment of expectations to past inflation by workers, which is more compatible with the data. But their model produces a slow trend to hyperinflation in the long run if the unemployment rate is smaller than the NAIRU.[19]

Another recent mainstream conflict inflation model by Ratner and Sim (2022) proposes a new-Keynesian Phillips curve with what they call 'Kaleckian assumptions'. They claim that the lower bargaining power of workers in the last decades in the U.S. reduced the volatility of inflation by changing the slope of the New-Keynesian Phillips curve. In our model, the flattening of the Phillips curve can be interpreted either as a fall in the parameter ρ^w, or as a reduction of the degree of real wage resistance as wage increases have become less frequent (the latter also decreasing inflation inertia)[20] or a bit of both, as a result of a long period of lower worker bargaining power and lower unionization rates. Ratner and Sim (2022) however do not establish a connection between distribution and the dynamics of nominal wage and price increases, as they introduce the effect of workers' bargaining power directly in the determination of firms' profit mark-ups.[21] The key issue for our purposes is that the introduction of the so-called Kaleckian assumptions does not bring this model closer to the notion of conflict inflation because distribution appears to be completely exogenous to the dynamics of nominal wages. Therefore, the effect of bargaining on distribution happens outside of the inflation part of the story.

We can also find NAIRU and accelerationist Phillips curves as a possibility in heterodox models. Rowthorn (1977) explicitly discusses the case that can be interpreted in our scheme as assuming $\alpha^w = \alpha^k = 1$.[22] As wage inflation depends on the unemployment rate, the compatibility between distributive claims is only possible with a unique unemployment rate, associated with a degree of workers' bargaining power which makes the distributive targets of workers and firms compatible. Any unemployment rate different from this heterodox NAIRU will produce accelerating or decelerating inflation, explained as a result of incompatible claims over income distribution. A model also based on conflicting claims over distribution, assuming $\alpha^w = \alpha^k = 1$ and with the same accelerationist properties can be found in Hein (2006).[23]

Levrero (2023) and Stirati (2001) base conflict inflation on a dispute between money wages and nominal profit rates, the latter seen as determined by the nominal interest rates set by the Central Bank, following Pivetti (1991).[24] As one particular case of their

---

[19]Notice that Blanchard and Bernanke (2023) use another indicator for the NAIRU, as they use the Beveridge Curve instead of the unemployment rate, so the 'NAIRU' here is given by the natural or steady-state vacancy-to unemployment ratio.

[20]See Setterfield and Blecker (2022) and Romaniello (2024) for evidence that the flattening of the Phillips curve happened during the period in which inflation inertia has fallen considerably.

[21]Steady-state mark-up therefore depends on two factors: the elasticity of substitution among final consumption goods produced by monopolistically competitive firms — as in New Keynesian mark-up pricing rule -, and inversely on workers' bargaining power. Curiously, the underlying reasoning is that unions would bargain for a lower relative price to increase consumers' demand and thus employment (Ratner and Sim 2022, p. 6). Workers are assumed capable of affecting firms' decisions on the price of the final good, and would do that in order to dispute a greater share in monopoly rents by increasing the employment level.

[22]The case could occur if inflation is above a certain threshold, and workers and firms fully take expected inflation into account (Rowthorn 1977, p. 226).

[23]See also an assessment of Hein (2006) by Hein and Häusler (2024).

[24]According to Pivetti (1991), the nominal interest rate on long-term riskless bonds, which is influenced by monetary policy, determines the opportunity cost of capital. The profit rate, in its turn, is determined by the opportunity cost of capital plus a factor of industry-specific risk premia, corresponding to the remuneration of the 'risk and trouble' of productive investment. Simply put, wage inflation reduces the real interest rate as well as the real profit rate, for increasing real wages and reproduction costs of capital. In this view, firms cannot autonomously react to wage inflation and protect their real mark-ups, since pricing decisions are constrained by competition and follow the

analyses, Levrero (2023) and Stirati (2001, p. 439) assume that Central Banks, by targeting real interest rates, can determine the real profit rate.[25] In our scheme, this would be represented by $\alpha^K = 1$. Central Banks thus deliberately and successfully fully protect the real profit rate from wage inflation. Beside this assumption of complete real profit rate resistance set by the Central Bank, Levrero (2023) and Stirati (2001) also assume in their models that workers fully pass on past price increases to their money wages and thus, which in our scheme would be represented by $\alpha^w = 1$. The combination of these two assumptions results in an accelerationist Phillips curve with a heterodox NAIRU at least as a theoretical possibility in this particular case analyzed by Levrero (2023) and Stirati (2001, p. 439). Of course, Stirati (2001, p. 434) clearly states that accelerating inflation is a very limited possibility, and in recent works she opposes the existence of a NAIRU (Stirati and Paternesi-Meloni 2018; Paternesi-Meloni, Romaniello, and Stirati 2022) explicitly referring to the partial inertia of money wages increases ($\alpha^w < 1$).

Note that this exercise depends on two strong assumptions. First, in practice the Central Bank would not be capable of adjusting the nominal interest rate continuously nor it would be likely that firms would also continuously pass those changes into their prices to stabilize the real profit rate. The assumption of full real profit rate resistance is therefore just a limiting case. The second problem is the assumption of full inflation inertia in money wage increases, which means assuming that workers' real wage resistance is also perfect and that workers can fully protect their real wages. The assumption of very strong bargaining power of the workers ($\alpha^w = 1$) is unrealistic for the economies they are discussing in the historical period they are analyzing, as these authors know better than anybody (Stirati and Paternesi-Meloni 2021; Fontanari, Levrero, and Romaniello 2022). Therefore, the NAIRU is an unlikely result since even perfect real profit rate resistance (with incomplete real wage resistance) would simply lead to a traditional downward-sloping Phillips Curve. Once again conflict only leads to inflation acceleration when there is both perfect real wage and perfect real profit rate resistance.

Thus, NAIRU models are based on quite extreme assumptions of perfect real income resistance of both firms and workers through continuous wage and price adjustments. Besides generating extreme and empirically implausible inflation dynamics, these models also imply that conflict inflation has a neutral impact in terms of distribution. As the NAIRU have been extensively criticized in the literature on both theoretical (Setterfield and Leblond 2003; Serrano 2019; Summa and Braga 2020) and empirical (Fair 2000, Lang et al. 2020; Paternesi-Meloni, Romaniello, and Stirati 2022) grounds, let us look to the old-type of Phillips curve as a more plausible framework for discussing conflict inflation.

5.2. Old-Type Phillips Curves

As we already discussed, an old-type Phillips curve (i.e., non-vertical and non-accelerationist Phillips curve) will occur if at least one of real resistance parameters from workers

---

historical costs of capital. However, increases in the nominal interest rate increase the opportunity cost of capital therefore allowing firms to increase prices more than proportionally to cost increases, recovering real profit margins.

[25] By targeting a real interest rate as in the Taylor rule, Central Banks implicitly target an outcome for income distribution (Levrero 2023).

and/or firms is smaller than 1. In the recent post-Keynesian debate, we can find two extreme positions compatible with this old-type Phillips curve.

On one side, Lavoie (2024, pp. 13–14) proposes a specific case with 'firms having the upper hand', that is, firms with the ability to fully index any wage increase, while workers are unable to fully index their wages.[26] In the long run, this means that the parameters of real resistance are $\alpha^k = 1$ for firms, and $\alpha^w < 1$ for workers. The result is an old-type Phillips curve, in which inflation, and not accelerating inflation, occurs as a result of conflict. However, this Phillips curve is only nominal, because as firms can fully protect their real profit rate (or mark-ups), workers cannot change distribution by increasing money wages, even if the employment ratio, and thus workers' bargaining power, is high.

The main theoretical problem with this kind of assumption has already been discussed in Section Four above. If firms have the capacity to fully index their real profits to the desired ones, why do either these firms or their workers care at all about money wage increases that have no effect on distribution? And the main empirical problem with this view is there is ample empirical evidence that the old-type Phillips curve is not only nominal, but 'real'. The employment rate has not only an impact on inflation, but also on the real wage (Stirati and Paternesi-Meloni 2018).

Contrary to this neutrality of changes in money wages on distribution, Hein and Häusler (2024) argue that the stronger bargaining power of workers, as a result of a higher employment rate, does have an impact on real wages and distribution.[27] In their model, workers have a target wage share, and can fully index their wages to price increases. This specification is equivalent of assuming $\alpha^w = 1$ in our own model.[28] The way they model firms' response through price inflation, however, is quite different from the standard model, as firms have no explicit profit rate (or profit share target). Also, firms are assumed not to be able to fully pass through 'excess wage inflation' into prices because of the heterogeneity among them.[29] Excess wage inflation is defined by the difference between wage inflation and expected price inflation, the latter equal to lagged price inflation. In this model what happens is that excess wage inflation tends to converge to zero because the wage share converges to workers' target. Therefore, despite the difference in modeling price inflation, the long run distributive result is similar to that of our own model with an explicit profit share target and $\alpha^k < 1$. In this case, workers will have the 'upper hand', and always get what they desire. The old-type Phillips curve, however, will be real, since changes in the employment rate will have an impact on the workers target real wage, and thus on the

[26] Lavoie (2022) argues that firms tending to have the upper hand in the long run is the usual assumption of most post-Keynesians. The case where 'firms do not let the margin of profit fall below its target level and they can respond immediately to any increase in their wage costs' corresponds to 'how mark-up pricing is viewed by most economists' (Lavoie 2022, p. 604).

[27] Hein and Häusler (2024) propose some possible amendments to Hein (2023) and compare the results with Blecker and Setterfield (2019) and Lavoie (2022). Lavoie (2024) and Hein and Häusler (2024) show that Hein (2023) produces unstable equilibrium regarding distribution if employment rate is different than the SIRE, and zero inflation if employment rate is equal to the SIRE.

[28] The only difference is that our specification is in terms of the real wage and real profit rate, while in Hein and Häusler (2024) the model is constructed in terms of the wage and profit shares.

[29] Firms are heterogeneous with respect to technology, management, and region. In fact, only the price-leading firm — i.e., the one with the lowest unit labor cost — could completely pass-through the nominal wage increase to prices. The other firms would increase prices less than proportionally to the increase in nominal unit labor costs, to preserve their market share (Hein 2023, p. 148).

equilibrium real wage. But then, the theoretical problem discussed above inevitably arises, if workers have perfect real wage resistance and can always get their desired real wage, why do firms keep increasing their prices and there is inflation at all?

In both cases discussed above, distribution is exogenously determined and solely influenced by one side of the conflict. The dynamics of inflation, therefore, do not affect the outcome of distribution, and cause no gains or losses at all neither to workers nor to firms. In our view, it is much a more reasonable to assume that while in certain periods the bargaining power and real resistance coefficients of either firms or of workers may be particularly high or particularly low, both firms and workers usually will have some limits in their capacity to protect their real profits and wages via changes in nominal variables. For this reason, they can influence distribution to a certain extent, either to obtain gains or at least to avoid losses, through nominal increases in prices and wages, giving them good reasons to push for such increases. In this case, the Phillips curve is from the old-type, and both inflation and real wages would be positively related to the employment rate (Serrano 2019; Summa and Braga 2020; Morlin and Pariboni 2023).

6. Final Remarks

The standard conflict inflation model, based on Dutt (1987) and disseminated in post-Keynesian textbooks (Blecker and Setterfield 2019; Lavoie 2022), provides a simple, flexible and useful framework compatible with different assumptions on its parameters. However, authors disagree with respect to the magnitude of these parameters (Hein 2023). Hein (2023) points out the inconsistency between the assumptions of incomplete 'indexation' and the assumptions that workers and firms have targets for their real wages and real (normal) rate of profits, respectively. This leads him to propose an alternative framework in which conflicting claims initially lead to inflation acceleration.

To that criticism we added that the 'bargaining power' coefficient can hardly be independent from to what extent workers (and firms) are able to react to previous price (or wage) increases, and hence of the values of the corresponding 'indexation' parameters.

Nevertheless, we argued that there is no need to abandon the simple framework proposed by Dutt (1987) if we reinterpret the 'bargaining power' and the 'indexation' parameters appropriately. In our view, there is a single objective element that is relevant to express simultaneously both the actual state of the bargaining power of firms and workers and their relative ability to protect their real incomes from the corresponding wage and prices increases. This element is the actual frequency of nominal wages and price increases. This relative frequency will determine the extent of real wage and profit resistance. And these real resistance parameters determine the degree of structural inflation inertia. Finally, we showed that the reason why the degree of 'indexation' of prices and wages is usually lower than one does not come from any departure from some notion of 'rationality', as implying that workers and firms ask for less than they seem to want, but instead is grounded on the fact that whenever there is an actual wage or price increase, workers and firms do ask for what they aspire, but they often are not able to have such wage and price increases as often as they could wish (and certainly not continuously).

This reinterpretation provides the foundations for our conflict-augmented Phillips curve. By varying the assumptions on the value of the real resistance (and thus inertia) parameters in this Phillips curve, we generated the different outcomes found in the literature. On the one hand, we have mainstream and heterodox NAIRU models, which require perfect real income resistance of both sides through continuous wage and price adjustments. On the other hand, in recent proposals by Lavoie (2024) and Hein and Häusler (2024), one of the two parties in the conflict (firms or workers, respectively) is assumed to be able to fully protect its real income in the long run, while the other side is not. In our terms this disparity arises from setting one real resistance parameter equal to one (and thus assuming the ability to adjust either price or wages continuously), while the other is smaller than one. Consequently, distribution converges towards the target associated with the class able to fully protect its income. However, in these models, the other class is implausibly assumed to keep asking for nominal increases with no distributive result. In our view, it is more realistic to assume that an intermediate situation is what usually prevails, with both workers and firms only partially being able to protect their real income, since neither price nor wage increases tend to be sufficiently frequent to generate perfect real wage nor profit rate resistance. Finally, in some extreme cases of very high inflation, the frequency of price and wage increases (measured in the local currency) tends to become very high. In that case, even a small distributive conflict can lead to accelerating inflation.[30]

Acknowledgements

The authors want to thank (but not implicate) Marc Lavoie, Gustavo Bhering, Eckhard Hein, Antonella Stirati, Nathalie Marins, Davide Romaniello, Pedro Machado and two anonymous referees for very useful discussions on and/or comments on an earlier draft, as well as other participants at presentations at the 4th International Demand-led Growth Workshop, Rio de Janeiro (July, 2023), 27th Annual Conference of the Forum Macroeconomics and Macroeconomic Policies, Berlin (October, 2023), 35th EAEPE Conference, Leeds (September, 2023), the 49th Annual Conference of the Eastern Economic Association (EEA), Boston (February, 2024), and the research seminars at the Graduate Program of Unicamp (August 2023) and UFF (November, 2023).

Disclosure Statement

No potential conflict of interest was reported by the author(s).

Funding

This work was supported by Conselho Nacional de Desenvolvimento Científico e Tecnológico [307273/2020-2; 315572/2021-3].

ORCID

Franklin Serrano http://orcid.org/0000-0002-9981-9029

[30]Historically, this kind of extreme situation has usually come together with economic and financial instability (for example, a severe Balance-of-Payments' crisis). Under such complex circumstances it seems unlikely that there would be a stable and definite relation between the employment rate and the rate of inflation (acceleration). Therefore, the notion of a NAIRU would hardly be of any policy relevance anyway.

Ricardo Summa http://orcid.org/0000-0002-4769-8974
Guilherme Spinato Morlin http://orcid.org/0000-0002-5010-5420

References

Blanchard, O. 2016. 'The Phillips Curve: Back to the '60s?' *American Economic Review* 106 (5): 31–34.

Blanchard, O. J., and B. S. Bernanke. 2023. 'What Caused the US Pandemic-Era Inflation? (No. w31417).' National Bureau of Economic Research, Working Paper No. 31417.

Blanchflower, D. G., and A. Bryson. 2023. 'Recession and Deflation?' *Review of Keynesian Economics* 11 (2): 214–231.

Blecker, R. A., and M. Setterfield. 2019. *Heterodox Macroeconomics: Models of Demand, Distribution and Growth*. Edward Elgar Publishing.

Braga, J., and F. Serrano. 2023. 'Post-Keynesian Economics: New Foundations by Marc Lavoie Chapter 8: Inflation Theory.' *Review of Political Economy*, 1–13.

Carlin, W., and D. Soskice. 1990. *Macroeconomics and the Wage Bargain* (Vol. 99). Oxford: Oxford University Press.

Coutts, K., R. Tarling, and F. Wilkinson. 1976. 'Wage Bargaining and the Inflation Process.' *Economic Policy Review* 2: 20–27.

Dutt, A. K. 1987. 'Alternative Closures Again: A Comment on 'Growth, Distribution and Inflation'.' *Cambridge Journal of Economics* 11 (1): 75–82.

Fair, R. C. 2000. 'Testing the NAIRU Model for the United States.' *Review of Economics and Statistics* 82 (1): 64–71.

Fair, R. C. 2022. 'A Note on the Fed's Power to Lower Inflation.' *Business Economics* 57 (2): 56–63.

Fontanari, C., E. S. Levrero, and D. Romaniello. 2022. 'A Composite Index for Workers' Bargaining Power and the Missing-Inflation Matter.' *Presented at 26th FMM Conference*, Berlin.

Forder, J. 2014. *Macroeconomics and the Phillips Curve Myth*. Oxford: Oxford University Press.

Garegnani, P. 1979. 'Notes on Consumption, Investment and Effective Demand: Part II, Monetary Analysis.' *Cambridge Journal of Economics* 3 (1): 63–82.

Godley, W., and F. Cripps. 1983. *Macroeconomics*. New York: Oxford University Press.

Hein, E. 2006. 'Wage Bargaining and Monetary Policy in a Kaleckian Monetary Distribution and Growth Model: Trying to Make Sense of the NAIRU.' *European Journal of Economics and Economic Policies* 3 (2): 305–329.

Hein, E. 2023. *Macroeconomics after Kalecki and Keynes: Post-Keynesian Foundations*. Edward Elgar Publishing.

Hein, E., and C. Häusler. 2024. 'Kaleckian Models of Conflict Inflation, Distribution and Employment: A Comparative Analysis.' IPE Working Paper No. 225/2024.

Hein, E., and E. Stockhammer. 2009. 'A Post Keynesian Alternative to the New Consensus Model.' In *Macroeconomic Theory and Macroeconomic Pedagogy*, 273–294. London: Palgrave Macmillan UK.

Hein, E., and E. Stockhammer. 2010. 'Macroeconomic Policy Mix, Employment and Inflation in a Post-Keynesian Alternative to the New Consensus Model.' *Review of Political Economy* 22 (3): 317–354.

Kurz, H. D., and N. Salvadori. 1997. *Theory of Production: A Long-Period Analysis*. Cambridge University Press.

Lang, D., M. Setterfield, and I. Shikaki. 2020. 'Is There Scientific Progress in Macroeconomics? The Case of the NAIRU.' *European Journal of Economics and Economic Policies* 17 (1): 19–38.

Lavoie, M. 2022. *Post-Keynesian Economics: New Foundations*. Edward Elgar Publishing.

Lavoie, M. 2023. 'Conflictual Inflation and Profit Inflation.' *27th Annual Conference of the Forum Macroeconomics and Macroeconomic Policies (FMM), 'Inflation, Distributional Conflict and Just Transition'*, Berlin.

Lavoie, M. 2024. 'Conflictual Inflation and the Phillips Curve.' *Review of Political Economy*, 1–23.

Levrero, E. S. 2023. 'The Taylor Rule and Its Aftermath: An Interpretation along Classical-Keynesian Lines.' *Review of Political Economy*, 1–19.

Lopes, F. 1986. *O choque heterodoxo: combate a inflação e reforma monetária*. Rio de Janeiro: Campus.

Lorenzoni, G., and I. Werning. 2023. 'Inflation is Conflict.' National Bureau of Economic Research, Working Paper No. 31099.

Modigliani, F., and T. Padoa-Schioppa. 1978. *The Management of an Open Economy with "100% Plus" Wage Indexation* (No. 130). International Finance Section, Department of Economics, Princeton University.

Morlin, G. S. 2023. 'Inflation and Conflicting Claims in the Open Economy.' *Review of Political Economy*, 1–29.

Morlin, G. S., and R. Pariboni. 2023. 'Conflict Inflation and Autonomous Demand: A Supermultiplier Model with Endogenous Distribution.' Department of Economics, University of Siena, Working Paper No. 902.

Okishio, N. 1959[1977]. 'Inflation as an Expression of Class Antagonism.' *Kobe University Economic Review* 23 (1): 17–29.

Palley, T. 2018. 'Recovering Keynesian Phillips Curve Theory: Hysteresis of Ideas and the Natural Rate of Unemployment.' *Review of Keynesian Economics* 6 (4): 473–492.

Paternesi-Meloni, W., D. Romaniello, and A. Stirati. 2022. 'Inflation and the NAIRU: Assessing the Role of Long-Term Unemployment as a Cause of Hysteresis.' *Economic Modelling* 113: 105900.

Pereira, L. B., and Y. Nakano. 1987. *The Theory of Inertial Inflation: The Foundation of Economic Reform in Brazil and Argentina*. Lynne Rienner Publishers.

Petri, F. 2021. *Microeconomics for the Critical Mind: Mainstream and Heterodox Analyses*. Springer.

Pivetti, M. 1991. *An Essay on Money and Distribution*. London: Macmillan.

Ratner, D., and J. W. Sim. 2022. *Who Killed the Phillips Curve? A Murder Mystery. Finance and Economics Discussion Series 2022-028*. Washington: Board of Governors of the Federal Reserve System.

Romaniello, D. 2024. 'The Longer, the Weaker? Considering the Role of Long-Term Unemployment in an 'Original' Phillips Curve.' *Review of Political Economy*, 1–34.

Ros, J. 1989. *On Inertia, Social Conflict, and the Structuralist Analysis of Inflation* (No. 128). Helen Kellogg Institute for International Studies, University of Notre Dame. of Governors of the Federal Reserve System (US).

Rowthorn, R. E. 1977. 'Conflict, Inflation and Money.' *Cambridge Journal of Economics* 1 (3): 215–239.

Serrano, F. 1986. 'Inflação inercial e indexação neutra.' In *Inflação Inercial, Teorias Sobre Inflação e o Plano Cruzado*, edited by J. M. Rego. São Paulo: Paz e Terra.

Serrano, F. 1993. 'Review of Pivetti's Essay on Money and Distribution.' *Contributions to Political Economy* 12: 117–123.

Serrano, F. 2010. 'O Conflito Distributivo e a Teoria da Inflação Inercial.' *Revista de Economia Contemporânea* 14 (2): 395–421.

Serrano, F. 2019. 'Mind the Gaps: The Conflict Augmented Phillips Curve and the Sraffian Supermultiplier.' IE-UFRJ, Working Paper No. 11-2019.

Serrano, F., G. Aidar, and G. Bhering. 2024. Tax Incidence and Distribution in a Sraffian Conflict Inflation Framework, *mimeo*, IE-UFRJ.

Setterfield, M., and R. A. Blecker. 2022. 'Structural Change in the US Phillips Curve, 1948–2021: The Role of Power and Institutions.' Post-Keynesian Economic Society, Working Paper No. 2208.

Setterfield, M., and K. Leblond. 2003. 'The Phillips Curve and US Macroeconomic Performance During the 1990s.' *International Review of Applied Economics* 17 (4): 361–376.

Sraffa, P. 1960. *Production of Commodities by Means of Commodities*. Cambridge: Cambridge University Press.

Stirati, A. 2001. 'Inflation, Unemployment and Hysteresis: An Alternative View.' *Review of Political Economy* 13 (4): 427–451.

Stirati, A., and W. Paternesi-Meloni. 2018. 'A Short Story of the Phillips Curve: From Phillips to Friedman ... and Back?' *Review of Keynesian Economics* 6 (4): 493–516.

Stirati, A., and W. Paternesi-Meloni. 2021. 'Unemployment and the Wage Share: A Long-Run Exploration for Major Mature Economies.' *Structural Change and Economic Dynamics* 56: 330–352.

Stockhammer, E. 2008. 'Is the NAIRU Theory a Monetarist, New Keynesian, Post Keynesian or a Marxist Theory?' *Metroeconomica* 59 (3): 479–510.

Summa, R., and J. Braga. 2020. 'Two Routes Back to the Old Phillips Curve: The Amended Mainstream Model and the Conflict-Augmented Alternative.' *Bulletin of Political Economy* 14 (1): 81–115.

Sylos-Labini, P. 1979. 'Prices and Income Distribution in Manufacturing Industry.' *Journal of Post Keynesian Economics* 2 (1): 3–25.

Sylos-Labini, P. 1982. 'Rigid Prices, Flexible Prices and Inflation.' *PSL Quarterly Review* 35 (140).

Tarling, R., and F. Wilkinson. 1985. 'Mark-Up Pricing, Inflation and Distributional Shares: A Note.' *Cambridge Journal of Economics* 9 (2): 179–185.

Index

Note: **Bold** page numbers refer to tables; *italic* page numbers refer to figures and page numbers followed by "n" denote footnotes.

For Product Safety Concerns and Information please contact our EU representative GPSR@taylorandfrancis.com Taylor & Francis Verlag GmbH, Kaufingerstraße 24, 80331 München, Germany